On This Day in Barangu
A Genealogical Calendar of Life Events

Front Cover: Simon Martinez

Simon Martinez is the oldest living Baranguna. This photo was taken at his 103rd birthday party in his home in Scotland. Here are some of his descendants:

Children

Gloria Martinez, Clinton Martinez, Jacqueline Martinez, Simon Martinez, Lorraine Martinez, Clifton Martinez, Carol Martinez, Francis Martinez

Grandchildren

Paul Martinez, Kenzie Martinez, Yutsil Hoyo, Alitzel Hoyo, Jordan Martinez, Ellie Martinez, Germaine Gloria Martinez, Elgin Martinez, Recilla Martinez, Jamie Martinez, Delia Gloria Martinez, James Simpson, Stacey Simpson, Carrie Simpson, Christopher Simpson

Great-grandchildren

Brigina Lopez, Elton Tyron Lopez, Kayla Gloria Lopez, Jamie Martinez, Jerille Martinez, Tiana Ebony Martinez, Mark Rayshawn Loredo, Marcia Loredo, Mischa Loredo, Sam Hobbs, Jac Hobbs, Nathan Simpson, Ellie-Mae Simpson

Great-great-grandchildren

Elaysia Lopez

Niúnagu (My Ancestors)

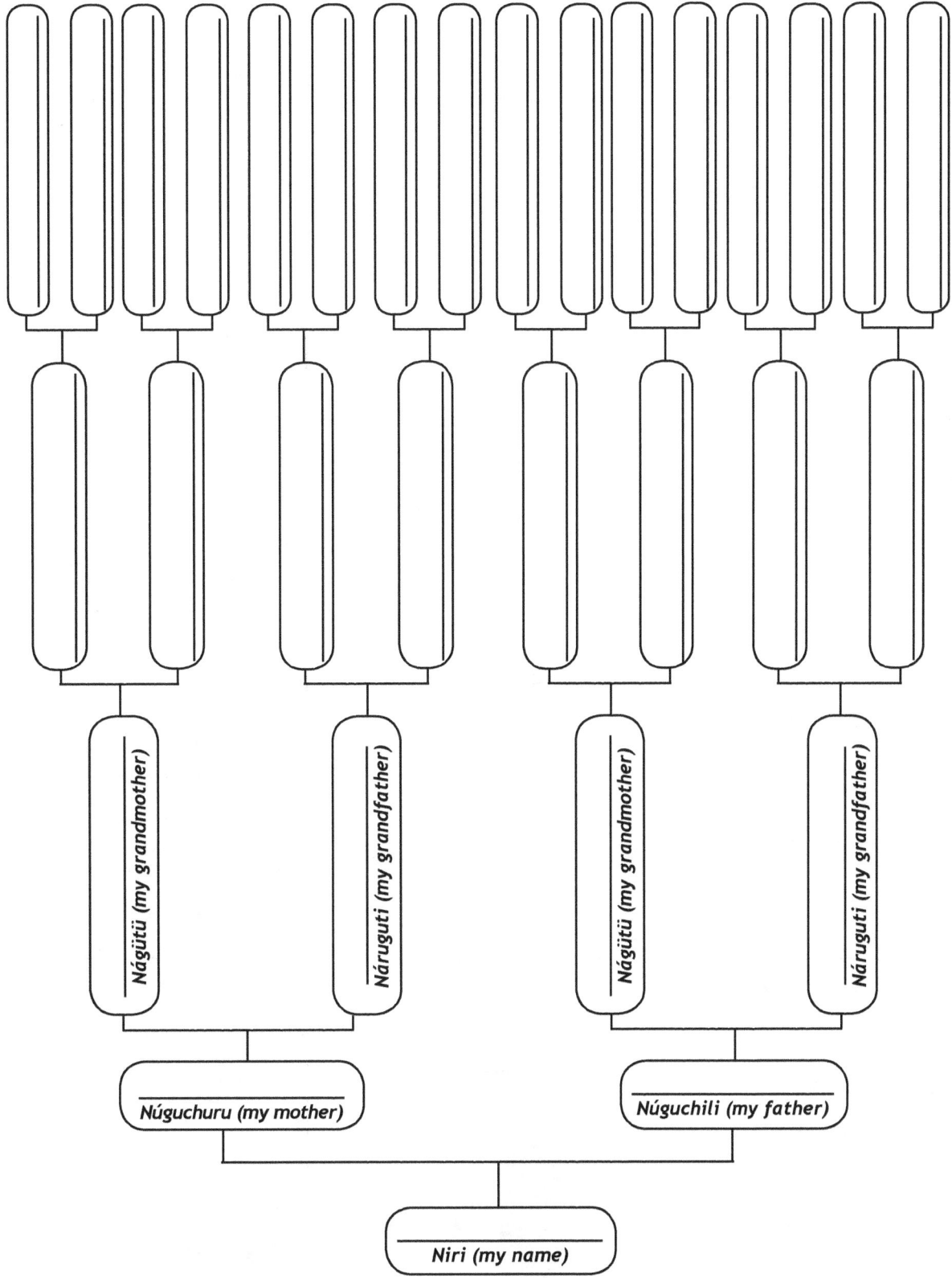

Nágütü *(my grandmother)*

Náruguti *(my grandfather)*

Nágütü *(my grandmother)*

Náruguti *(my grandfather)*

Núguchuru *(my mother)*

Núguchili *(my father)*

Niri *(my name)*

Ninebafan (My Descendants)

_____

Númari *(my spouse)*

Nisanigu *(my children)*	***Nibayani*** *(my grandchildren)*	***Nílawagu*** *(my great-grandchildren)*
_____	_____	_____
		_____
		_____
	_____	_____
		_____
		_____
		_____
	_____	_____
		_____
_____		_____
		_____
		_____
	_____	_____
		_____
		_____
	_____	_____
		_____
		_____
_____		_____
	_____	_____
		_____
		_____
	_____	_____
		_____
		_____

On This Day in Barangu:
A Genealogical Calendar of Life Events

Carlson John Tuttle

Edited by Joseph Orlando Palacio and Judy Lumb
Barranco Village
Toledo District, Belize
April 1, 2013

Cover: *The front cover shows the oldest living Baranguna (person belonging to Barangu), Simon Martinez, while the back cover shows the youngest Baranguna, Ominique Castillo.*

Published by *Producciones de la Hamaca*, Caye Caulker, Belize <producciones-hamaca.com>

ISBN: 978-976-8142-52-8

The Barranco Genealogical database is published online at <mccourry.net/webtrees>.

Photo Credits: Except for those listed below, the photos were taken by Carlson Tuttle, Joseph Palacio, or Judy Lumb, or they are in our collections because they were given to one of us. We have included the year the photos was taken in the captions, if it is known. Sources of other photos are as follows:

p. 7 **Candido Arzu and Clotildo Zuniga,** *Courtesy Kevin Zuniga*

p. 19 **Nicanora Garcia** *Guatemala immigration records*

p. 28 **John Jacob Zuniga** *funeral service programme*

p. 38 **Balbina Williams nee Arzu** *Guatemala immigration records*

p. 45 **Victor Garcia** *Guatemala immigration records*

p. 48 **Olivia Avila nee Palacio** *Courtesy Olivia Avila*

p. 50 **Bonifacio Petillo** *Guatemala immigration records*

p. 52 **Petrona Joseph nee Palacio** *Courtesy Rose Joseph*

p. 54 **Bernardina Martinez nee Santino** *Courtesy Victorina Nolberto nee Martinez*

p. 68 **Estanislao Martinez** *Courtesy Paul Palacio*

p. 74 **Frederick Nicholas,** 2005, *Greg Pinel*

p. 90 **Vilma Petrona Chimilio** *Courtesy Chimilio family*

p. 91 **Jacinta Palacio,** 2005, *Greg Pinel*

p. 99 **Brigida Paulino and Aparicio Santiago Marin** *Courtesy E. Roy Cayetano*

p. 108 **Diego Benguche** *Guatemala immigration records*

p. 109 **Florentina "Flora" Avila,** *Carlson Tuttle*

p. 124 **Manuela Marin,** 1938, *Courtesy E. Roy Cayetano*

p. 128 **Hilario Nolberto and Victoriana "Vicky" Martinez** *Courtesy Victorina Nolberto nee Martinez*

Producciones de la Hamaca is dedicated to:

—Celebration and documentation of Earth and all her inhabitants,
—Restoration and conservation of Earth's natural resources,
—Creative expression of the sacredness of Earth and Spirit.

Contents

Niúnagu (My Ancestors) iii
Ninebafan (My Descendants) iv
Foreword ix
Preface xi
Editor's Note xiii
JANUARY 1
FEBRUARY 16
MARCH 27
APRIL 39
MAY 49
JUNE 60
JULY 70
AUGUST 78
SEPTEMBER 87
OCTOBER 98
NOVEMBER 107
DECEMBER 117
Family Charts 129
Descendants of Desideria 129
Descendants of Juan Pedro Cayetano and Nicolasa Moralez 130
Descendants of Alexander Nicholas and Eugenia Delavez 131
Descendants of Francisco Nolberto and Serapia Alvarez 132
Descendants of Apolinario Garcia and Marcelina Martinez 133
Descendants of Rufino Ariola 134
Descendants of Diego Paulino 135
Descendants of Ascenciona Paulino 136
Descendants of Eulalio Loredo 137
Descendants of Narciso Bermudez 138
Descendants of Philip Santino 139
Descendants of Paula Noralez 140
Descendants of Simon Mejia 141
Descendants of Concepcion Arana 142
Descendants of Pedro John Avila 143
Descendants of Martin Benjamin Noralez 144
Descendants of Santiago Lopez 144
Descendants of Eulogio Marin 145
Descendants of Joseph Ramirez 145
Descendants of Francisco Nunez 146
Descendants of Juan Avilez 146
Descendants of Francisco Ellis Arzu 147
Descendants of Victoriano Castillo 147
Descendants of Mariano Zuniga 148
Descendants of Joanis Blas 148
Afterword 149
Index 150

Baranguna attending Father Callistus Cayetano's 40th Anniversary Celebratory Mass August 4, 2013
(from left) Alberita Enriquez nee Avila, Sebastian Cayetano, Maria Rash nee Makin, Alfredo Rash, Jason Sandoval, Olivia Avila nee Palacio, "Pants" Ramos, DeLane Ogaldez nee Nicholas, Elston Zuniga, Father Callistus Cayetano, Noni Arana, Kevaughn Enriquez, Pia Arana nee Magdelano, Valentina Alvarez, Amanda Ramos nee Zuniga, Irma Gonzalez nee Ariola, Rhea Arnold, Catherine Castillo, Francisco Ariola, Evaristo Lopez, Reina Rash, Dercy Sandoval, Elena Rash, Adriana "Tuntunata or Tun" Casimiro, Anthony Ogaldez, Marivel Rash

Foreword

This book on family linkages on which Carlson Tuttle has been working for several years is a gem for the gathering of pages and pages of what had previously been his daily postings on *Barangu* (the name of the village of Barranco in Garifuna). Any person reading it will be fascinated with how it has been possible to amass so much about so many people for such a long time. For all these accomplishments the book is an unusual contribution that all persons interested in family relations, especially within a rural community, should read.

In this Foreword I show to the reader that there are three platforms that together augment the book's usefulness to the student, the Garifuna nation, and the reader who may want to follow through and work on his/her own family tree. I refer to these as three pillars on which the book stands—the intellectual, social and cultural, and the personalized.

The Intellectual Grounding

In asking questions about the science of genetics, most people could immediately refer to the laboratory skills useful to correct allegations of paternity or also useful to trace one's origins from a short time period as well as going back hundreds of years to parts of Africa, Europe, and Asia. Refinements in molecular biology and other fields in the so-called hard sciences continue to open new avenues to pinpoint what has made the Garinagu what we are.

There is another component of the scientific study of human continuity which is confined to ethnology, a branch of social anthropology. The term most often used is kinship studies. Tuttle's book introduces us to some of the basic elements of this science.

Firstly, it builds on the primary approach to the study of social structure that dominated ethnology up to the 1950s. Under the leadership of Nancie Gonzalez, Mary Helms, and Douglas Taylor, in its beginning stages Garifuna studies acquired both a theoretical underpinning and a substantial database on which Tuttle and others have built.

Secondly, Tuttle uses the rigourous methodology of collecting and constantly re-checking data originating from archival and oral sources. He has spent many hours re-checking the notes for each day before posting them on his daily message board. A special word needs to be said about his use of oral history sources. At several moments he will leave his computer to speedily validate a given bit of information from an elder. Taking advantage of such opportunities is a rare treat for someone who is compiling ethnological information to share with the reading public. The fact is that in most cases, having done her/his fieldwork, the researcher retires to her/his ivory tower to analyse and publish her/his findings. Tuttle, on the other hand, has remained mostly in the field with dedicated access to his sources.

Finally, Tuttle maintains a conceptual justification for the study that is usually not articulated in ethnological research but for which many of our informants are demanding—giving back to the community the fruits of the research being done among them for their own benefit. This way he has built a bridge between science and community well-being that most scholars seriously need to emulate. And I should add that the community here refers not only to Barangu but also to *Peine* (Punta Gorda), *Labuga* (Livingston), as well as, of course, to the larger Garifuna nation wherever we are.

The Social and Cultural Grounding

It is worth asking the question why the Garifuna and *Baranguna* (those belonging to Barangu) deserve so much attention about their genealogy. Here we refer to the discipline of ethnohistory where people provide information about the past linking both tradition as well as remembered facts. The Garifuna are unusual for taking much pride in the details of their history as a people and furthermore taking pleasure in sharing it, writing about it, and generally documenting it.

When the indigenous peoples write their own version of the history of the New World they will do so from the viewpoint of genocide—who were killed out by the Europeans, where, and what measures were most used. Within the Circum-Caribbean the Garifuna are among those who saw their annihilation happening before their very eyes. They were exiled from their home island of St. Vincent and dumped by the British on the island of Roatan in 1797. The contribution of the Garifuna to the history of the New World is inevitably that of surviving genocide and re-constituting peoplehood within a new setting.

Survival in Roatan and starting anew within the adjacent portions of mainland Central America depended to a large extent on re-activating the small group organization that the Garifuna had formed in St. Vincent. *Iduheguo* (loosely translated as "kinship") was a primary principle that our forefathers used to organize who would go to settle in different parts of the coastal mainland from Belize to Nicaragua. *Iduheguo* entailed not only blood but also affinal (in-law) ties. Partners for potential spouses were selected from close relatives (at the level of first cousins). Tuttle shows many examples of the overlaps of interrelations between couples across blood ties, a practice not as common today as it was earlier.

Barangu is a good example of the re-articulation so necessary to survive not only the impact of genocide among its early inhabitants but also to re-inforce themselves using their own inner strength within the overwhelming challenges confronting them in Central America. As the last coastal community in territory claimed by the British, Barangu benefitted by attracting immigrants and trade across the border, resulting in an early population coming from further north in Belize and from south in Guatemala and Honduras. Besides, totally by chance the first settlers found themselves on public lands, not privately owned lands like other Garifuna communities. This became another major drawing card for settlement in the community. Kinship became a strong glue that wove through the waves of early settlers as Baranguna adpated to their new environment and built a new settlement for themselves and their descendants.

Personalized Grounding

This book breaks through a primary irony in traditional knowledge within Garifuna communities—the deep regard for the ancestors but limitations in human memory to recall connections with given ancestors. As children we were told by our parents,

"Yes, we are related to that person but don't ask me how. I wish your grandfather were still living, he would know."

This book covers the memories of scores of grandfathers. Furthermore, it invites the reader to write information about one's family tree to make it easy for the grandchildren and great grandchildren in the future. Tuttle personalizes genealogy in two ways. There are charts at the beginning of the book on which the reader can record the names of one's ancestors and descendants. At the end of each month, there is space for the reader to record one's own family events. As a result, there should be less of a demand to rely on grandfather's failing memory on the link to the relative to be honoured, for example, in an upcoming dügü.

For several years Carlson, Judy, and I have been mulling over what should be the content of this book, its formatting, and methods of presentation. We were not too certain what the outcome would be. We were certain, on the other hand, that we did not want a study/analysis that would be beyond the grasp of the layperson. The aim was to provide access to the dozens of persons, who have given us information so readily.

Following the format of the postings that Tuttle had done daily for more than one year was fairly easy. To embellish the narrative and introduce the reader to the meaning of kinship as an intricate but understandable pattern, there are several tables in the text. These tables, for example, show how two persons can be related to each other up to three different ways. The methods of relationship follow lines of descent, marriage ties, as well as the never-ending web formed among cousins in varying degrees of distance both over time as well as among the living. Other tables depict the preferential marriage rules, more common earlier than now, between cross-cousins. This way Tuttle achieves his objective not to overwhelm the reader but to provide him/her with the introductory nuts and bolts of genealogy that s/he can apply in any society.

To break the flow of data the pages are beautifully adorned with the pictures of some of the persons mentioned. By themselves the pictures are priceless and give the reader the privilege of being invited to take a peek into the family album. Not only are they the proverbial icing on the cake; they bring to life images that close relatives and others would like to see over and over again. Later in the text there are also charts of several families, which provide a helpful longitudinal view of family members and their ties to each other.

Joseph Orlando Palacio

Preface

For the past thirty years I have been collecting genealogical information on the residents of Barangu. It began for me as a way of understanding this village. I had moved to Barangu from the mountains of rural North Carolina in 1986. In the past I had worked on my family genealogy with its New York Dutch and Kentucky Appalachian roots. I also did a genealogical study in the valley where I lived in North Carolina.

When E. Roy Cayetano showed me the ancestor chart that he had done with his family, I saw the opportunity for me to better understand this village of Barangu. My interest was heightened with my marriage in 1989 to Valerie Delcy Valencio, who is related to Roy three different ways. This study describes Delcy's family, but goes way beyond that to include the whole village. Her family becomes a reflection of the village as the village becomes a reflection of Delcy's family. Thus began a systematic gathering of genealogical information that goes on to this day.

Genealogy helps me to put this village life into a perspective that goes over a period of time. Understanding the past generations helps me understand who has helped make the village what it is today. It has helped me understand the nature of how the past generations have helped to define the present and how the future is perceived. My genealogical studies also give other Baranguna the opportunity to look at the village with a different perspective.

The village of Barangu developed from a turtle camp founded by Santiago Avilez on a piece of high land within a coastal mangrove swamp that stretches from Peine (Punta Gorda) to the Guatemalan border. Some of the original settlers were from Jonathan Point further north in the British Colony and from Peine. Both of these groups of Garinagu had come from Unduru (Honduras). Other Garinagu came from Labuga (Livingston, Guatemala) and Unduru. All of these Garinagu are descendants of indigenous people who intermarried with Africans on Yurumein (St. Vincent Island in the West Indies). They were rounded up by the British and dumped on the coast of Central America, one of many barbarous acts of the British toward the indigenous peoples of the Caribbean. The British policy of genocide toward indigenous people and their policy of chattel slavery toward the African population left the Garinagu an isolated and marginalized people on the coast of Central America.

The Garifuna term "aban rasa" means "one people." That is a description of Barangu—one people, which is shown in this genealogical database without a doubt. Everyone in this database is related to someone else in this database through either affinal or consanguinal relations. This is not just true for the majority Garifuna. The Q'echi, Creole (a mix of Afro- and Euro-descendants) and Euro-descendant members of the community also are part of this aban rasa. Through marriage they have become part of this larger whole.

The residents of Barangu (Baranguna) see life as obligations to past and present generations, and also to future generations. Within Garifuna spirituality one's ancestors are very important. This recognition of ancestors and how important they are to present daily activities is a distinctive part of the Garifuna world. It is hoped that this work will help in identifying and putting into context Baranguna ancestors.

The research began with visiting the St. Peter Claver Church rectory in Peine and copying by hand the relevant citations in the sacramental records (baptism and marriage). This was very limiting because I could not simply go back over the records to check something without going back to Peine. The government civil records (birth, marriage, and death) had been copied onto microfilm and were housed in Belmopan at the Government Archives. These were very helpful but, like the church records, I had only limited access because of the distance to Belmopan. This was overcome when E. Roy Cayetano digitized the St. Peter Claver sacramental records. I could spend weeks at home going over and over these records checking and rechecking the data.

In 2010 E. Roy Cayetano and Surusia (Dr.) Joseph Palacio digitized some of the Izabal sacramental records with the kind permission of Monsignor Gabriel Peñata at the Puerto Barrios Diocesan Office. Through the work of E. Payne of Costa Rica, the 1821 Trujillo census has become available online. The San Juan Bautista Church records of Trujillo, Honduras, are now available online. More recently other genealogical source materials have become available online, first the Livingston Nuestra Señora del Rosario Church records and then the Guatemalan civil records for Livingston.

Surusia Peitra Arana uncovered the immigration papers of numerous Baranguna and others who immigrated to Guatemala in the late 1920s to work for United Fruit Company. These give not only information, but photos, several of which are included in this book.

Along with other records and numerous oral interviews I have been able to reconstruct a fairly complete record of the various Baranguna families. By its nature this work is never finished, but what has been completed allows one the rare opportunity to begin doing ethno-genealogical work based on the data collected. Most genealogical collection is motivated by the desire to trace an individual back through his/her ancestors. This genealogical database is not about one individual or even one family. This database is rather a complex interwoven set of relationships among numerous families that are woven into a whole, a whole village. This intertwining of affinal and consanguineal relationships shows a multi-layer set of relationships that help define a community.

There are problems with the ethnocentricity of genealogical programmes. Western European cultures emphasize the importance of legally sanctioned marriages. Garifuna generally do not distinguish between legal and extralegal spouses, though a legal marriage carries more prestige. Nor is there a distinction between legitimate and illegitimate children. By the Western European definition the "illegitimate" children do not exist, but for Garifuna the acknowledgement of paternity is the important factor. "What is important is not the nature of the parents' relationship but the acknowledgment of paternity." Virginia Kerns (*Woman and the Ancestors*, 1983, Urbana: University of Illinois Press, p. 113).

In the genealogical programme I use, and in most others, one only has two choices in a relationship between a man and a woman, i.e., married or not married. This does not cover the range of relationships between a man and a woman in Garifuna communities. Within Barangu there exist a variety of conjugal relationships: serial relationships, legal marriage (usually a church-sanctioned relationship), common-law, concurrent relationships between a man and more than one woman, and various forms of short-term relationships that produce children.

Uxorilocal residence is when the man moves to the location of the woman, which is very common in Barangu. This brings in new males and new names to the village, which is an important factor in the history of the village.

Cross-cousin (brother and sister's children forming a union) relationships were often practiced in the village. The church viewed these as "sinful" relationships, so they were actively opposed by the Jesuits and taught as being evil and sinful. The Jesuits' primary concern seemed to be to ensure that children were baptized and that conjugal relationships were sanctified by the church. The British colonial authorities exerted their power to stamp out the practice of cross-cousin marriages.

This work is multi-dimensional, beginning with the vertical direction of one's immediate ancestors and descendants, which is information that is very important to each and every Baranguna. One's second, third and fourth cousins comprise the horizontal direction of relationships, as each Baranguna celebrates and enjoys niduheñu (my people). Affinal relationships through one's spouse have great value in Garifuna culture.

This book comes out of the 150th anniversary of the founding of Barangu. With the birth and baptism of Maria Loreta Palacio in December of 1862, we have the start of recorded information about Barangu. My contribution to this anniversary was to do a daily email and Facebook posting of births, marriages, and deaths occurring on that day with additional information about the person, such as nicknames; their parents, spouses, children; past roles in the village; and how the person is related to Maria Loreta Palacio and to someone living in the village now. *On this Day in Barangu* is a compilation of those daily postings.

To get a history of the village and its events, one can read this book daily. By using the index, one can search for one's family or another family of interest. One can find one's ancestors among the family charts that include three generations from the first settler with that name.

While I was doing these postings I got responses with additional information and corrections from some readers. I hope this book also generates similar responses. It will have much more meaning if a dialogue is created. Charts are included in the beginning to document one's ancestors and descendants. At the ends of some months is space where additional events can be recorded.

I am very grateful for the partnership of Surusia Joseph Palacio in this work. He brings both his experience of having grown up as a member of the Barangu community and his anthropological training and experience. We have spent countless hours discussing these genealogical data. Our third partner is Judy Lumb who takes care of the unseen technical details of editing, presentation, and publishing.

My high school English teacher and debate coach, Laurence LeCapelain, introduced me to the concept that there is a multiplicity of ways of looking at the world in which I find such joy. I thank Larry McCourry, the webmaster of the Barranco genealogical website, for introducing me to genealogical programmes and giving me lots of technical advice. My friend Ann Kieffer has supported me and my work, listening, tolerating, and acting as a sounding board.

I want to thank all those Baranguna who have given generously of their time in many, many interviews. I am especially grateful to Lucille "Chilagu" and Raymond Valencio, my mother- and father-in-law for their patience as I bothered them often when they were in the midst of cooking, knitting cast nets, or other activities. They answered all my questions and gave me crucial information so willingly and lovingly.

All Baranguna are part of the whole genealogical structure. This family tree doesn't just get bigger, it folds over on itself and has many layers. This book and the exercise of daily genealogical posting hopefully have contributed to a better understanding, placing Baranguna in the parade of generations. The genealogy of Barangu is an ever changing project. Baranguna still get married, have children, and die. New information is added. Corrections are made. Things change. So add your own information to this book and look online <www.mccourry.net/barranco> or search for "Barranco genealogy" to keep up to date with other new additions and changes.

Carlson John Tuttle

Editor's Note: Using this Book

I begin with a major apology for names misspelled. This database was formed from interviews, and church and government records that were made by priests and government workers writing the names. Whether the information comes from oral or official sources, someone other than the individual involved wrote the name. We have done our best to use consistent and the most logical spellings. In earlier times, Spanish spellings were commonly used by Garinagu, so we have used Spanish spellings preferentially for persons born in the nineteenth and early twentieth centuries.

Where possible we have included nicknames, as they help to distinguish individuals who have the same name. In earlier times Baranguna followed the precedent of naming children according to the Saint days in the Catholic calendar, resulting in several people with the same first name. Nicknames are indicated by quotation marks "name." We have used phonetic spellings of nicknames as best as we could determine. In some cases the surname was not known, or seemed inappropriate. In those cases, we have added a name in parentheses (name) to further identify the individual. In some cases a person was also known by another name. Those are also indicated in parentheses (name).

Throughout we have used a few Garifuna words, *Barangu* (Barranco), *Baranguna* (those belonging to Barangu), *Indura* (Honduras), *Labuga* (Livingston), *Peine* (Punta Gorda), *Wadimalu* (Guatemala).

Scattered throughout the text are photographs. Many are very old and not in good condition, but we present them for the image of particular people that they represent. Most are from the collections of Carlson Tuttle, Joseph Palacio, or Judy Lumb, either taken or collected by us. Other sources are indicated on the copyright page.

The Index includes all names in alphabetical order by their surname. Married women are indexed by both their maiden name and married name in the "nee" form.

The data used for this book are as of April, 2013, so events after that time are not included. Carlson Tuttle's genealogical database, on which this book is based, is on the Internet <mccourry. net/webtrees>. In order to expand this collection of genealogical data to keep it useful for Baranguna, we request that information be submitted to Carlson Tuttle in Barangu or via email <carlsontuttle@ yahoo.com>.

Judy Lumb

JANUARY

1st January

In the Catholic calendar today is the Feast Day of St. Fulgentius of Ruspe.

Antonia Palacio nee Ariola died on this day in 2004 in Barangu. She is the daughter of **Catarino Patricio Ariola** and **Benita Nunez**. She married **Ruben Palacio** in 1945. Antonia was a bread baker in the village.

Mary Martha Cayetano died on this day in 1999 in Belmopan. She is the daughter of **Pascacio Cayetano** and **Eustaquia Satuye**. Mary is the granddaughter of **Maria Loreta Palacio**. She married **Leonard Petillo** in 1959. She was a trained nurse.

On this day **Hazel Elinor Arzu** was born. She is the daughter of **Candido Arzu** and **Bernadette Arzu nee Loredo**. Hazel married **Michael Alejandro Martinez**. **Maria Loreta Palacio** is the great-great-aunt of Hazel and also the first cousin thrice removed of Hazel.

Crescencio Nicholas was born on this day in Barangu in 1929. He is the son of **Pablo Nicholas** and **Aniceta Nicholas nee Blas**. Crescencio is **Victor Nicholas's** uncle.

Francis Benedict Cayetano and **Florencia Lucas** were married on this day in Barangu in 1938. Francis is the grandson of **Maria Loreta Palacio**. He was a schoolteacher. **Nathaniel "Shorty" Cayetano** is the son of Francis and Florencia.

Aurelia Enriquez and **Emmanuel Arzu** were married on this day in Peine in 1966. Aurelia is the daughter of **Nazaria Zuniga** and **Lino Enriquez**.

Epifania Petillo was born on this day in Peine in 1900. She is the daughter of **Bonifacio Petillo** and **Carmen Enriquez**. Epifania is the eldest sister of **Leonard "Mr. Pete" Petillo**.

Francis Casimiro was born in 1933. He is the son of **Erasmo Casimiro** and **Paula Noralez**. Francis married **Gloria Mejia**. Francis died in 1994 in Dangriga. **Maria "Mari" Zuniga nee Casimiro** is the daughter of Francis.

Yvonne Lopez was born on this day in Peine. She is the daughter of **Patrick Lopez** and **Josephine Palacio**. **Maria Loreta Palacio** is the great-great-aunt of Yvonne. **Hermenehilda "Maria" Lopez** is the sister of Yvonne.

O'Dillan Petillo was born on this day in 1918 in Peine. He is the son of **Bonifacio Petillo** and **Carmen Enriquez**. O'Dillan married **Antonia King** in 1944 in Peine. **Leonard "Mr. Pete" Petillo** is the brother of O'Dillan.

On this day there is an instance of the birth of triplets, **Fulgencio Avilez**, **Fulgencia Avilez** and **Justina Avilez**. They are the children of **Casimiro Avilez** and **Simeona Teo**. All three of the children died within the week. The three children are the great-grandchildren of **Santiago "Gaünbü" Avilez**, the founder of the village.

Hazel Elinor Arzu Relationship-1 to Maria Loreta Palacio		
Teodoro Palacio	common ancestor	Teodoro Palacio
Maria Loreta Palacio	siblings	Nolberto Palacio
Maria Loreta Palacio	aunt	Patrocinia Palacio
Maria Loreta Palacio	great-aunt	Candido Arzu
Maria Loreta Palacio	great-great-aunt	Hazel Elinor Arzu
Hazel Elinor Arzu Relationship-2 to Maria Loreta Palacio		
Francisco Palacio	common ancestor	Francisco Palacio
Teodoro Palacio	siblings	Anastacio Palacio
Maria Loreta Palacio	first cousins	Gregoria Palacio
Maria Loreta Palacio	first cousin, once removed	Henry Loredo
Maria Loreta Palacio	first cousin, twice removed	Bernadette Loredo
Maria Loreta Palacio	first cousin, thrice removed	Hazel Elinor Arzu

2nd January

In the Catholic calendar today is the Feast Day of St. St. Macarius the Younger.

Trina Maria Zuniga was born on this day in Peine. She is the daughter of **Derrick Zuniga** and **Maria Zuniga nee Casimiro**. **Maria Loreta Palacio** is the first cousin four times removed of Trina.

On this day in 1976 in Barangu **Epifania Loredo** died. She is the daughter of **Eulalio Loredo** and **Gregoria Palacio**. She was born in 1894. Epifania is the mother of **Gladys Lino nee Loredo** with **Patricio Ariola**. Epifania married **Sotero Arana** in 1917. **Maria Loreta Palacio** is the first cousin once removed of Epifania.

Macario Chimilio was born on this day in Mango Creek. **Eduviges Ramirez** and **Crispulo Chimilio** are his parents. **Claude Zuniga** and Macario are brothers.

Evan Stephen Cayetano was born on this day in Barangu. He is the son of **Eugenio Cayetano** and **Manuela Cayetano nee Marin**. Evan is the first cousin thrice removed of **Maria Loreta Palacio**. At present he works for the International Development Bank in Trinidad.

Evilia Gonzalez was born on this day in Labuga. Her parents are **Justo Gonzalez** and **Ursula Arana**. Evilia married **Martin Martinez** in 1970 in Belize City. Evilia is the sister-in-law of **Irma Gonzalez nee Ariola**.

In 1901 in Barangu on this day **Casimira Nicholas** died. She is the daughter of **Joseph Alexander Nicholas** and **Maria Eugenia Delavez**. Casimira was born in 1868 in Barangu. She married **Pio Nolberto** in Barangu in 1883. Casimira is the grandmother of **Paula Nolberto**. **Alvin Loredo** is the great-grandson of Casimira.

On this day in 1941 **John Noralez** and **Damiana Lopez** were married in Peine. **John Noralez** is the son of **Felix "Aska" Noralez** and **Juana Nolberto**. John was known as "John Box." Damiana is the daughter of **Nicolas Caballero** and **Barbara Lopez**. John is **Teresa "Tandu" Noralez**'s uncle.

Angelina Alvarez was born on this day in Tiquisate, Guatemala. She is the daughter of **Feliciano "Felix" Alvarez** and **Pantaleona Mejia**. She married **Victor Joseph Nicholas**. Angelina is a retired educator who taught school and was the principal teacher at St. Joseph R.C. School in Barangu. Perhaps because of her association with the school Angelina has many nicknames, "T," "Angie" and "Teacher Angie." At present she operates a small shop in the village.

On this day **Carlos Ramirez** was born in Labuga. He is the son of **Luciano Mejia** and **Florencia Mejia**. **Maria Loreta Palacio** is the great-great-aunt of Carlos. **Catarino "Claudi" Zuniga** is the first cousin of Carlos.

John Paul Alvarez was born on this day in Peine. John is the son of **David Alvarez** and **Martina Cornelia Palacio**. **Maria Loreta Palacio** is the great-great-great-aunt, the first cousin four times removed and the first cousin six times removed of John. **Paul Palacio** is the grandfather of John.

3rd January

Daniel Ramirez was born on this day in Barangu in 1897. He is the son of **Carmen Ramirez** and **Eustaquia "Bilacu" Palacio**. Daniel is the uncle of **Eduviges "Auntie Bea" Ramirez**. Daniel is the nephew of **Maria Loreta Palacio**.

On this day in 1888 in Peine **John Lambey** and **Gregoria Nolberto** were married. John is the son of **Joseph Antonio Lambey** and **Maria Juana Socorro**. This is another example of a Baranguna woman attracting a spouse to the village. They had eleven children. Gregoria is the great-aunt of **Paula Nolberto**.

Francisco Xavier Sanchez was baptized in Peine in 1866 on this day. He had been born the month before in Barangu. His parents are **Sebastian Sanchez** and **Vinciona Cayetano**. His mother, Vinciona, is the daughter of **Juan Pedro Cayetano** and was known as "Beltrana." Both parents were from Labuga.

On this day **Ignacia Cayetano** was born in Barangu. She is the daughter of **Francis Benedict Cayetano** and **Florencia Lucas**. Ignacia is known as "Yaka." Ignacia is a retired ecducator and an active lay minister in the Roman Catholic Church. **Maria Loreta Palacio** is the great-grandmother of Ignacia.

Justina Avilez died on this day in 1921 in Peine. She is the daughter of **Casimiro Avilez** and **Simeona Teo**. Justina was one of a set of triplet born two days earlier.

On this day **Lambert Joseph** died in 1979 in Caye Caulker. He is the son of **Ambrosio Joseph** and **Petrona Palacio**. He died in a drowning accident. He was born in 1964 in Barangu. **Maria Loreta Palacio** is the great-great-aunt of Lambert.

4th January

On this day in 1888 in Barangu **Santita Reyes** was born. She is the daughter of **Martin Reyes** and **Luisa Roches**. Santita is the great-aunt of **Roy Cayetano** and **Raymond Valencio**.

Procopio Arzu

Procopio Arzu was born on this day in Barangu in 1920. Procopio is the son of **Francisco Ellis Arzu** and **Patrocinia Palacio**. His parents are an example of a Baranguna woman attacting a spouse to the village. Procopio is the father of **Dr. Francis Arzu**. He is the grandnephew of **Maria Loreta Palacio**. He died in Labuga.

Abraham Bernard Mejia and **Victoriana Santino** were married on this day in 1917 in Peine. Abraham is the son of **Cirilo Mejia** and **Margarita Rivas**. Abraham was born in Labuga.

On this day **Carmelo Nunez** and **Genevieve Martinez** were married in 1897 in Barangu. Carmelo is the son of **Jose Maria Nunez** and **Marta Bernardez**. Genevieve is the daughter of **Liborio Martinez** and **Romalda Avila**. **Jacinta Palacio** is the great-granddaughter of Carmelo and Genevieve.

Fulgencia Avilez died on this day in Peine in 1921. Fulgencia is the daughter of **Casimiro Teo** and **Simeona Teo**. Fulgencia is the second of the triplets that were born on the first of January to die.

5th January

In the Catholic calendar today is the Feast Day of St. Telesphorus.

On this day **Colin Marlon Enriquez** was born in Belmopan. He is the son of **Lloyd Enriquez** and **Rita Enriquez nee Avila**. **Maria Loreta Palacio** is the great-great-great-aunt of Colin. **Eugenia "Jean" Zuniga nee Noralez** is a grandmother of Colin.

Telesflora Martinez was born on this day in 1928 in Barangu. **Francisco Martinez** and **Estefania Avila** are her parents. Telesflora died in 1945 in Peine. She had been brought to Peine from Barangu in the middle of the night in a rain storm because of difficulties in childbirth and died.

Telesforo Palacio was born in Barangu on this day in 1909. He is the son of **Hipolito Palacio** and **Josefa Zuniga**. **Maria Loreta Palacio** is the first cousin once removed of Telesforo. Telesforo is an elder brother of **Ruben Palacio**.

Telesflora "Stella" Simeona Mejia was born in Barangu in 1919. She is the daughter of **Abraham Bernard Mejia** and **Victoriana Santino**. Stella married **John Jacob Zuniga** in 1939 in Barangu. Stella died in 1980 in Peine.

On this day **Telesforo Lambey** was born in Barangu in 1894. Telesforo is the son of **John Lambey** and **Gregoria Nolberto**. Telesfloro is the first cousin twice removed of **Alvin Loredo**.

Ethel Loredo was born on this day in 1905 in Barangu. She is the daughter of **Eulalio Loredo** and **Gregoria Palacio**. **Maria Loreta Palacio** is the first cousin once removed of **Ethel**.

On this day **Ian Dane Valerio** was born in San Ignacio. He is the son of **Peter Valerio** and **Hermenehilda "Maria" Lopez**. **Maria Loreta Palacio** is the great-great-great-aunt of Ian. Ian is the grandson of **Josephine Palacio**.

6th January

In the Catholic calendar today is the Feast Day of the Epiphany of the Lord (*El Dia de Reyes*).

Basilia Luis died on this day in Belmopan in 1981. She was born in Peine in 1913 to **Basilio Luis** and **Canuta Lucas**. Basilia married **Adriano Natividad Arana**. **Francisco Bonifacio "Frank" Arana**, a farm demonstrator in Barangu, is the son of Basilia.

Epifania Martinez and **Macrina Martinez**, a set of twins, were born on this day in Peine in 1907. They are the daughters of **Brown Prudencio Martinez** and **Gabina Zuniga**. They died when young. Epifania and Macrina are aunts of **Viola Martinez**.

Epifania Polonio was born on this day in Barangu in 1911. She is the daughter of **Apolonio Polonio** and **Damiana Garcia**. Epifania is the aunt of **Madeline Loredo**.

Rafael Zuniga and Catarina Paulino were married on this day in 1916 in Peine. Rafael's parents are Mauricia Cayetano and Claro Zuniga. Catarina's parents are Cirilo Gutierrez and Bonifacia Paulino. Rafael and Catarina had two children, Felix Zuniga and Marcelo Zuniga. Rafael is the brother of Inocente "Mafia" Zuniga.

Myra Moreira was born on this day in Barangu. She is the daughter of Lucille Zuniga and Santos Moreira.

Fulgencio Avilez died on this day in 1921 in Peine, He is the son of Casimiro Avilez and Simeona Teo. This is the third of the set of triplets that were born on New Year's Day to die. His mother had a set of twins in 1922 and died in childbirth.

7th January

In the Catholic calendar today is the Feast Day of St. Lucian of Antioch.

Benita Nunez died on this day in 1981 in Barangu. She was born in 1899 in Peine to Carmelo Nunez and Genevieve Martinez. She married Catarino Ariola in 1929 in Peine. Benita was known as "Lobi." Benita is the grandmother of Jacinta Palacio.

Luciano Ramirez was born on this day in 1924 in Labuga. He is the son of Evangelista Nunez and Bonifacio Ramirez. Maria Loreta Palacio is the great-aunt of Luciano. Luciano is the brother of "Auntie Bea" Eduviges Ramirez and Justina Nicholas nee Ramirez.

Macario Nolberto and Josefa Alvarez were married on this day in 1925 in Dangriga. Macario was born in Barangu in 1864. Macario and Josefa are the grand-parents of Lorenzo "Thunder" Nolberto.

On this day Esmith Garcia and Blacina Apolonio were married in Peine in 1890. Esmith is the son of Apolinario Garcia and Marcelina Augustina Martinez. The Garcia family came from Jonathan Point as did many of the other early settlers of Barangu. Blacina is the daughter of Francisco Apolonio and Leonarda Nunez. The Garcia family were noted for their tailoring.

Sebastian Ramirez and Manuela Ariola were married on this day in 1910 in Barangu. Sebastian is the son of Loreto Ramirez and Aniceta Palacio. Manuela Ariola is the daughter of Patricio Ariola and Florencia Lambey.

Pantaleon Odway Polonio died on this day in 1927 in Peine. He is the son of Eusebio Polonio and Lucia Ordonez. Pantaleon was born in 1891 in Peine. Pantaleon was a deputy registrar of births and deaths in the village. This is a little unusual because the post of registrar was usually given to the principal teacher in the village. But with the constant changing of principal teachers in the early part of 20th century in Barangu, the colonial authorities decided to give this post to a permanent resident of the village. Pantaleon is the uncle of Bartolo Polonio and grandfather of Bobby Polonio.

8th January

In the Catholic calendar today is the Feast Day of St. Lucian of Beauvais.

Maria Makin holding her granddaughter Lumar Valencio (2009)

Maria Makin was born on this day in Barangu. She is the daughter of Matildo Makin and Santa Bebe. Maria is the grandmother of Lumar Valencio. Maria married Alfredo Rash. Maria Loreta Palacio is the great-great-aunt of Maria's first cousin.

Seferina Castillo was born on this day in 1915 in Barangu. She is the daughter of Inez Castillo and Martha Fuentes. She was confirmed in Barangu in 1924. She is the sister of Margarita Castillo who is James Avilez's wife.

Luciana Nolberto was born on this day in 1896 in Barangu. She is the daughter of Pio Nolberto and Casimira Nicholas. Luciana married Inocente Zuniga in 1916 in Peine. Lucille "Chilagu" Valencio nee Zuniga.

Vicenta Blas died on this day in 1991 in Barangu. She is the daughter of Macario Blas and Leonarda Nunez. Vicenta married Eusebio Santino in 1922 in Barangu. Jacinta Trigueno nee Santino is the daughter of Vicenta.

9th January

In the Catholic calendar today is the Feast Day of St. Basilissa of Antioch.

George Hill died on this day in 1997 in Dangriga. **Isabela Mejia** is his mother. **Leslie Colon** is the son of **George Hill**.

Keron Cacho was born on this day in Belize City. He is the son of **Daniel Cacho** and **Celestina Enriquez**.

On this day **Basilia Luis** was born in 1913 in Peine. She is the daughter of **Basilio Luis** and **Canuta Lucas**. Basilia married **Adriano Natividad Arana**. **Francisco Bonifacio "Frank" Arana**, a farm demonstrator in Barangu, is the son of Basilia.

Julian Paulino and **Nicolasa Palacio** were married on this day in 1900 in Barangu. They had one child, **Leandra Paulino** before Julian died in 1903. **Nicolasa Palacio** then married **Simon Mejia**.

On this day **Feliciano Garcia** was born in 1890 in Peine. His parents are **Esmith Garcia** and **Blacina Apolonio**. **Esmith Garcia** was a tailor as was his father. Esmith's father's name is Apolinario, one of the early pioneers with his wife **Marcelina (Magiri) Martinez**.

Apolonio Polonio was born on this day in 1888 in Peine. He is the son of **Eusebio Polonio** and **Lucia Ordonez**. Apolonio is the father of **Ursula Polonio** who married **Henry Loredo**. Apolonio is the great-grandfather of **Alvin Loredo**.

Santiago Labriel was born on this day in 1883 in Peine and baptized later in Labuga. He is the son of **Domingo Labriel** and **Ferdinanda Cruz**. He married **Crecencia Zuniga** in 1904 in Peine. Secondly he married **Serapia Avilez**, **Ambrosio Avilez**'s daughter, in 1920 in Peine.

10th January

In the Catholic calendar today is the Feast Day of St. Guillaume de Bourges.

Gonzalez Casimiro was born on this day in Barangu in 1911. Gonzalez is the son of **Pablo Casimiro** and **Bernadina Nolberto**. In 1944 he married **Mary Flores**. Gonzalez died in 1983 in Barangu. He was a farmer and a fisherman. **Adriana "Tun" Casimiro** is the daughter of Gonzalez.

Shevaughn King was born on this day in Peine. He is the son of **Clifford King** and **Agnes Lino**. **Maria Loreta Palacio** is the great-great-great-aunt of Shevaughn.

On this day **Guillermo Avila** was born. He is the son of **Reginald Avila** and **Georgiana Palacio**. **Maria Loreta Palacio** is the great-great-aunt and first cousin twice removed of Guillermo. Guillermo is the uncle of **Lynn Zuniga nee Arnold**.

On this day in 1890 in Barangu **Jeronima Garcia** was born. Her parents are **Apolinario Garcia** and **Marcelina "Magiri" Martinez**. Jeronima's parents as well as a number of other early Baranguna settlers were from Jonathan Point.

11th January

Evaristo Nunez died on this day 1989 in Peine. He is the son of **Francisco Nunez** and **Martina "Obispa" Martinez**. Evaristo married **Alexine Loredo** in 1938 in Barangu. Evaristo was known as "Bob Steele." Evaristo had worked for the United Fruit Company in Wadimalu. **Elorine Nunez** is the daughter of Bob Steele.

Eusebio Santino was born on this day in 1897 in Barangu. He is the son of **Philip Santino** and **Justina Cayetano**. Eusebio married **Vicenta Blas** in 1922 in Barangu. **Clifford Marin** is the grandson of Eusebio.

12th January

In the Catholic calendar today is the Feast Day of St. Arcadius of Mauretania.

Raheem Martinez was born on this day in Belize City. He is the son of **Martin Martinez** and **Joy Young**. Raheem is the grandson of **Martin Martinez** and **Evilia Gonzalez**. **Maria Loreta Palacio** is the great-great-great-aunt of Raheem.

Gonzalez Casimiro (1979)

Emeri Palacio was born on this day in Belize City. He is the son of **Timothy Palacio** and **Gaynor Ferguson**. **Maria Loreta Palacio** is the great-great-great-aunt of Emeri. Emeri is also the first cousin four times removed of **Maria Loreta Palacio**. Emeri is the grandson of **Theodore Palacio** and **Bridget Palacio nee Marin**.

Ellis Henry Arzu was born on this day. He is the son of **Candido Arzu** and **Bernadette Arzu nee Loredo**. **Maria Loreta Palacio** is the great-great-aunt of Ellis. Ellis is also the first cousin thrice removed of **Maria Loreta Palacio**. He worked for the Lands Department. Since his retirement he has run a private surveying business.

Arcadio Palacio was born on this day in 1892 in Barangu. He is the son of **Liberato Palacio** and **Florencia Blas**. **Gumercinda Palacio** is the sister of Arcadio. **Maria Loreta Palacio** is the first cousin once removed of Arcadio.

On this day **Kareen Casimiro** was born in Corozal. She is the daughter of **Dionisio Casimiro** and **Alice Nicholas**. Kareen married **Dwight Cadle** in 2000 in Roaring Creek. **Maria Loreta Palacio** is the great-great-great-aunt and the great-great-aunt of Kareen.

On this day in Barangu in 1922 **Stephen Gibbons** and **Estena Blanco** were married. Steven is from Barangu. His parents are **Isaac Gibbons** and **Ascenciona Paulino**. Estena is from Labuga, a reversal of the usual order of a Baranguna woman attracting an outside man. **Naomi Colon** is the granddaughter of Steven with **Paula Paulino**.

Pedro John Avila and **Viviana Palacio** were married in 1898 in Barangu. Pedro's parents are **Victoriano Avila** and **Cesaria Zuniga**. **Anastacio Palacio** and **Sotera Gutierrez** are Viviana's parents. **Reginald Avila** is the son of Pedro and Viviana. **Marti Cain nee Arana** is the granddaughter of Pedro and Viviana.

Clement Satuye and **Eluteria Cayetano** were married in 1888 in Peine. Clement is the son of **Jacob Satuye** and **Juana Castillo**. Eluteria is the daughter of **Sebastian Sanchez** and **Vinciona Cayetano**. **Sheridan Arzu nee Petillo** is the great grandchild of Clement and Eluteria.

James Satuye and **Andrea Arana** were married on this day in 1935 in Barangu. James is the son of **Clemente Satuye** and **Eluteria Cayetano**. Andrea is from Puerto Cortez and the daughter of **Daniel Arana** and **Cleofa Nunez**. **Sheridan Arzu nee Petillo** is the grandniece of James.

On this day in 2010 in Belize City **Rodney Robert Zuniga** died. He is the son of **John Ray Zuniga** and **Vicenta "Lulu" Sanchez**. Rodney was born in Barangu in 1962. **Maria Loreta Palacio** is the great-great-aunt of Rodney.

Karlie Lorraine Guerra was also born in Los Angeles on this day. She is the daughter of **Opal Arzu** and **Carlos Guerra**. Opal is the youngest child of **Candido Arzu** and **Bernadette Arzu nee Loredo**. **Maria Loreta Palacio** is the great-great-great-aunt of Karlie and also the first cousin four times removed of Karlie.

13th January

In the Catholic calendar today is the Feast Day of St. Gumesinus of Cordoba.

Gregorio Ruben Palacio died on this day in 2003 in Peine. He is the son of **Hipolito Palacio** and **Josefa Zuniga**. Ruben was born in 1918 in Barangu. Ruben is the first cousin once removed of **Maria Loreta Palacio**. He married **Antonia Ariola** in Barangu in 1945. **Jacinta Palacio** is the daughter of Ruben and Antonia. Ruben is the father of **Andy Palacio** with **Cleofa Avilez**.

On this day a set of twins was born in Monkey River, **Fabian Cayetano** and **Sebastian Cayetano**. They are the sons of **Francis Benedict Cayetano** and **Florencia**

Sebastian (left) and Fabian Cayetano (1994)

Lucas. They are the great-grandsons of **Maria Loreta Palacio**. Fabian married **Agnes Felicita Palacio**. Sebastian married **Isabel Nunez**. Both Sebastian and Fabian are retired educators and lay ministers in the Catholic Church.

Eric Loredo was born on this day in Barangu. He is the son of **Henry Loredo** and **Ursula Polonio**. Eric is the first cousin twice removed of **Maria Loreta Palacio**. He served a term as mayor of Peine. Eric is the uncle of **Alvin Loredo**.

On this day in 1898 in Barangu **Gumercinda Palacio** was born. Her parents are **Liberato Palacio** and **Florencia Blas**. Gumercinda is the first cousin once removed of **Maria Loreta Palacio**. She is the mother of **Dominica Noralez**. Gumercinda was also known as "Sindagu."

Bernardo Baltazar and **Dominica Colindres** were married on this day in 1929 in Barangu. Dominica is the niece of **Maria Loreta Palacio**.

Francisco Ellis Arzu and **Patrocinia Palacio** were married on this day in Barangu in 1914. Francisco is the daughter of **Eusebio Arzu** and **Zoila Mejia**. Patrocinia is the daughter of **Nolberto Palacio** and **Ignacia Arana**. Franisco and Patrocinia are the great-grandparents of **Nadeth Michelle Martinez**.

On this day **Orson Lucious Nicholas** was born in 1979. He is the son of **Godfrey Marin** and **Avelina Nicholas**. Orson died in 2005. **Maria Loreta Palacio** is the first cousin five times removed and also the great-great-great-aunt of Orson.

Epifania Avilez was born on this day in 1886 in Peine. She is the daughter of **Ambrosio Avilez** and **Justa Polonio**. Epifania is the granddaughter of **Santiago "Gaünbü" Avilez**, the founder of Barangu.

Xavier "Harvey" Sandoval died on this day in Belize City in 2013. He is the son of **Felicita Zuniga**. Xavier was known as "Harvey." **Maria Loreta Palacio** is the first cousin thrice removed of Xavier. Harvey always had a smile and a joke to give.

14th January

In the Catholic calendar today is the Feast Day of St. Hilary of Poitiers.

Clotildo Zuniga died on this day in 2006 in Peine. His parents are **Marcos Zuniga** and **Juliana Castillo**. He was born 1917 in Barangu. He married **Eugenia Jean Noralez** in 1966. Clotildo was the second alcalde of Barangu between 1948-1951 and first alcalde of Barangu between 1951-53. He was the Roman Catholic Church mayordomo for many years in the village.

Kenrick Gilbert Marin was born on this day in Belize City. He is the son of **Gilbert Marin** and **Loretta Williams**. **Maria Loreta Palacio** is the first cousin four times removed of Kenrick.

James Marin was born in Barangu on this day in 1934. James is the son of **Clarence Marin** and **Victoria Zuniga**. **Maria Loreta Palacio** is the first cousin thrice removed of James. **Orson Lucious Nicholas** is the grandson of James. Orson's father **Godfrey Marin** is James' son.

Claro Zuniga and **Mauricia Cayetano** were married on this day in 1875 in Barangu. Claro is the son of **Mariano Zuniga** and **Juana Paula Celertina**. **Mauricia Cayetano** is the daughter of **Anacleto Cayetano** and **Dominga Martila Arzu**. Lucille "Chilagu" Valencio nee Zuniga is the granddaughter of Claro and Mauricia.

John de Malha Palacio and **Nicanora Garcia** were married on this day in 1917. John is the son of **Teodoro Palacio** and **Petrona Cayetano**. Nicanora is the daughter of **Apolinario Garcia** and **Marcelina Augustina Martinez**. John died the same day he was married.

On this day **John de Malha Palacio** died in 1917 in Peine. He is the son of **Teodoro "Joe Young" Palacio** and **Petrona Cayetano**. He was born in 1884 in Barangu. John married **Nicanora Garcia** earlier the same day he died. **Maria Loreta Palacio** is the aunt of John.

Hilaria Mejia was born on this day in 1906 in Barangu. She is the daughter of **Simon Mejia** and **Andrea Nicholas**. Hilaria married **Joseph Pollard Palacio** in 1924 in Barangu. **Angela Palacio** is the granddaughter of Hilaria.

Candido Arzu (left) and Clotildo Zuniga

15th January

In the Catholic calendar today is the Feast Day of Our Lord of Esquipulas (*El Senor de Esquipulas*), an important day in the Catholic church calendar in Barangu.

Clayton Chavez was born on this day in Peine. His parents are **Joycelyn Miller** and **Gilroy Chavez**. **Maria Loreta Palacio** is the great-great-great-aunt of Clayton.

Jerry Patrickjean Arzu was born on this day in Belize City. He is the son of **Hazel Arzu**. Jerry is the grandson of **Candido Arzu** and **Bernadette Arzu nee Loredo**. **Maria Loreto Palacio** is the great-great-great-aunt of Jerry and the first cousin four times removed of Jerry.

On this day **Paul Morgan** was born in Peine. He is the son of **Govel Morgan** and **Virginia Patricia Martinez**. Paul is one of the founders of the VIP political party. His father, Govel, was a rural primary school teacher.

16th January

In the Catholic calendar today is the Feast Day of Pope St. Maecellius I.

Basilia Lucas was born on this day in Peine in 1914. She is the daughter of **Fernando Lucas** and **Diega "Cocona" Benguche**. Basilia was confirmed in Barangu in 1923. She married **Anastacio Reyes** in 1944 in Barangu.

On this day in 1961 **Ambrosio Joseph** and **Petrona Palacio** were married in Corozal. Ambrosio is the son of **Francis Joseph and Juliana Castillo**. Petrona is the daughter of **Augustine Palacio** and **Simeona Mejia**. **Maria Loreta Palacio** is the great-aunt of Petrona. Ambrosio and Petrona moved from Barangu to Caye Caulker many years ago. Petrona has been very involved in the Catholic Church ministry. Petrona died in 2012.

Agnes Alvarez was born on this day in 1944. She is the daughter of **Eustacio Alvarez** and **Elvira Cris Velasquez**. Agnes is the first cousin once removed of **Maria Loreta Palacio**.

Marcelo Colindres was born on this day in Barangu in 1909. he is the son of **Victoriano Colindres** and **Pasquala Ramirez**. **Maria Loreta Palacio** is the great-aunt of Marcelo. **Claude Zuniga** is the first cousin once removed of Marcelo.

On this day in 1918 in Peine **Martin Bernardez** and **Apolinaria Ogaldez** were married. Their daughter **Silveria Bernardez** married **Felix "Aska" Noralez** in 1943 in Peine.

Joseph Velasquez and **Eulalia Arana** were married on this day in 1935 in Barangu. Joseph is from Ironia, Indura and is the son of **Faustino Velasquez** and **Gregoria** (unknown last name). Eulalia "Lala" is the daughter of **Alejandro Arana** and **Gregoria Bermudez**.

On this day **Elma Yvonne Martinez** was born. She is the daughter of **Francis Benedict Martinez** and **Victoria Barcelona**. Elma married **Ellis Henry Arzu**.

17th January

In the Catholic calendar today is the Feast Day of St. Anthony the Abbot.

Egbert Anthony Valencio (2004)

Egbert Anthony Valencio was born on this day in Peine. He is the son of **Raymond Valencio** and **Lucille Zuniga**. He served as a member of the village council. He was the first resident of the village to ever be issued a logging concession and one of the few Garinagu to be issued one. Egbert is the first cousin thrice removed of **Maria Loreta Palacio**.

On this day in 1918 in Barangu **Marcelo Zuniga** was born. He is the son of **Rafael Zuniga** and **Catarina Paulino**. **Lucille Valencio nee Zuniga** is the first cousin of Marcelo.

Francisca Serapia died on this day in 1910. She was one of the founders of Barangu along with her spouse **Francisco Nolberto**. We don't know the names of her father or mother or even her family name. Most if not all of the Nolbertos of Barangu are descended from **Francisca Serapia**. She is the great-grandmother of **Paula Nolberto**.

In 1914 on this day in Peine **Antonia Noralez** was born. She is the daughter of **Martin Benjamin Noralez** and **Modesta Lucas**. Antonia is **Eugenia "Jean" Zuniga nee Noralez**'s mother's sister with a different mother.

Michael Anthony Arana was born on this day. He is the son of **Francisco Bonifacio "Frank" Arana** and **Narcisa Esther Contreras**. His father, Frank, was a farm demonstrator for a number of years in Barangu.

18th January

On this day in 1944 **Carmela Arzu** died in Peine. She is the daughter of **Andrea Avelina Santiago**. Carmela had one child, **Modesto Zuniga**, with **Clotildo Zuniga** in 1942.

Juliana Guevara was born on day. She is the daughter of **Joseph Guevara** and **Teodora Nicholas**. Teodora is the aunt of **Frederick Nicholas**.

In Peine on this day in 1913 **Pedro Petillo** was born. He is the son of **Bonifacio Petillo** and **Carmen Enriquez**. Pedro is the uncle of **Sheridan Arzu nee Petillo**.

Petrona Juliana Avila was born on this day in 1908 in Barangu. She is the daughter of **Pantaleon Avila** and **Juliana Garcia**. **Marti Cain nee Arana** is the first cousin once removed of Petrona. **Victoriano Avila** is the common ancestor of Petrona and Marti with Pantaleon and Pedro John are brothers.

19th January

Today in the Catholic calendar is the Feast Day of St. Canute IV.

Canuto Zuniga was born on this day in 1895 in Barangu. He is the son of **Natividad Zuniga** and **Christina Nolberto**. He married **Loriana Ramirez**. Canuto is the first cousin of **Clotildo Zuniga** and the father of **Abraham Zuniga**.

On this day **Derona Requena** was born in Belize City. She is the daughter of **Esme Requena**. **Lauruni Lucille Valencio** is the daughter of Derona and **Egbert Valencio**.

On this day in 2008 Andy Vivien Palacio died. He is the son of **Gregorio Ruben Palacio** and **Cleofa Avilez**. Andy was a very well known musician, composer, and public servant. His album, *Watina*, won numerous awards, including the World Music Award in Seville, Spain, October 28th, 2007.

Canuta Martinez was born on this day in 1902 in Barangu. She is the daughter of **Liborio Martinez** and **Romalda Avila**. Canuta is the aunt of **Paula Nolberto**.

20th January

In the Catholic calendar today is the Feast Day of St. Fabian.

On this day in 2001 in Peine **John Jacob Zuniga** died. He died less than two months before his one hundredth birthday. He was born in Barangu in 1901. John is the son of **Ascencion Zuniga** and **Eluteria Cayetano**. John was an educator most of his working life. He also worked as a tally man for United Fruit Company. He was a well known herb doctor. **Dercy Sandoval** is the granddaughter of John.

Florencia Cayetano nee Lucas died on this day in 1990 in Peine. She is the daughter of **John Nipalmson Lucas** and **Benita Nunez**. Florencia married **Francis Benedict Cayetano** in 1938. **Fabian Cayetano** and **Sebastian Cayetano** are children of Florencia.

Fabiana Nolberto was born on this day in 1933 in Barangu. She is the daughter of **Dionisio Nolberto** and **Nicolasa Martinez**. She was a noted singer of traditional Garifuna music both sacred and secular. She died in 1995 in Labuga. She was known as "Chiquita." She is the aunt of **Irma Gonzalez nee Ariola**.

Andy Vivien Palacio (2003)

9

On this day in 1913 in Barangu **Peter Canuto Paulino** was born. He is the son of **Eugenio Paulino** and **Nicolasa Zuniga**. Peter is the great-uncle of Surusia **Peitra Arana**.

Gabian Sebastian Palacio was born on this day in 1884 in Barangu. He is the son of **Anastacio Palacio** and **Magdalena Cesaria**. Maria Loreta Palacio is the first cousin of Gabian. **Raymond Valencio** is the grandnephew of Gabian.

On this day in 1873 in Barangu **Policarpio Paulino** was born. He is the son of **Diego Paulino** and **Dominga "Waganga" Cayetano**. Policarpio is the grandson of **Juan Pedro Cayetano**.

21st January

In the Catholic calendar today is the Feast Day of St. Agnes.

Edgar Wayne Joseph was born on this day in Barangu. He is the son of **Ambrosio Joseph** and **Petrona Palacio**. Maria Loreta Palacio is the great-great-aunt of Edgar Wayne.

On this day in 1923 in Barangu there was a set of twins born, **Leonarda Polonio** and **Timoteo Polonio**. They were the children of **Cecilio "Dick" Polonio** and **Camila Contreras**. **Bartolo Polonio** is the brother of Leonarda and Timoteo.

Juan Avilez died on this day in 1922 in Barangu. He was 69 when he died. After her first husband **Narciso Bermudez** died, **Dominga "Gadu" Marin** had eight children with **Juan Avilez**. Andy Palacio is the great-grandson of **Juan Avilez** through his maternal grandfather.

Andy Palacio Relationship to Juan Avilez		
Juan Avilez	common ancestor	Juan Avilez
Juan Avilez	son	Ufamio Avilez
Juan Avilez	granddaughter	Clofa Avilez
Juan Avilez	great-grandson	Andy Vivien Palacio

Eulalio Loredo died on this day in Barangu in 1918. He was 49 when he died. His spouse is **Gregoria Palacio**. She had a couple of nicknames. "Ponana" was one and the other was "Go Da Night." This is another example of a Baranguna woman attracting an outside man to the village. Eulalio was from Dangriga and before moving to Barangu he was a police constable. In Barangu he was a tailor. Eulalio was elected first alcalde twice, once in 1906 and again the following year in 1907. **Melquiades Julius Loredo**, better known as "Jimbo," is the great-grandson of Eulalio.

On this day in 1904 **Maria Eugenia Delavez** died in Barangu. She along with her spouse, **Joseph Alexander Nicholas**, were early settlers of Barangu. Eugenia was 64 when she died. Nearly all of the Nolbertos of Barangu and all of the Nicholases of Barangu are descended from her.

Ignacia "Inez" Arana was born on this day in Barangu in 1900. She is the daughter of **Alejandro Arana** and **Gregoria Bermudez**. She was known in the village as "Dadi." She married **William Grant** in 1933 in Barangu. She married **Pascacio Cayetano** in 1939 in Barangu. **Zita Arzu nee Alvarez** is the granddaughter of Inez. Inez may of also had a twin sister named **Teresa Arana**. I have her in the government birth records but can not find her baptism but I have Ignacia's. Teresa may have died soon after birth.

On this day in Barangu in 1892 **Claudio Ariola** died. He is the son of **Rufino Ariola** and **Ascenciona "Da Sola" Paulino**. Claudio was born in 1890. **Francisco "Chico" Ariola** is the grandnephew of Claudio.

In 1904 on this day in Barangu **Eugenio Paulino** and **Nicolasa Zuniga** were married. Eugenio was elected second alcalde in 1915. Eugenio and Nicolasa are the great-grand-parents of Surusia **Peitra Arana**.

Patricio Ariola and **Vicenta Castillo** were married on this day in 1904. Patricio is the son of **Rufino Ariola** and **Ascenciona Paulino**. Vicenta is the daughter of **Rafael Castillo**. Patricio had eleven children with Vicenta and two other women. Patricio was elected first alcarde for 1912. Patricio is the great-grandfather of **Trevor Ariola**.

Harold Arzu was born on this day. He is the son of **Bernadette Loredo** and **Candido Arzu**. Harold is known as "Greg." He married **Sheridan Petillo**. Maria Loreta Palacio is the great-great-aunt of Harold and also the first cousin thrice removed of Harold.

In Peine on this day **Dale Gutierrez** was born. He is the son of **Steven Gutierrez** and **Valentina "Flora" Lorenzo**. Maria Loreta Palacio is the great-great-aunt of Dale.

Agnes Lopez was born on this day in Barangu. She is the daughter of **Patrick Lopez** and **Josephine Palacio**. Maria Loreta Palacio is the great-great-aunt of Agnes.

On this day Orson **Lucius Nicholas** died on this day in 2005. He is the son of **Godfrey Marin** and **Avelina Nicholas**. Orson was born in 1979. **Maria Loreta Palacio** is the first cousin five times removed and also the great-great-great-aunt of Orson.

22nd January

In the Catholic calendar today is the Feast Day of St. Vincent of Saragozza.

Michael Luke Loredo died on this day in 2002 in Belize City. He is the son of **Hector Loredo** and **Anacleta "Da" Nolberto**. Michael has a twin brother, Mark. Michael was born in 1975. He was a member of the Belize Defence Force.

John Justo Avilez died on this day in Barangu in 1946. He was the grandson of **Santiago Avilez**, the founder of the village. He married **Paula Noralez** in Peine in 1894. He was a storekeeper in the village. He was one of the first village residents to own his village lot and to also own farm land. During the colonial period he was one of the few Baranguna who could vote in colonial elections which he qualified for because of his land ownership.

On this day in 1934 **Martin Benjamin Noralez** and **Andrea Avelina Santiago** were married in Peine. Martin was known as "Sasu." He died in 1948 in Guatemala City. Martin was described as a businessman. **Eugenia "Jean" Zuniga nee Noralez** is the daughter of Martin with her mother, **Jane Lino**.

Ivan Avilez was born on this day in Indura and baptized about three months later in Peine. He is the son of **Bernard Avilez** and **Anacleta Castro**. He is the grandson of **Ambrosio "Sabigi" Avilez** and the great-grandson of **Santiago "Gaünbü" Avilez**, the founder of Barangu. Ivan is retired from the U.S. and now lives in Peine.

Andres Sebastian and **Romalda Zuniga** were married on this day in 1906 in Barangu. This is Romalda's second marriage. She had married **Liberato Palacio** in 1903. He died 11 months later in June 1904. This again is an instance of a Baranguna woman attracting a man from outside. **Inocente "Mafia" Zuniga** is the brother of Romalda. Andres is from Indura.

On this day in Barangu in 1907 **Vicente Gutierrez** was born. He is the son of **Crescente Gutierrez** and **Felipa Bermudez**. **Dominga "Gadu" Marin** is his grandmother on his mother's side.

23rd January

Today in the Catholic calendar is he Feast Day of St. Ildefonso. The name has Germanic origins. The name comes from when the Visigoth invaded what is now called Spain in 415AD. The two citation below are examples of using the calendar to name the children.

On this day in Barangu in 1910 **Ildefonsa Arzu** was born. She is the daughter **Isidro Arzu** and **Maxima Ariola**.

Ildefonso Lambey was born on this day in 1914 in Peine. He is the son of **Severiano Lambey** and **Romana Arana**. Ildefonso is **Almira "Irma" Ariola**'s second cousin twice removed through her Nolberto side.

Almira Ariola Relationship to Ildefonso Lambey		
Francisco Nolberto	common ancestor	Francisco Nolberto
Pio Nolberto	siblings	Gregoria Nolberto
Dionicio Nolberto	first cousins	Severiano Lambey
Paula Nolberto	second cousins	Ildefonso Lambey
Almira Ariola	second cousin once removed	Ildefonso Lambey

Alfonsa Zuniga was born on this day in 1920 in Peine. She is the daughter of **Inocente Zuniga** and **Luciana Nolberto**. Alfonsa married **Eugenio Cayetano** in 1938 in Barangu. She died in 1939 in Belize City.

Laruni Lucille Valencio was born on this day in Belize City. She is the daughter of **Egbert Valencio** and **Derona Requena**. **Maria Loreta Palacio** is the first cousin four times removed of Laruni.

Peter Palacio and **Tranquilina Zuniga** were married on this day in Peine in 1896. Peter is the son of **Anastacio "Baibai" Palacio** and **Magdalena Cesaria**. Tranquilina is the daughter of **Antolino Zuniga** and **Isidora Nunez**. **Maria Loreta Palacio** is the first cousin of Peter.

Ambrose Arana died on this day in Dangriga in 1983. He is the son of **Cipriano Arana** and **Leonora Avila**. He was born in 1937 in Barangu. He married **Juliana "Linda" Lopez**. Ambrose taught school in Barangu and was an educational officer. **Maria Loreta Palacio** is the first cousin twice removed of Ambrose.

24th January

Today in the pre-1969 Catholic calendar is the Feast Day of St. Tomothy.

Timoteo Chimilio was born on this day in 1911 in Barangu. He is the son of **John Chimilio** and **Delfina Blas**. He died in a boating accident in 1982. **Vilma Petrona Chimilio** is the daughter of Timoteo. **Maria Loreta Palacio** is the first cousin twice removed of Timoteo. **Crispulo Chimilio** is the brother of Timoteo.

On this day in 1906 **Macario Martinez** and **Escolastica Santino** were married in Barangu. Macario is the son of **Nolberto Martinez** and **Francisca Nunez**. Escolastica is the daughter of **Philip Santino** and **Justina Cayetano**. Here again is an example of a Baranguna woman attracting a man to the village. Escolastica is from Barangu and Macario is from Peine. Escolastica is known as "Ka." **Jacinta Trigueno nee Santino** is the niece of Escolastica.

Agapito Bernardez and **Venancia Nolberto** were married on this day in Barangu in 1905. Agapito is the son **Francisco Bernardez** and **Francisca** (last name unknown). Venancia is the daughter of **Francisco Nolberto** and **Francisca Serapia**. This too is an example of a Baranguna woman attracting a man from outside.

Vicente Apolonio was born on this day in 1903 in Barangu. Vicente is the son of **Macario Apolonio** and **Venancia Nolberto**. Vicente married Felicita Bernardez in 1960 in Dangriga. **Alvin Loredo** is the first cousin twice removed of Vicente on the Nolberto side.

25th January

In the Catholic calendar today is the Feast Day of Conversion of Paul the Apostle.

Philip Nicholas was born on this day in Barangu in 1932. He is the son of **Victor Leonard Nicholas** and **Paula Lopez**. Philip is the brother of **Martin "Game and Gone"** or **"Tin-Tin" Nicholas**.

Timoteo Noralez was born on this day in Barangu in 1920. He is the son of **Felix "Aska" Noralez** and **Juana Nolberto**. Timoteo is the uncle of **Teresa "Tandu" Noralez**.

Andres Patricio Enriquez died on this day in Peine. He is the son of **Joseph Victoriano Enriquez** and **Maria Genera Colindres**. Andres was born in Peine in 1886 in Peine. He married **Jane Victoriana Villafranco** in 1912 in Peine. Andres died in 1951 in Peine. Andres was a schoolteacher. He taught for a short time in Barangu but spent most of his teaching career in San Antonio Toledo.

Kelvin Casimiro was born on this day in 1947 in Barangu. He is the son of **Gonzalez Casimiro** and **Mary Flores**. Kelvin died in 1950. He is the brother of **Fermin Casimiro**.

Paul A. M. Williams was born on this day in Peine. He is the son of **Dionisio Williams** and **Eugenia "Henny" Martinez**. Paul married **Cecilia Rhys** in 1977 in Dangriga. Paul is the grandson of **Prudencio "Brown" Martinez**.

26th January

In the Catholic calendar today is the Feast Day of St. Paula.

Martha Ramirez was born on this day in 1934 in Barangu. She is the daughter of **Bonifacio Ramirez** and **Evangelista Nunez**. **Maria Loreta Palacio** is the great-aunt of Martha. Martha is the sister of **Eduviges "Auntie Bia" Ramirez**.

Melvinia Martinez was born on this day in Barangu in 1912. She is the daughter of **Pedro Nicasio Martinez** and **Augustina Nunez**. Melvinia is better know as "Grandma Mi." **Roy Rogers** is the son of Melvinia.

On this day in 1898 in Barangu **Daniel Ariola** and **Alberta Nicholas** were married. Daniel is the son of **Rufino Ariola**. Alberta is the daughter of **Leoncio Nicholas** and **Christina Garcia**. Daniel died two years later in 1900. Alberta remarried in 1908 to **Philip Santino**. Daniel and Alberta had one son, Branlio who was born in 1899 and died six months later. Daniel is the great-uncle of **Francisco "Chico" Ariola**. Alberta is the aunt of **Victor Joseph Nicholas**.

Paula Ramirez was born on this day in Barangu in 1916. She is the daughter of **Sebastian Ramirez** and **Manuela Ariola**. Paula is the first cousin of "Chico" **Francisco Ariola**.

Policarpio Zuniga was born on this day in 1889 in Barangu. He is the son of **Natividad Zuniga** and **Christina Nolberto**. Policarpio died on the same day as he was born. He is the uncle of **Clotildo Zuniga**.

27th January

In the Catholic calendar today is the Feast Day of St. John Chrysostom.

Paula Paulino was born on this day in 1917. She is the daughter of **Eusebio Paulino** and **Pasquala Ramirez**. She died in 2005 in Peine. With **Jerome Alvarez** she is the mother of **Tim Alvarez** and **Emma Alvarez**.

On this day **Sadie Nolasca Alvarez** was born in Barangu. She is the daughter of **Eustacio Alvarez** and **Toribia Garcia**.

On this day in Peine in 1916 **Feliciano Lopez** and **Vicenta Palacio** were married. Feliciano is from Dangriga and the son of **Eugenio Lopez** and **Cornelia Martinez**. Vicenta is from Barangu and the daughter of **Teodoro "Joe Young" Palacio** and **Petrona Cayetano**. **Maria Loreta Palacio** is the sister of Vicenta with a different mother.

Juan Christomo Gregorio was born on this day in 1911 in Barangu. He is the son of **Viviano Gregorio** and **Bernardina Santino**. Juan is **Petrona "Petu" Gregorio**'s brother. He is the uncle of **Victoriana "Vicky" Nolberto**.

On this day in Barangu in 1917 **Pablo Paulino** was born. He is the son of **Eusebio Paulino** and **Pasquala Ramirez**. Eusebio was the grandson of "Big Ease." **Maria Loreta Palacio** is the great-aunt of Pablo. **Eduviges "Auntie Bia" Ramirez** is the first cousin of Pablo with **Carmen Ramirez** as a common ancestor.

28th January

On this day in 1900 in Barangu there was a set of twins born **John Garcia** and **William Garcia**. They are the sons of **Esmith Garcia** and **Blacina Apolonio**. Esmith Garcia was a tailor and so were many other members of the Garcia family.

Otilda Avilez was born on this day in Peine. She is the daughter of **Lucio Avilez** and **Dorotea "Sista" Ramirez**. **Cherry-Mae Avilez** is the daughter of Otilda and **Govel Morgan**. **Cleofa Avilez** is the first cousin of Otilda.

In Barangu in 1897 on this day **Francisco Sales Paulino** was born. He is the son of **Augustin "Big Ease" Paulino** and **Juana Luis**. Juana's mother is **Clara Martinez**. Clara was an early midwife in Barangu.

Juana Martinez was born on this day in 1903. Juana is the daughter of **Anacleto Martinez** and **Juliana Garcia**. Juana's mother Juliana married **Pantaleon Avila** in 1905. Juana is the first cousin thrice removed of **Kevin Zuniga**.

Kevin Zuniga Relationship to Juana Martinez		
Apolinario Garcia	common ancestor	Apolinario Garcia
Carmen Garcia	siblings	Juliana Garcia
Juliana Castillo	first cousins	Juana Martinez
Clotildo Zuniga	first cousins once removed	Juana Martinez
Isaac Zuniga	first cousin twice removed	Juana Martinez
Kevin Zuniga	first cousin thrice removed	Juana Martinez

Teodoro "Joe Young" Palacio and **Petrona Cayetano** were married on this day in Barangu in 1880. Teodoro is the son of **Francisco Palacio** and **Desideria**. This was Teodoro's second marriage. Petrona is the daughter of **Juan Pedro Cayetano** and **Maria Nicolasa Moralez**.

On this day **Narciso Bermudez** and **Dominga "Gadu" Marin** were married on this day in 1880 in Barangu. Narciso is the son of **Santiago Bermudez** and **Rosa Angela** (unknown last name). **Erlinda Ogdalez nee Nicholas** is the great-great-grand-daughter of Narciso and Dominga.

29th January

In the Catholic calendar today is the Feast Day of St. Francis de Sales.

Rita Avila was born on this day in Peine. She is the daughter of **Olivia Prudencia Palacio** and **Cirilo Avila**. Rita married **Lloyd Enriquez**. Rita is an educator and founder of the Garifuna Museum in Barangu. **Maria Loreta Palacio** is the great-great-aunt of Rita.

John Justo Avilez and **Paula Noralez** were married on this day in 1894 in Peine. John Justo was a store keeper in Barangu. The land for the present Roman Catholic was donated by John Justo. **James Avilez** is the son of John and Paula.

On this day in 1925 **Anita Marin** was born in Barangu. She is the daughter of **Aparicio Santiago Marin** and **Brigida Paulino**. Anita is the aunt of **Clifford Marin**.

Pedro Ramirez and **Juana Ariola** were married on this day in 1901. Juana is from Barangu and the daughter of **Rufino Ariola** and **Ascenciona Paulino**

On this day in 1886 **Francisca Palacio** was born. She is the daughter of **Teodoro "Joe Young" Palacio** and **Petrona Cayetano**. **Maria Loreta Palacio** is the sister of Francisca.

Luis Majin Villafranco and **Antonia Zuniga** were married on this day in 1894 in Peine. Luis is the son of **Juan Villafranco** and was from Indura. Antonia is the daughter of **Marti Zuniga** and **Maria Petrona Labriel**. **Jerry Enriquez** is the great-grand-son of Luis and Antonia.

Luciano Arzu and **Eulogia Palacio** were married on this day in Barangu in 1916. Luciano is from Labuga while Eulogia is from Barangu, another example of Baranguna woman attracting an outside male. Eulogia is the daughter of **Nolberto Palacio** and **Ignacia Arana**. **Maria Loreta Palacio** is the aunt of Eulogia. Luciano is the cousin of **Francisco Ellis Arzu**, their fathers both coming from Labuga and marrying two Palacio sisters.

Claudio Martinez died on this day in Quirigua, Guatemala. He is the son of **Ireneo Martinez** and **Bernardina Santino**. His body was sent to Peine from Guatemala and the Heron H took the body to Barangu. **Victoriana "Vicky" Nolberto nee Martinez** is the daughter of Claudio.

30th January

In the Catholic calendar today is the Feast Day of St. Martina of Rome.

Joseph Cayetano (2005)

Joseph Cayetano was born on this day in Peine. He is the son of **Francis Benedict Cayetano** and **Florencia Lucas**. Joseph married **Hazel Castro**. Joseph was the first Baranguna to be elected as an Area Representative in the National Assembly. Joseph is an educator. **Maria Loreta Palacio** is the great-grandmother of Joseph.

Inebessi Sandoval was born on this day in Peine. He is the son of **Augusto Castillo** and **Dercy Sandoval**. **Maria Loreta Palacio** is the first cousin four times removed of Inebessi.

Francis Nunez was born on this day in Labuga. He is the son of **Evaristo "Bob Steele" Nunez** and **Juanita Cayetano**. He has two nicknames in the village, "Chico" and "Cronic."

On this day in Commerce Bight **Govel Morgan** was born in 1932. Govel was a career educator. **Govel Morgan** was one of the first group of Garifuna young men that the Catholic Church selected for secondary school education at St. Johns College in Belize City

and to return to teach in primary schools after graduation. **Govel Morgan** is the father of **Cherry-Mae Avilez** with **Otilda Avilez**.

Martina Noralez was born on this day in Barangu in 1922. She is the daughter of **Felix "Aska" Noralez** and **Juana Nolberto**. Martina is the aunt of Teresa "Tandu" Noralez.

Martin Polonio was born on this day in Peine in 1921. He is the son of **Cecilio "Dick" Polonio** and **Camila Contreras**. Martin is the brother of **Bartolo Polonio**.

On this day in 1929 in Peine **John Paulino** and **Santiaga Enriquez** were married. John is the son of **Augustin "Big Ease" Paulino** and his second wife, **Martina Arzu**. Santiaga is from Peine.

Saturnino Palacio and **Felicita Reyes** were married in Barangu in 1906. Saturnino is the first cousin of **Maria Loreta Palacio**. Saturnino was noted for his knowledge of distillation which he used in making "drinking alcohol." **Raymond Valencio** is grandson of Saturnino and Felicita. Saturnino was a first alcalde in 1919 in Barangu. Saturnino was one of the several farmers who did banana cash-cropping along the Temash River.

31 January

Victoria Barcelona was born on this day in 1919. She is the daughter of **Isabel Barcelona** and **Fecunda Gabriel**. Victoria married **Francis Benedict Martinez** in 1935 in Peine. Francis' father, Francisco, lived in Barangu adjoining **Henry Loredo**'s lot. **Elma Yvonne Arzu nee Martinez** is the daughter of Victoria.

On this day in Barangu **Henry Peter Zuniga** was born in 1934. He is the son of **John Jacob Zuniga** and **Tomasine Loredo**. **Derrick Zuniga** is the son of **Henry Moriera** and **Sotera Moriera**. **Maria Loreta Palacio** is the first cousin twice removed of Henry. **Felicita "Cita" Zuniga** is the sister of Henry.

Alexine Loredo was born on this day in Barangu in 1912. She is the daughter of **Eulalio Loredo** and **Gregoria Palacio**. She married **Evaristo Nunez** in 1938 in Barangu. Another example of a Baranguna woman attracting an outside man. **Maria Loreta Palacio** is the first cousin once removed of Alexine. **Elorine Nunez** is the daughter of Alexine.

Erasmo Casimiro and **Paula Noralez** were married in Barangu in 1962 on this day. There were twelve children from this marriage. This is a family that started in Barangu but moved to Peine. Erasmo was also known as "Amos." **Ricorda Geraldine Casimiro** is the daughter of Erasmo and Paula.

In Peine on this day **Manuel Carmen Paulino** married **Zeferina Ortiz** in 1883. Manuel is the son of **Diego Paulino** and **Maria Victoria Gamboa**. Manuel's father Diego was one of the early pioneers of the village.

In Barangu on this day **Carmen Ramirez** and **Eustaquia "Bilacu" Palacio** were married in 1889. Here is another example of Baranguna woman attracting an outside man. Carmen was known as "Bulan." **Maria Loreta Palacio** is the sister of Eustaquia. **Eduviges "Auntie Bea" Ramirez** is the granddaughter of Carmen and Eustaquia.

More Life Events in January

FEBRUARY

1st February

In the Catholic calendar today is the Feast Day of St. Ignatius of Antioch and also St. Cecilius of Granada.

Emelda Marin was born on this day in Barangu in 1909. She is the daughter of **Aparicio Marin** and **Brigida Paulino**. In 1937 Emelda married **Toribio Joseph Lopez**. **Maria Loreta Palacio** is the first cousin twice removed of Emelda. **Erlinda "Delane" Ogaldez nee Nicholas** is the granddaughter of Emelda.

On this day in 1915 **Cecilia Ramirez** was born in Peine. She is the daughter of **Pedro Ramirez** and **Juana Ariola**.

Dionisio Noralez was born on this day in 1908 in Barangu. He is the son of **Felix Noralez** and **Juana Nolberto**. Juana is the daughter **Pio Nolberto** and **Casimira Nicholas**. **Teresa "Tandu" Noralez** is the niece of Dionisio.

On this day **Averill Arzu** was born in Belize City. He is the son of **Stephen Arzu** and **Barbara Andrews**. **Maria Loreta Palacio** is the first cousin five times removed of Averill. **Vilma Chimilio** is the grandmother of Averill.

In 1916 in Barangu **Ignacio Nunez** was born. He is the son of **Felix Nunez** and **Albina Cayetano (Avilez)**.

Ivan Arzu was born on this day in Barangu in 1943. His mother is **Cecilia Flores**. He is the nephew of **Procopio Flores**. **Adriana "Tun" Casimiro** is his first cousin.

Macaria Gutierrez was born this day in 1915 in Peine. She is the daughter of **Crescente Gutierrez** and **Felipa Bermudez**. Macaria is the granddaughter of **Dominga "Gadu" Marin**.

Mildred Hernandez was born on this day in Dangriga. She is the daughter of **Peter Egbert Hernandez** and **Paula Serano**. Mildred married **Rudy Concepcion Arana** in Belize City in 1969. Surusia **Peitra Arana** is the daughter of Mildred and Rudy.

On this day **Ignacia Arana** was born in 1872 in Peine. She is the daughter of **Dionisio Arana** and **Basilia Labriel**. Ignacia was known as "Glessima." She married **Nolberto Palacio** in 1890 in Barangu. Surusia **Tim Palacio** is the great-grandson of Ignacia.

Nicolasa Martinez was born on this day in 1907 in Peine. She is the daughter of **Liborio Martinez** and **Eluteria Cayetano**. Nicolasa married **Dionisio Nolberto** in 1924 in Peine. Nicolasa died in 1991 in Barangu. **Anacleta "Da" Nolberto** is the daughter of Nicolasa.

Nicolasa Martinez was born on this day in 1907 in Peine. She is the daughter of **Liborio Martinez** and **Eluteria Cayetano**. Nicolasa married **Dionisio Nolberto** in 1924 in Peine. Nicolasa died in 1991 in Barangu. **Anacleta "Da" Nolberto** is the daughter of Nicolasa.

2nd February

Darina Martinez was born in Belize City on this day. She is the daughter of **Martin Martinez** and **Joy Young**. **Maria Loreta Palacio** is the great-great-great-aunt of Darina. **Martin Martinez** and **Evilia Martinez nee Gonzalez** are the grandparents of Darina.

Andres Avila was born in Peine on this day in 1903. He is the son of **Pantaleon Avila** and Nolasca Colindres. Andres is the first cousin once removed of **Marti Cain nee Arana**. Cecilia Sebastian was born on this day in 1907 in Barangu. She is the daughter of **Andres Sebastian** and **Romalda Zuniga**. Cecilia is the first cousin of **Lucille "Chilagu" Valencio nee Zuniga**.

On this day **Francisco Nunez** and **Martina "Obispa" Martinez** were married in Peine. Francisco is the son of **Alfonso Nunez** and **Felipa Blanco**. Martina is the daughter of **Pedro Martinez** and **Regina Virgen Luis**. **Evaristo "Bob Steele" Nunez** is the son of Francisco and Martina. **Melvinia "Grandma Mi" Martinez** is the niece of Martina.

Emry Casimiro was born on this day in Corozal. He is the son of **Dionisio Casimiro** and **Alice Nicholas**. **Maria Loreta Palacio** is the great-great-great-aunt of Emry on his mother's side and also the great-great-aunt of Emry on his father's side (*see next page*). Emry is the father of **Rashad Casimiro**.

3rd February

Stephen Arzu was born on this day in Barangu. He is the son of **Julian Arzu** and **Vilma Petrona Chimilio**. He married **Elida Palacio**. Stephen is the first cousin four times removed of **Maria Loreta Palacio**.

On this in Barangu in 1945 **Paul Casimiro** was born. He is the son of **Petrona Ariola** and **Peter Casimiro**. Paul died in Barangu in 2002. He was a fisherman.

Antonio Avilez and **Juana Palacio** were married on this day in 1904. **Juana Palacio** is the daughter of **Anastacio Palacio**. **Santiaga Avilez** is the daughter of Antonio and Juana. Juana is the niece of **Maria Loreta Palacio**.

Emry Casimiro Relationship-1 to Maria Loreta Palacio		
Teodoro Palacio	common ancestor	Teodoro Palacio
Maria Loreta Palacio	siblings	Nolberto Palacio
Maria Loreta Palacio	aunt	Josephine Palacio
Maria Loreta Palacio	great-aunt	Alice Nicholas
Maria Loreta Palacio	great-great-aunt	Emry Casimiro

Emry Casimiro Relationship-2 to Maria Loreta Palacio		
Teodoro Palacio	common ancestor	Teodoro Palacio
Maria Loreta Palacio	siblings	Juana "Jane" Palacio
Maria Loreta Palacio	aunt	Margarita Lorenzo
Maria Loreta Palacio	great-aunt	Dionisio Casimiro
Maria Loreta Palacio	great-great-aunt	Emry Casimiro

On this day in Orange Walk in 1969 **Secundino Martinez** and **Bonifacia Avilez** were married. This was a late in life marriage. Secundino is the son of **Saturnino "Senerial" Martinez**. Secundino had married his first wife, Anastacia Santiago, in 1929.

Nicolasa Zuniga was born on this day in 1887 in Barangu. She is the daughter of **Natividad Zuniga** and **Christina Nolberto**. Nicolasa married **Eugenio Paulino** in 1904 in Barangu.

On this day **Presentacion Nunez** was born in 1914 in Peine. He is the son of **Francisco Nunez** and **Martina "Obispa" Martinez**. Presentacion married **Gregoria "Gogo" Paulino** in 1938 in Peine. He died in 1946.

4th February

In the Catholic calendar today is the Feast Day of St. Andrew Corsini.

Petrona Gregorio died on this day in 2002 in Barangu. She was born in 1912 in Barangu. Petrona's parents are **Viviano Gregorio** and **Bernardina Santino**. Petrona was better known as "Petu." She is the aunt of **Victoriana "Vicky" Nolberto nee Martinez**.

Catarino Patricio Ariola died on this day in Barangu in 1973. He is the son of **Patricio Ariola** and **Florencia Lambey**. Catarino was born in Barangu in 1895. He married **Benita Nunez** in 1929 in Peine. Catarino was the second alcalde in Barangu in 1904. He was first alcalde in 1909, 1923, 1929 and 1930. Catarino is the grandfather of **Jacinta Palacio** and the father of **Francisco "Chico" Ariola**.

Eluteria Cayetano died on this day in Barangu in 1927. Her parents are **Sebastian Sanchez** also known as "Sebastian Nunez" and **Vinciona Cayetano**. Eluteria married **Clemente Satuye** in 1888 in Peine. She was 53 years old when she died. Besides Clemente she also had children with **Liborio Martinez**,

Ascencion Zuniga, **Simon Mejia** and **Sebastian Arzu**. There were other instances of multiple male and female spouses at this time in the village, which had not been too often earlier. One possibility was the onset of cash income from banana cropping in the late 1880s to the early 1900s resulting in the inflow of more men and women into the community.

On this day in 1863 in Barangu **Andrea Cayetano** was born. This is the second birth recorded in Barangu. Andrea was born a little less than two months after Maria Loreta Palacio was born. Andrea's parents are **Anacleto Cayetano** and **Dominga Martila Arzu**.

Andrea Palacio was born on this day in 1911 in Monkey River. She is the daughter of **Catarino T. Palacio** and **Francisca Sacasa (Ortiz)**. On her baptism paper it indicates that both her parents were residents of Barangu when she was born. She married **Antonio Palacio** in 1934 in Peine. **Maria Loreta Palacio** is the aunt of Andrea. The presence of Baranguna in the Monkey River area is reflection of the inflow of persons from Seine Bight to the area of Monkey River during the heyday of banana cash cropping. There are several overlapping kinship ties between Baranguna and persons from Seine Bight.

On this day **Tom Andrew Casimiro** was born in Barangu. He is the son of **Gonzalez Casimiro** and **Mary Flores**. Tom is the brother of **Fermin Casimiro**.

On this day **Zaira Mierelli Martinez** was born in Belmopan. Zaira is the daughter of **Lywelyn Martinez** and **Dativa Elizabeth Melendrez**.

John Nipalmson Lucas died on this day in 1961 in Peine. He is the son of **Joseph Robert Lucas** and **Alfonsa Gabriel**. John was born in 1900 in Peine. He married **Clotilda Nunez** in 1926 in Peine. John is the grandfather of **Fatima Cayetano**.

On this day **Paula Noralez** died in Peine in 2012. She is the daughter of **Luis Nunez** and **Tomasa Noralez**. Paula was born in 1920 in Spanish Lookout. **Erasmo Casimiro** married Paula in 1962 in Barangu. **Muriel Williams nee Casimiro** is the daughter of Paula.

Gilbert Nicholas was born on this day. He is the son of **Victor Leonard Nicholas** and **Paulina Lopez**. **Maria Loreta Palacio** is the first cousin twice removed of Gilbert. **Martin "Game and Gone" or "Tin-Tin" Nicholas** is the brother of Gilbert.

On this day **Nolberto Palacio** and **Ignacia "Glessima" Arana** were married in 1890. Ignacia is the daughter of **Dionisio Arana** and **Basilia Labriel**. Nolberto is the son of **Teodoro "Joe Young" Palacio** and **Maria Tomasa Martinez**. He later married **Bernadina Casimiro nee Nolberto** in 1935 in Barangu. Nolberto raised his grandson, **Paul Palacio**.

Cecilio "Dick" Polonio and **Camila Contreras** were married in Peine in 1920. Cecilio is the son of **Eusebio Polonio** and **Lucia Ordonez**. Camila is the daughter of **Andres Contreras** and **Secundina Colindres**. **Bartolo Polonio** is the son of Cecilio and Camila.

5th February

Felipe Castillo was born in Barangu in 1899. He is the son of **Victoriano Castillo** and **Carmen Garcia**. Felipe is the uncle of **Clotildo Zuniga**.

Virgen M. Martinez was born in Barangu in 1903. Virgen is the daughter of **Bernardo Martinez** and **Felipa Bermudez**. She married **Felix Gonzalez** in 1920 in Peine. This family moved to Peine.

On this day in 1927 **Nicolasa Zuniga** died in Barangu. She was the daughter of **Natividad Zuniga** and **Christina Nolberto**. Nicolasa was born in Barangu in 1887. She married **Eugenio Paulino** in Barangu in 1904. **Clotildo Zuniga** is the nephew of Nicolasa.

Philip Casimiro was born on this day in Barangu in 1921. He is the son of **Pablo Casimiro** and **Bernadina Nolberto**. Philip died in accident in Peine when he tried to "hop" a truck for a ride. He died in Peine early in the morning of the 24th of April 1938 and was buried the same day in Barangu. **Fermin "Rama" Casimiro** is nephew of Philip.

Marcelo Cayetano and **Maria Loreta Palacio** were married on this day in 1883 in Barangu. Marcelo is the son of **Anacleto Cayetano** and **Dominga Martila Arzu**. **Maria Loreta Palacio** is the daughter of **Teodoro "Joe Young" Palacio** and **Maria Tomasa Martinez**. **Sebastian Cayetano** is the great-grandson of Marcelo and Maria Loreta.

6th February

Today in the pre-1969 Catholic calendar is the Feast Day of St. Dorothy.

Elliot Martinez was born on this day. He is the son of **Samuel Hipolito Martinez** and **Regina Lorenzo**. **Maria Loreta Palacio** is the great-aunt of Elliot.

Dorotea Ramirez was born on this day in Barangu. She is the daughter of **Bonifacio Ramirez** and **Eulalia Arana**.

On this day **Doroteo Labriel** was born in 1872 in Peine. He is the son of **Domingo Labriel** and **Ferdinanda Cruz**. Doroteo married **Josefa Arzu** in 1896 in Peine. He again married in 1922 in Peine to **Prudencia Lopez**.

7th February

Today in the pre-1969 Catholic calendar is the Feast Day of St. Romauld the Abbot.

Shermaine Amber Zuniga was born on this day in Barangu. She is the daughter of **Derrick Zuniga** and **Maria Casimiro**. Shermaine's parents are fourth cousins once removed. Shermaine is the first cousin four times removed of **Maria Loreta Palacio**.

Romalda Zuniga was born on this day in 1894 in Barangu. She is the daughter of **Claro Zuniga** and **Mauricia Cayetano**. She married twice, first to **Liberato Palacio** in 1903 and secondly to **Andres Sebastian** in 1906. Romalda is an older sister of **Inocente "Mafia" Zuniga**. She is the aunt of **Lucille "Chilagu" Valencio nee Zuniga**.

On this day in 1978 **Hector Loredo** died in Barangu in a drowning accident. He is the son of **Henry Loredo** and **Ursula Polonio**. **Anacleta Nolberto** is the common-law-wife of Hector. He is the first cousin twice removed from **Maria Loreta Palacio**. **Alvin Loredo** is the son of Hector.

8th February

In the Catholic calendar today is the Feast Day of St. John de Matha.

John de Malha Palacio was born on this day in 1884 in Barangu. He is the son of **Teodoro "Joe Young" Palacio** and **Petrona Cayetano**. He married **Nicanora Garcia** (*next page*) in 1917 in Peine and he died later the same day. **Maria Loreta Palacio** is the brother of John.

On this day **John Nicholas** was born in 1917 in Barangu. He is the son of **Philip Nicholas** and **Fabiana Palacio**. John died in 1937 in San Pedro

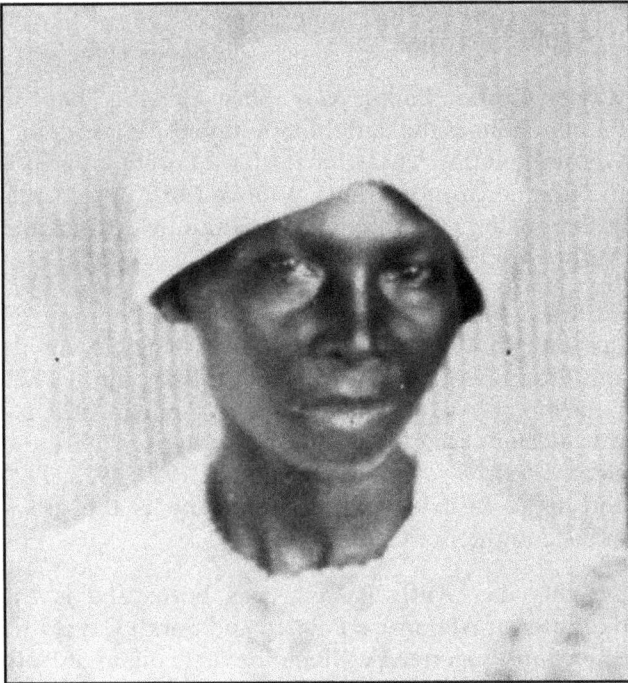

Nicanora Garcia

Sarstoon. **Maria Loreta Palacio** is the first cousin once removed of John.

9th February

Guillermo Valencio was born on this day in 1930. He is the son of **Eufamio Valencio** and **Beatrice Palacio**. **Maria Loreta Palacio** is the first cousin twice removed of Guillermo. **Raymond Valencio** is the brother of Guillermo.

Arreini Paula Palacio was born on this day in Belize City. She is the daughter of **Joseph Orlando Palacio** and **Myrtle Cacho**. **Maria Loreta Palacio** is the great-great-aunt of Arreini.

Policarpio Cayetano and **Maria Gregorio** were married on this day in Barangu. Policarpio is the son of **Juan Pedro Cayetano** and **Maria Nicolasa Moralez**. Maria is the daughter of Jose **Maria Gregorio**.

On this day **David Alvarez Jr.** was born in Belize City. He is the son of **David Alvarez** and **Martina Cornelia Palacio**. **Maria Loreta Palacio** is the great-great-great-aunt of David.

10th February

In the Catholic calendar today is the Feast Day of St. Scholastica.

Escolastica Santino was born on this day in Barangu in 1888. She is the daughter of **Philip Santino** and **Justina Cayetano**. She was known as "Ka" in the village. Escolastica married **Macario Martinez** in 1906 in Barangu. For years Ka or Escolastica made the best buns in Barangu. For the younger children of Barangu, she lived across from the Marins in Louba. Her daughter Encarnacion (Canu) lived with her for years along with Canu's children, Tensie, Martha, Raymond, and Clifford. Escolastica is the great-aunt of **Jacinta Trigueno nee Santino**.

Wayne Kenny Castillo was born on this day in Peine. He is the son of **Joseph Castillo** and **Ricorda Geraldine Casimiro**.

On this day in 1936 in Barangu **Frank Dean Arana** and **Bonifacia Ramirez** were married. Frank is the son of **Alejandro Arana** and **Gregoria Bermudez**. Bonifacia was better known as Evangelista. **Nazaria Zuniga** is the mother of Bonifacia. **Victor "Bobby" Arana** is the son of Frank and Bonifacia.

11th February

In the Catholic calendar today is the Feast Day of St. Saturninus of Albatina the Elder and also the Feast Day of St. Saturninus of Albatina the Younger.

Saturnino Paulino was born on this day in Barangu in 1922. He is the son of **Eusebio "Macoshin" Paulino** and **Pasquala Ramirez**. **Irene Gibbons** is the second cousin of Saturnino with **Diego Paulino** being the common ancestor.

On this day in 1916 **Julio Arzu** was born in Barangu. He is the son of **Francisco Ellis Arzu** and **Patrocinia Palacio**. **Maria Loreta Palacio** is the great-aunt of Julio. **Candido Arzu** is the brother of Julio.

Julia Palacio was born in Barangu on this day in 1900. She is the daughter of **Teodoro "Joe Young" Palacio** and **Petrona Cayetano**. She died five days after her birth on the 16th of February. **Maria Loreta Palacio** is the sister of Julia from a different mother.

Ermeterio Romero and **Crecencia Zuniga** were married in San Pedro Columbia on this day in 1924. Ermeterio is from Labuga and **Crecencia Zuniga** is from Barangu and is the daughter of **Claro Zuniga** and **Mauricia Cayetano**. This marriage is another example of a Baranguna woman attracting a man from outside. The couple was in San Pedro Colombia probably to do logging wage labour or to work on chicle extraction—an indication that persons and couples left Barangu to work close and far away for wage labour. This is worth highlighting as marriage is a male/female event that could take place where they happen to be.

12th February

In the Catholic calendar today is the Feast Day of St. Eulalia of Barcelona.

Martina Lorraine Arzu died on this day in 1973. She is the daughter of Candido Arzu and Bernadette Loredo. She was born in 1948. Martina Lorraine was a school teacher. Maria Loreta Palacio is the great-great-aunt of Martina Lorraine. Hazel Martinez nee Arzu is the sister of Martina Lorraine. Cynthia Leanne Cayetano is the daughter of Martina Lorraine.

On this day in 1896 Diego Paulino died in Barangu. Diego is the patriarch of the Paulino family. He had children with two women, Dominga "Waganga" Cayetano and Maria Victoria Gamboa who was from Labuga. Diego is the father of Augustin "Big Ease" Paulino.

Abraham Zuniga was born on this day in Barangu. He is the son of Canuto Zuniga and Loriana Ramirez. Abraham was a fisherman. Maria Loreta Palacio is the great-aunt of Abraham. He is the first cousin twice removed of Kevin Zuniga.

Eulalio "Bidun" Arana was born on this day in 1914. He is the son of Concepcion Arana and Simeona Flores. Rudy Concepcion Arana is the son of Eulalio Arana and Gregoria "Gogo" Paulino.

Eulalia Martinez was born on this day in Peine in 1905. She is the daughter of Macario Martinez and Escolastica Santino. She is the first cousin once removed of Clifford Marin.

13th February

In the Catholic calendar today is the Feast Day of St. Catherine d'Ricci.

Gonzalez Casimiro died in Barangu on this day in 1983. He is the son of Pablo Casimiro and Bernadina Nolberto. Gonzalez was born in 1911. Mary Flores married him in 1944. Fermin "Rama" Casimiro is the son of Gonzalez.

On this day Toribia Garcia was born in 1934. She is the daughter of Bonifacio Garcia from Dangriga and Geronima Martinez. Toribia married Eustacio Alvarez in 1961 in Barangu. Zita Arzu nee Alvarez is the daughter of Toribia.

Luisa Santino was born in Barangu on this day in 1928. She is the daughter of Augustin Santino and Pauline Palacio. She is known as "My Blood." Maria Loreta Palacio is the aunt of Luisa. Jacinta Trigueno nee Santino is the first cousin of Luisa.

On this day Catalina Santino was born in Barangu in 1928. She is the daughter of Eusebio Santino and Vicenta Blas. Dionisia Marin nee Santino is the sister of Catalina.

Pio Nolberto and Cipriana Gregorio were married on this day in 1921 in Peine. Pio is the son of Francisco Nolberto and Francisca Serapia. This was Pio's third marriage.

Kayla Gloria Lopez was born on this day in Barangu. She is the daughter of Raymond Lopez and Germaine Gloria Martinez. Maria Loreta Palacio is the first cousin four times removed of Kayla. Kayla is the great-granddaughter of Simon Martinez and Ambrosine Mejia.

Catarino Patricio Ariola was born in Barangu on this day in 1895. He is the son of Patricio Ariola and Florencia Lambey. He died in Barangu in 1973. Catarino married Benita Nunez in Peine in 1929. He was elected second alcalde in Barangu in 1904 and elected first alcalde for Barangu in 1909, 1923, 1929 and 1930. Beatrice "Tricia" Mariano is the great-granddaughter of Catarino.

On this day Ruth Palacio was born. She is the daughter of Alejandro Palacio and Sarah Cayetano. Sheridan Arzu nee Petillo is the first cousin of Ruth with Pascacio Cayetano as the common ancestor. Maria Loreta Palacio is the great-aunt of Ruth and also the great-grandmother of Ruth.

14th February

In the Catholic calendar today is the Feast Day of Saint Valentine.

Valentina Lorenzo was born on this day. She is the daughter of Victoriano "Father" Lorenzo and Virgilia Ariola. Valentina is better known as "Flora." Steven "Junior" Gutierrez is the son of Valentina. Maria Loreta Palacio is the great-aunt of Valentina.

Valentina Baltazar was born on this day in Labuga. Her parents are Pablo Baltazar and Adriana Lauriano. Valentina married Gilbert Marin in Belize City in 1968.

Valentin Zuniga was born on this day in Labuga. He is the son of John Jacob Zuniga and Jane "Wana" Alvarez. He is the brother of Felicita "Nitu" Zuniga from a different mother.

Valentina Palacio was born in Barangu on this day in 1911. She is the daughter of Nolberto Palacio and Ignacia "Glessima" Arana. She died in Labuga. Maria Loreta Palacio is the aunt of Valentina. Vicenta "Lulu" Sanchez is the niece of Valentina.

Valentina Alvarez was born on this day. She is the daughter of Feliciano "Felix" Alvarez and Pantaleona Mejia. Maria Loreta Palacio is the first cousin twice removed of Valentina. Lascelle Alvarez is the son of Valentina.

On this day Valentina Jovita Casimiro was born. She is the daughter of Paul Casimiro and Margarita

Gladys Clarice Loredo	Relationship to Maria Loreta Palacio	
Francisco Palacio	common ancestor	Francisco Palacio
Teodoro Palacio	siblings	Anastacio Palacio
Maria Loreta Palacio	first cousins	Gregoria Palacio
Maria Loreta Palacio	first cousins, once removed	Epifania Loredo
Maria Loreta Palacio	first cousins, twice removed	Gladys Clarice Loredo

Lorenzo. Mara **Loreta Palacio** is the great-aunt of Jovita. **Steven "Junior" Gutierrez** is the first cousin once removed of Jovita with **Timoteo Lorenzo** as the common ancestor.

The above six notations are another example of Baranguna using the calendar to name their children. This tradition is seen very seldom in Barangu 2012.

Nolasca Avila was born in Peine on this day in 1912. She is the daughter of **Pedro John Avila** and **Viviana Palacio**. **Maria Loreta Palacio** is the first cousin once removed of Nolasca. She is the aunt of **Marti Cain nee Arana**.

On this day in Barangu in 2010 **Gladys Clarice Loredo** died. Gladys is the daughter of **Patricio Ariola** and **Epifania Loredo**. She was born in Barangu in 1921. Gladys married **Daniel Lino** in 1945 in Barangu. In 1950 her husband and daughter, Mary, drowned in a boating accident. **Maria Loreta Palacio** is the first cousin twice removed of Gladys with **Francisco Palacio** as the common ancestor (*see above*). **Felicita "Nitu" Zuniga** is the first cousin of Gladys.

15th February

In the Catholic calendar today is the Feast Day of St. Faustina of Monte Cassino.

Prudencio "Brown" Martinez and **Gabina Zuniga** were married in Peine on this day in 1905. Prudencio is the son of **Jose Martinez** and **Luisa Zuniga**. Gabina is the daughter of **Claro Zuniga** and **Mauricia Cayetano**. Prudencio and Gabina are the grandparents of **Viola Martinez**.

On this day in Barangu **Faustina Zuniga** was born in 1919. **Marcos Zuniga** and **Juliana Castillo** are the parents of Faustina. **Clotildo Zuniga** is the brother of Faustina. **Kevin Zuniga** is the grand nephew of Faustina.

Faustino Petillo was born on this day in 1922 in Peine. He is the son of **Bonifacio Petillo** and **Carmen Enriquez**. **Leonard "Mr. Pete" Petillo** is the brother of Faustino.

Valentino Santos Nolberto was born in Dangriga on this day in 1897 and baptized in Peine in April of 1897. He is the son of **Macario Nolberto** and **Josefa**

Alvarez. Valentino is the first cousin once removed of **Paula Nolberto** and **Lucille "Chilagu" Valencio nee Zuniga**.

On this day **Brigid Cayetano** was born in Crique Arena. She is the youngest daughter of **Eugenio Cayetano** and **Manuela Marin**. Brigid's father was the principal of Holy Trinity R.C. School in Crique Arena. Many Garifuna children were born in non-Garifuna villages because of the number of families that had followed the Garifuna school teacher to their rural postings. **Maria Loreta Palacio** is the first cousin thrice removed of Brigid.

16th February

In the Catholic calendar today is the Feast Day of Juliana of Nicomedia.

Julia Palacio died in Barangu on this day in 1900. She is the daughter of **Theodore Palacio** and **Petrona Cayetano**. She was five days old when she died. She is the sister of **Maria Loreta Palacio** from a different mother.

Juliana Garcia was born in Barangu on this day in 1892. She is the daughter of **Apolinario Garcia** and **Marcelina "Magiri" Martinez**. She married **Pantaleon Avila** in 1905.

Juliana Castillo was born in Peine in 1896 on this day. She is the daughter of **Victoriano "Weibayua" Castillo** and **Carmen Garcia**. Juliana's father, Victoriano, was a buyei and her uncle is the reknown buyei, "Ding." She married **Marcos Zuniga**. Juliana died in Barangu in 1975. **Clotildo Zuniga** is the son of Juliana. **Kevin Zuniga** is her great-grandson.

Shirley Nicholas was born on this day. She is the daughter of **Ignacio Nicholas** and **Perfecta Avilez**. Master **Victor Nicholas** is the brother of Shirley.

On this day in 1899 **Benigno Avila** was born in Peine. He is the son of **Pedro John Avila** and **Viviana Palacio**, Benigno married **Faustina Chavez** in Monkey River in 1922. Monkey River was in the middle of a banana boom, Benigno may have been up there working. **Maria Loreta Palacio** is the first cousin once removed of Benigno. Benigno is the uncle of **Marti Cain nee Arana**.

17th February

Alexander Avilez was born on this day in 1928. He is the son of **Lucio Avilez** and **Dorotea "Sista" Ramirez**. Alexander is the uncle of **Cherry-Mae Avilez**. **Cleofa Avilez** is the first cousin of Alexander. Alexander's grandfather is **Juan Avilez** who is from Jonathan Point like many other early **Baranguna**.

Ziolyne Miranda was born on this day in Belize City. She is the daughter of **Thomas Miranda** and **Rhoda Alvarez**. Ziolyne is the great-granddaughter of **Jerome Alvarez**.

On this day in 1890 **Pedro Martinez** and **Regina Virgen Luis** were married in Barangu. Pedro and Regina are grandparents of **Melvinia "Grandma Mi" Martinez** and great-grandparents of **Victoriana Victoriana "Vicky" Martinez**.

Inocente Zuniga and **Luciana Nolberto** were married on this day in 1916 in Peine. Inocente is the son of **Claro Zuniga** and **Mauricia Cayetano**. Luciana is the daughter of **Pio Nolberto** and **Casimira Nicholas**. **Lucille "Chilagu" Valencio nee Zuniga** is the daughter of Inocente and Luciana.

18th February

In the Catholic calendar today is the Feast Day of St. Simeon.

Simon Martinez serving drinks on his 103rd birthday

On this day in 1910 **Simon Martinez** was born in Peine. He is the son of **Francisco Martinez** and **Estefania Avila**. He married **Ambrosine Mejia** in Barangu in 1938. **Gloria Martinez** and **Clinton Martinez** are the children of Simon and Ambrosine. He went to Scotland with a group of British Hondurans during WWII to cut timber. He remained in Scotland and had a second family there.

Joan Palacio was born on this day in Mango Creek. She is the daughter of **Antonia Palacio nee Ariola**. Joan is the aunt of **Antonette "Neti" Zuniga** and the granddaughter of **Ruben Palacio**.

Rosa Zuniga was born on this day in in 1933 in Chacalte, Wadimalu. She was adopted by **John Jacob Zuniga** and **Tomasine Loredo**. She is of Q'eq'chi heritage. Her father died in Wadimalu and her mother moved to Dolores with Rosa and then married another man. John adopted Rosa when she was three while teaching in Dolores. There were other cases of Baranguna adopting Q'eq'chi children and having them live as Garifuna; Rosa died around 1979. She is the sister of **Felicita "Nitu" Zuniga**.

Alejandro Arzu was born in Barangu on this day in 1926. He is the son of **Benito Arzu** and **Crecencia Zuniga**.

Francisco Martinez and **Estefania Avila** were married in Peine on this day in 1914. These two are the parents of **Simon Martinez**. **Zaira Martinez** is the great-granddaughter of Francisco and Estefania.

On this day **Simeona Teo** was born in Peine. She is the daughter of **Juan Bautista Teo** and **Bonlea Martina Sanchez**. Simeona married **Casimiro Avilez** in 1919 in Peine. She died in 1922 in Peine.

Gabina Lopez was born on this day in 1918 in Barangu. She is the daughter of **Santiago Lopez** and **Felicita Bermudez**. Gabina is the granddaughter of **Narciso Bermudez** and **Dominga "Gadu" Marin**.

19th February

In the Catholic calendar today is the Feast Day of St. Gabinus.

Joseph Palacio was born in Barangu on this day in 1930. He is the son of **Carlos Palacio** and **Luisa Nunez**. **Maria Loreta Palacio** is the great-aunt of Joseph.

On this day in 1921 **Pio Nolberto** died in Barangu. He is the son of **Francisco Nolberto** and **Francisca Serapia**. He married **Casimira Nicholas** in Barangu in 1883. Pio married again in 1903 in Barangu to **Florencia Blas**. Pio married a third time to **Cipriana Gregorio** in 1921 in Peine. He is the grandfather of **Paula Nolberto**. The Nolbertos likely came to Barangu through Dangriga and/or the Jonathan Point area.

Gabina Zuniga was born on this day in Barangu in 1888. She is the daughter of **Claro Zuniga** and **Mauricia Cayetano**. She married **Prudencio "Brown" Martinez** in Peine in 1905. Gabina is **Elliot Martinez**'s grandmother.

Almira Ariola was born in Barangu on this day. She is the daughter of **Francisco "Chico" Ariola** and **Paula Nolberto**. She is better known as "Irma" in the village. She married Macario "Fino" Gonzalez in Barangu in 1970. **Maria Loreta Palacio** is the great-great-aunt of Irma.

Casimiro Avilez and **Simeona Teo** were married on this day in 1919 in Peine. Casimiro is the son of **Ambrosio Avilez** and **Justa Polonio**. Simeona is the daughter of **Juan Bautista Teo**.

20th February

In the Catholic calendar today is the Feast Day of St. Eleutherius of Tournai.

Diega Benguche died on this day in 1980 in Peine. She is the child of **Gregorio Benguche** and **Teofila "Wana" Martinez**. She was known as "Cocona." She was born in 1893 in Peine. Diega is the great-great-grandmother of **Kevin Zuniga**. In the 1920's Diega legally migrated to Guatemala to work as a domestic for the United Fruit Company. Many Garifuna and other Belizeans migrated to work for the United Fruit Company. Diega was one of the few single women to have migrated. She later returned to Belize.

On this day **Eldred Roy Cayetano** was born in Barangu. He is the son of **Eugenio Cayetano** and **Manuela Marin**. Roy married **Phyllis Miranda** in 1971 in Dangriga. He has been a school teacher, an education officer, a linguist, a CEO in the Ministry of Rural Development, a senator and author of many Garifuna papers and books. Roy is an outstanding Baranguna, Gariifuna, Belizean, and international person.

Silvan Joseph Chimilio was born in Barangu in 1919. He is the son of **John Chimilio** and **Delfina Blas**. Silvan married Claudia Casimiro. **Maria Loreta Palacio** is the first cousin twice removed of Silvan. **Carol Garcia** is the daughter of Silvan and **Josephine Garcia**.

Eluteria Mejia was born on this day in 1917. She is the daughter of **Abraham Bernard Mejia** and **Victoriana Santino**. She married **Casimiro Castillo** in 1946 in Peine. In 1998 she married **Nolberto Flores** in Dangriga. Eluteria is the first cousin once removed of **Victoriana "Vicky" Nolberto nee Martinez**.

On this day **Gabriel Velasquez** and **Mercedes Paulino nee Palacio** were married in 1893 in Peine. Gabriel is the son of **Faustino Velasquez**. Gabriel "Roo" was not from Barangu. Mercedes "Bata" is the daughter of **Anastacio "Baibai" Palacio** and **Magdalena Cesaria**. This was Mercedes' second marriage.

Leon Mejia was born on this day in 1903. He is the son of **Simon Mejia** and **Augustina Nunez**. Leon is the third cousin once removed of Sheridan Arzu Petillo with **Juan Pedro Cayetano** as the common ancestor.

Eleuterio "Linford" Williams was born on this day in Peine. He is the son of **Dionisio Williams** and **Eugenia "Henny" Martinez**. Eleuterio is the grandson of **Prudencio Brown Martinez** and **Gabina Zuniga**.

On this day **Germaine Gloria Martinez** was born in Mango Creek. She is the daughter of **Gloria Martinez**. Germaine is the granddaughter of **Simon Martinez** and **Ambrosine Mejia**.

On this day in Barangu **Paula Nolberto** was born. She is the daughter of **Dionisio Nolberto** and **Nicolasca Martinez**. Paula is a village dance and singing leader. For many years Paula has been a member of a gayusa group that participated as singers in dügüs.

21st February

In the Catholic calendar today is the Feast Day of St. Felix of Hadrumetum and St.Fel ix of Metz.

Felicita Bermudez was born on this day in 1895 in Barangu. She is the daughter of **Narciso Bermudez** and **Dominga "Gadu" Marin**. **Erlinda "Delane" Ogaldez nee Nicholas** is the great-granddaughter of Felicita.

Cindy Nicole Martinez was born on this day in Belize City. She is the daughter of **Melquiades Julius "Jimbo" Loredo** and **Viola Martinez**. Cindy is the first cousin four times removed of **Maria Loreta Palacio**. **Maria Loreta Palacio** is also the great-great-aunt of Cindy.

Phyllis Palacio was born on this day in Wadimalu. She is the daughter of **Alejandro Palacio** and **Sarah Cayetano**. **Maria Loreta Palacio** is the great-aunt of Phyllis through **Catarino T. Palacio**. **Maria Loreta Palacio** is also the great-grandmother of Phyllis. **Alvin Loredo** is the third cousin once removed of Phyllis. Alvin is also the fourth cousin of Phyllis with **Juan Pedro Cayetano** as the common ancestor. Thirdly Alvin is the second cousin of Phyllis with **Eluteria Cayetano** as the common ancestor. The reason for including all these geneaological ties is to show how convoluted the kinship ties are that are found among Baranguna. Two persons can be related to each other in so many ways (*see the next page*).

Felix Martinez and **Serveriano Martinez** were a set of twins born on this day in Barangu in 1910. They are the sons of **Pedro Nicasio Martinez** and **Augustina**

Alvin Loredo Relationship-1 to Phyllis Palacio		
Francisco Palacio	common ancestor	Francisco Palacio
Anastacio Palacio	siblings	Teodoro Palacio
Gregoria Palacio	first cousins	Catarino T. Palacio
Henry Loredo	second cousins	Alejandro Palacio
Hector Loredo	third cousins	Phyllis Palacio
Alvin Loredo	third cousins once removed	Phyllis Palacio

Alvin Loredo Relationship-2 to Phyllis Palacio		
Francisco Palacio	common ancestor	Francisco Palacio
Anastacio Palacio	siblings	Teodoro Palacio
Gregoria Palacio	first cousins	Maria Loreta Palacio
Henry Loredo	second cousins	Pascacio Cayetano
Hector Loredo	third cousins	Sarah Cayetano
Alvin Loredo	fourth cousins	Phyllis Palacio

Alvin Loredo Relationship-3 to Phyllis Palacio		
Eleuteria Cayetano	common ancestor	Eleuteria Cayetano
Nicolasa Martinez	siblings	Eustaquia Satuye
Anacleta Nolberto	first cousins	Sarah Cayetano
Alvin Loredo	second cousins	Phyllis Palacio

Nunez. Felix and Serveriano are the brothers of **Melvinia "Grandma Mi" Martinez**.

Agnus Castillo was born on this day in Barangu in 1871. He is the son of **Rafael Castillo** and **Simona Garcia**. Simona is daughter of **Apolinario Garcia** and his wife **Marcelina (Magiri) Martinez**, who were among the early pioneers of the village.

Cecilio Ramirez and Matilda Arana were married on this day in 1928 in Peine. Cecilio is the son of **Peter Ramirez** and **Juana Gonzalez**. **Mauricio Linford "Linsy" Ramirez** is the son of Cecilio and Matilda.

22nd February

In the Catholic calendar today is the Feast Day of St. Margaret of Cortona.

Pascacio Cayetano was born on this day in 1891 in Barangu. He is the son of **Marcelo Cayetano** and **Maria Loreta Palacio**. Pascacio married **Apolinaria Mejia** in 1912 in Barangu. He married again in 1920 in Barangu to **Eustaquia Satuye**. Thirdly, he married **Ignacia "Inez" Arana**. He died in 1985 in Barangu. **Sheridan Arzu nee Petillo** is the granddaughter of Pascacio.

Margarito Lorenzo was born on this day in 1909 in Barangu. He is the son of **Timoteo Lorenzo** and **Juana**

"Jane" Palacio. Margarita married **Paul Casimiro** in 1933 in Barangu. Margarita died in 1997 in Peine. **Valentina Jovita Casimiro** is the daughter of Margarita.

On this day **Clarence "Cally" Coffin** was born in 1929 in Belize City. He died in Brooklyn, New York, in 2008. Clarence is the father of **Sylvia Coffin** with **Vilma Petrona Chimilio**.

Margarita Garcia was born in Barangu on this day in 1907. She is the daughter of **Esmith Garcia** and **Cornelia Martinez**. The Garcia family was thought of as a family of tailors.

Pantaleon Avila and **Juliana Garcia** were married on this day in Peine in 1905. Pantaleon is the son of **Victoriano Avila** and **Cesaria Zuniga**. Juliana was from Barangu and her parents are **Apolinario Garcia** and **Marcelina Augustina Martinez**. Apolinario and Marcelina were early settlers of Barangu coming from Jonathan Point.

Marcos Zuniga and **Juliana Castillo** were married on this day in 1916 in Barangu. Marcos is the son of **Natividad Zuniga** and **Christina Nolberto**. Juliana is the daughter of **Victoriano Castillo** and **Carmen Garcia**. **Clotildo Zuniga** is the son of Marcos and Juliana.

23rd February

In the Catholic calendar today is the Feast Day of St. Peter Damien.

Eusebio Polonio was born in Peine on this day in 1924. He is the son of **Cecilio "Dick" Polonio** and **Camila Contreras**. He was named after his grandfather **Eusebio Polonio**. Eusebio is the brother of **Bartolo Polonio**.

Damiana Paulino was born in Barangu in 1923 on this day. She is the daughter of **Eusebio Paulino** and **Pasquala Ramirez**. Damiana is the sister of **Paula Paulino**. Damiana is the aunt of **Irene Gibbons**

On this day in 1923 **Florencia Lucas** was born in Peine. She is the daughter of **John Nipalmson Lucas** and **Benita Nunez**. She married **Francis Benedict Cayetano** in Barangu in 1938. She died in 1990 in Peine. Florencia is the mother of our former area representative, **Joseph Cayetano**, the twins, "Sab" and "Fab," the school teacher Mrs. Reyes, "Shorty" and many more.

Florencia Blas was born in 1908 in Barangu on this day. She is the daughter of **Macario Blas** and **Felipa Zuniga**. Her father, Macario, was from Jonathan Point as were many other early settler of the village.

On this day **Daril Avila** was born in Peine. He is the son of **Darius Avila** and **Lisa Woodye**. **Maria Loreta Palacio** is the great-great-great-aunt of Daril.

Apolonia Virginia Labriel died on this day in 1952. She is the daughter of **Santiago Labriel** and **Crecencia Zuniga**. Apolonia married **Thomas Paulino** in 1935 in Peine. Apolonia's father was a school teacher in Barangu.

24th February

In the Catholic calendar today is the Feast Day of St. Matthias the Apostle.

Aniki Patrick Palacio was born on this day in Belize City. He is the son of **Joseph Orlando Palacio** and **Myrtle Cacho**. **Maria Loreta Palacio** is the great-great-aunt of Aniki. **Darius Avila** is the first cousin of Aniki.

On this day in Barangu in 1942 **Modesto Edilberto Zuniga** was born. He is the son of **Clotildo Zuniga** and **Carmela Arzu**. His mother died in 1944, a month before Modesto's second birthday. Modesto is the uncle of **Kevin Zuniga**.

Matias Gutierrez was born on this day in 1909 in Peine. He is the son of **Crescente Gutierrez** and **Felipa Bermudez**. He married **Veronia Gabriel** in 1967 in Peine. Matias is the grandson of **Dominga "Gadu" Marin**.

Sebastiana Valencia was born on this day in 1906 in Limon, Induru. She is the daughter of **Luis Valencia** and **Alfonsa Gomez**. Sebastiana married a Melendrez. Sebastiana is the aunt of **Raymond Valencio** (the name Valencia had changed to Valencio in the move from a Spanish-speaking country to an English-speaking country).

Paulina Reyes died on this day in 1969 in Barangu. She is the daughter of **Martin Reyes** and **Luisa Roches**. She was born in Barangu in 1892. Paulina married **Luis Cayetano**. Later in life she married **George McKensie**. George was from Jamaica. During the banana boom of the 1930's Jamaicans from Wadimalu came to the Barangu area to raise bananas. Their farms were mainly between Boyo Creek and the Temash River. Paulina is the grandmother of **Roy Cayetano**.

Sebastian Sanchez and **Vinciona Cayetano** were married on this day in 1865 in Labuga. Sebastian is the son of **Vicenta Sanchez** and **Hilaria** (unknown last name). Vinciona is the daughter of **Juan Pedro Cayetano** and **Maria Celestina**. Vinciona was known as "Beltrana." **Sheridan Arzu nee Petillo** is the great-great-granddaughter of Sebastian and Vinciona.

25th February

Today in the Catholic calendau it is the Feast Day of Sebastian of Aparicio.

Sebastian Arzu was born on this day in 1862 in Peine. He is the son of **Augustin Arzu** and **Cayetana Gonzalez**. Sebastian had children with **Luciana Enriquez** and **Eluteria Cayetano**. Eluteria is the granddaughter of **Juan Pedro Cayetano** through her mother Vinciona.

Sebastian Gonzalez was born on this day in 1922 in Peine. He is the son of **Felix Gonzalez** and **Virgen M. Martinez**. His mother, Virgen, is the granddaughter of **Dominga "Gadu" Marin**. Dominga was one of the first born in Barangu.

On this day **Isidora "Manu" Arana** died in 2005 in Dangriga. She is the daughter of **Atanacio Arana** and **Leona Garcia**. "Manu" was a buyei who often led dugus in Barangu. Manu is the aunt of **Marti Cain nee Arana**.

26th February

In the Catholic calendar today is the Feast Day of St. Nestor.

Vinton Colon was born on this day. He is the son of **Naomi Colon** and **Charles Marin**. **Maria Loreta Palacio** is first cousin four times removed of Vinton.

Ernesto Martinez was born in 1907 on the Sarstoon Bar. He is the son of **Saturnino "Senerial" Martinez** and **Josefa Paulino**. Many Baranguna moved back and forth between Barangu and the Sarstoon Bar in Wadimalu. The Sarstoon Bar and San Martin (called "San Juan" in Wadimalu) were satellite communities of Barangu, smaller outposts that depended upon the services of the village. Sometimes the parents lived on the Sarstoon and their children lived in the village with a grandparent or other family member and went to school in the village. Some lived on the Bar for extended periods of time planting or harvesting. The Martinez family dominated this area with family ties also in Barangu, Labuga, and Peine.

On this day **John Jacob Zuniga** and **Tomasine Loredo** were married in 1927 in Barangu. John is the son of **Ascencion Zuniga** and **Eluteria Cayetano**. **Tomasine Loredo** is the daughter of **Eulalio Loredo** and **Gregoria Palacio**. John was a rural school teacher. **Amanda Ramos nee Zuniga** is the child of John and Tomasine.

27th February

Sebastiana Zuniga was born on this day in Peine in 1909. She is the daughter of **Faustino Zuniga** and **Estanislada Arzu**. Faustino is the brother of Claro and **Natividad Zuniga**. Sebastiana is the first cousin once removed of **Lucille "Chilagu" Valencio nee Zuniga**.

On this day **Emily Miranda** was born in Brooklyn, New York. She is the daughter of **Thomas Miranda** and **Rhoda Alvarez**. **Geronima Martinez** is the great-grandmother of Emily.

28th February

Macaria Chimilio was born on this day in Barangu in 1914. She is the daughter of **John Chimilio** and **Delfina Blas**. Marcaria died when she was young. She is the sister of Crispulo "Polo" Chimilio. **Maria Loreta Palacio** is the first cousin once removed of Marcaria.

On this day in 1900 in Barangu **Juana Paulino nee Luis** died. She was the daughter of **Pedro Luis** and **Clara Martinez**. Her mother, Clara, was a midwife in the 1880's and 1890's in Barangu. Juana married **Augustin "Big Ease" Paulino** in Barangu in 1883. While Augustin married a Martinez woman, **Saturnino "Senerial" Martinez** married a Paulino woman. It was one way of linking blood ties with marriage ties over generations in earlier Garifuna society. Another set of family names that exchanged ties over generations were the Arzus and Cayetanos. Juana is **Victor Paulino**'s great-grandmother.

29th February

Erlett Lozano was born in Dangriga. She is the daughter of **Yvonne Lopez**. **Maria Loreta Palacio** is the great-great-great-aunt of Erlett.

More Life Events in Febuary

_____

_____

_____

_____

_____

_____

_____

_____

MARCH

1st March

Iris Palacio was born on this day in 1931 in Barangu. She is the daughter of **Augustine Palacio** and **Simeona Mejia**. **Maria Loreta Palacio** is the great-aunt of Iris.

On this day a set of twins, **Angel Ramirez** and **Angela Ramirez** were born in Peine in 1908. They are the sons of **Pedro Ramirez** and **Juana Ariola**. **Francisco "Chico" Ariola** is the first cousin once removed of the twins with **Rufino Ariola** as the common ancestor.

Angel Arzu was born on this day in 1938 in Peine. He is the son of **Benito Arzu** and **Crecencia Zuniga**. Angel was a district superintendent in the malaria control programme.

Luis Rosedo Martinez was born on this day. He is the son of **Francis Benedict Martinez** and **Victoria Barcelona**. Luis is the brother of Elma Arzu nee Martinez.

2nd March

Lucio Avilez was born on this day in 1900 in Barangu. He is the son of **Juan Avilez** and **Dominga "Gadu" Marin**. He married Losanta Cacho in 1933 in Peine. Lucio is the great-great-uncle of **Erlinda "Delane" Ogaldez nee Nicholas** with **Dominga "Gadu" Marin** as the common ancestor.

On this day **Paul Avila** was born in Peine in 1908. He is the son of **Alcardio Avila** and **Justa Gonzalez**. Paul is the uncle of **Rita Enriquez nee Avila**.

Ron Nunez was born on this day in Belize City. He is the son of **Mackie Nunez** and **Joycelyn Miller**. **Maria Loreta Palacio** is the great-great-great-aunt of Ron.

Nolbert Joseph Arzu died on this day in 2002. He is the son of **Candido Arzu** and **Bernadette Loredo**. He was born in Barangu in 1942. Nolbert married Esther, a native of Winnipeg, Canada in 1967. They had a daughter, **Eileen Arzu**. Besides Eileen, Nolbert had five other children: Giovanni Javier, Arlene, Sherette, Natalie, and Victor. He worked for many years as an agronomist for the government until he decided to open up an agricultural supply store in Dangriga. He had moved from Belmopan to Dangriga with the idea of leading the Garifuna people to mechanize the production of cassava as he had seen in South America. Nolbert is related to **Maria Loreta Palacio** in two ways through both his mother and his father. Maria is her great-great-aunt on his father's side and Maria is his first cousin thrice removed on his mother's side. **Harold "Greg" Arzu** is his brother.

3rd March

Simeona Mejia was born on this day in 1905 in Barangu. She is the daughter of **Simon Mejia** and **Petrona Severia** (could be a form of Chavaria). She married **Augustine "Baba Titi" Palacio** in 1923 in Peine. She died in Barangu in 1982. Simeona is the grandmother of Surusia **Ludwig Palacio**.

Emeteria Noralez was born in 1905 on this day in Peine. She is the daughter of **Venancio Noralez** and **Juliana Colindres**. Emeteria is the sister of **Martin Benjamin Noralez**. Martin is the father of **Eugenia "Jean" Zuniga nee Noralez**. Martin is an example of a Peinena moving his family to Barangu.

On this day **Marciana Paulino** was born in 1912 in Barangu. She is the daughter of **Eusebio "Macoshin" Paulino** and **Telesflora Bermudez**. Eusebio "Macoshin" and Telesflora are second cousins. Relationships between second cousins are often seen in Barangu. Perhaps it is a response to the church's ban on cross-cousin marriages (a form of first cousin marriage).

Pablo Arzu was born on this day in 1924 in Barangu. He is the son of **Isidro Arzu** and **Maxima Ariola**. Pablo is the first cousin once removed of **Francisco "Chico" Ariola**.

Augustin Santino and **Pauline Palacio** were married in 1917 in Barangu. Augustin 's parents are **Philip Santino** and **Justina Cayetano**. Pauline's parents are **Teodoro "Joe Young" Palacio** and **Petrona Cayetano**. Augustin and Pauline had to get a dispensation from the church before they could marry. Augustin's mother is the niece of Pauline's mother. So the married couple are first cousins once removed.

On this day **Leonard Petillo** and **Mary Martha Cayetano** were married in 1959 in Crique Sarco. Leonard is the son of **Bonifacio Petillo** and **Carmen Enriquez**. Mary is the daughter of **Pascacio Cayetano** and **Eustaquia Satuye**. Sheridan Arzu nee Petillo is the daughter of Leonard and Mary.

4th March

In the Catholic calendar today is day of St. Casimir which you can see by all the children born on this day named after him. It was a common practice in the past for parents of Baranguna to name their children after the saint of the day they were born.

Ethel Dee Loredo was born in 1925 in Barangu. She is the daughter of **Henry Loredo** and **Martina Avilez**. She married **Paul Palacio**. In 1995 she died in Peine. **Bernadette Arzu nee Loredo** is the sister of Ethel and **Martina Alvarez nee Palacio** is her daughter.

Adriano Nicholas was born in 1922 in Barangu. He is the son of Pablo Nicholas and Aniceta Blas. Adriano married Felicita Valencio in Belize City in 1961. Felicita is the sister of Raymond Valencio.

On this day Amelia Chimilio was born in 1922 in Barangu. She is the daughter of John Chimilio and Delfina Blas. Amelia is the sister of Crispulo Chimilio. Maria Loreta Palacio is the first cousin twice removed of Amelia.

Casimira Nicholas was born on this day in Barangu in 1868. She is one of the early first generation to be born in Barangu. She is the daughter of Joseph Alexander Nicholas and Maria Eugenia Delavez. Casimira married Pio Nolberto in 1883 in Barangu. She died in Barangu in 1901. Alvin Loredo is the great-grandson of Casimira.

Casimiro Avilez was born in Peine on this day in 1888. He is the son of Ambrosio "Sabigi" Avilez and Justa Polonio. Casimiro married Simeona Teo in 1919 in Peine. Casimiro is the grandson of Santiago Avilez.

Casimiro Nunez was born on this day in Peine in 1892. He is the son of Thomas Nunez and Tomasa Ortiz. Thomas Nunez had land near Barangu around Wellis Creek. Casimiro married Gertrude Villafranco in 1914.

Lucia Nunez was born on this day in Peine in 1895. She is the daughter of Thomas Nunez and Tomasa Ortiz.

Casimiro Ariola was born on this day in Barangu in 1899. He is the son of Patricio Ariola and Florencia Lambey. Casimiro died a little over two years later in November of 1901 in Barangu. Casimiro is the uncle of Francisco "Chico" Ariola.

On this day James Alfred Arzu was born in Barangu. He is the son of Slvan Arzu and Tolentina Palacio. Alfred made and sold perfume in the village. He presently lives on Rubadan, Indura. Maria Loreta Palacio is the great-great-aunt of Alfred. Vicenta "Lulu" Sanchez is the aunt of Alfred.

Elisa Ariola was born on this day in Belize City. She is the daughter of Cardinal George Rodriguez and Elswith Frances Ariola. She is the granddaughter of Francisco "Chico" Ariola. Elisa is related to Maria Loreta Palacio two ways on her mother's side. First Maria is the great-great-great-aunt of Elisa and secondly Maria is the first cousin four times removed of Elisa.

Santiago Labriel and Serapia Avilez were married on this day in 1920 in Peine. Santiago is the son of Domingo Labriel and Ferdinanda Cruz. Serapia is the daughter of Ambrosio Avilez and Justa Polonio.

On this day Teresa Nunez was born in 1917 in Peine. She is the daughter of Francisco Nunez and Martina "Obispa" Nunez. Evaristo "Bob Steele" Nunez is the brother of Teresa.

5th March

Balbino Zuniga was born on this day in 1918 in Peine. He is the son of Viviano Zuniga and Filomena Paulino. Viviano and Filomena are second cousins through the Cayetano line. Balbino had a child, Exzine Martinez, with Rosalia "Baby Rose" Martinez who is Balbino's third cousin once removed also through the Cayetano line. Lucille "Chilagu" Valencio nee Zuniga is the first cousin of Balbino.

On this day in 1897 Eusebio Santino was born in Barangu. He is the son of Philip Santino and Justina Cayetano. He married Vicenta Blas in Barangu in 1922. Eusebio died in Barangu in 1970. Jacinta Trigueno nee Santino is the daughter of Eusebio and Vicenta. Clifford Marin is the grandson of Eusebio.

Tomasine Loredo was born on this day in 1908 in Barangu. She is the daughter of Eulalio Loredo and Gregoria "Ponana" or "Go da Night" Palacio. Tomasine married John Jacob Zuniga in Barangu in 1927. She died in 1937 in Barangu. Tomasine is the first cousin once removed of Maria Loreta Palacio. Dercy Sandoval is the granddaughter of Tomasine.

On this day in Barangu Alvin Loredo was born. He is the son of Hector Loredo and Anacleta Nolberto. Sharon Nunez is Alvin's common-law-wife and is also both Alvin's second cousin and Alvin's third cousin once removed. Alvin is a builder in the village. He has served as village chairperson and chairman of the board of SATIIM.

Alvin Loredo (2004)

Rose Maria Arana was born on this day in Barangu. She is the daughter of **Francisco Bonifacio "Frank" Arana** and **Narcisa Esther Contreras**. Rose's father was the farm demonstrator in Barangu. **Hayworth Sabala** married Rose in 1984 in New York.

America Garcia died on this day in 1912 in Barangu. She is the daughter of **Esmith Garcia** and **Cornelia Martinez**. America had been born nine months earlier along with her twin sister, **Georgiana Garcia** in June 1911 in Barangu.

6th March

Luwani Frances Cayetano was born on this day in Belize City. She is the daughter of **Marion Cayetano** and Surusia **Claudina Elington**. Her mother, Claudina is from Labuga. Luwani is the first cousin four times removed of **Maria Loreta Palacio**. **Roy Cayetano** is the uncle of Luwani.

On this day in 1920 **Robert Lucas** was born in Peine. He is the son of **John Nipalmson Lucas** and **Benita Nunez**. In 1996 Robert died in Labuga. Robert is the uncle of **Jacinta Palacio**.

Secundino Avilez died on this day in 1958 in Peine. He is the son of **Ambrosio Avilez** and **Justa Polonio**. Secundino was born in 1900 in Peine. **Bonifacia Ramirez** married Secundino in 1922 in Peine. **Santiago "Gaünbü" Avilez**, the founder of Barangu, is the grandfather of Secundino.

7th March

Josephine Genevieve Arana was born on this day in Hopkins. She is the daughter of **Cipriano Arana** and **Leonora Avila**. She was born in Hopkins while her father was teaching there. **Maria Loreta Palacio** is the first cousin twice removed of Josephine. Josephine is a younger sister of **Marti Cain nee Arana**.

Polonia Zuniga died on this day in 1924 in Barangu. She is the daughter of **Claro Zuniga** and **Mauricia Cayetano**. When she died she was 34 years old. Polonia is the aunt of **Lucille "Chilagu" Valencio nee Zuniga**.

Joycelyn Miller was born on this day in Belize City. She is the daughter of **Denzel Miller** and **Josephine Palacio**. **Maria Loreta Palacio** is the great-great-aunt of Joycelyn.

On this day **Damien Tingling** was born in Dangriga. He is the son of **Edward Tingling** and **Rosita Miller**. **Maria Loreta Palacio** is the great-great-great-aunt of Damien. **Augustine "Baba Titi" Palacio** is the great-grandfather of Damien.

In the Catholic calendar today is the Feast Day of St. John of God.

John Jacob Zuniga was born on this day in 1901 in Barangu. He is the son of **Ascencion Zuniga** and **Eluteria Cayetano**. He married **Tomasine Loredo** in Barangu in 1927 and, after his first wife died, he married **Telesflora "Stella" Simeona Mejia** in Barangu in 1939. John was a rural primary school teacher. He died in Peine in January 2001 just shy of his 100th birthday. **Felicita "Nitu" Zuniga** is John's and Tomasine's daughter. **Sharron Gelobter nee Williams** is John's and Telesflora "Stella's" granddaughter.

John Jacob Zuniga

Macario Nolberto was born in Barangu in 1864. He is the son of **Francisco Nolberto** and **Francisca Serapia**. He married **Josefa Alvarez** in 1925 in Dangriga. This was a marriage later in life to the woman by whom he had most of his children. Macario is the grandfather of **Lorenzo "Thunder" Nolberto**. Macario is the great-uncle of **Paula Nolberto**.

Juana "Jane" Palacio was born in 1888 in Barangu. She is the child of **Teodoro "Joe Young" Palacio** and **Petrona Cayetano**. Juana married **Timoteo Lorenzo** in 1903 in Barangu. **Maria Loreta Palacio** is the sister of Juana from a different mother. Juana is the mother of **Victoriano "Fada" Lorenzo**. She is the great-grandmother of **Steven "Junior" Gutierrez**.

On this day in Barangu in 1901 **Martha Palacio** was born. She is the daughter of **Catarino T. Palacio** and

Francisca Sacasa (Ortiz). Martha married **Fabiano Arzu** in Peine in 1921. **Maria Loreta Palacio** is Martha's aunt.

Victor Leonard Nicholas was born on this day in Barangu in 1909. He is the son of **Philip Nicholas** and **Fabiana Palacio**. He married **Paulina Lopez** who was from Seine Bight. He died in 1996 in Bridgeport, Connecticut. **Maria Loreta Palacio** is the first cousin once removed of Victor.

On this day in Peine in 1915 **John Palacio** was born in Peine. He is the son of **Catarino T. Palacio** and **Francisca Sacasa (Ortiz)**. John married **Zenobia Enriquez** in 1941 in Peine. **Maria Loreta Palacio** is John's aunt.

9th March

In the Catholic calendar today is the Feast Day of St. Frances of Rome.

Francisca Santino was born on this day in Barangu in 1930. She is the daughter of **Eusebio Santino** and **Vicenta Blas**. Francisca died when she was four or five years old. **Jacinta Trigueno nee Santino** is the sister of Francisca.

On this day in 1915 in Barangu a set of twins were born, **Victoria Cayetano** and **Francis Benedict Cayetano**. They are the children of **Pascacio Cayetano** and **Apolinaria Mejia**. Victoria died as an infant in a boating accident as well as her mother. Francis married **Florencia Lucas** in 1938 in Barangu. Francis was a rural primary school teacher. He was known as "Dun Dun" in the village. Sab and Fab are children of Francis and Florencia.

On this day in Barangu **Sandra Casimiro** was born. She is the daughter of **Francis Casimiro** and **Evelyn Enriquez**. Sandra is the sister of **Maria Zuniga nee Casimiro**.

Fabiana Nolberto died on this day in 1995 in Labuga. She is the daughter of **Dionisio Nolberto** and **Nicolasa Martinez**. Fabiana was born in 1933 in Barangu. Fabiana married **Tom Alvarez** who was from Labuga. Fabiana was a noted singer of arumahani and abeimahani songs.

10th March

Victoria Mejia was born on this day in 1899 in Barangu. She is the daughter of **Simon Mejia** and **Andrea Nicholas**. Victoria is the aunt of **Olivia "Aunti Olive" Avila nee Palacio**.

On this day in 1926 **Benito Arzu** was born. He is the son of **Gregorio Arzu** and **Teodora Nicholas**. Benito is the first cousin of **Frederick Nicholas**.

Myrna Martinez was born on this day. She is the daughter of **Fred Martinez** and **Anacleta Nolberto**. **Keila Sharlene Martinez** is the daughter of Myrna.

11th March

In the Catholic calendar today is the Feast Day of St. Eulogius of Cordoba and you will see below the influence of the Saints' days on the calendar in naming of children in Barangu. Today's posting shows another aspect of Garifuna naming. Using the calendar to name children results in the village having a number of people with the same first name. The use of nicknames is one way of dealing with this problem.

Eulogia Palacio was born on this day in 1893 in Barangu. She is the daughter of **Nolberto Palacio** and **Ignacia Arana**. Eulogia married **Luciano Arzu** in 1916 in Barangu. She also had a child, **Bernabe Apostol Palacio** with **John Castillo**. **Maria Loreta Palacio** is the aunt of Eulogia.

On this day in 1904 **Casimiro Castillo** was born in Barangu. He is the son of **Victoriano Castillo** and **Carmen Garcia**. Casimiro's father, Victoriano was a buyei in the village. Casimiro was known as "Cundu" or "Cundumi." He married **Eluteria Mejia** in 1946 in Peine. Casimiro died in Peine.

Eulogia Nicholas was born in 1912 in Barangu. She is the daughter of **Philip Nicholas** and **Fabiana Palacio**. Eulogia Nicholas was locally known as "Ma Logie." Eulogia married **Stephen Paulino** in 1942 in Peine. **Maria Loreta Palacio** is the first cousin once removed of Eulogia. Eulogia is the mother of **Victor Paulino**.

Eulogia Avilez was born on this day in 1914. She is the daughter of **John Justo Avilez** and **Paula Noralez**. Eulogia was known as "Toti" in the village. Eulogia is the aunt of **Bernadette Arzu nee Loredo**. Eulogia Avilez had two daughters, **Veronica "Dindina" Avilez**, and **Leonie Avilez**, both raised by her brother, **James J. Avilez**. Eulogia died in Dangriga during Hurricane Hattie in 1961.

Agatha Santino was born on this day in 1922 in Barangu. She is the daughter of **Augustin Santino** and **Pauline Palacio**. **Maria Loreta Palacio** is the aunt of Agatha. **Jacinta Trigueno nee Santino** is the first cousin of Agatha.

12th March

In the Catholic calendar today is the Feast Day of Pope St. Gregory the Great.

Gregorio Garcia was born on this day in Barangu in 1909. He was the son of **Esmith Garcia** and **Cornelia**

Martinez. Esmith had six children with his wife and seven children with **Cornelia Martinez**.

On this day **Gregoria Gutierrez** was born in 1913 in Peine. She is the daughter of **Crescente Gutierrez** and **Felipa Bermudez**. Gregoria is the granddaughter of **Dominga "Gadu" Marin**.

Gregorio Ruben Palacio

Gregorio Ruben Palacio was born on this day in 1918 in Barangu. He is the son of **Hipolito Palacio** and **Josefa Zuniga**. Ruben died in 2003 in Peine. **Antonia Ariola** married Ruben in 1930. **Andy Palacio** is the son of Ruben and **Cleofa Avilez**. Ruben was the postmaster in the village for a number of years.

Gregoria Arzu was born on this day in Peine in 1920. She is the daughter of **Fabiano Arzu** and **Martha Palacio**. Martha is the daughter of **Catarino T. Palacio**. **Maria Loreta Palacio** is the great-aunt of Gregoria.

Lloyd Arana was born on this day. He is the son of **Agnes Alvarez**. **Maria Loreta Palacio** is the first cousin four times removed. Lloyd is the nephew of **Zita Arzu nee Alvarez**.

13th March

Solomon Velasquez was born on this day in either Indura or Nicaragua. He is the son of **Faustino Velasquez**. Solomon married **Cristobel Loredo** in Peine in 1925. Solomon was a cook on ships and was also a cook for United Fruit Company.

Asenciona Lorenzo was born on this day in 1913 in Barangu. She is the daughter of **Timoteo Lorenzo** and **Juana "Jane" Palacio**. **Maria Loreta Palacio** is

the aunt of Asenciona. She is the great-aunt of **Dale Gutierrez**.

On this day in 1909 **John Paulino** was born in Peine. He is the son of **Augustin "Big Ease" Paulino** and **Martina Arzu**. This child for "Big Ease" is with his second wife, Martina. "Big Ease" second marriage was to a Peinina. After his second marriage he moved to Peine. This may be reflected in John's birth in Peine.

Leandra Paulino was born on this day in 1902 in Barangu. She is the daughter of **Julian Paulino** and **Nicolasa Palacio**. **Maria Loreta Palacio** is the first cousin once removed of Leondra.

On this day in 1924 in Barangu **Anastacio Palacio** died. He is the son of **Francisco Palacio** and **Desideria**. He came to Barangu probably from Dangriga via Jonathan Point. He was known as "Baibai." He had concurrent relationships with two women, **Magdalena Cesaria** and **Sotera Gutierrez**. Anastacio was the uncle of **Maria Loreta Palacio**. Anastacio was the last survivor of the original settlers of Barangu that came in the early 1860's. **Egbert Valencio** is the great-great-grandson of Anastacio.

14th March

In the Catholic calendar today is the Feast of St. Matilda of Saxony.

Sebastiana Arzu was born on this day. She is the daughter of **Domingo Arzu** and **Eugenia "Henny Girl" Nicholas**. **Maria Loreta Palacio** is the first cousin once removed of Sebastiana.

Matildo Zuniga was born in Barangu in 1928. He is the son of **John Jacob Zuniga** and **Tomasine Loredo**. **Maria Loreta Palacio** is the first cousin twice removed of Matildo. Matildo is brother of **Felicita "Nitu" Zuniga**.

Matildo Zuniga was born in Barangu in 1929. He is the son of **Inocente Zuniga** and **Luciana Nolberto**. He died as an infant. He is the brother of **Lucille "Chilagu" Valencio nee Zuniga**.

On this day **Josephine Palacio** was born in Barangu. She is the daughter of **Augustine Palacio** and **Simeona Mejia**. **Maria Loreta Palacio** is the great-aunt of Josephine. **Lynette Valerie Valerio** is the granddaughter of Josephine.

Max Alvarez and **Ciriaca Lucas** were married on this day in 1935 in Peine. Ciriaca is the daughter of **Joseph Robert Lucas** and **Alfonsa Gabriel**. **John Nipalmson Lucas** is the brother of Ciriaca.

On this day in 1996 in Peine **Crispino Martinez** and **Florencia Avila** were married in Peine. This was a late in life union. "Crispin" is the son of **Victoriano Martinez** and **Isabela Zuniga**. He was sent as a child to live with a Creole family in Belize City.

Martin Polonio and **Archangela Ogaldez** were married on this day in Mango Creek in 1955. Martin is the son of **Cecilio "Dick" Polonio** and **Camila Contreras**. Martin died in Dangriga. **Bartolo Polonio** is the brother of Martin.

15th March

Hazel Loredo was born on this day in 1930 in Barangu. She is the daughter of **Henry Loredo** and **Ursula Polonio**. This child was with Henry's second wife. Hazel is the first cousin once removed of **Maria Loreta Palacio**.

Emelda Rash was born on this day in Conejo. She is the daughter of **Alfredo Rash** and **Maria Makin**. Emelda has two children with **Egbert Valencio**. Over the years the Makin family has had relationships with a number of Baranguna individuals. **Maria Loreta Palacio** is the great-great-aunt of Emelda's first cousin once removed.

Julia Petillo was born on this day in 1907 in Peine. She is the daughter of **Bonifacio Petillo** and **Carmen Enriquez**. Julia married **Pedro Juan Avila**. Pedro signed a pupil teacher contract in Barangu for 12.07.1917-02.07.1920.

Dorla Marian Casimiro was born on this day in Peine. Dorla is the daughter of **Ricorda Geraldine Casimiro**. Dorla is the granddaughter of **Paula Casimiro nee Noralez**.

Dercy Sandoval was born on this day. She is the daughter of **Felicita Zuniga** and the granddaughter

Dercy Sandoval (2009)

of **John Jacob Zuniga**. **Maria Loreta Palacio** is first cousin thrice removed of Dercy.

16th March

Today in the pre-1969 Catholic calendar is the Feast Day of St. Abraham the Hermit.

Abraham Bernard Mejia was born on this day in 1885 in Labuga. He is the son of **Cirilo Mejia** and **Margarita Rivas**. Abraham married **Victoriana Santino** in 1917 in Peine. This is another case of a Baranguna woman attracting a outside man to Barangu.

On this day in 1899 **Benigno Avila** was born in Peine. He is the son of **Pedro John Avila** and **Viviana Palacio**. Benigno married Faustina Chavez in 1922 in Monkey River. **Maria Loreta Palacio** is the first cousin once removed of Benigno. **Marti Cain nee Arana** is the niece of Benigno.

Leon Cacho was born on this day in Belize City. He is the son of **Daniel Cacho** and **Celestina Enriquez**. Leon's maternal grandmother is **Vilma Petrona Chimilio**. **Maria Loreta Palacio** is the first cousin five times removed of Leon.

On this day in 1983 **Dominica Noralez** died in Barangu. She is the daughter of **Venancio Noralez** and **Gumercinda Palacio**. She was born in 1914 in Peine. Dominica married **Domingo Arzu** in 1942 in Belize City. She died in a fire in Barangu. **Maria Loreta Palacio** is the first cousin twice removed of Dominica.

17th March

In the Catholic calendar today is the Feast Day of St. Patrick.

Cherry-Mae Avilez was born on this day in 1969 in Benque Viejo. She is the daughter of **Govel Morgan** and **Otilda Avilez**. **Juan Avilez** and **Dominga "Gadu" Marin** are the great-grandparents of Cherry-Mae. **Andy Palacio** is the second cousin of Cherry-Mae.

On this day in 1864 **Patricio Ariola** was born. He is the son of **Rufino Ariola** and **Acenciona Paulino**. Patricio had children with **Florencia Lambey**, **Vicenta Castillo** and **Epifania Loredo**. He died in Barangu in 1959. He was a first alcalde for Barangu in 1912.

Margarita Castillo was born on this day in 1911 in Barangu. Margarita is the daughter of **Inez Castillo** and **Martha Fuentes**. Margarita married **James J. Avilez** in 1934 in Peine.

Patrick Lopez was born on this day in 1925 in Peine. He is the son of **Antonio Lopez** and Loreta Brown. He died in 1998 in Belize City. Patrick is **Yvonne Lopez's** father.

Adriano Natividad Arana died on this day in 1948 in Peine. He is the son of **Concepcion Arana** and **Simeona Flores**. Adriano was born in 1903 in Peine. Adriano is the father of **Francisco Bonifacio "Frank" Arana**. Adriano's son Frank was a farm demonstrator in Barangu.

18th March

Clarence Nunez was born in 1935. He is the son of **Evaristo "Bob Steele" Nunez** and **Alexine Loredo**. **Maria Loreta Palacio** is the first cousin once removed of Clarence. **Elorine Nunez** is the brother of Clarence.

On this day **Joseph Avilez** was born in 1896. He is the first child of **John Justo Avilez** and **Paula Noralez**. Joseph is the great-grandson of **Santiago Avilez**. **James J. Avilez** is the brother of Joseph.

Gabriel Nicholas was born in Barangu on this day in 1908. He is the son of **Leoncio Nicholas** and his second wife, **Alberta Nolberto**. **Ignacio Nicholas** is the brother of Gabriel.

19th March

Today in the religious year of the village, it is the Feast of St. Joseph. St. Joseph is the patron saint of Barangu.

Curt Nunez was born on this day in Belize City. He is the son of **Mackie Nunez** and **Joycelyn Miller**. **Maria Loreta Palacio** is the great-great-great-aunt of Curt.

On this day in Barangu **Amanda Zuniga** was born. She is the daughter of **John Jacob Zuniga** and **Tomasine**

Amanda Ramos nee Zuniga (2003)

Loredo. She married **"Pants" Ramos** in Barangu. She makes dolls in the village. **Loma Rodriguez nee Sanchez** is the daughter of Amanda. **Maria Loreta Palacio** is the first cousin twice removed of Amanda.

On this day in 1902 **Joseph Pollard Palacio** was born in Barangu. He is the son of **Nolberto Palacio** and **Ignacia Arana**. He married **Hilaria Mejia** in 1924 in Barangu. Hilaria died in 1946. He remarried in 1947 to **Carlotta Marin** in Barangu. He was a rural primary school teacher and farmer. Joseph died in Peine in 1975. **Maria Loreta Palacio** is the aunt of Joseph. **Darius Avila** is the grandson of Joseph.

Josefa Paulino was born on this day in Barangu in 1887. She is the daughter of **Augustin Paulino** and **Juana Luis**. She married **Cayetano Amaya** in 1908 in Barangu and later married **Felix Lucas** in 1934 in Peine. She also had four children with **Saturnino "Senerial" Martinez**.

20th March

Eufemio Gutierrez was born on this day in 1911 in Peine. He is the son of **Crescente Gutierrez** and **Felipa Bermudez**. Eufemio married **Juliana Lambey** (granddaughter of **Gregoria Nolberto**) in Peine in 1940. **Narciso Bermudez** and **Dominga "Gadu" Marin** are the grandparents of Eufemio. **Steven Gutierrez** is the grandson of Eufemio.

Filomena Chimilio was born on this day in Barangu in 1909. She is the daughter of **John Chimilio** and **Delfina Blas**. She is the older sister of **Crispulo "Polo" Chimilio**. **Maria Loreta Palacio** is the first cousin once removed of Filomena.

On this day **Bernardina Arzu** was born in Peine in 1909. She is the daughter of **Juan Bautista Arzu** and **Obispa Florentina Paulino**. Bernardina married **Crescencio Roches** in 1933 and she died eight days later. She is the granddaughter of **Augustin "Big Ease" Paulino** and **Juana Luis**.

21st March

In the Catholic calendar today is the Feast Day of Saint Benedicta Cambiagio Frassinello.

Benedictina Polonio was born on this day in 1922. She is the daughter of **Pantaleon Odway Polonio** and **Petrona Paulino**. Benedictina married **Filomeno Lorenzo,** "Father's" brother, in 1939 in Barangu. She is the first cousin of **Bartolo Polonio**.

On this day in Peine in 1920 **Benedicto Martinez** was born. He is the son of **Secundino Joseph Martinez** and **Anastacia Vicenta Santiago**. Benedicto married **Francisca Palacio** in Peine in 1945. He is the grandson of **Saturnino "Senerial" Martinez** and **Josefa**

Paulino. **Emily Ramirez nee Martinez** who taught school in Barangu is the daughter of **Benedicto**.

Liselle Celine Valencio was born on this day in Belize City. She is the daughter of **Leroy Bradley** and **Leolin Elma Valencio**. **Maria Loreta Palacio** is the first cousin four times removed of Liselle.

Benita Nunez was born on this day in Peine in 1899. She is the daughter of **Carmelo Nunez** and **Genevieve Martinez**. She was known as "Lobi" in the village. Benita had children with **John Nipalmson Lucas** in Peine. She married **Catarino Ariola** in 1929 and moved to Barangu where she had children with him as well as raising children of Catarino that he had with other women. Benita died in 1981 in Barangu.

Hipolito Martinez died on this day in 2003 in Barangu. He is the son of **Prudencio "Brown" Martinez** and **Gabina Zuniga**. Hipolito was born in 1920 in Peine. He married **Regina Lorenzo** in Barangu in 1939. **Viola Martinez** is Hipolito's daughter.

22nd March

Today in the pre-1969 Catholic calendar is the Feast Day of St. Catherine of Sweden.

On this day in Mango Creek **Catherine Joseph** was born. She is the daughter of **Ambrosio Joseph** and **Petrona Palacio**. **Maria Loreta Palacio** is the great-great-aunt of Catherine.

Victoriano Lorenzo was born on this day in Barangu in 1923. He is the son of **Timoteo Lorenzo** and **Juana "Jane" Palacio**. Victoriano was known as "Father." He married **Virgilia Ariola** and they had one child **Valentina "Flora" Lorenzo**. **Maria Loreta Palacio** is the aunt of Victoriano. He is remembered for his fudge. "Father" died in 1994 in Peine. **Dale Gutierrez** is his grandson.

23rd March

In the Catholic calendar today is the Feast Day of St. Victorian.

Victoriano Garcia was born on this day in Barangu in 1895. He is the son of **Esmith Garcia** and **Blacina Apolonio**. The Garcia family had a number of tailors among them. Store-bought clothes were a luxury and difficult to find in Barangu. So the village had its own seamstresses and tailors.

Victoriana Vargas was born in 1918 on this day in Barangu. She is the daughter of **Nicasio "Yao Daguwasi" Vargas** and **Isidora "Mama Daguwasi" Garcia**. Nicasio was a fisherman and farmer in Barangu. The Vargas family moved into Barangu

and then left, so we have little information on the Vargas family.

On this day **Erlinda Nicholas** was born. She is the daughter of **Frederick Nicholas** and **Joyce Lopez**. Erlinda is known as "Delane" in the village. She married **Anthony Alexander Ogaldez**. Erlinda is the first cousin four times removed of **Maria Loreta Palacio**.

Martila Cayetano was born on this day in 1933 in Barangu. She is the daughter of **Pascacio Cayetano** and **Eustaquia Satuye**. Martila is the granddaughter of **Maria Loreta Palacio**. Martila's parents are second cousins so she is her own third cousin with **Juan Pedro Cayetano** as the common ancestor.

Dolores Castillo was born on this day in 1934 in Barangu. She is the daughter of **"Showno" Castillo** and **Valentina Palacio**. Dolores was known as "Olga." She had children with **"Nimla" Nunez**. **Maria Loreta Palacio** is the great-aunt of Dolores.

Nicodemus Castillo died on this day in 1978 in Seine Bight. He is the son of **Inez Castillo** and **Martha Fuentes**.

Victor Enriquez was born on this day in Indura. He married **Vilma Petrona Chimilio** in 1981 and died one and a half months later.

Aniceto Reyes was born on this day in 1924. His parents are **Evangelisto "16" Reyes** and **Ascenciona Arzu**. He died in Peine in 1999. **Patrick Mariano**, the Ebu, is the grandson of Aniceto. Aniceto is the first cousin once removed of **E. Roy Cayetano**.

Leroy Leo Palacio was born on this day in Peine. He is the son of **Paul Palacio** and **Ethel Dee Loredo**. **Maria Loreta Palacio** is the great-great-aunt of Leroy and also the first cousin thrice removed of Leroy.

On this day **Brigina Lopez** was born on this day in Barangu. She is the daughter of **Raymond Lopez** and **Germaine Gloria Martinez**. **Maria Loreta Palacio** is the first cousin four times removed. Brigina is the great-granddaughter of **Simon Martinez**.

24th March

Delvarene Zuniga was born on this day. She is the daughter of **John Jacob Zuniga** and **Telesflora "Stella" Simeona Mejia**. Delvarene married **Claudio Alonzo Williams**. Her parents John and "Stella" were second cousins once removed with **Juan Pedro Cayetano** as common ancestor. **Sharron Williams** is the daughter of Delvarene.

Simeon Chimilio was born on this day in 1930. He is the son of **Marcial Chimilio** and **Inocenta Nicholas**. **Simeon Chimilio** is the first cousin twice removed of **Maria Loreta Palacio**. Simeon is the father well known football administrator Surusia **Bertie Chimilio**.

Gilbert Marin and **Valentina Baltazar** were married on this day in Puerto Barrios in 1968. Gilbert is the son of **Clarence Marin** and **Dionisia Santino** of Barangu. Valentina parents are from Labuga and Dangriga. Gilbert is the nephew of **Jacinta Trigueno nee Santino**.

25th March

Maria Mariano was born on this day in Dangriga in 1958. She is the daughter of **Angelina Diego**. Maria died in 2003 in Dangriga. **Patrick Mariano**, the Ebu, is the son of Maria Mariano.

Felix Lucas and **Josefa Paulino** were married on this day in 1934 in Peine. This was a later in life marriage. Felix is the son of **William Lucas** and **Isabel Nunez**. Josefa is the daughter of **Augustin "Big Ease" Paulino** and **Juana Luis**. This was Josefa's second marriage.

On this day **Gabriel "Dimas" Arana** was born in 1923 in Peine. Gabriel is the son of **Concepcion Arana** and **Simeona Flores**.

Eugenia "Henny" Martinez died on this day in 1996 in Peine. She is the daughter of **Prudencio "Brown" Martinez** and **Gabina Zuniga**. **Dionisio Williams** married Eugenia in 1941.

26th March

In the Catholic calendar today is the Feast Day of St. Braulio of Saragossa.

Severiano Lambey and **Romana Arana** were married on this day in 1913 in Peine. Severiano's parents, **John Lambey** and **Gregoria Nolberto** lived in Barangu. Roma was from Peine. Severiano settled in Peine and many of the Lambeys of Peine are descended from this union.

Ricorda Geraldine Casimiro was born on this day in Barangu. She is the daughter of **Erasmo Casimiro** and **Paula Noralez**. Geraldine married **Joseph Castillo**.

On this day in Barangu in 1892 **Braulio Paulino** was born. He is the son of **Augustin "Big Ease" Paulino** and **Juana Luis**.

Byron Leo Thomas was born on this day in New York City. He is the son of **Rosanna Martinez Rogers**. Byron is the great-grandson of **Melvinia "Grandma Mi" Martinez**.

On this day **Braulio Ariola** was born in 1899 in Barangu. He is the son of **Daniel Ariola** and **Alberta Nicholas**. Braulio died later the same year in October in Barangu.

Castro Cayetano was born on this day in 1894. He is the son of **Marcelo Cayetano** and **Maria Loreta Palacio**. **Pascacio Cayetano** is the brother of Castro.

27th March

In the Catholic calendar today is the Feast Day of St. Alexander of Driziara and also the Feast Day of Alexander of Pannonia.

Eusebio Paulino and **Telesflora Bermudez** were married on this day in 1907 in Barangu. Eusebio is the son of **Augustin "Big Ease" Paulino** and **Juana Luis**. Telesflora is the daughter of **Narciso Bermudez** and **Dominga Marin**.

On this day **Eugenia "Henny" Martinez** was born in 1916 in Barangu. She is the daughter of **Prudencio "Brown" Martinez** and **Gabina Zuniga**. **Ceona Lucas nee Williams** is the daughter of Eugenia.

Eugenia Williams nee Martinez

Stephen Palacio was born on this day in Peine. He is the son of **Theodore Palacio** and **Bridget Marin**. **Maria Loreta Palacio** is the great-great-aunt of Stephen and the first cousin thrice removed of Stephen.

Roberto Sanchez was born on this day in 1889 in Barangu. He is the son of **Sebastian Sanchez** and

Vinciona "Beltrana" Cayetano. Roberto is the grandson of **Juan Pedro Cayetano**.

Santos Reyes was born on this day in 1898 in Barangu. He is the son of **Martin Reyes** and **Luisa Roches**. Santos is the great-uncle of both **E. Roy Cayetano** and **Raymond Valencio**.

On this day **Alexander Palacio** was born in Barangu in 1902. He is the son of **Peter Palacio** and **Tranquilina Zuniga**. Alexander is the first cousin once removed of **Maria Loreta Palacio**. He is the grandson of **Anastacio "Baibai" Palacio**.

Petrona Cayetano died on this day in 1908. Her parents are **Juan Pedro Cayetano** and **Maria Nicolasa Moralez**. She married **Teodoro "Joe Young" Palacio** in 1880 in Barangu. This was Teodoro's second marriage. The Cayetano and Palacio families have had numerous marriages between the families. Three years later **Marcelo Cayetano** (Petrona's nephew) married **Maria Loreta Palacio** (Teodoro "Joe Young" Palacio's daughter from his first marriage).

Pablo Gonzalez died on this day in 1992 in Peine and was buried in Barangu. He is the son of **Justo Gonzalez** and **Ursula Arana**. He lived with **Isolene Loredo** before he died. He is the brother of **Evilia "Ivy" Martinez nee Gonzalez**.

On this day **Patricio Ariola** died in Barangu in 1959. He is the son of **Rufino Ariola** and **Ascenciona Paulino**. He was born in 1864. He married in 1904 to **Vicenta Castillo**. He also had children with **Florencia Lambey** and **Epifania Loredo**. Patricio is the grandfather of **Francisco "Chico" Ariola**.

28th March

Roberta Nolberto was born on this day in Barangu in 1872. She is the daughter of **Francisco Nolberto** and **Francisca Serapia**. Roberta's parents were founding settlers of Barangu. Roberta is the great-aunt of **Anacleta "Da" Nolberto**.

Sixta Cayetano was born on this day in Barangu in 1898. She is the daughter of **Marcelo Cayetano** and **Maria Loreta Palacio**. She died in Barangu in 1903. The government death records say that she died from "heart heating."

On this day in 1920 in Barangu **Eustacio Alvarez** was born. He is the son of **Jerome Alvarez** and **Ignacia "Inez" Arana**. Eustacio was known as "Tacho" in the village. He was a fisherman in Barangu, very active in the credit union, and also one of Barangu's very talented musicians. He played the clarinet. He married **Toribia Garcia** in 1961 and died within the month.

Marsha Margaret Suazo was born on this day. She is the daughter of **Errol Suazo** and **Claudia Avila**. **Maria Loreta Palacio** is the great-great-great-aunt of Marsha. **Rita Enriquez** is the aunt of Marsha.

29th March

Beatrice Sanchez died on this day in 2011 in Belize City. She is the daughter of **Amanda Zuniga**. Beatrice married **Robert Cayetano**. **Maria Loreta Cayetano** is the first cousin thrice removed of Beatrice.

Loma Sanchez was born on this day. Loma is the daughter of **Amanda Zuniga**. Loma married **John Rodriguez**. Loma was the principal teacher at the St. Joseph R.C. School in Barangu for a number of years. **Maria Loreta Palacio** is the first cousin thrice removed of Loma, who is the sister of **Beatrice Cayetano nee Sanchez**.

Loma Rodriguea nee Sanchez (2011)

Ophelia Loredo was born on this day in 1933 in Barangu. She is the daughter of **Henry Loredo** and **Ursula Polonio**. Ophelia is the first cousin twice removed of **Maria Loreta Palacio**. Ophelia is the aunt of **Alvin Loredo**.

Sista Avila was born on this day in Peine in 1910. She is the daughter of **Juliana Garcia** and **Pantaleon Avila**. Sista's grandfather, **Apolinario Garcia** was on of the early settlers in Barangu.

On this day **Sonya Nicholas** was born. She is the daughter of **Victor Leonard Nicholas** and **Paulina Lopez**. **Maria Loreta Palacio** is the first cousin twice removed of Sonya. Sonya married a Mr. Harris. They had no issue between the two of them. She had children with **Perfecto Makin** and **Guillermo Plummer**. **Egbert Nicholas** is a child of Sonya.

Balbina Nicholas was born on this day in 1935 in Barangu. She is the daughter of **Tiburcio Nicholas** and **Candida Palacio**. Balbina is the sister of **Frederick Nicholas**.

Benito Martinez and **Eudora Zuniga** were married on this day in 1986 in Orange Walk. Eudora is the daughter of **Clotildo Zuniga** and **Eugenia "Jean" Zuniga nee Noralez**. Eudora died in 2007 in Orange Walk. She was known as "Dora." She made red recado, which is used by Baranguna in preparing chicken for stewing.

On this day **Victoriana Nolberto** was born in 1927 in Barangu. She is the daughter of **Dionisio Nolberto** and **Nicolasa Martinez**. She married **Lauriano Arana**.

30th March

In the Catholic calendar today is the Feast Day of St. Pastor.

Patrick Lopez died on this day in Peine in 1998. He is the son of **Antonio Lopez** and **Loreta Brown**. He was born in 1925 in Peine. He had children with **Josephine Palacio**. **Yvonne Lopez** is the daughter of Patrick.

Gladys Clarice Loredo was born on this day in 1921. She is the daughter of **Patricio Ariola** and **Epifania Loredo**. She married **Daniel Lino** in Barangu. She had one child, Mary, who died as a school girl in a boating accident along with her father. Gladys fostered a number of children. She died in 2010 in Barangu.

Daniel Lino and **Gladys Clarice Loredo** were married on this day in Barangu in 1945. Daniel is the son of **Obispo Lino** and **Diega Benguche**. Daniel was born in Savanna Bank, Belize River.

On this day **Martin Reyes** and **Luisa Roches** were married in 1883 in Barangu. Luisa is the daughter of **Yuancio Roches** and **Sotera Gutierrez**. **Egbert Valencio** is the great-grandson of Martin and Luisa.

Augustin "Big Ease" Paulino and **Juana Luis** were married on this day in 1883 in Barangu. "Big Ease" is the son of **Diego Paulino** and **Dominga "Waganga" Cayetano**. **Victor Paulino** is the great-grandson of Augustin and Juana.

Fabiano Arzu and **Martha Palacio** were married on this day in 1921 in Peine. Fabiano is the son of **Sebastian Arzu** and **Luciana Enriquez**. **Martha Palacio** is the daughter of **Catarino T. Palacio** and **Francisca Sacasa (Ortiz)**. **Gregoria Arzu** is the daughter of Fabiano and Martha.

On this day in 1899 in Barangu **Pastora Lambey** was born. She is the daughter of **John Lambey** and **Gregoria Nolberto**. She died about five month later in October of 1899. Pastora is the first cousin twice removed of **Almira "Irma" Gonzalez nee Ariola**.

Pascacio Cayetano died on this day in Barangu in 1985. He is the son of **Marcelo Cayetano** and **Maria Loreta Palacio**. Pascacio was born 22 February 1891. He married **Apolinaria Mejia** in 1912 in Barangu. He then married **Eustaquia Satuye** in 1920 in Barangu. Finally he married **Ignacia "Inez" "Grandma Dadi" Arana**. **Sheridan Arzu nee Petillo** is the granddaughter of Pascacio.

31st March

In the Catholic calendar today is the Feast of Saint Balbina of Rome.

Victoriana Santino was born on this day in 1895 in Barangu. She is the daughter of **Philip Santino** and **Justina Cayetano**. She died in 1962. She had a child, **Estanislada Rodriguez**, in 1910 with **Benjamin Rodriguez**. She married **Abraham Bernard Mejia** in Peine in 1917 with whom she also had children.

Andaiye Colynn McAndrew was born on this day in Belize City. She is the daughter of **Neville McAndrew** and **Leolin Elma Valencio**. Her father is from Guyana. **Maria Loreta Palacio** is the first cousin four times removed of Andaiye. She is the granddaughter of **Lucille "Chilagu" Valencio nee Zuniga**.

Pastora Villafranco was born on this day in 1911 in Peine. She is the daughter of **Luis Majin Villafranco** and **Antonia Zuniga**. **Geronimo Avilez** married Pastora in 1934 in Peine.

Zuleesa Mireya Arzu was born on this day in Belmopan. She is the daughter of **Harold "Greg" Arzu** and **Sheridan Petillo**. Her parents, Harold and Sheridan are third cousins with **Teodoro "Joe Young" Palacio** being the common ancestor and also fourth cousins with **Francisco Palacio** being the common ancestor. **Maria Loreta Palacio** is related to Zuleesa three different ways. Maria is the great-great-great-aunt of Zuleesa. Maria is also the first cousin four times removed of Zuleesa. Finally **Maria Loreta Palacio** is the great-great-grandmother of Zuleesa.

Adranie Miranda was born on this day in Belmopan. She is the daughter of **Thomas Miranda** and **Rhoda Alvarez**.

On this day **Pastora Paulino** was born in 1907 in Barangu. She is the daughter of **Eugenio Paulino** and **Nicolasa Zuniga**. **Clotildo Zuniga** is the first cousin of Pastora.

On this day in 1914 **Balbina Arzu** was born in Barangu. She is the daughter of **Francisco Ellis Arzu** and **Patrocinia Palacio**. She married **Andrew Williams** in 1936 in Barangu. **Maria Loreta Palacio** is the great-aunt of Balbina.

Balbina Williams nee Arzu

On this day **George McKensie** and **Paulina Reyes** were married in 1934 in Barangu. George is from Portland, Jamaica and is the son of **William D. McKensie** and **Acilla Withworth**. Paulina is the daughter of **Martin Reyes**. This is **Paulina Reyes'** second marriage.

More Life Events in March

APRIL

1st April

Ambrosio Avilez and **Justa Polonio** were married on this day in 1883 in Peine. Ambrosio was known as "Sabigi." His parents are **Santiago Avilez** and **Francisca Gonzalez**. Santiago, his father, is the founder of Barangu.

Faustino Zuniga and **Estanislada Arzu** were married on this day in 1883 in Peine. Estanislada was known as "Garangadili." Faustino is the son of **Mariano Zuniga** and **Juana Paula Celertina**. Faustino is the brother of **Claro Zuniga**, Mafia's father, and **Natividad Zuniga**, Abe's grandfather, both early settlers of Barangu. It is a good example of siblings settling both here as well as simultaneously in Peine during the early years of the village.

On this day in Barangu **Philip Santino** and **Justina Cayetano** were married in 1883. Philip is the son of **Tomas Santino** and **Marta Bernardez**. Justina is the daughter of **Anacleto Cayetano** and **Dominga Martila Arzu**. **Jacinta Trigueno nee Santino** is the granddaughter of Philip and Justina.

Xavier "Harvey" Sandoval was born on this day in Labuga in 1955. He is the son of **Felicita Zuniga**. Xavier was known as "Harvey." **Maria Loreta Palacio** is the first cousin thrice removed of Xavier. April Fools Day is an appropriate birthday for Harvey because he was a stand-up comedian. After he moved back home to Barangu he continued entertaining with ready jokes.

Xavier "Harvey" Sandoval (2009)

Venancio Noralez was born on this day in 1869 in Peine. He is the son of **Florencio Noralez** and **Gregoria Mena**. Venancio died in 1926 in Barangu. **Martin Benjamin Noralez** is the son of Venancio.

Eusebio Lorenzo died on this day in 1905 in Barangu. He is the son of **Timoteo Lorenzo** and **Juana Palacio**. He was four months old when he died having been born in December of 1904. He is **Victoriano "Fada" Lorenzo**'s brother. **Maria Loreta Palacio** is the aunt of Eusebio. He is the great-uncle of **Steven "Junior" Gutierrez**.

2nd April

In the Catholic calendar today is the Feast of Francis of Paola and it can be seen in some of the names below.

Francisco Lorenzo was born on this day in Barangu in 1918. He is the son of **Timoteo Lorenzo** and **Juana "Jane" Palacio**. He is the brother of **Victoriano "Fada" Lorenzo**. **Maria Loreta Palacio** is the aunt of Francisco. He is the great-uncle of **Dale Gutierrez**.

On this day **Francisco Palacio** was born in Peine in 1907. He is the son of **Peter Palacio** and **Tranquilina Zuniga**. Francisco married **Escolastica Gomez** in 1936 in Dangriga. Francisco is the grandson of **Anastacio "Baibai" Palacio**. **Maria Loreta Palacio** is the first cousin once removed.

Frank Dean Arana was born on this day in 1909 in Barangu. He is the son of **Alejandro Arana** and **Gregoria Bermudez**. Frank married **Bonifacia Ramirez** in Barangu in 1936. Frank died in Barangu in 1984. **Victor "Bobby" Arana** is the son of Frank.

On this day **Elaysia Lopez** was born in New York City. She is the daughter of **Elton Tyron Lopez** and **Asia Benjamin**. Elaysia is the great-great-granddaughter of **Simon Martinez** and **Ambrosine Mejia**

Elroy Tucker was born on this day in Belize City. He is the son of **Antonia Palacio nee Ariola**. Elroy is the brother of **Jacinta Palacio**.

Reginald Avila died on this day in Peine in 1995. He is the son of **Pedro John Avila** and **Viviana Palacio**. He was born in 1921. He married **Georgiana Palacio**, his second cousin once removed in 1944. **Maria Loreta Palacio** is his first cousin once removed. **Lynn Zuniga nee Arnold** is the granddaughter of Reginald.

On this day **Estanislao Arzu** and **Cecilia Sanchez** were married in Barangu in 1934. Estanislao's parents are **Isidro Arzu** and **Maxima Ariola**. Cecilia's parents are **John Sanchez** and **Isidora Bermudez**.

3rd April

Anastacio Castillo was born on this day in Barangu in 1901. He is the son of **Inez Castillo** and **Martha Fuentes** (she is also known as **Martha Nunez**). Anastacio is the brother of **Cornelio Castillo** and **Nicodemus Castillo**

On this day **Ricardo Rash** was born in Peine. He is the son of **Alfredo Rash,** who is from El Estor, Wadimalu, and **Maria Makin,** who is from Conejo.

Petrona Cayetano was born on this day in Labuga in 1868. She is the daughter of **Juan Pedro Cayetano** and **Maria Nicolasa Moralez**. She married **Teodoro "Joe Young" Palacio** in 1880 in Barangu. This was Teodoro's second marriage. She died in 1908. Petrona is the step-mother of **Maria Loreta Palacio**. **Steven "Junior" Gutierrez** is the great-great-grandson of Petrona.

4th April

In the Catholic calendar today is the Feast Day of Isidore of Seville.

Theodore Palacio was born on this day in 1930 in Barangu. He is the son of **Joseph Pollard Palacio** and **Hilaria Mejia**. He married **Bridget Marin**. He was a principal of the Belize Teacher Training College. The Garifuna Choir was led by Theodore for a number of years. Theodore died in 2012 in Belize City. **Maria Loreta Palacio** is the great-aunt of Theodore.

Theodore Palacio (2002)

On this day **Isidora Bermudez** was born in Barangu in 1887. She is the daughter of **Narciso Bermudez** and **Dominga "Gadu" Marin**. She died in 1950 in Barangu. She had children with two men, **John Sanchez** and **Candido Flores**. **Procopio Flores** and **Mary Casimiro nee Flores** are children of Isidora.

Isidora "Manu" Arana was born on this day in 1921 in Newtown. She is the daughter of **Atanacio Arana** and **Leona Garcia**. She died in 2005 in Dangriga. "Manu" was a buyei who conducted many dügüs over the years.

Isidoro Chimilio was born on this day in Barangu in 1927. He is the son of **John Chimilio** and **Delfina Blas**. Isidoro is the brother of **Crispulo "Polo" Chimilio**.

Isidora Martinez was born on this day in Barangu in 1899. She is the daughter of **Liborio Martinez** and **Romalda Avila**.

On this day in 1922 **Marcos Zuniga** died in Barangu. He is the son of **Natividad Zuniga** and **Christina Zuniga**. He was born in 1892 in Barangu. He is the father of **Clotildo Zuniga**. He died a few days before his thirtieth birthday and was the first person buried in the present cemetery. The previous cemetery was down the coast and the first cemetery of the village was behind the present church.

Isidora Garcia was born on this day in 1899 in Barangu. She is the daughter of **Esmith Garcia** and **Cornelia Martinez**. Isidora married **Nicasco Vargas** in 1924 in Barangu. This is an example of a Baranguna woman attracting a man from outside. She was known as "Mama Daguwasi."

5th April

In the Catholic calendar today is the Feast Day of St. Vincent Ferrer.

Vicente Palacio was born on this day in 1882. He is the son of **Teodoro "Joe Young" Palacio** and **Petrona Cayetano**. Vicente is the brother of **Maria Loreta Palacio** with a different mother.

Vicente Rebide Palacio was born on this day in 1920 in Barangu (This looks like a strange name to me but it is what is listed in the baptism record.). He is the son of **Hipolito Palacio** and **Josefa Zuniga**. He was known as "Shente Boy." Vicente is the brother of **Ruben Palacio**. **Maria Loreta Palacio** is the first cousin once removed of Vicente.

Andrew Williams and **Balbina Arzu** were married on this daty in 1934 in Barangu. Andrew was from the Toledo Settlement. Balbina was from Barangu.

Vicenta Luisa Sanchez (*next page*) was born on this day in Barangu. She is the daughter of **Seferino Sanchez** and **Carciana Palacio**. Vicenta is known as "Lulu." **Maria Loreta Palacio** is the great-aunt of Lulu. Vicenta is the sister of **Paul Palacio**.

On this day in 1972 **Carciana Palacio** died in Barangu. She is the daughter of **Nolberto Palacio** and **Ignacia**

Vicenta Luisa "Lulu" Sanchez (2011)

Arana. Carciana was born in 1904 in Barangu. Carciana is **Paul Palacio**'s and "Lulu's" mother

Tomas Noralez and **Felicita Nunez** were married on this day in 1866 in Labuga. Tomas is the son of **Jose Lino Sebastian** and **Maria Teresa**. Felicita is the daughter of **Sebastian Nunez** and **Maria Leondre Carmen**. Tomas and Felicita are the great-grandparents of Teresa "Tandu" Noralez.

Eleanor Arana was born on this day in Barangu. She is the daughter of **Cipriano Arana** and **Leonora Avila**. **Maria Loreta Palacio** is the first cousin twice removed of Eleanor. **Marti Cain nee Arana** is the sister of Eleanor.

6th April

Wilfred Harold Lino was born on this day in 1920 in Cacao Bank, Rio Bravo, Orange Walk District. He was baptised in 1922 in Barangu. Wilfred was known as "Man Man." He is the son of **Diega "Cocona" Benguche** and **Obispo Lino**. Wilfred is the uncle of **Eugenia "Jean" Zuniga nee Noralez**.

Vicenta Palacio was born on this day in 1890 in Barangu. She is the daughter of **Teodoro "Joe Young" Palacio** and **Petrona Cayetano**. She married **Feliciano Lopez** in Peine in 1916. Vicenta is the sister of **Maria Loreta Palacio** with a different mother.

Julian Paulino died on this day in Barangu in 1903. He is the son of **Obispo Paulino**. He was married to **Nicolasa Palacio** in 1900 in Barangu.

On this day **Cirilo Avila** died in Peine in 1997. He is the son of **Alcardio Avila** and **Justa Gonzalez**. He married **Olivia Prudencia Palacio** in 1995 in Peine. **Rita Enriquez nee Avila** is the daughter of Cirilo.

Tiburcio Nicholas died on this day in 1940 in Peine. He is the son of **Sotero Nicholas** and **Paula Nunez**. He was born in 1898 in Barangu. He married **Candida Palacio**. Tiburcio was a carpenter. In 1930 with his sons he completed the third tower of the church (this church was "kitty-corner" to the police station).

7th April

In the Catholic calendar today is the Feast Day of Epiphanius the Martyr.

Cyril Alvarez was born on this day. He is the son of **Feliciano "Felix" Alvarez** and **Pantaleona Mejia**. He is the first cousin twice removed of **Maria Loreta Palacio**. Cyril is the brother of **Victor Alvarez**.

Joseph Martinez was born on this day. He is the son of **Hipolito Martinez** and **Regina Lorenzo**. **Maria Loreta Palacio** is the great-aunt of Joseph. He is the brother of **Viola Martinez**.

Epifania Loredo was born on this day in 1894 in Barangu. She is the daughter of **Eulalio Loredo** and **Gregoria Palacio**. Epifania married **Sotero Arana** in 1917 in Peine. **Maria Loreta Palacio** is the first cousin once removed of Epifania.

On this day in Labuga **Eric Arzu** was born. He is the son of **Procopio Arzu** and **Catalina Castillo**. **Maria Loreta Palacio** is the great-great-aunt of Eric. He is the first cousin of **Hazel Martinez nee Arzu**.

Hipolito Martinez and **Regina Lorenzo** were married on this day in 1939. Hipolito is the son of **Prudencio "Brown" Martinez** and **Gabina Zuniga**. Regina is the daughter of **Timoteo Lorenzo** and **Juana "Jane" Palacio**. **Elliot Martinez** is the son of Hipolito and Regina.

8th April

In the Catholic calendar today is the Feast Day of St. Dionysius of Corinth.

Dionisio Avilez was born on this day in Barangu in 1898. He is the son of **Juan Avilez** and **Dominga "Gadu" Marin**. Dionisio is the uncle of **Cleofa Avilez**.

Maximo Nicholas was born on this day. He is the son of **Ignacio Nicholas** and **Perfecta Avilez**. He is known as "Maxie." **David Nicholas** is the brother of "Maxie."

On this day **Jane "Kim" Sanchez** was born. She is the daughter of **Beatrice Sanchez**. **Maria Loreta Palacio** is the first cousin four times removed of Jane.

Benedictina Arana died on this day in 1990 in Barangu. **Frank Dean Arana** and **Bonifacia "Banje" Ramirez** are the parents of Benedictina. She was known as "Chunga." She is the sister of **Victor "Bobby" Arana**.

9th April

Dionisio Nolberto was born on this day in Barangu in 1900. He is the son of **Pio Nolberto** and **Casimira Nicholas**. He married **Nicolasa Martinez** in 1924 in Peine. Dionisio had a farm up the Temash River during the banana boom called "Quiripi." He was elected second alcalde in Barangu in 1927 and again in 1928. He was elected first alcalde in Barangu in 1933 and again in 1934. **Irma Gonzalez nee Ariola** is the granddaughter of Dionisio.

10th April

Santos Leon Avila was born on this day in Peine in 1914. He is the son of **Pantaleon Avila** and **Juliana Garcia**. Pantaleon was from Peine and his wife Juliana was from Barangu. After marrying they lived in both Barangu and Peine. Pantaleon is grandfather of the boatman "Memo" who currently travels between Peine and Labuga-Barrios. Santos married **Eulogia Cacho** in Peine in 1938.

Runulfo "Roman" Nelson Palacio died on this day in 1984 in Labuga. He is the son of **Nolberto Palacio** and **Ignacia Arana**. He was born in Barangu in 1907. He married **Estela Rubio** from Labuga. Roman was one of the last arumahani composers and singers in Belize and Guatemala. Roman is the father of the buyei (Sinabei), **Esteban Palacio**.

On this day in 1998 in New York City **Amenigi Arzu** was born. He is the son of **Stephen Arzu** and **Elida Palacio**. **Maria Loreta Palacio** is the great-great-great-aunt of Amenigi.

Opal Arzu was born on this day. She is the daughter of **Candido Arzu** and **Bernadette Loredo**. **Maria Loreta Palacio** is the great-great-aunt of Opal and also the first cousin thrice removed of Opal.

11th April

Leolin Elma Valencio was born on this day in Barangu. She is the daughter of **Raymond Valencio** and **Lucille "Chilagu" Zuniga**. **Maria Loreta Palacio** is the first cousin thrice removed of Elma.

Leona Martinez was born on this day in 1908 in Peine. She is the daughter of **Ireneo Martinez** and **Bernardina Santino**. She married **Feliciano Jimenez** in 1937 in Peine. Leona is the aunt of **Victoriana "Vicky" Nolberto nee Martinez**.

On this day **Maxwell Makin** was born in Barangu. He is the son of **Perfecto Makin** and **Vicenta "Lulu" Sanchez**. **Maria Loreta Palacio** is the great-great-aunt of Maxwell.

12th April

Victor Paulino was born on this day in Peine. He is the son of **Stephen Paulino** and **Eulogia Nicholas**. He married Berta Petillo in 1985. Victor is the first cousin twice removed of **Maria Loreta Palacio**. He is the great-grandson of **Augustin "Big Ease" Paulino**. Victor and his family operate a glass business in Peine.

Alejandro Palacio and **Sarah Cayetano** were married on this day in 1947 in Belize City. Sarah is the granddaughter of **Maria Loreta Palacio** and Alejandro is the son of **Catarino T. Palacio**. Maria Loreta and Catarino are brother and sister. Therefore Aleandro and Sarah are first cousins once removed. This marriage is another example of the Cayetano/Palacio exchange through marriage. Other examples of this exchange are **Harold Arzu** and **Sheridan Petillio** and **Teodoro "Joe Young" Palacio** and **Petrona Cayetano**.

Sarah Cayetano and Alejandro Palacio		
Maria Loreta Palacio	siblings	Catarino T. Palacio
Pascacio Cayetano	first cousins	Alejandro Palacio
Sarah Cayetano	first cousins once removed	Alejandro Palacio
Sheridan Petillo and Harold Arzu		
Pascacio Cayetano	first cousins	Patrocinia Palacio
Mary Martha Cayetano	second cousins	Candido Arzu
Sheridan Petillo	third cousins	Harold Arzu
Petrona Cayetano and Teodoro "Joe Young" Palacio		
marriage, but no prior relationship		

13th April

In the Catholic calendar today is the Feast Day of St. Hermengild.

Nora Arana was born on this day in Belize City. She is the daughter of **John "Shamba" Dominquez** and **Marthy "Marti" Arana**. Nora teaches at St. John's College.

Merejilda Blanco was born on this day in 1922. She is the daughter of **Ciriaco Blanco** and **Matea Paulino**. She is the granddaughter of **Augustin "Big Ease" Paulino**.

Merejildo Nicholas was born on this day in 1914 in Barangu. He is the son of **Sotero Nicholas** and **Paula Nunez**. He was one of the men that left the village and went overseas to assist the war effort.

Santo Williams and Monica Martinez were married on this day in 1946 in Peine. Santo and Monica are grandparents of **Sharron Williams**.

Hermenehilda "Maria" Lopez was born on this day in Barangu. She is the daughter of **Patrick Lopez** and **Josephine Palacio**. Maria Loreta Palacio is the great-great-aunt of Hermenehilda.

14th April

Tiburcio Zuniga was born on the day in 1890 in Barangu. He is the son of **Natividad Zuniga** and **Christina Nolberto**. Tiburcio is the great-uncle of **Clotildo Zuniga**.

Sharday Loredo was born on this day in Barangu. She is the daughter of **Alvin Loredo** and **Sharon Nunez**. Sharday is the first cousin four times removed of **Maria Loreta Palacio**. Since her parents are related Sharday is her own third cousin and also her own fourth cousin once removed.

On this day in 1941 John Palacio and Zenobia Enriquez were married in Peine. John is the son of **Catarino T. Palacio** and **Francisca Sacasa (Ortiz)**. Zenobia is the daughter of **A.P. Enriquez** and **Jane Villafranco**. Zenobia's father **A.P. Enriquez** taught in Barangu for a short period of time in 1918. Zenobia was the government nurse in Barangu for a period of time.

Peter Casimiro was born on this day in Barangu in 1916. He is the son of **Pablo Casimiro** and **Bernadina Nolberto**. **Petrona Ariola** married Peter. Peter died in 1958 in Barangu. Peter is the father of **Paul Hudson Casimiro**.

15th April

In the Catholic calendar today is the Feast of Anastasia of Rome.

Victoriana Martinez was born on this day in Dangriga. She is the daughter of **Claudio Martinez**

and **Bonifacia Francois**. She is known as "Vicky" in the village. "Vicky" died in 2007 in Belize City. She was the community health worker for a number of years in the village. She also was involved with crafts in the village. She married **Hilario Nolberto**.

Victoriana "Vicky" Martinez (2006)

On this day **Anastacia Christina Ramirez** was born in Hopkins. She is the daughter of **Cecilio "Nudi" Ramirez** and **Natividad Palacio**. Anastacia married **Peter Castillo** in 1982 in Belize City. Anastacia is the first cousin thrice removed of **Maria Loreta Palacio**. She is the first cousin once removed of **Andy Palacio** with **Hipolito "Puludu" Palacio** as the common ancestor.

Anastacio Reyes was born on this day in 1908 in Barangu. He is the son of **Martin Reyes** and **Luisa Roches**. Anastacio married **Basilia Lucas** in Barangu in 1944. He is the great-uncle of **E. Roy Cayetano** and **Raymond Valencio**.

Eusebia (Toribia) Lambey was born on this day in 1893 in Barangu. She is the daughter of **John Lambey** and **Gregoria Nolberto**. **Alvin Loredo** is the first cousin twice removed with **Francisco Nolberto** as the common ancestor.

On this day **Ignacio Nicholas** and **Perfecta Avilez** were married in 1925 in Barangu. Ignacio is the son of **Leoncio Nicholas** and **Alberta Nolberto**. Perfecta is the daughter of **John Justo Avilez** and **Paula Noralez**. Ignacio was the mayordomo of the St. Joseph Church in Barangu. Ignacio was also the last first alcalde in Barangu before the office was abolished. Perfecta and **Ignacio Nicholas** had many children who contributed to Belize's development and took Barangu to the next level. First of all, they are the parents of

Benjamin Nicholas, Belize's first Garifuna artist. They are also the parents of **Victor Joseph Nicholas**, who contributed many years to Barranco R.C. School serving for many years as a teacher and a principal, and was principal of Belize Teachers' College. Most importantly, he paved the way for many Barangunas by returning home to retire. Ignacio and Perfecta are also the parents of school teachers, Christina and Maxie, and Belize's first Garifuna policewoman, Shirley.

16th April

In the Catholic calendar today is the Feast Day of Toribio of Astorga.

Toribio Joseph Lopez was born on this day in 1908 in Barangu. He is the son of **Santiago Lopez** and **Felicita Bermudez**. He was known as "Jeff." He married **Emelda Marin** in 1937. **Erlinda "Delane" Ogaldez nee Nicholas** is the granddaughter of Toribio.

On this day **Cordelia Casimiro** was born. She is the daughter of **Erasmo Casimiro** and **Paula Noralez**. She is the second cousin of **Paula Nolberto**.

Luis Palacio died on this day in 1974. He is the son of **Augustine Palacio** and **Simeona Mejia**. He was born in 1945. He was a school teacher.

Toribia Zuniga was born on this day in 1914 in Barangu. She is the daughter of **Viviano Zuniga** and **Filomena Paulino**. Toribia's parents are second cousins. **Lucille "Chilagu" Valencio nee Zuniga** is the first cousin of Toribia.

Tiana Ebony Martinez was born on this day in New York City. She is the daughter of **Recillia Martinez**. **Maria Loreta Palacio** is the first cousin four times removed of Tiana. Tiana is the great-granddaughter of **Simon Martinez** and **Ambrosine Mejia**.

17th April

In the Catholic calendar today is the Feast Day of St. Anicetus.

Aniceto Nicholas was born on this day in 1885 in Barangu. He is the son of **Leoncio Nicholas** and **Christina Garcia**. Aniceto is the uncle of Master **Victor Nicholas**.

On this day **Leslie Carlton Colon** was born in Barangu. He is the son of **George Hill** and **Naomi Colon**. Leslie is a noted muscian.

Salvatore Basil "S.B." Daniels and **Victoria Ogaldez** were married on this day in 1922 in Peine. Salvatore is the son of **Miguel Daniels** and **Tomasa Martinez**.

Victoria is the daughter of **Secundino Ogaldez** and **Alberta Ciego**. Mr. Daniels was the principal teacher in Barangu from the early 1930's to 1950. Under his tutelage many of his students became rural school teachers.

18th April

In the Catholic calendar today is the Feast Day of Sts. Eleutherius and Anthia.

Kevin Zuniga was born on this day in Barangu. He is the son of **Isaac Zuniga** and **Julia Alvarez**. He married **Lynn Arnold**. Kevin is an educator.

On this day in 1868 **Eluteria Cayetano** was born in Barangu and a month later was baptised in Labuga. She is the daughter of **Vinciona Cayetano** and **Sebastian Sanchez**. Multiple generations of the Cayetano family went back and forth between Labuga and Barangu during this period of time. A few of Eluteria's children were **John Jacob Zuniga**, **Isabela Mejia**, **Nicolasa Martinez** and **Eustaquia Satuye**.

Nicolasa Palacio died on this day in 1919 in Barangu. She is the daughter of **Anastacio Palacio** and **Magdalena Cesaria**. Nicolasa married **Julian Paulino** in 1900 in Barangu. She also married **Simon Mejia**. **Maria Loreta Palacio** is the first cousin of Nicolasa.

Angel Jimenez and **Faustina Villafranco** were married in 1917 in Peine. Angel is the son of **Fermin Jimenez** and **Petrona Cayetano**. Faustina is the daughter of **Luis Majin Villafranco** and **Antonia Zuniga**. Angel was from Barangu and Faustina was from Peine.

On this day **Kevin Zuniga** and **Lynn Arnold** were married in 2001 in Barangu. Kevin is the grandson of **Clotildo Zuniga** and **Jean Zuniga** and Lynn is the granddaughter of **Reginald Avila** and **Georgiana Palacio**.

19th April

In the Catholic calendar today is the Feast Day of St. Hermogenes.

Leroy Ramos was born on this day in Belize City. He is the son of **Eudora Zuniga**. Leroy is the first cousin of **Kevin Zuniga**.

Hermogenes Castillo was born on this day in 1918 in Barangu. She is the daughter of **Nicodemus Castillo** and **Ramona Marin**. Ramona was known as "Sagu" and was from Seine Bight.

20th April

In the Catholic calendar today is the Feast Day of St. Agnes of Montepulciano.

Inez Martinez was born on this day in 1899 in Barangu. She is the daughter of **Liborio Martinez** and **Romalda Avila**. Inez is the great-aunt of **Alvin Loredo**.

On this day **Hilario Nolberto** died in Peine in 1997. He is the son of **Dionisio Nolberto** and **Nicolasa Martinez**. Hilario was born in 1929 in Barangu. He married **Victoriana Martinez** . Hilario was a carpenter. Hilario is the father of **Hilma "Nana" Nolberto**.

On this day in 1892 **Marcos Zuniga** was born. He is the son of **Natividad Zuniga** and **Christina Nolberto**. He died in 1922 in Barangu. He married **Juliana Castillo** in 1916 in Barangu. Marcos is the father of **Clotildo Zuniga** and the great-grandfather of **Kevin Zuniga**.

Agnes Felicita Palacio was born on this day in 1952. **Fabian Cayetano** married Agnes in 1976. Agnes died in 2006.

Ines Lucas was born on this day in 1919 in Peine. She is the daughter of **Ireneo Lucas** and **Gertrude Labriel**. **Felix Garcia** married Ines in 1936 in Barangu. Ines died in 1945 in Belize City

Apolinaria Garcia was born on this day in 1897. She is the daughter of **Esmith Garcia** and **Blacina Apolonio**. Apolinaria died in 1901 in Barangu.

Jane Lino died on this day in 1987 in Peine. She is the daughter of **Obispo Lino** and **Diega Benguche**. She was born in 1916 in the Sarstoon River Community, a small Garifuna village on the Guatemalan side of the river that was basically a satellite village of Barangu. People were moving back and forth between Barangu and the Sarstoon community. This village started around the first banana boom in the 1880's and continued as a Garifuna community into the 1950's. Jane was a midwife and made herbal medicines. She is the mother of **Eugenia "Jean" Zuniga nee Noralez**.

Secundino Maximo and **Fabiana Sebastiana Daniels** were married on this day in Peine in 1921. Fabiana is the sister of **S.B. Daniels** who was a principal for many years in Barangu. **S.B. Daniels** has a daughter Fabiana named after his sister.

Aniceta Blas was born on this day in 1895 in Barangu (*top of the next colomn*). She is the daughter of **Macario Blas** and **Leonarda Nunez**. She married **Pablo Nicholas** in 1912 in Barangu. **Alice Casimiro nee Nicholas** is the granddaughter of **Aniceta Blas**.

Aniceta Blas at 103 years old (1998)

21st April

Victor Garcia and **Estanislada Rodriguez** were married in 1935 in Peine. Victor is the son of **Esmith Garcia** and **Blacina Apolonio**. Victor got his Guatemalan immigration papers on 22nd May 1928. At that time he was living in Los Quebrados, Izabal, Guatemala with his first wife, **Victoria Colon**, from Labuga and their daughter, **Patrocinia Marcelina Garcia**. Victor was working for United Fruit Company when he formally immigrated to Wadimalu, as were many other Baranguna.

Victor Garcia

22nd April

Today in the Catholic calendartis The Feast Day of Pope St. Soter.

Sotero Arana was born on this day in 1886 in Peine. He is the son of **Dionisio Arana** and **Basilia Labriel**. Sotero married **Epifania Loredo** in 1917 in Peine. Sotero died in Barangu in 1930. Sotero is the brother of **Ignacia "Glessima" Arana** who married **Nolberto Palacio**.

On this day in 1920 **Cirila Marin** was born in Barangu. She is the daughter of **Aparicio Santiago Marin** and **Brigida Paulino**. Cirila is the sister of **Clarence Marin**.

Ambrosio Joseph was born on this day in 1931 in Barangu. He is the son of **Francis Joseph and Juliana Castillo**. He married **Petrona Palacio** in 1961 in Corozal. **Michael Joseph** is the son of Ambrosio.

Victoriano Martinez was born on this day in 1894 in Peine. He is the son of **Liborio Martinez** and **Romalda Avila**. Victoriano died in Labuga in 1962. **Crispino Martinez** is the son of Victoriano.

Sotera Nicholas was born on this day in 1910 in Barangu. She is the daughter of **Sotero Nicholas** and **Paula Nunez**. She married **Peter Avila**. Sotera is the aunt of **Frederick Nicholas**. **Peter Anthony Avila** and **Sotera Nicholas Avila** are parents of **Peter Avila, Sr. Mary Avila, OSP, Gloria Avila Hernandez, Dr. Marvin Avila, Magna Avila Gibbs,** and **Joannem Avila Baker**. All five of her children are educators with the exception of Joannem who is a social worker.

23rd April

Gregorio Ruben Palacio and **Antonia Ariola** were married on this day in 1945. They had one child between them, **Jacinta Palacio**.

On this day **Lavern Bernice Loredo** was born in Peine. She is the daughter of **Hector Loredo** and **Anacleta Nolberto**. Lavern is a primary school teacher in Belize City. **Maria Loreta Palacio** is the first cousin thrice removed of Lavern.

Peter Valerio was born on this day in 1949 in Seine Bight. He is the son of **Santiago Valerio** and **Santiaga** (unknown last name). He died in 1993 in Belize City. **Lynette Valerie Rodriguez nee Valerio** is the daughter of Peter.

Catarino T. Palacio died on this day in 1940. He is the son of **Teodoro "Joe Young" Palacio** and **Maria Tomasa Martinez**. He married **Francisca Sacasa (Ortiz)**. Catarino is the brother of **Maria Loreta Palacio**.

24th April

In the Catholic calendar today is the Feast of Alexander of Lyon.

Alejandro Ramirez was born on this day in 1919 in Peine. He is the son of **Sebastian Ramirez** and **Manuela Ariola**. Alejandro is the first cousin of **Francisco "Chico" Ariola**.

On this day in 1919 **Alejandro Palacio** was born in Peine. He is the son of **Catarino T. Palacio** and **Francisca Sacasa (Ortiz)**. Alejandro married **Sarah Palacio** in 1947 in Belize City. **Maria Loreta Palacio** is the aunt of Alejandro.

Philip Casimiro died on this day in 1938 in Peine. He is the son of **Pablo Casimiro** and **Bernadina Nolberto**. He was born in 1921 in Barangu. He died as a result of an accident when "he tried to hop a truck." Philip is the uncle of **Adriana "Tun" Casimiro**.

Gilbert Michael Marin was born on this day in Los Angeles, California. He is the son of **Gilbert Marin** and **Valentina Baltazar**. Gilbert is the first cousin four times removed of **Maria Loreta Palacio**.

StephAnn Cayetano was born on this day in Los Angeles, California. She is the daughter of **Evan Stephen Cayetano** and **Sylvia Sampson**. StephAnn is the first cousin four times removed of **Maria Loreta Palacio**. StephAnn is the niece of **E. Roy Cayetano**.

25th April

Alexandra Mejia was born on this day in 1896. She is the daughter of **Simon Mejia** and **Andrea Nicholas**. She is the great-aunt of **Rita Enriquez nee Avila**.

Gregorio Nolberto was born on this day in 1900 in Peine. He is the son of **Macario Nolberto** and **Seferina Arana**. Gregorio's father, Macario was one of the first children born in Barangu, his parents being **Francisco Nolberto** and **Francisca Serapia**. **Paula Nolberto** is the first cousin once removed of Gregorio.

On this day in 1945 **Marcos Oliver Casimiro** was born in Barangu. He is the son of **Gonzalez Casimiro** and **Mary Flores**. He died in 1983. Marcos is the brother of **Fermin "Rama" Casimiro**.

Sheridan Petillo was born on this day. She is the daughter of **Leonard Petillo** and **Mary Martha Cayetano**. She married **Harold "Greg" Arzu**. Sheridan and Harold are both third and fourth cousins. **Maria Loreta Palacio** is the great-grandmother of Sheridan.

Arnold Nicholas was born on this day. He is the son of **Madeline Loredo** and **David Nicholas**. Arnold

Nicholas is the first cousin thrice removed of **Maria Loreta Palacio.**

26th April

Today in the pre-1969 Catholic calendar is the Feast Day of Pope St. Marcellus.

Zenobia Enriquez was born on this day in 1921 in El Cayo. She is the daughter of **A.P. Enriquez** and **Victoriana Villafranco.** Zenobia's father Andres was teaching school in the area and that explains the birth location. She married **John Palacio** in Peine in 1947. Zenobia was a rural health nurse who was stationed in Barangu for a period of time.

Julius Casimiro was born on this day in 1950 in Barangu. He is the son of **Gonzalez Casimiro** and **Mary Flores.**

On this day **Marge Avila** was born. She is the daughter of **Cirilo Avila** and **Olivia Prudencia Palacio.** Maria Loreta Palacio is the great-aunt of Marge. **Darius Avila** is the brother of Marge.

Leroy Owen Marin was born on this day in San Ignacio. He is the son of **Gilbert Marin** and **Valentina Baltazar.** Maria Loreta Palacio is the first cousin four times removed of Leroy. He is the great-grandson of **Augustin Baltazar** better known as "Ding." Ding was a famous buyei stationed in Chewecha in the early 20th century.

On this day **Marcelino Castillo** was born in 1887 in Peine. He is the son of **Alejandro Castillo** and **Victoriana Cayetano.** Marcelino's grandfather is **Anacleto Cayetano** of one of the founding families of Barangu.

Wilhemina "Mina" Loredo and **Matildo Martinez Leiva** were married in 1942 in Barangu. Wilhemina is the daughter of **Eulalio Loredo** and **Gregoria Palacio**

Darlene McDonald was born on this day in Belize City. She is the daughter of **Sadie Nolasca Alvarez.** Darlene is the great-granddaughter of **Jerome Alvarez.**

Zena Palacio was born on this day. She is the daughter of **Stephen Palacio.** Zena is the granddaughter of **Theodore Palacio** and **Bridget Palacio nee Marin.** Maria Loreta Palacio is the great-great-great-aunt of Zena.

27th April

Today in the pre-1969 Catholic calendar is the Feast Day of St. Peter Canisius.

Elorine Nunez was born on this day in Peine. She is the daughter of **Evaristo Nunez** and **Alexine Loredo.** Elorene's father worked for United Fruit Company in Guatemala.

Clarence Marin died on this day in 2006. He is the son of **Aparicio Marin** and **Brigida Paulino.** He was born in 1910 in Peine. Clarence married **Dionisia Santino** in 1967 in Barangu. **Maria Loreta Palacio** is the first cousin twice removed of Clarence.

On this day **Anastasia Avilez** was born in 1904 in Peine. She is the daughter of **Ambrosio Avilez** and **Justa Polonio.** Anastasia married **William Santino** in 1925 in Peine.

Pedro Nunez was born on this day in 1899 in Peine. He is the son of **Tomas Nunez** and **Tomasa Ortiz.** Pedro's father Tomas Nunez had a farm near Wellis Creek.

Rosita Miller was born on this day. She is the daughter of **Denzel Miller** and **Josephine Palacio.** Rosita married Edward Tingling in 1989 in Dangriga. **Maria Loreta Palacio** is the great-great-aunt of Rosita.

28th April

In the Catholic calendar today is the Feast Day of Prudentius of Tarazona in the Catholic calendar.

Prudencia Paulino was born on this day in 1883. She is the daughter of **Augustin "Big Ease" Paulino** and **Juana Luis.** Prudencia is the great-granddaughter of **Juan Pedro Cayetano.**

On this day in 1920 **Paul Nicholas** was born in Barangu. He is the son of **Philip Nicholas** and **Fabiana Palacio.** He married **Melvinia Noralez** in 1962 in Peine. Paul is the first cousin once removed of **Maria Loreta Palacio.**

Olivia Prudencia Palacio *(next page)* was born on this day in Barangu. She is the daughter of **Joseph Pollard Palacio** and Hilario and **Hilaria Mejia.** She married **Cirilo Avila** in Peine in 1995. **Maria Loreta Palacio** is the great-aunt of Olivia.

Lucille Luciana "Chilagu" Zuniga and **Raymond Valencio** *(next page)* were married in Barangu on this day in 2006. Lucille is the daughter of **Inocente Zuniga** and **Luciana Nolberto.** Raymond is the son of **Eufamio Valencio** and **Beatrice Palacio.**

29th April

Julius Santino was born on this day in 1920 in Barangu. He is the son of **Philip Santino** and **Nicasia Martinez.** He is the brother of **Eusebio Santino** with a different mother.

On this day **Prudencia Nicholas** was born in 1926 in Barangu. She is the daughter of **Pablo Nicholas** and **Aniceta Blas.** Prudencia is the aunt of **Alice Casimiro nee Nicholas.**

Petrona Zuniga was born on this day in Labuga in 1891. She is the daughter of Nicholas Zuniga and Mariana Rodriguez. Petrona is the sister of Nazaria Enriquez nee Zuniga.

On this day Peter Anthony Avila was born in 1907 in Peine. He is the son of Antonio Albert "Yuboo" Avila and Alberta Enriquez. Peter married Sotera Nicholas in 1932 in Peine. Peter died in 1989.

Olivia Avila nee Palacio (2006)

Lucille "Chilago" Zuniga and Raymond Valencio (2006)

30th April

In the Catholic calendar today is the Feast Day of St. Catherine of Siena.

Catalina Paulino was born on this day in 1926 in Barangu. She is the daughter of Eugenio Paulino and Nicolasa Zuniga. She was the youngest of ten children.

Catarina Enriquez was born on this day in 1920 in Peine. She is the daughter of Clotildo Enriquez and Andrea Nunez.

Victoriano Castillo and Carmen Garcia were married on this day in 1894 in Peine. Victoriano was a buyei in Barangu. Clotildo Zuniga is the grandson of Victoriano and Carmen.

More Life Events in April

_____
_____
_____
_____
_____
_____
_____
_____
_____
_____
_____
_____
_____
_____
_____
_____
_____
_____
_____
_____
_____
_____

MAY

1st May

Today in the pre-1969 Catholic calendar is the Feast Day of Sts. Philip and James, Apostles.

Michael Luke Loredo and **Mark Loredo**, a set of twins, were born on this day. They are the sons of **Hector Loredo** and **Anacleta Nolberto**. Michael and Mark had careers in the Belize Defence Force. Michael died in 2002 in Belize City. Michael and Mark are the first cousin thrice removed of **Maria Loreta Palacio**.

On this day **Henry Loredo** died in 1982 in Barangu. He is the son of **Eulalia Loredo** and **Gregoria Palacio**. He was born in 1897 in Dangriga. Henry married **Martina Avilez** in 1920 in Barangu and after she died he married **Ursula Polonio** in 1928. Mark and Michael Loredo, above, are the grandchildren of Henry. Henry is the first cousin once removed of **Maria Loreta Palacio**. Henry was a school teacher in Barangu in the 1920's.

Felipa Garcia was born on this day in 1884 in Barangu. She is the daughter of **Apolinario Garcia** and **Marcelina Augustina Martinez**. She was known as "Bache." Felipa married **Luis Palacio** in 1903. **Emily Ramirez nee Martinez** who taught school in Barangu is the great-granddaughter of Felipa.

Alejandra Arana was born on this day in 1904 in Barangu. She is the daughter of **Alejandro Arana** and **Gregoria Bermudez**.

James J. Avilez was born on this day in 1905 in Peine. He is the son of **John Justo "Bangi" Avilez**. He married **Margarita Castillo** in 1934 in Peine. There was no issue from their marriage, but they raised a daughter of James' sister. He was considered to be an agricultural innovator in the village. He grew rice commercially and hired a number of Baranguna to help with the harvest. He also raised cattle.

On this day **Philip "Percy" Palacio** was born in 1908 in Barangu. He is the son of **Luis Palacio** and Maria Lino. **Maria Loreta Palacio** is the aunt of Philip.

Alberta Felipa Labriel was born on this day in 1921 in Peine. She is the daughter of **Santiago Labriel** and **Serapia Avilez**. Alberta married **Morris Castro** in 1947 in Peine. Alberta was known as "Alba." **Hazel Castro** is the daughter of Alberta and Morris.

Beatrice Barcelona was born on this day in 1912 in Peine. Beatrice is the daughter of **Isabel Barcelona** and **Fecunda Gabriel**. **Elma Yvonne Arzu nee Martinez** is the niece of Beatrice.

Nicodemus Palacio and **Victoria Zuniga** were married on this day in 1945 in Peine. Nicodemus "Fast" is from Dangriga and is the son of **Agapito Palacio**. Victoria is the daughter of **Viviano Zuniga** and **Filomena Paulino**.

On this day **Maximo Avilez** and Eugenia (last name unknown) were married in 1913 in Belize Town. Maximo is the son of **Ambrosio Avilez** and **Justa Polonio**.

2nd May

In the Catholic calendar today is the Feast Day of St. Athanasius.

Atanacio Noralez was born on this day in 1916 in Peine. He is the son of **Martin Benjamin Noralez** and **Modesta Lucas**. Atanacio married **Nicasia Lambey** in Peine in 1938. He is the brother of **Eugenia "Jean" Zuniga nee Noralez** with a different mother.

Philip Nicholas and **Fabiana Palacio** were married on this day in 1908 in Peine. Philip is the son of **Leoncio Nicholas** and **Christina Garcia**. Fabiana is the daughter of **Anastacio Palacio** and **Magdalena Cesaria**. Philip and Fabiana are the grandparents of **Martin "Game and Gone" or "Tin-Tin" Nicholas**.

3rd May

In the Catholic calendar today is the Feast Day of St. Alexander.

Mary Flores and **Gonzalez Casimiro** were married on this day in 1944. Mary is the daughter of **Candido Flores** and **Isidora Bermudez**. Gonzalez is the son of **Pablo Casimiro** and **Bernadina Nolberto**. They had eleven children. **Procopio "Prook" Flores** is Mary's brother and **Adriana "Tun" Casimiro** is the daughter of Mary and Gonzalez.

Pedro Juan Avila and **Julia Petillo** were married on this day in 1903. Pedro is the son of **Pedro John Avila** and **Viviana Palacio**. Julia is the daughter of **Bonifacio Petillo** (*see next page*) and **Carmen Enriquez**.

On this day **Facundo Martinez** and **Inocenta Nicholas** were married in 1939. Inocenta is the daughter of **Sotero Nicholas** and **Paula Nunez**. Inocenta had an earlier marriage to **Marcial Chimilio**.

On this day in Dangriga **Anthony Alexander "Tony" Ogaldez** was born. He is the son of **Cyril Ogaldez** and **Cayetana Arana**. He was raised by **Paula Paulino**, his grandmother. Anthony was a school teacher and then a principal teacher at St. Joseph R. C. School in Barangu. He married **Erlinda "Delane" Nicholas**.

Cruz Avilez was born in 1884 in Peine. He is the son of **Ambrosio Avilez** and **Justa Polonio**. Cruz is the grandson of **Santiago "Gaünbü" Avilez**, the founder of Barangu.

Eugene Alexander Ariola was born on this day. He is the son of **Francisco Ariola** and **Almira Cayetano**. Eugene's parents are fourth cousins with **Juan Pedro Cayetano** as the common ancestor, third cousins with **Diego Paulino** as the common ancestor and third cousins once removed with **Francisco Palacio** as the common ancestor.

On this day **Alejandro Jimenez** was born in 1893 in Barangu. He is the son of **Fermin Jimenez** and **Petrona Cayetano**. Alejandro's parents are first cousin (cross-cousins, brother and sister's children marrying). This is an example of a traditional practice that was brought from St. Vincent and still persisted into the late nineteenth century and early twentith century.

On this day **Alexandra Nicholas** was born in 1864 in Barangu. She is the daughter of **Joseph Alexander Nicholas** and **Maria Eugenia Delavez**. Alexandra was one of the first children born in Barangu. Her parents were early settlers of Barangu. Alexandra is the great-aunt of **Frederick Nicholas**.

Paula Paulino died on this day. She is the daughter of **Liborio Martinez** and **Francisca Cayetano**. Paula was born in 1899 in Barangu. **Irene Gibbons** is the daughter of Paula.

Bonifacio Petillo

4th May

Today in the pre-1969 Catholic calendar is the Feast Day of St. Monica.

Pasqual Martinez was born on this day in 1894 in Barangu. He is the son of **Liborio Martinez** and **Romalda Avila**. Pasqual is the brother of Nicolasa Nolberto nee Martinez from a different mother and the uncle of **Paula Nolberto**.

Victoriana Santino died on this day in Barangu in 1962. She is the daughter **Philip Santino** and **Justina Cayetano**. She was born in 1895 in Barangu. She married **Abraham Mejia** in 1917 in Peine. Victoriana is the aunt of **Jacinta Trigueno nee Santino**.

Monico Santino was born on this day in Peine in 1900. He is the son of **Philip Santino** and **Nicasia Martinez**. Monico married **Christina Moreria** in 1959 in Peine.

Monica Martinez was born on this day in 1908 in Peine. She is the daughter of **Crescencio Martinez** and **Epifania Avilez**. Monica married **Santo Williams** in 1946 in Peine. **Claudio Alonzo Williams** is the son of Monica and Santo.

Santiago Labriel and **Crecencia Zuniga** were married on this day in 1904 in Peine. Santiago is the son of **Domingo Labriel** and **Ferdinanda Cruz**. Santiago later married **Serapia Avilez** in 1920 in Peine.

Francis Benedict Martinez and **Victoria Barcelona** were married on this day in 1935 in Peine. Francis is the son of **Francisco Martinez** and **Estefania Avila**. Victoria is the daughter of **Isabel Barcelona** and **Fecunda Gabriel**. **Llwelyn Martinez** and **Elma Yvonne Arzu nee Martinez** are children of Francis and Victoria.

5th May

On this day **Anthony Lino** was born in Dangriga. He is the son of **Mary Lino** and **Paul Hudson Casimiro**. Anthony is the second cousin of **Beatrice "Tricia" Mariano**.

Anastacio Martinez was born on this day in 1918 in Barangu. He is the son of **Pedro Nicasio Martinez** and **Augustina Nunez**. Anastacio is the brother of **Melvinia "Grandma Mi" Martinez**.

On this day in 1906 **Jacob Palacio** was born in Barangu. He is the son of **Hipolito Palacio** and **Josefa Zuniga**. He married **Tomasa Polonio**. He moved from Barangu and spent the rest of his life in Hopkins where he died. He is the brother or **Ruben Palacio** and uncle of **Andy Palacio**. **Anastacia Christina Castillo nee Ramirez** of Hopkins is the granddaughter of Jacob. **Maria Loreta Palacio** is first cousin once removed of Jacob.

Augustin Santino was born on this day in 1890 in Peine. He is the son of **Philip Santino** and **Justina Cayetano**. He married **Paulina "Mayo" Palacio** in 1917 in Barangu. Augustin is the great-uncle of **Clifford Marin**.

6th May

Glen Garrett Gutierrez was born on this day in Peine. He is the son of **Valentina "Flora" Lorenzo** and **Steven Gutierrez**. **Maria Loreta Palacio** is the great-great-aunt of Glen. **Dale Gutierrez** is the brother of Glen.

Ireneo Frazer Francisco and **Otilia Lucia Martinez** were married on this day in 1934 in Barangu. **Ireneo** was born in Peine but baptised in Barangu. Otilia was from Peine. Ireneo's mother is **Juana Nolberto** who is **Dionisio Nolberto's** sister. **Paula Nolberto** is Ireneo's first cousin.

Dwayne Michael Rodriguez was born on this day in Belize City. He is the son of **Clinton Rodriguez** and **Lynette Valerie Valerio**. **Maria Loreta Palacio** is the great-great-great-great-aunt of Dwayne.

7th May

Today in the pre-1969 Catholic calendar is the Feast Day of St. Stanislaus of Cracow.

Claudio Nunez was born on this day. He is the son of **Claudina Nunez**. Claudio was one of the many children fostered by **Gladys Lino nee Loredo**. **Maria Loreta Palacio** is the first cousin four times removed of Claudio. Claudio is the great-grandson of **Evaristo "Bob Steele" Nunez** and Alexine Nunez nee Loredo.

On this day in 1947 **Marcus Lambert Arzu** and **Fermina Nicholas** were married in Puerto Cortez, Indura. Fermina is the daughter of **Pablo Nicholas** and **Aniceta Blas**. Fermina is the second cousin of **Frederick Nicholas**.

Stanislar Arzu was born on this day in 1908 in Barangu. He is the son of **Isidro Arzu** and **Maxima Ariola**. He married **Cecilia Sanchez** in 1934 in Barangu.

8th May

Patrocino Colindres was born on this day in 1915 in Barangu. He is the son of **Victoriano Colindres** and **Pasquala Ramirez**. **Maria Loreta Palacio** is the great-aunt of Patrocino.

Cipriano Arana died on this day in Peine in 1989. He is the son of **Atanacio Arana** and **Leona Garcia**. Cipriano was born in 1918 in Newtown. He married **Leonora Avila** in 1937 in Barangu. Cipriano was a rural school teacher. He is the father of **Marti Cain nee Arana**.

On this day **Rufino Ariola** and **Ascenciona Paulino** were married in 1888 in Peine. Rufino was born in Indura and Ascenciona is the daughter of **Diego Paulino** and **Dominga "Waganga" Cayetano**. Ascenciona is the brother of **Augustin "Big Ease" Paulino**. This is another example of a Baranguna women attracting a man from another place to Barangu. Another interesting thing to note is that Rufino's father is **Ariola Gonzalez**. Thus Rufino took his father's first name for his last name. **Francisco "Chico" Ariola** is the great-grandson of Rufino and Ascenciona.

John Nipalmson Lucas and **Clotilda Nunez** were married in 1926 in Peine. John was known as "Hepu." John had a shop in Peine and also in San Pedro Sarstoon.

On this day **Francis Arana** and **Helen Reynolds** were married in 1993 in Clemson, South Carolina. Francis is the son of **Francisco Bonifacio "Frank" Arana** and **Narcisa Esther Contreras**. Francis' father was a farm demonstrator in Barangu.

9th May

Leoncio Nicholas and **Alberta Nolberto** were married in 1899 in Barangu. This was Leoncio's second marriage after his first wife, **Christina Garcia**, died. Leoncio was a mayordomo in Barangu. "Tiger" was the nickname that Leoncio was known by in the village. **Victor Nicholas** is the grandson of Leoncio. Leoncio and his brother Sotero had farms up Boyo Creek. Leoncio was also one of the first Baranguna to purchase his lot in Barangu rather than lease it.

10th May

Today in the pre-1969 Catholic calendar is the Feast Day of St. Antonius.

Gregoria Paulino was born on this day in 1916 in Barangu. She is the daughter of **Eugenio Paulino** and **Nicolasa Zuniga**. Gregoria is known as "Gogo." She had **Rudy Concepcion Arana** and Earl Arana with **Eulalio "Bidun" Arana**. Surusia **Peitra Arana** is the granddaughter of Gregoria. Gregoria married **Presentacion Nunez** in 1938 in Peine. There was no issue from this union. Gregoria raised her niece, **Hazel Lino**, after her sister Basilia's death. Gregoria died in 1991.

On this day **Antonia Noralez** was born in 1900 in Peine. She is the daughter of **Venancio Noralez** and **Juliana Colindres**. Antonia is the aunt of **Eugenia "Jean" Zuniga nee Noralez**.

Victoriana Nolberto nee Martinez died on this day in Belize City in 2007. She is the daughter of **Claudio Martinez** and **Bonifacia Francois**. Victoriana was born in 1929 in Dangriga. She married **Hilario Nolberto**. She was known as "Vicky" in the village. She was the Community Health Worker in Barangu for many years. Vicky also was a skilled craft person. She died in 2007 in Belize City.

Benigno Avila and **Faustina Chavez** were married on this day in 1922 in Monkey River. Benigno is the son of **Pedro John Avila** and **Viviana Palacio**. He is the older brother of **Reginald Avila**. **Maria Loreta Palacio** is the first cousin once removed of Benigno.

11th May

In the Catholic calendar today is the Feast Day of Sts. Mamertius and Francis Jerome.

Geronima Martinez was born on this day in 1911 in Barangu. She is the daughter of **Prudencio "Brown" Martinez** and **Gabina Zuniga**. She died in 1986. She is the sister of **Hipolito Martinez**. Geronima is the mother of **Vilma Petrona Chimilio**.

On this day in 1906 **Francisca Paulino** was born in Barangu. She is the daughter of **Eusebio Paulino** and **Telesflora Bermudez**. Francisca's parents are second cousins with **Juan Pedro Cayetano** being the common ancestor. She is the granddaughter of **Augustin "Big Ease" Paulino**.

Maria Ascencion Palacio was born on this day in 1899 in Barangu. She is the daughter of **Catarino T. Palacio** and **Francisca Sacasa (Ortiz)**. **Maria Loreta Palacio** is the aunt of Maria Ascencion.

On this day in 1910 **Mamerta Avilez** was born. She is the daughter of **John Justo Avilez** and **Paula Noralez**. Mamerta is the great-granddaughter of **Santiago Avilez**. She is the aunt of **Bernadette Arzu nee Loredo**.

Antonio Flores was born on this day in 1919 in Barangu. He is the son of **Candido Flores** and **Isidora Bermudez**. Antonio is the older brother of **Procopio Flores** and **Mary Casimiro nee Flores**.

On this day in 1952 **Gilbert Arana** was born. He is the son of **John Arana** and **Alberta**. He died in 2004. Gilbert is the great-great-grandson of **Benita Ariola nee Nunez**. He is also the second cousin once removed of **Beatrice "Tricia" Mariano**.

12th May

Daniel Lino was born on this day in Savanna Bank, Belize River in 1918. He is the son of **Obispo Lino** and **Diega Benguche**. He married **Gladys Clarice Loredo** in 1945 in Barangu. He died in 1950 along with his daughter Mary in a boating accident. Daniel is the uncle of **Eugenia "Jean" Zuniga nee Noralez**.

13th May

Today in the pre-1969 Catholic calendar is the Feast Day of St. Robert Bellarmine.

Pedro John Avila was born on this day in Peine in 1872. He is the son of **Victoriano Avila** and **Cesaria Zuniga**. He married **Viviana Palacio** in 1898 in Barangu. Pedro is the great-grandfather of **Lynn Zuniga nee Arnold** and the grandfather of **Marti Cain nee Arana**.

On this day in 1934 a set of twins, **Petrona Palacio** and **Robert Palacio**, was born in Barangu. They were the children of **Augustine Palacio** and **Simeona Mejia**. Robert died three months later in August 1934. Petrona died in 2012 in Caye Caulker. She was an active member of the Catholic Parish in Caye Caulker. **Maria Loreta Palacio** is the great-aunt of Pertrona. She was known as "Peti." She married **Ambrosio Joseph** in 1961 in Corozal.

Petrona Joseph nee Palacio

Rachel Mejia was born on this day in Belize City. She is the daughter of **Yvonne Lopez**. **Maria Loreta Palacio** is the great-great-aunt of Rachel.

Llwelyn Martinez was born on this day in Peine. He is the son of **Francis Benedict Martinez** and **Victoria Barcelona**. He married **Dativa Elizabeth Melendrez** in 1979 in Belize City. **Zaira Mierelli Martinez** is the daughter of Llwelyn and Dativa.

On this day **Herman Tenk Daniels** was born. He is the son of **Salvatore Basil "S.B." Daniels** and **Victoria Ogaldez**. He is named after Father Herman Tenk, S.J., who is credited with recruiting many Garifuna men to be rural primary school teachers. Fr. Tenk served in Peine from 1913 to 1938.

14th May

Jerroll Giovani Arana was born on this day. He is the son of **Earl Adrian Arana** and **Marina Egzine Cayetano**. **Francisco Bonifacio "Frank" Arana** (a farm demonstrator in Barangu) is the grandfather of Jerroll.

15th May

Bonifacio Ramirez was born on this day in 1892. He is the son of **Carmen Ramirez** and **Eustaquia Palacio**. Bonifacio married **Evangelista Nunez** in 1925. He died in 1975 in Barangu. **Maria Loreta Palacio** is the aunt of Bonifacio. He is the father of **Eduviges "Auntie Bea" Ramirez** and **Justina Nicholas nee Ramirez**.

On this day **Joseph Orlando Palacio** was born in Barangu. He is the son of **Joseph Pollard Palacio** and **Hilaria Mejia**. He married **Myrtle Cacho**. He is an educator and has written a number of articles and books on Garifuna and Baranguna history and culture. **Maria Loreta Palacio** is the great-aunt of Joseph.

16th May

John Noralez was born on this day in 1910 in Peine. He is the son of **Felix Noralez** and **Juana Nolberto**. He married **Damiana Lopez** in 1941. He was known as "John Box."

On this day in 1864 **Isidro Arzu** was baptized in Peine. He is the son of **Augustin Arzu** and **Cayetana Gonzalez**. He married **Maxima Ariola** in 1903 in Barangu.

Esmith Garcia died on this day in 1924 He is the son of **Apolinario Garcia** and **Marcelina Augustina Martinez** who were both from Jonathan Point. Esmith and a number of other family members were tailors in the village. He married **Blacina Apolonio** in 1890 in Peine. He was also known as "Maximiliano." He was a second alcalde for Barangu in 1893 and a first alcalde for Barangu in 1920.

Clinton Rodriguez was born on this day in Belize City. **Lynette Valerie Valerio** married Clinton in 1998 in Ladyville.

17th May

In the Catholic calendar today is the Feast Day of St. Paschal Baylon.

Bridget Marin was born on this day in Barangu. She is the daughter of **Aparicio Santiago Marin** and **Brigida Paulino**. Bridget married **Theodore Palacio**. She and Theodore were third cousins with **Francisco Palacio** being the common ancestor. **Bridget Marin** is the sister of **Clarence Marin**. **Maria Loreta Palacio** is the first cousin twice removed.

Bridget Marin and Theodore Palacio (2006)

Pasqualo Colindres was born on this day in 1913 in Barangu. He is the son of **Victoriano Colindres** and **Pasquala Ramirez**. His father, Victoriano, was a first alcade for Barangu in 1914. **Maria Loreta Palacio** is the great-aunt of Pasqualo.

Florencio Nunez and **Anastacia Petillo** were married on this day in 1923 in Peine. Anastacia is the granddaughter of **Justo "Bangi" Avilez** through her mother **Francisca Avilez**.

18th May

On this day in 1916 **Jane Lino** was born on the Sarstoon River. Her parents are **Obispo Lino** and **Diega Benguche**. She died in Peine in 1987. She was a bush doctor and maker of herbal medicine. She is the mother of **Eugenia "Jean" Zuniga nee Noralez**. Jane is the great-grandmother of **Kevin Zuniga**.

Peter Castillo was born on this day in Hopkins Village. He is the son of **Aurelio Castillo** and Emelia Ariola. He married **Anastacia Christina Ramirez** in 1982. Peter is an educator and worked with the buyei, "Manu." Both he and his wife have family ties with

Barangu, Peter to the Ariola family and Anastacia to the Palacio family. Ruben is her great-uncle.

On this day **Angus Claude Cayetano** was born in 1919 in Dangriga. He is the son of **Gregorio Cayetano** and **Teofila Flores**. He married **Adela Jaime** in 1949. Angus was a bookkeeper, accountant and a lay minister in the Methodist faith. He was a veteran of WWII serving in the Panama Canal. He was made a Justice of Peace in 1992. **Maria Loreta Palacio** is the grandmother of Angus.

Celestino Ramirez was born on this day in 1914 in Barangu. He is the son of **Sebastian Ramirez** and **Manuela Ariola**. He is the first cousin of **Francisco "Chico" Ariola** with **Patricio Ariola** as the common ancestor.

19th May

Patrocinia Palacio was born on this day in 1895 in Barangu. She is the daughter of **Nolberto Palacio** and **Ignacia Arana**. Patrocinia married **Francisco Ellis Arzu** in 1914 in Barangu. She died in 1946 in Barangu. **Maria Loreta Palacio** is the aunt of Patrocinia. Patrocinia is the grandmother of Surusia **Francis Arzu** and Surusia **Harriet Scarborough nee Arzu**.

On this day **Loreta Cayetano** was born in 1927 (This information is from the St. Joseph school registry. The government birth records has her being born on the 29th of May). She is the daughter of **Pascacio Cayetano** and **Eustaquia Satuye**. She died in 1946. **Maria Loreta Palacio**, her namesake, is the grandmother of Loreta. Loreta is the aunt of **Sheridan Arzu nee Petillo** Martinez.

James Wilfred Alexander Martinez was born on this day in 1920 in Peine. James is the son of **Francisco Martinez** and **Estefania Avila**. **Francis Benedict Martinez** is the brother of James.

On this day **Eugene Pacelli Denny Martinez** was born. He is the son of **Francis Benedict Martinez** and **Victoria Barcelona**. Eugene is the brother of **Elma Yvonne Arzu nee Martinez**.

Carol Garcia died on this day in 2012. She is the daughter of **Silvan Joseph Chimilio** and **Josephine Garcia**. Carol was raised by **Felicita "Nitu" Zuniga**. **Maria Loreta Palacio** is the first cousin thrice removed of Carol.

20th May

In the Catholic calendar today is the Feast Day of St. Bernardine of Siena.

Sylvia Sampson was born on this day in Belize City. She is the daughter of **Simeon Sampson**. She married **Evan Stephen Cayetano**. Sylvia's family has a long relationship with Barangu. Her grandfather, **Simeon Sampson**, was a teacher in Barangu. Between 1914 and 1922 Simeon was stationed in Barangu as the principal teacher numerous times.

On this day **Thomas Loredo** was born in 1940. He is the son of **Henry Loredo** and **Ursula Polonio**. Thomas is the uncle of **Melquiades Julius "Jimbo" Loredo**.

Bernardina Santino was born on this day in Barangu in 1885. She is the daughter of **Philip Santino** and **Justina Cayetano**. Bernardina married **Ireneo Martinez** in 1907 and later married **Viviano Gregorio** in 1919. She died in 1968. **Victoriana Victoriana "Vicky" Nolberto nee Martinez** is the granddaughter of Bernardina. Bernardina is the aunt of **Jacinta Trigueno nee Santino**.

Bernardina Martinez nee Santino

Solomon Velasquez and **Cristobel Loredo** were married on this day in 1925 in Peine. **Elswith Frances Ariola** is the granddaughter of Solomon and Cristabel. **Kareem Davon Underwood** (who was raised by **Irma Gonzalez**) is the great-great-granddaughter of Solomon and Cristabel.

On this day **Leonora Avila** was born in 1918. Her baptism record says she was born on the 20th May but in the declaration before marriage it says she was born on the 24th of May. She is the daughter of **Pedro John Avila** and **Viviana Palacio**. She married **Cipriano Arana** in 1937 in Barangu. She died in Peine in 1981. As the wife of a teacher she spent many years in various rural villages with her husband. **Maria Loreta Palacio** is the first cousin once removed of Pedro.

Bernard Avilez was born on this day in 1898 in Peine. He is the son of **Ambrosio "Sabigi" Avilez** and **Justa Polonio**. He married **Anacleta Castro** in 1924 in Peine.

Salvatore Daniels was born on this day. He is the son of **Salvatore Basil "S.B." Daniels** and **Victoria Ogaldez**. Salvatore's father taught for many years as the principal teacher in Barangu.

Pio Nolberto was born on this day in 1888 in Peine. He is the son of **Francisco Nolberto** and **Francisca Serapia**. Pio married **Casimira Nicholas** in 1883 in Barangu. His second marriage was to **Florencia Blas** in 1903 in Barangu. His third marriage was to **Cipriana Gregorio** in 1921 in Peine. Pio died in 1921 in Barangu. **Dionisio Nolberto** is the son of Pio.

21st May

In the Catholic calendar today is the Feast Day of St. Secundinus.

Secundino Avilez was born on this day in 1900 in Peine. He is the son of **Ambrosio "Sabigi" Avilez** and **Justa Polonio**. He married **Bonifacia Ramirez** in 1922 in Peine. Secundino died in Peine in 1950. Secundino is the grandson of **Santiago "Gaünbü" Avilez**, the founder of Barangu.

On this day in 1904 **Martires Coronado Palacio** died in Barangu. He is the son of **Anastacio Palacio** and **Magdalena Cesaria**. He was born in 1881 in Barangu. **Maria Loreta Palacio** is the first cousin of Martires.

Eugenio Cayetano and **Alfonsa Zuniga** were married on this day in 1938 in Barangu. Eugenio is the son of **Luis Cayetano** and **Paulina Reyes**. Alfonsa is the daughter of **Inocente Zuniga** and **Luciana Nolberto**. Alfonsa died in October of 1939. Eugenio then married **Manuela Marin** in Peine in 1941. Alfonsa is the sister of **Lucille "Chilagu" Valencio nee Zuniga**. E. Roy Cayetano is the son of Eugenio with Manuela.

Francisco Bonifacio "Frank" Arana died on this day in Belmopan in 2005. He is the son of **Adriano Natividad Arana** and **Basilia Luis**. He was born in Peine in 1931. He married **Narcisa Esther Contreras** in 1955 in Peine. Frank was a Farm Demonstrator in Barangu.

On this day **Rosendo Lino** died in Peine in 1959. He is the son of **Nievi Lino** and **Polonia Santino**. He married **Clemencia Nunez** in Peine in 1907. **Faith Daniels** married Rosendo and Clemencia's son **Barbarin Nunez**.

Abeline Shashta Zelaya was born this day. Abeline is the daughter of **Ernie Zelaya** and **Genevieve Mariano**. Abeline is the granddaughter of **Jacinta Palacio**. **Maria Loreta Palacio** is the first cousin four times removed of Abeline.

22nd May

Paulina Reyes was born on this day in Barangu in 1892. She is the daughter of **Martin Reyes** and Luisa Roches. She married **Luis Cayetano** and after his death she married **George McKensie** in 1934. George was from Jamaica. **Marion Cayetano** is the grandson of Paulina and Luis.

On this day in Barangu **Feliciano "Felix" Alvarez** and **Pantaleona Mejia** were married in 1937 in Barangu. Feliciano was from Labuga, Wadimalu. He was a clerk with United Fruit Company. Pantaleona is the daughter of **Simon Mejia** and **Nicolasa Palacio**. **Angelina "Angie" Nicholas nee Alvarez** is the daughter of Feliciano and Pantaleona.

23rd May

Andrea Nicholas was baptised on this day in Peine in 1872. She is the daughter of **Leoncio Nicholas** and **Christina Garcia**. Andrea married **Simon Mejia** in 1890 in Barangu. **Angela Palacio** is the great-granddaughter of Andrea through her grandmother **Hilaria Palacio nee Mejia**.

On this day in 1901 **Sebastian Garcia** died in Barangu. He is the son of **Apolinario Garcia** and **Marcelina Augustina Martinez**. He was born in 1879 in Barangu. His parents had moved from Jonathan Point to Barangu.

Carciana Palacio was born in 1904 in Barangu. She is the daughter of **Nolberto Palacio** and **Ignacia Arana**. She died in 1972 in Barangu. **Maria Loreta Palacio** is the aunt of Carciana. Carciana is the mother of **Paul Palacio** and **Vicenta "Lulu" Sanchez**.

On this day **Dawn Joseph** (*next page*) was born in Peine. She is the daughter of **Ambrosio Joseph** and **Petrona Joseph**. **Maria Loreta Palacio** is the great-great-aunt of Dawn. Dawn lives in Caye Caulker.

Pedro Nolasco Cayetano and **Benita Pascual** were married on this day in 1877 in Peine. Pedro is the son of **Juan Pedro Cayetano**. Anacleto and Vinciona, Pedro's siblings were early settlers of Barangu. Pedro is the great great-great-uncle of **Egbert Valencio** with **Juan Pedro Cayetano** being the common ancestor.

On this day **Aparicio Santiago Marin** was born in 1884 in Dangriga. He married **Brigida Paulino**. Aparicio worked for over 10 years for United Fruit Company in Wadimalu. He is the grandfather of **Angela Palacio** through her mother **Bridget Palacio nee Marin**. Many Garifuna men and women immigrated to Wadimalu to work for United Fruit Company in the 1920's.

24th May

In the Catholic calendar today is the Feast Day of St. Joanna.

Susanne Palacio was born on this day in 1912 in Barangu. She is the daughter of **Hipolito Palacio** and **Josefa Zuniga**. **Thelma Arzu** (the daughter of **Bima Arzu**) is the granddaughter of Susanne. **Ruben Palacio** is the brother of Susanne. **Maria Loreta Palacio** is the first cousin once removed of Susanne.

On this day **Juana Nolberto** was born in 1884 in Barangu. She is the daughter of **Pio Nolberto** and **Casimira Nicholas**. Juana married **Felix Noralez** in 1903 in Barangu. **Teresa "Tandu" Noralez** is the granddaughter of Juana. **Paula Nolberto** is the niece of Juana.

Juan Bautista Arzu and **Obispa Florentina Paulino** were married in 1901 in Peine. Obispa is the daughter of **Augustin "Big Ease" Paulino** and **Juana Luis**. One of their children, **Santos Arzu**, taught school for a number of years in Barangu in the early 1930's.

On this day **Leonora Avila** was born in 1918 in Barangu. She is the daughter of **Pedro John Avila**

Dawn Joseph (2013)

and **Viviana Palacio**. Leonora married **Cipriano Arana** in 1937 in Barangu. Leonora died in 1981 in Peine.

25th May

Today in the pre-1969 Catholic calendar is the Feast Day of Pope St. Gregory VII.

Gregoria Nolberto was born on this day in 1866 in Barangu. She is the daughter of **Francisco Nolberto** and **Francisca Serapia**. She married **John Lambey** in 1888 in Peine. This marriage marked one of several close linkages between the Nolberto/Lambey family groups that still persists to the present. Gregoria is the great-aunt of **Isabel "Beans" Nolberto**.

On this day **Alcardio Avila** and **Justa Gonzalez** were married in 1904 in Peine. He is the son of **Victoriano Avila** and **Cesaria Zuniga**. Justa is the daughter of **Carlos Zuniga**. They are the grandparents of **Rita Enriquez nee Avila**.

26th May

Bernardina Arzu died on this day in 1933. She is the daughter of **Juan Bautista Arzu** and **Obispa Florentina Paulino**. She was born in Peine in 1909. She married **Crescencio Roches** in 1933 a week before she died.

Elbert Karle Castillo was born on this day in Peine. He is the son of **Joseph Castillo** and **Ricorda Geraldine Casimiro**. **Erasmo Casimiro** and **Paula Noralez** are the grandparents of Elbert.

27th May

Martina "Obispa" Martinez was born on this day in 1884. She is the daughter of **Pedro Martinez** and **Regina Virgen Luis**. She married **Francisco Nunez** in 1911 in Peine. **Evaristo "Bob Steele" Nunez** is the son of Martina and Francisco. Martina is the aunt of **Melvinia "Grandma Mi" Martinez** and the great-aunt of **Victoriana Victoriana "Vicky" Nolberto nee Martinez**.

On this day **Thomas Zuniga** was born. He is the son of **John Jacob Zuniga** and **Telesflora "Stella" Simeona Mejia**. Thomas is the brother of **Delvarene Zuniga**.

Ashley Gamboa was born on this day in Belize City. He is the son of **Antonio Gamboa** and **Leolin Elma Valencio**. He is the grandson of **Lucille "Chilagu" Valencio nee Zuniga** and **Raymond Valencio**.

Justo Polonio and **Justina Martinez** were married on this day in 1938 in Peine. Justo is the son of **Pantaleon**

Odway Polonio and Petrona Paulino. Justina is the daughter of George Martinez and Luisa Nunez. Justo's father, Pantaleon was Deputy Registrar of Births and Deaths (a position usually held by the principal teacher but not in this case) in Barangu in the late teens of the twentieth century.

28th May

Raheem Mariano was born on this day in San Ignacio. He is the son of Austin Aranda and Beatrice Mariano. He is the second cousin once removed of Steven "Junior" Gutierrez. Maria Loreta Palacio is the first cousin four times removed of Raheem.

On this day Felipa Carlota Marin was born in Barangu in 1916. She is the daughter of Aparicio Santiago Marin and Brigida Paulino. She married Joseph Pollard Palacio in 1947 after his first wife

Felipa Carlota Marin (1979)

died. Carlota died in 1995 in Belize City. Juliana "Linda" Arana nee Lopez is the daughter of Carlota with a different father.

Angel Baltazar was born on this day. He is the son of Valentine Baltazar and Gregoria Noralez. Teresa "Tandu" Noralez is the first cousin of Angel with Felix Noralez being the common ancestor.

On this day in 1929 Hilario Nolberto was born in Barangu. He is the son of Dionisio Nolberto and Nicolasa Martinez. He married Victoriana "Vicky" Martinez. Hilario died in 1997 in Peine. He is the father of Hilma "Nana" Nolberto. Hilario was a school teacher when he was young and later became a carpenter.

Felipa Nolberto was born in 1925 in Barangu. She was the daughter of Dionisio Nolberto and Nicolasa Martinez. Felipa is the sister of Paula Nolberto.

On this day Joyce Lopez was born. She is the daughter of Toribio Joseph Lopez and Emelda Marin. Joyce's parents are third cousins with Juan Pedro Cayetano as the common ancestor. Maria Loreta Palacio is the first cousin thrice removed of Joyce. Erlinda "Delane" Ogaldez nee Nicholas is the daughter of Joyce.

On this day Presentacion Nunez and Gregoria "Gogo" Paulino were married in 1938. Francisco Nunez and Martina Martinez are Presentacion's parents. Gregoria's parents are Eugenio Paulino and Nicolasa Zuniga. Presentacion's brother is Evaristo "Bob Steele" Nunez.

29th May

In the Catholic calendar today is the Feast Day of Saint Maximinus of Trier.

Runulfo "Roman" Palacio was born on this day in 1907 in Barangu. He is the son of Nolberto Palacio and Ignacia Arana. He died in 1984 in Labuga. He was a composer and performer of Arumahani songs. He is the father of Esteban Palacio, the Buyei. Maria Loreta Palacio is the aunt of Roman.

On this day Nathaniel Cayetano was born in Orange Walk. He is the son of Francis Benedict Cayetano and

Nathaniel "Shorty" Cayetano (2003)

Florencia Lucas. He is known as "Shorty" in the village. **Maria Loreta Palacio** is the great-grandmother of Nathaniel. He is at present a farmer in Midway village.

Loreta Cayetano was born on this day in 1927. She is the daughter of **Pascacio Cayetano** and **Eustaquia Satuye**. She died in 1946. **Maria Loreta Palacio** is the grandmother of Loreta.

Michael Angelo Daniels was born on this day. He is the son of **Salvatore Basil "S.B." Daniels** and **Victoria Ogaldez**. His father, **S.B. Daniels**, was a long time principal teacher in Barangu.

On this day in 1910 **Maximino Lino** was born in Peine. He is the son of **Rosendo Lino** and **Clemencia Nunez**. He married **Santiaga Avilez** (the granddaughter of **Anastacio Palacio**) in 1933 in Peine. Maximino is the brother of **Barbarin Lino**.

Maximo Avilez was born on this day in 1890. He is the son of **Ambrosio "Sabigi" Avilez** and **Justa Polonio**. He married **Eugenia** (unknown last name) in 1913 in Belize Town. Maximo is the grandson of **Santiago Avilez**, the founder of Barangu.

Jose Apolinario Garcia was born on this day in 1870 in Barangu. He is the son of **Apolinario Garcia** and **Marcelina Augustina Martinez**. He is the brother of **Nicanora Palacio nee Garcia**.

Evaristo Nunez and **Alexine Loredo** were married in 1938 in Barangu. Evaristo is the son of **Francisco Nunez** and **Martina "Obispa" Martinez**. Alexine is the daughter of **Eulalio Loredo** and **Gregoria Palacio**. Evaristo and his wife had a shop in Barangu. **Elorine Nunez** and **Leonard Nunez** are two of their children.

On this day **Andres Patricio Enriquez** and **Jane Victoriana Villafranco** were married in 1912 in Peine. Andres was a long time teacher in San Antonio Toledo and retired from teaching while teaching in San Antonio Cayo. He taught for a short time in Barangu between 1916 and 1918. For more information on Andres and Jane, look out for their autobiography being edited by their grandson, **Jerry Enriquez**.

Eugenio Cayetano and **Manuela Marin** were married on this day in 1941 in Barangu. Eugenio is the son of **Luis Cayetano** and **Paulina Reyes**. Manuela is the daughter of **Aparicio Santiago Marin** and **Brigida Paulino**. **Judith Cayetano** is the daughter of Eugenio and Manuela.

30th May

Martin Martinez and **Evilia Gonzalez** were married in 1970 in Belize City. Martin is the son of **Hipolito Martinez** and **Regina Lorenzo**. Evila is the daughter of **Justo Gonzalez** and **Ursula Arana**. Evila is know as "Ivy" in the village. Martin is the brother of **Elliot Martinez**.

Geronimo Avilez and **Pastora Villafranco** were married on this day in 1934 in Peine. Geronimo is the son of **Ambrosio "Sabigi" Avilez** and **Justa Polonio**. Pastora is the daughter of **Luis Majin Villafranco** and **Antonia Zuniga**. Geronimo is the grandson of **Santiago "Gaünbü" Avilez**, the founder of Barangu.

Barbarin Lino married **Faith Daniels** on this day in 1945 in Peine. Faith is the daughter of **Salvatore Basil "S.B." Daniels** and **Victoria Ogaldez**. Barbarin is the son of **Rosendo Lino** and **Clemencia Nunez**.

On this day **Richard Cayetano** was born in Dangriga. He is the son of **Solomon Cayetano** and **Felicita Flores**. Richard was known as "Shadigo." His spouse is **Merline Alvarez**. Richard is the second cousin of **Sebastian Cayetano** with **Marcelo Cayetano** as the common ancestor. **Maria Loreta Palacio** is the great-grandmother of Richard.

Kenroy Cayetano was born on this day in Belize City. He is the son of **Richard Cayetano** and **Merlene Alvarez**. Kenroy is the great-great-grandson of **Maria Loreta Palacio**. Kenroy is the third cousin of **Hanjai Gregory Arzu** with **Marcelo Cayetano** as the common ancestor. He is the fourth cousin of **Hanjai Gregory Arzu** with **Teodoro "Joe Young" Palacio** as the common ancestor and Kenroy is the fifth cousin of **Hanjai Gregory Arzu** with **Francisco Palacio** as the common ancestor.

On this day (unknown first name) **Paulino** was born in Labuga in 1868. He is the son of **Diego Paulino** and **Dominga "Waganga" Cayetano**. This is **Augustin "Big Ease" Paulino**'s brother. This couple had children in both Laguga and Barangu, showing the close relationship betwn the two Garifuna communities.

31st May

Henry Loredo and **Martina Avilez** were married on this day in 1920 in Barangu. Henry is the son of **Eulalio Loredo** and **Gregoria Palacio**. Martina is the daughter of **John Justo Avilez** and **Paula Noralez**. Henry taught school in Barangu beginning in 1923. He was a first alcalde for Barangu in 1945. Martina died during childbirth in 1927. Henry remarried in 1928 to **Ursula Polonio**. **Harold "Greg" Arzu** is the grandson of Henry and Martina.

Joseph Pollard Palacio and **Hilaria Mejia** were married on this day in Barangu in 1924. Joseph is the son of **Nolberto Palacio** and **Ignacia Arana**. Hilaria is the daughter of **Simon Mejia** and **Andrea Nicholas**. Hilara died in 1946 in Peine. **Theodore Palacio** is the son of Joseph and Hilaria.

Robert Cayetano was born on this day in Peine. He is the son of **Robert Cayetano** and **Beatrice Sanchez**. **Maria Loreta Palacio** is the great-great-grandmother of Robert.

On this day in 1962 **Rodney Robert Zuniga** was born in Barangu. He is the son of **John Ray Zuniga** and **Vicenta "Lulu" Sanchez**. Rodney died in 2010 in Belize City. **Maria Loreta Palacio** is the great-great-aunt of Rodney.

Fernando Arzu was born on this day in 1922. He is the son of **Juan Bautista Arzu** and **Obispa Florentina Paulino**. Fernando is the grandson of **Augustin "Big Ease" Paulino**. Fernando is the brother of **Santos Arzu** who was a school teacher in Barangu from 1930 to 1932.

On this day **Angel Jimenez** was born in 1895 in Labuga. He is the son of **Fermin Jimenez** and **Petrona Cayetano**. His parents are first cousins, carrying on the cross cousin tradition that was brought from St. Vincent where a child of a sister marries a child of her brother. **Faustina Villafranco** married Angel in 1917 in Peine.

Cross Cousin Marriage		
Juan Pedro Cayestano	common ancestor	Juan Pedro Cayetano
Anacleto Cayetano	siblings	Rafaela Cayetano
Petrona Cayetano	first cousins	Fermin Jimenez

More Life Events in May

_____   _____
_____   _____
_____   _____
_____   _____
_____   _____
_____   _____
_____   _____
_____   _____
_____   _____
_____   _____
_____   _____
_____   _____
_____   _____
_____   _____
_____   _____
_____   _____

JUNE

1st June

In the Catholic calendar today is the Feast Day of St. Fortunatus of Spoleto.

Santiago Martinez died on this day in Peine. He is the son of **Florentino Martinez** and **Apolonia Francisca (Foster)**. He was born in 1893 in Barangu. Santiago married **Florentina Avila** in 1945 in Peine.

Fortunata Avila was born on this day. She is the daughter of **Reginald Avila** and **Georgiana Palacio**. Her parents are second cousins once removed. **Maria Loreta Palacio** is the great-great-aunt of Fortunata with **Teodoro Palacio** as the common ancestor. **Maria Loreta Palacio** is also the second cousin once removed of Fortunata. **Lynn Zuniga nee Arnold** is the niece of Fortunata.

Erwin Martinez was born on this day. He is the son of **Benito Martinez** and **Eudora Zuniga**. Erwin is the grandson of **Eugenia "Jean" Zuniga nee Noralez**.

2nd June

In the Catholic calendar today is the Feast Day of St. Marcellinus.

Victoriano Lorenzo and **Virgilia Ariola** were married on this day in 1947. They are second cousin twice removed with **Juan Pedro Cayetano** as the common ancestor. Victoriano is the son of **Timoteo Lorenzo** and **Juana "Jane" Palacio**. Virgilia is the daughter of **Catarino Patricio Ariola** and **Benita Nunez**. Victoriano was known as "Father." He was noted for his fudge. "Father" died in 1994 in Peine. Virgilia worked for many years with the St. Joseph Credit Union. **Dale Gutierrez** is the grandson of Victoriano and Virgilia.

On this day **Leoncio Nicholas** and **Christina Garcia** were married in 1877 in Peine. Leoncio is the son of **Joseph Alexander Nicholas** and **Maria Eugenia Delavez**. Christina is the daughter of **Venturo Garcia** and **Maria Antonia Isidora** (last name unknown). Leoncio and Christina are the great-grand parents of **Victor Paulino** and the great-great-grandparents of **Rita Enriquez nee Avila**.

Nicasio Vargas and **Isidora Garcia** were married on this day in 1924 in Barangu. Nicasio was known as "Yao Daguwasi" and Isidora was known as "Mama Daguwasi."

On this day **Peter Anthony Avila** and **Sotera Nicholas** were married in 1932 in Peine. Peter is the son of **Antonio Albert Avila** and **Alberta Enriquez**. Sotera is the daughter of **Sotero Nicholas** and **Paula Nunez**. **Albertha Magna Gibbs nee Avila** is the daughter of Peter and Sotera.

Marcelina Lambey was born on this day in 1895 in Barangu. She is the daughter of **John Lambey** and **Gregoria Nolberto**. Marcelina married **Seferino Marin** in Dangriga in 1914. She is the first cousin twice removed of **Alvin Loredo**.

On this day **Trinidad Martinez** was born in 1912 in San Francisco, Indura. Twenty days later she was baptised in Peine. This indicates the movement of Garinagu over great distances even with very young children. She is the daughter of **Crescencio Martinez** and **Epifania Avilez**. She married **Luis Baltazar** in 1944 in Peine. Trinidad is the granddaughter of **Ambrosio "Sabigi" Avilez**. **Santiago "Gaünbü" Avilez**, founder of Barangu, is her great-grandfather.

John Luis Medina was born on this day in the Sarstoon area of Wadimalu. He is the son of **Antonio Medina** and **Miriam Maldonado**.

On this day **Carmela Cayetano** was born in Barangu in 1921. She is the daughter of **Gregorio Cayetano** and **Teofila Flores**. **Maria Loreta Palacio** is the grandmother of Carmela. **Angus Cayetano** is the brother of Carmela.

Liberato Palacio died on this day in 1904 in Barangu. He is the son of **Anastacio Palacio** and **Magdalena Cesaria**. He was 36 when he died of "consumption." He married **Romalda Zuniga** in 1903 in Barangu. **Gumercinda Palacio** is Liberato's daughter with **Florencia Blas**. **Maria Loreta Palacio** is the first cousin of Liberato.

3rd June

In the Catholic calendar today is the Feast Day of St, Clotilde.

Julio Luis and **Lorenza Avilez** were married on this day in 1925 in Peine. Julio was from Indura. Lorenza (baptism paper has her name as Laurentia) is the daughter of **John Justo Avilez** and **Paula Noralez**. Lorenza is the great-granddaughter of **Santiago "Gaünbü" Avilez**, the founder of Barangu. Julio died in 1926 in Peine.

On this day **Clotilda Nunez** was born in 1901 in Peine. She is the daughter of **Thomas Nunez** and **Tomasa Ortiz**. Clotilda married **John Nipalmson "Hepu" Lucas** in 1926 in Peine. John was a shopkeeper in Peine.

Angela Palacio was born on this day. She is the daughter of **Theodore Palacio** and **Bridget Marin**. Her parents are third cousins. **Maria Loreta Palacio** is the great-great-aunt and the first cousin thrice removed of Angela. Many of Angela's ancestors were original settlers of Barangu, **Teodoro "Joe Young" Palacio, Maria Tomasa Martinez, Anastacio "Baibai" Palacio, Magdalena Cesaria, Diego Paulino,** and **Dominga "Waganga" Cayetano**.

On this day **Clotildo Zuniga** was born in 1917 in Barangu. He is the son of **Marcos Zuniga** and **Juliana Castillo**. He married **Eugenia "Jean" Noralez** in 1966 in Peine. Clotildo was a mayordomo of the Catholic Church in Barangu and was a leader of the Barranco Farmer's Co-op. **Kevin Zuniga** is the grandson of Clotildo.

Clotildo Zuniga (2005)

Apolonio Polonio died on this day in 1915 in Barangu. He is the son of **Eusebio Polonio** and **Lucia Ordonez**. Apolonio was born in Peine in 1888. His father Eusebio had a shop in Peine and later in Barangu. Apolonio married **Damiana Garcia** in 1915 in Barangu. Apolonio is the grandfather of **Madeline Loredo**. **Bartolo Polonio** is the nephew of Apolonio.

4th June

In the Roman Catholic calendar today is the Feast Day of Saint Francis Caracciolo.

Elswith Frances Ariola was born on this day in Barangu. She is the daughter of **Francisco "Chico" Ariola** and **Elsie Velasquez**. Elswith's parents are third cousins. Elswith is an educator. **Maria Loreta Palacio** is the great-great-aunt of Elswith and the first cousin thrice removed of Elswith with **Francisco Palacio** as the common ancestor. **Elisa Ariola** is the daughter of Elswith with **Cardinal George Rodriguez**.

On this day **Francisco Petillo** was born in 1901 in Peine. He is the son of **Cosme Petillo** and **Francisca Avilez**. Francisco married **Francisca Castro** in 1928 in Peine. Francisco is the grandson of **Justo "Bangi" Avilez** and **Suzanna Arana**. **Santiago "Gaünbü" Avilez** is the great-grandfather of Francisco. **Leonard "Mr. Pete" Petillo** is the first cousin of Francisco.

Francisco Arsido Paulino was born on this day in 1920 in Barangu. He is the son of **Eugenio Paulino** and **Nicolasa Zuniga**. Francisco is the brother of **Gregoria "Gogo" Nunez nee Paulino**.

5th June

In the Catholic calendar today is the Feast Day of St. Boniface I of Mainz.

Mauricio Linford "Linsy" Ramirez was born on this day in 1942. He is the son of **Cecilio Ramirez** and **Matilda Arana**. He married **Emily Martinez** who taught school for a few years in Barangu in the 1990's.

Marion Cayetano was born on this day in Barangu. He is the son of **Eugenio Cayetano** and **Manuela Marin**. **Claudina Elington** of Labuga married Marion. His parents are third cousins with **Juan Pedro Cayetano** as the common ancestor. **Maria Loreta Palacio** is the first cousin thrice removed.

Nolberta Avila and **Bonifacia Avila**, a set of twins, were born on this day in 1914 in Peine. They are the daughters of **Antonio Albert Avila** and **Alberta Enriquez**. Bonifacia was known as "Carlota." Nolberta and Bonifacia are the sisters of **Peter Anthony Avila**.

Tremaine Ariola was born on the day. He is the son of **Valerie Dawn Ariola**. **Maria Loreta Palacio** is the great-great-great-aunt of Tremaine and also the first cousin four times removed of Tremaine. Tremaine is the grandson of **Francisco "Chico" Ariola**.

6th June

In the Roman Catholic calendar today is the Feast Day of St. Nolbert of Magdeburg.

Olivia Justiniana Enriquez and **Henry H. Hartman** were married on this day in Peine in 1956. Justiniana was the daughter of **Andres "A.P." Patricio Enriquez** and **Jane Victoriana Villafranco**. Justiniana's father taught school for a short period of time in Barangu.

Nolberto Palacio was born on this day in Barangu in 1868. He is the son of **Teodoro "Joe Young" Palacio** and **Maria Tomasa Martinez**. Nolberto married **Ignacia Arana** in 1890 in Barangu and married a second time to **Bernadina Casimiro nee Nolberto** in 1935 in Barangu. Nolberto died in 1944 in Barangu. **Maria Loreta Palacio** is the sister of Nolberto. He is the grandfather of **Paul Palacio** and the great-grandfather of Surusia **Ludwig Palacio**.

On this day **Lisa Woodye** was born. She is the daughter of **Douglas Fairweather** and **Marjorie Woodye**. Lisa married **Darius Avila**.

7th June

In the Catholic calendar today is the Feast Day of St. Paul of Constantinople.

Pablo Jimenez was born on this day in 1888 in Barangu. He is the son of **Fermin Jimenez** and **Petrona Cayetano**. His parents are first cousins with the common ancestor being **Juan Pedro Cayetano**. Cross cousin marriage (marriage between children of a sister and a brother) was a common practice within the Garifuna community in the past. The Catholic Church worked hard to end this practice. This marriage was one of the last examples of this practice in Barangu. Pablo married **Cristobel Loredo** in 1922 in Peine. They were married at 5:45 pm and Pablo died at 7:30 pm the same evening.

On this day **Celestino Paulino** and **Mercedes Palacio** were married in 1886 in Peine. This is an example of one of the many Palacio/Cayetano marriage exchanges. Celestino is the son of **Diego Paulino** and **Dominga "Waganga" Cayetano**. Mercedes is the daughter of **Anastacio Palacio** and **Magdalena Cesaria**. Celestino died in 1887 (15 months after his marriage to Mercedes). **Clifford Joseph Marin** is the great-grandson of Celestino and Mercedes.

Pablo Baltazar was born on this day in 1913 in Labuga. He is the son of **Augustin "Ding" Baltazar** and **Faustina Mariano**. His father Augustin "Ding" is the renowned buyei from Labuga. Pablo married **Adriana Lauriano** in 1945 in Dangriga. He died in 1986 in Los Angeles, California. **Valentina Marin nee Baltazar** is the daughter of Pablo.

On this day **Pablo Nicholas** was born in 1891 in Barangu. He is the son of **Leoncio Nicholas** and **Christina Garcia**. **Aniceta Blas** married Pablo in 1912 in Barangu.

8th June

Philip "Kamuru Kamuru" Santino and **Alberta Nicholas** were married in 1908 in Barangu. Philip is the son of **Thomas Santino** and **Marta Bernardez**. Marta Bernardez had earlier been married to **Jose Maria Nunez**, one of the early pioneers of Peine and the leader of the St. Vincent (Cerro) Block initiative, showing the traditionally close links between Peine and Barangu as neigbouring communities. **Alberta Nicholas** is the daughter of **Leoncio Nicholas** and **Christina Garcia**. This marriage is the second for both of them. Philip was first married to **Justina Cayetano** in 1883 and Alberta was married to **Daniel Ariola** in 1898. This marriage had no issue. Philip was a mayordomo for the St. Joseph R. C. Church in Barangu.

On this day **Valerie Delcy Valencio** was born in Barangu. She is the daughter of **Raymond Valencio** and **Lucille "Chilagu" Zuniga**. Delcy married **Carlson John Tuttle** in 1989 in Barangu. She is known for the tabletas that she makes and sells. **Maria Loreta Palacio** is the first cousin thrice removed of Delcy.

Paula Noralez was born on this day in Spanish Lookout in 1920. She is the daughter of **Luis Nunez** and **Tomasa Noralez**. She married **Erasmo Casimiro** in 1962 in Barangu. Paula died in 2012 in Peine. She had 12 children with Erasmo, two of whom are **Ricorda Geraldine Casimiro** and **Muriel Casimiro**.

On this day **Jarreen J. Ramos** was born in Belize City. She is the daughter of **Wellington Ramos** and **Sylvia Coffin**. Jarreen is the granddaughter of **Vilma Petrona Chimilio** and she is the great-great-great-great-great-granddaughter (or the 5th great-granddaughter) of **Juan Pedro Cayetano**.

John Nicholas died on this day in 1937 in San Pedro Sarstoon. He is the son of **Philip Nicholas** and **Fabiana Palacio**. **Maria Loreta Palacio** is the first cousin once removed. John is the uncle of **Martin "Game and Gone"** or **"Tin-Tin" Nicholas**.

9th June

Feliciano Noralez was born on this day in 1913 in Barangu. He is the son of **Venancio Noralez** and **Gumercinda Palacio**. **Maria Loreta Palacio** is the first cousin twice removed. Feliciano is the brother of **Dominica Arzu nee Noralez**.

On this day **Pamela Palacio** was born in Belize City. She is the daughter of **Leroy Leo Palacio** and **Sharon Humes**. **Maria Loreta Palacio** is the great-great-great aunt of Pamela. **Paul Palacio** is the grandfather of Pamela.

10th June

In the Catholic calendar today is the Feast Day of St. Crispulus of Rome.

Crispulo Chimilio was born on this day in 1916 in Barangu. He is the son of **John Chimilio** and **Delfina Blas**. His mother was from Indura. He went to Indura with his grandfather, **Macario Blas**. He had children in both Indura and Belize. He was living in one country or the other for family reason or work availability showing his ease of moving back and forth between these two countries. This mobility was shown by many Garinagu of that period. In 1963 he moved to Mango Creek because of the availability of work. Crispulo lived off and on in Barangu. He died in Masca, Indura. **Maria Loreta Palacio** is the first cousin twice removed of Crispulo. **Eduviges "Auntie Bia" Ramirez** was the common-law wife of Crispulo.

On this day **Margaret Buckley** was born. She is the daughter of **Ursula Polonio**.

Antonio Luis was born on this day in 1920 in Peine. He is the son of **Julio Luis** and **Lorenza Avilez**. He is the grandson of **John Justo Avilez** and **Paula Noralez**. Antonio is the great-great-grandson of **Santiago Avilez**, the founder of Barangu. He is the great-uncle of **Harold "Greg" Arzu**.

11th June

In the Catholic calendar today is the Feast Day of St. Barnabas the Apostle.

Teodoro "Joe Young" Palacio died on this day in 1909 in Barangu. He is the son of **Francisco Palacio** and **Desideria "Maga Gidei."** According to the government death records, he was 65 when he died from "shortness of breathe." He married **Maria Tomasa Martinez** before he came to Barangu. After her death he married **Petrona Cayetano** in 1880 in Barangu. He came to Barangu with his brother Anastacio following his mother who was with **Santiago Avilez**. He was one of the first settlers in the transformation of Santiago's fishing camp to the village of Barangu. Teodoro was known as "Joe Young." **Maria Loreta Palacio** was the daughter of Teodoro with **Maria Tomasa Martinez**. He is the ancestor or uncle of nearly all those related to the Palacio family. A few of those related to him are **Theodore Palacio, Fabian Cayetano, Austin Arzu, Lynn Zuniga nee Arnold, Alice Nicholas nee Casimiro, Rita Enriquez nee Avila, Vicenta Sanchez, Erick Moreira, Tim Alvarez** and **Charlotte Lorenzo**. We have in our database 429 descendants of Teodoro, so this is only a small fraction of his descendants.

Bernabe Apostol Palacio was born on this day in 1913 in Barangu. He is the son of **John Castillo** and **Eulogia "Nitu Mamie" Palacio** (she was **Candido Arzu**'s aunt). Bernabe died when he was eight years old. **Maria Loreta Palacio** is his great-aunt.

On this day **Henrietta Enriquez** was born in 1931 in Peine. She had a son, **Martin Petillo,** with **Leonard "Mr. Pete" Petillo**. Henrietta died in 2001 in Peine.

Margarita Ariola was born on this day in 1921 in Barangu. She is the daughter of **Patricio Ariola** and **Vicenta Castillo**. She was known as "Dodo" (pronounced with the accent on the first "o"). She is the aunt of **Francisco "Chico" Ariola**.

On this day in 1892 **Manuela Ariola** was born in Peine. She is the daughter of **Patricio Ariola** and **Florencia Lambey**. She married **Sebastian Ramirez** in 1910 in Barangu. She is the aunt of **Francisco "Chico" Ariola**.

12th June

Ambrosine Mejia was born on this day in 1914 in Barangu. She is the daughter of **Simon Mejia** and **Nicolasa Palacio**. She married **Simon Martinez** in 1938 in Barangu. Ambrosine died in New York City. **Maria Loreta Palacio** is the first cousin once removed of Ambrosine.

On this day **John Herbert Earl Arana** was born on this day in 1950. He is the son of **Eulalio "Bidun" Arana** and **Gregoria "Gogo" Paulino**. He died in 2003. Earl is the first cousin once removed of **Irene Gibbons** and the uncle of Surusia **Peitra Arana**.

Clifford Joseph Marin was born on this day in Barangu. He is the son of **Clarence Marin** and **Dionisia Santino**. Clifford is an educator. **Maria Loreta Palacio** is the first cousin thrice removed of Clifford. He is the third cousin of **Alvin Loredo** with **Anastacio Palacio** as the common ancestor and the fourth cousin of **Alvin Loredo** with **Juan Pedro Cayetano** as the common ancestor.

On this day **John Polonio** was born in 1896 in Peine. He is the son of **Eusebio Polonio** and **Lucia Ordonez**. He died in 1901 in Barangu. His father Eusebio had a shop in Barangu. John is the uncle of **Bartolo Polonio**.

13th June

Pablo Jimenez and **Cristobel Loredo** were married on this day in 1922 in Peine. Pablo is the son of **Fermin Jimenez** and **Petrona Cayetano**. **Eulalio Loredo** and **Gregoria Palacio** are the parents of Cristobel. They were married at 5:45 pm and Pablo died at 7:30 pm the same evening. Cristobel later married **Solomon Velasquez**.

On this day **Pascual Cayetano** and **Maria Los Angeles Montero (Juana Nunez)** were married in 1862 in Labuga. Pascual is the son of **Juan Pedro Cayetano** and **Maria Celestina**. Maria's parents are **Jose Maria**

Montero and **Narcisa Nunez**. Pascual and his wife never lived in Barangu. Some of the children of **Juan Pedro Cayetano** moved to Barangu (Anacleto, Vinciona, Raphaela, etc.) and some remained in Labuga (Luis Tomas Leopoldo, Luciano, Augustin, etc.). This is an example of a family straddling two countries, which was often seen in this period among Garinagu of Barangu and Labuga.

Nolbert Joseph Arzu was born on this day in 1942 in Peine. He is the son of **Candido Arzu** and **Bernadette Loredo**. Nolbert was an agriculturalist. He died in 2002. **Maria Loreta Palacio** is the great-great-aunt of Nolbert. Nolbert was named for his great-grandfather, **Nolberto Palacio** "Concote," and his great-uncle, **Joseph Pollard Palacio**, thus **Nolbert Joseph Arzu**. He was the father of Javier Giovanni, Eileen, Arlene, Sherette, Natalie, and Victor Arzu.

On this day **Erick Dionisio Moreira** was born in Labuga. He is the son of **Juan Fernando Castillo** and **Olga "Lettie" Ramirez**. Erick is a school teacher in Belize City and is also a noted drummer. **Maria Loreta Palacio** is the great-great-great-aunt of Erick. **Apolonia Cayetano** (*above right*) is the great-grandmother of Erick.

Apolonia Cayetano (2009)

14th June

Valentino Ramirez and **Marcelina Jimenez** were married on this day in 1883 in Barangu. Valentino is the son of **Joseph Ramirez** and **Maria Candelaria**. **Marcelina Jimenez** is the daughter of **Marcelino Jimenez** and **Rafaela Cayetano** and the granddaughter of **Juan Pedro Cayetano**. Valentino and his brother, **Carmen Ramirez** both came from Labuga and moved to Barangu and married Baranguna women.

On this day **Pasquala Ramirez** was born in 1890 in Barangu. She is the daughter of **Carmen Ramirez** and **Eustaquia Palacio**. Pasquala married **Victoriano Colindres** in 1908 in Barangu. **Maria Loreta Palacio** is the aunt of Pasquala. **Tim Alvarez** is the grandson of Pasquala.

Nicholas Rogers was born on this day. He is the son of **Melvinia "Grandma Mi" Martinez**. He is the brother of **Roy Rogers**.

On this day **Nazaria Zuniga** died in 1988 in Barangu. She is the daughter of **Nicholas Zuniga** and **Mariana Diego**. Nazaria was born in 1897 in Labuga. She married **Lino Enriquez** in 1913 in Peine. She was a lay leader in the St. Joseph Church in Barangu. She led "Posada" during Advent and led the reciting of the Rosary in Spanish during Novenas in the village. Nazaria is the grandmother of **Elodia "Loya" Nolberto nee Palacio**.

Maria Loreta Palacio and Erik Dionisio Moreira		
Teodoro Palacio	common ancestor	Teodoro Palacio
Maria Loreta Palacio	siblings	Eustaquia Palacio
	aunt	Bonifacio Ramirez
	grand-aunt	Ricardo Ramirez
	great-grand-aunt	Olga "Lettie" Ramirez
	great-great-grand-aunt	Erik Dionisio Moreira
Erik Dionisio Moreira and Apolonia Cayetano		
Apolonia Cayetano		Apolonia Cayetano
	daughter	Benita ?
	grand-daughter	Olga "Lettie" Ramirez
	great-grandson	Erik Dionisio Moreira

Candida Palacio died on this day in Peine in 1957. She is the daughter of **Dionisio Palacio** and **Catarina Nunez**. She was born in 1902 in Peine. **Tiburcio Nicholas** married Candida. **Frederick Nicholas** is the son of Candida.

On this day **Victor Joseph Nicholas** died in Barangu. He is the son of **Ignacio Nicholas** and **Perfecta Avilez**. Victor married **Sarah Arzu**. He latter married **Angelina Alvarez**. Victor was an educator, he taught and was a principal teacher in Barangu. Later he was principal of the Belize Teachers College.

15th June

Pio Nolberto and **Casimira Nicholas** were married on this day in 1883 in Barangu. Pio is the son of **Francisco Nolberto** and **Francisca Serapia**. Casimiro is the daughter of **Joseph Alexander Nicholas** and **Maria Eugenia Delavez**. This was the first of three marriages for Pio. Pio was elected first alcalde for Barangu in 1897. Pio and Casimiro are the grandparents of **Paula Nolberto**.

On this day **Vela Nolberto** was born in 1891 in Barangu. She is the daughter of **Pio Nolberto** and **Casimiro Nicholas**. Vela was known as "Vita" in the village. Vita is the great-aunt of **Alvin Loredo**.

Basilia Palacio was born on this day in 1936 in Barangu. She is the daughter of **Jacob Palacio** and **Tomasa Polonio**. **Maria Loreta Palacio** is the first cousin twice removed of Basilia. Basilia is the first cousin of **Andy Palacio**.

16th June

In the Catholic Calendar today is the Feast Day of St. Francois Micheneau veuve Gillot and St. Francois Suhard veuve Menard.

Francis Zuniga was born on this day in 1929 in Barangu. He is the son of **John Jacob Zuniga** and **Tomasine Loredo**. He was known as "Lü." Francis had a family in Belize and moved to England and has a daughter there named **Francesca Thomasina Zuniga**. Francis is the brother of **Felicita "Cita" Zuniga**.

On this day **Antonio Palacio** was born in 1909 in Peine. He is the son of **Dionisio Palacio** and **Catarina Nunez**. Antonio married **Andrea Palacio**, the daughter of **Catarino T. Palacio** and **Francisca Sacasa (Ortiz)**, in 1934 in Peine. His wife Andrea is his second cousin with **Francisco Palacio** as the common ancestor.

On this day **Francisco Zuniga** was born in 1868 in Peine. He is the son of **Mariano Zuniga** and **Juana Paula Celertina**. Francisco is the brother of **Claro Zuniga** and **Natividad Zuniga**. Francisco is the great-uncle of **Lucille "Chilagu" Valencio nee Zuniga** and the great-uncle of **Clotildo Zuniga**.

17th June

Manuela Flores was born on this day in 1917 in Barangu. She is the daughter of **Candido Flores** and **Isidora Bermudez**. Manuela is the sister of **Procopio Flores** and **Mary Casimiro nee Flores**.

On this day in 1893 **Romana Nolberto** died Barangu. She is the daughter of **Macario Nolberto** and **Josefa Alvarez**. Romana was born in 1890 in Barangu. Her father, Macario was elected second alcalde in 1892. Macario is the brother of **Pio Nolberto**. Romana is the great-aunt of **Lorenzo "Thunder" Nolberto**.

18th June

Martina Avilez was born on this day in 1900 in Peine. She is the daughter of **John Justo Avilez** and **Paula Noralez**. She married **Henry Loredo** in 1920 in Barangu. She died in 1927 in Barangu. Martina is the great-granddaughter of **Santiago Avilez**, the founder of Barangu. **Bernadette Arzu nee Loredo** is the daughter of Martina.

On this day in 1920 **Macrina Petillo** was born in Peine. She is the daughter of **Bonifacio Petillo** and **Carmen Enriquez**. Macrina is the aunt of **Sheridan Arzu nee Petillo**.

Telesflora Martinez died on this day in Peine in 1945. She is the daughter of **Francisco Martinez** and **Estefania Avila**. Telesflora was born in Barangu in 1928. She was brought to Peine in the middle of the night in a rainstorm because of her having trouble in childbirth. She died after arriving in Peine. Telesflora is the great-aunt of Surusia **Ludwig Palacio**.

19th June

Marcial Chimilio and **Inocenta Nicholas** were married on this day in 1923. Marcial was the son of **Benito Chimilio** and **Saturnina Palacio**. Inocenta was the daughter of **Sotero Nicholas** and **Paula Nunez**. Inocenta married a second time in 1939 to **Facundo Martinez**. Surusia **Bertie Chimilio**, the former Belize football administrator, is the grandson of Marcial and Inocenta.

Carlette Alvarez was born on this day in 1970. She is the daughter of **Simon Aloysius Alvarez** and **Phyllis Palacio**. Her parents are third cousins with **Francisco Palacio** as the common ancestor. **Maria Loreta Palacio** is Carlette's great-great-aunt and also her first cousin thrice removed with **Francisco Palacio** as the common ancestor. Also her great-grandparents **Pascacio Cayetano** and **Eustaquia Satuye** are second cousins with **Juan Pedro Cayetano** as the common ancestor. Carlette is the sister of **Michelle Alvarez** and the niece of **Angelina "Angie" Nicholas nee Alvarez**.

20th June

Fabiano Arzu was born on this day in 1892 in Peine. He is the son of **Sebastian Arzu** and **Luciana Enriquez**. He married **Martha Palacio**, daughter of **Catarino T. Palacio** and **Francisca Sacasa (Ortiz)**, in 1921 in Peine.

21st June

Anthony Lopez and **Jacqueline Regina Martinez** were married on this day in 1997 in Belize City. **Martin Martinez** and **Evilia Gonzalez** are the parents of Jacqueline.

Celestina Enriquez was born on this day. She is the daughter of **Victor Enriquez** and **Vilma Petrona Chimilio**. She had children with **Daniel Cacho** and **Moses Aranda**. **Maria Loreta Palacio** is the first cousin four times removed of Celestina with **Francisco Palacio** as the common ancestor. **Hanjai Arzu** is the fifth cousin of Celestina. As shown in the table below, it takes seven generations to obtain a fifth cousin.

Hanjai Arzu and Celestina Enriquez		
Francisco Palacio	common ancestor	Francisco Palacio
Teodoro Palacio	siblings	Anastacio Palacio
Nolberto Palacio	first cousins	Saturnina Palacio
Patrocinia Palacio	second cousins	John Chimilio
Candido Arzu	third cousins	Timoteo Chimilio
Harold Arzu	fourth cousins	Vilma Petrona Chimilio
Hanjai Arzu	fifth cousins	Celestina Enriquez

Lorenzo Arana died on this day in 1947 in Peine. He is the son of **Concepcion Arana** and **Simeona Flores**. Lorenzo was born in 1909 in Peine. Lorenzo is the brother of **Gabriel "Dimas" Arana** and **Eulalio "Bidun" Arana**.

22nd June

Peter Amaya was born on this day in 1908 in Barangu. He is the son of **Cayetano Amaya** and **Josefa Paulino**. Cayetano and Josefa married in December of 1908 in Barangu. Josefa then married **Saturnino "Senerial" Martinez** and lived on the Sarstoon Bar. Then at age 40 she married **Felix Lucas** in Peine in 1934.

Juliana Lambey was born on this day in 1917 in Peine. She is the daughter of **Severiano Lambey** and **Romana Arana**. She is the granddaughter of **Gregoria Nolberto**, **Pio Nolberto**'s sister, and **John Lambey**. Her grandparents were early residents of Barangu. Juliana married **Eufemio Gutierrez** in 1940. Juliana is the second cousin once removed of **Alvin Loredo**.

Silveria Bernardez was born on this day in 1920 in Dangriga. She is the daughter of **Martin Bernardez** and **Apolinaria Ogaldez**. She married **Felix Noralez** in 1943 in Peine. This was **Felix Noralez**'s second marriage.

Ethel Arana was born on day in Barangu in 1941. She is the daughter of **Cipriano Arana** and **Leonora Avila**. Ethel died in 1954 in Barangu. She is the sister of **Marti Cain nee Arana**. **Maria Loreta Palacio** is the first cousin twice removed of Ethel.

On this day **Odelma Casimiro** was born in Corozal. She is the daughter of **Dionisio Casimiro** and **Alice Nicholas**. Odelma's parents are third cousins with **Joseph Alexander Nicholas** as the common ancestor and Odelma's parents are also second cousins once removed with **Teodoro "Joe Young" Palacio** as the common ancestor. **Maria Loreta Palacio** is the great-great-great-aunt and the great-great-aunt of Odelma.

23rd June

Albina Cayetano (Avilez) was born on this day in 1893 in Barangu. She is the daughter of **Juan Avilez** and **Dominga "Gadu" Marin**. **Juan Avilez** comes from Jonathan Point, whereas **Santiago Avilez** is said to come from Santa Fe (Griga) on the outskirts of Trujillo. Santiago's family claims no relationship with the **Juan Avilez** family. The rest of Albina's brothers and sisters use the Avilez surnames but Albina in the "Marin" style uses the Cayetano surname. This naming was more a case of personal preference as against the presence or absence of kinship ties. Albina is the aunt of **Cleofa Avilez**.

On this day **Martin Martinez** was born in Belize City. He is the son of **Martin Martinez** and **Evilia Gonzalez**. Martin married **Parlet McFadzean** in 1997 in Belize City. **Maria Loreta Palacio** is the great-great-aunt of Martin. Martin's parents are cousins in two ways both with **Juan Pedro Cayetano** as the common ancestor. Martin and Evilia are fourth cousins and third cousins once removed (*table on the next page*).

24th June

In the Catholic calendar today is the Feast Day of the Birth of St. John the Baptist.

John "Shamba" Dominguez was born on this day in 1936 in Belize City. He died in 1999 in Belize City. He is the father of **Nora Arana** with **Marthy "Marti" Arana**, now **Marti Cain nee Arana**.

On this day **John Ogaldez** was born in 1923 in Barangu. He is the son of **Agapito Ogaldez** and **Paula Paulino**. John is the uncle of **Anthony "Tony" Ogaldez** and the brother of **Irene Gibbons**.

Evilia Gonzalez and Martin Martinez I		
Juan Pedro Cayetano	common ancestor	Juan Pedro Cayetano
Luisa Cayetano	siblings	Anacleto Cayetano
Dominga Marin	first cousins	Mauricia Cayetano
Gregoria Bermudez	second cousins	Gabina Zuniga
Ursula Arana	third cousins	Hipolito Martinez
Evilia Gonzalez	fourth cousins	Martin Martinez

Evilia Gonzalez and Martin Martinez II		
Juan Pedro Cayetano	common ancestor	Juan Pedro Cayetano
Luisa Cayetano	siblings	Petrona Cayetano
Dominga Marin	first cousins	Juana "Jane" Palacio
Gregoria Bermudez	second cousins	Regina Lorenzo
Ursula Arana	third cousins	Martin Martinez
Evilia Gonzalez	third cousins once removed	Martin Martinez

Alice Arana was born on this day in Barangu. She is the daughter of **Cipriano Arana** and **Leonora Avila**. Alice is an educator as was her father, Cipriano. **Maria Loreta Palacio** is the first cousin once removed of Alice. Alice is the sister of **Marti Cain nee Arana**.

25th June

In the Catholic calendar today is the Feast Day of St. William the Abbot.

David William Nicholas was born on this day in 1927. He is the son of **Ignacio Nicholas** and **Perfecta Avilez**. He married **Justina Ramirez** in Peine. **Stanley Nicholas** is the son of David.

On this day **Guillerma Chimilio** was born in 1924 in Barangu. She is the daughter of **Marcial Chimilio** and **Inocenta Nicholas**. **Maria Loreta Palacio** is the first cousin twice removed of Guillerma.

Georgiana Garcia and **America Garcia** were born on this day in 1911 in Barangu. They are the twin children of **Esmith Garcia** and **Cornelia Martinez**. America died in 1912 when she was six months old.

On this day **Pablo Roches** was born in 1920 in Barangu. He is the son of **Elijio Roches** and **Francisca Lucas**.

Stephen Francis Hecker died on this day in in 2005. He is the son of **Naomi Colon**. He was born in 1974.

26th June

Carla Tucker was born on this day in Belize City. She is the daughter of **Antonia Ariola**. Carla is the sister of **Jacinta Palacio**.

27th June

In the Catholic calendar today is the Feast Day of Cordova.

Cipriano Arana and **Leonora Avila** were married on this day in 1937 in Barangu. Cipriano is the son of Atanacio Arana and **Leona Garcia**. Leonora is the daughter of **Viviana Palacio** and **Pedro John Avila**. Cipriano was a rural school teacher. Leonora and her husband had eight children with Ambrose being the oldest and Alice being the youngest.

On this day **Joseph Margarito Petillo** and **Adriana Lopez** were married. Joseph is the son of **Bonifacio Petillo** and **Carmen Enriquez**. Adriana is the daughter of **David Lopez** and **Rosa**. Joseph is the brother of **Leonard "Mr. Pete" Petillo**. **Sheridan Arzu nee Petillo** is the niece of Joseph.

Estanislao Reyes was born on this day in 1889 in Barangu. He is the son of **Martin Reyes** and **Luisa Roches**. Estanislao died in 1900 in Barangu. He is the great-uncle of **E. Roy Cayetano**.

On this day **Zoilo Arzu** and **Zoila Arzu** were born in 1913 in Peine. This set of twins are the children of **Juan Bautista Arzu** and **Obispa Florentina Paulino**. They are the brother and sister of **Santos Arzu** who taught school in Barangu. Zoilo and Zoila are the grandchildren of **Augustin "Big Ease" Paulino**.

Augustin "Big Ease" Paulino died on this day in 1931 up the Temash River. He died of a snake bite. He is the son of **Diego Paulino** and **Dominga "Waganga" Cayetano**. Augustin first married **Juana Luis** in 1883 in Barangu and later married **Martina Arzu** in 1902 in Peine.

28th June

In the Catholic calendar today is the Feast Day of St. Paul I, Pope.

Paul Casimiro was born on this day in 1908 in Barangu. He is the son of **Pablo Casimiro** and **Bernadina Nolberto**. He married **Margarita Lorenzo** in 1933 in Barangu. He died in 1977 in Puerto Barrios. **Jovita Casimiro** is the daughter of Paul.

Emily Williams Ramirez was born on this day. She is the daughter of **Maurice Linford "Linsy" Ramirez** and **Emily Martinez**. Her son **Andres Dion Makin** schooled in Barangu for a year and her mother, Emily taught for a few years in Barangu.

Celestina Lambey was born on ths day in 1916 in Barangu. She is the daughter of **Dionisia Lambey**. Her grandparents, **Joseph Antonio Lambey** and **Francisco Nolberto**, were early settlers of Barangu.

Salvatore Basil "S.B." Daniels died on this day in 1963 in Belize City. He is the son of **Miguel Daniels** and **Tomasa Martinez**. He was born in 1898 in Peine. His first name probably came from the name of Fr. Salvatore di Pietro, one of the early Jesuit missionaries in southern Belize. Father Pietro was an Italian priest hence the Italian name Salvatore. S.B. married **Victoria Ogaldez** in 1922 in Peine. He was a long time principal teacher in Barangu. Salvatore received an MBE from the British Crown.

Ambrosio Noralez died on this day in 1931 at Topco Camp. He is the son of **Venancio Noralez** and **Juliana Colindres**. He was born in 1912 in Peine. It is reported that he committed suicide. He is the uncle of **Eugenia "Jean" Zuniga nee Noralez**.

On this day **Victoria Ogaldez** died in 1963 in Dangriga. She is the daughter of **Secundino Ogaldez** and **Alberta Ciego**. Victoria was born in Peine in 1903. She married **Salvatore Basil "S.B." Daniels** in 1922 in Peine.

29th June

In the Catholic calendar today is the Feast Day of St. Peter the Apostle.

Vicente Apolonio and Felicita Bernardez were married on this day in 1960 in Dangriga. Vicente is the son of **Macario Apolonio** and **Venancia Nolberto**. Vicente is the first cousin once removed of **Paula Nolberto**.

On this day **Devon Cacho** was born in Belize City. He is the son of **Daniel Cacho** and **Celestina Enriquez**. **Maria Loreta Palacio** is the first cousin five times removed of Devon with **Francisco Palacio** as the common ancestor. **Vilma Petrona Chimilio** is the grandmother of Devon.

Paula Martinez was born on this day on the Sarstoon Bar. The settlement on the Sarstoon was a satellite community of Barangu. She is the daughter of **Pedro Nicasio Martinez** and **Augustina Nunez**. She married **Isidro Trigueno**. Paula is the sister of **Melvinia "Grandma Mi" Martinez**.

On this day **Carlson John Tuttle** was born in New York City. He is the son of **Farice Tuttle** and **Marion Elizabeth Lent**. He married **Valerie Delcy Valencio** in 1989 in Barangu. He makes rugumas and other traditional Garifuna baskets.

Rudolph "Rudy" Valencio was born on this day in Barangu. He is the son of **Raymond Valencio** and **Lucille "Chilagu" Zuniga**. Rudy works with the Belize Coast Guard. **Maria Loreta Palacio** is the first cousin thrice removed of Rudy.

On this day **Peter Arzu** was born. He is the son of **Catrino Arzu** and **Santiaga Mejia**. Peter is the brother-in-law of **Victor Joseph Nicholas** through his first wife, **Sarah Arzu**.

Pedro Garcia was born on this day in 1894. He is the son of **Esmith Garcia** and **Cornelia Martinez**.

On this day **Pablo Arzu** was born in 1920 in Peine. He is the son of **Benito Arzu** and **Crecencia Zuniga**. Pablo married **Sotera Franzria Benguche** in 1966 in Dangriga. He died in 1997.

Basilio Palacio was baptised in 1891 in Peine. He is the son of **Nolberto Palacio** and **Ignacia Arana**. Basilio is the uncle of **Theodore Palacio**.

30th June

Today in the pre-1969 Catholic calendar is the Feast Day of the Commemoration of St. Paul.

Paul Palacio (*next page*) was born on this day in Barangu. He is the son of **Estanislao Martinez** (*below*) and **Carciana Palacio**. He was raised by his grandfather, **Nolberto Palacio**. Paul was a member of a group of men who went out of the country to contribute to the war effort during the Second World War. He is the father of **Martina Cornelia Alvarez nee Palacio**, a member of the St. Peter Parish Council and a school teacher. **Maria Loreta Palacio** is the great-aunt of Paul.

Estanislao Martinez

Justin Vivian Gregorio was born on this day in 1933. He is the son of **Petrona "Petu" Gregorio**. Justin is the first cousin once removed of **Jacinta Trigueno nee Santino**.

Paul Palacio (2003)

More Life Events in June

JULY

1st July

In the Catholic calendar today is the Feast Day of Sts. Castus and Secundinus.

Clarence Marin and **Dionisia Santino** were married in 1967 in Barangu. Clarence is the son of **Aparicio Marin** and **Brigida Paulino**. Dionisia is the daughter of **Eusebio Santino** and **Vicenta Blas**. **Gilbert Marin** is the son of Clarence and Dionisia.

Secundino Noralez was born on this day in 1896 in Peine. He is the son of **Venancio Noralez** and **Juliana Colindres**. Secundino is the brother of **Martin Benjamin Noralez**. Eugenia "Jean" Zuniga nee Noralez is the niece of Secundino.

On this day **Margarita Palacio** was born in 1895 in Barangu. She is the daughter of **Teodoro "Joe Young" Palacio** and **Petrona Cayetano**. **Maria Loreta Palacio** is the sister of Margarita with a different mother.

Francis Benedict Martinez was born on this day in 1915 in Peine. He is the son of **Francisco Martinez** and **Estefania Avila**. Francis married **Victoria Barcelona** in 1935 in Peine. **Zaira Mierelli Martinez** is the granddaughter of Francis.

2nd July

John Arzu and **Gladys Palacio** were married on this day in 1941 in Peine. John is the son of **Isidro Arzu** and **Maxima Ariola** and was born in Barangu. Gladys is the daughter of **Francisco Palacio** and **Sixta** (last name unknown) and was from Peine.

Secundino Joseph Martinez was born on this day in 1896 in Barangu. He is the son of **Saturnino "Senerial" Martinez** and **Josefa Paulino**. Secundino married **Anastacia Vicenta Santiago** in 1929 in Peine and he then married **Bonifacia Avilez** in 1969 in Orange Walk. He lived along the Sarstoon River with his parents for a number of years. Various members of the Martinez family lived along the Sarstoon and in the Guatemalan village of San Martin (San Juan). Secundino is the grandson of **Augustin "Big Ease" Paulino**.

3rd July

On this day **Ethel Dee Loredo** died in 1995 in Peine. She is the daughter of **Henry Loredo** and **Martina Avilez**. Ethel was born in Barangu in 1925. She married **Paul Palacio**. **Maria Loreta Palacio** is the first cousin twice removed of Ethel. **Bernadette Arzu nee Loredo** is the sister of Ethel.

On this day **Pantaleona Mejia** died in 1980 in Barangu. She is the daughter of **Simon Mejia** and **Nicolasa Palacio**. She was born in 1917 in Barangu. She married **Feliciano "Felix" or "Banjie" Alvarez** in 1937 in Barangu. **Maria Loreta Palacio** is the first cousin once removed of Pantaleona. **Victor Alvarez** is the son of Pantaleona.

Andres Nicholas was born on this day in 1933. He is the son of **Cipriano Nicholas** and **Ursula Arana**.

On this day **Saturnina Chimilio** was born in 1929. She is the daughter of **John Chimilio** and **Delfina Blas**. Saturnina died in 1948. **Maria Loreta Palacio** is the first cousin twice removed of Saturnina. **Crispulo Chimilio** is the brother of Saturnina.

4th July

In the Catholic calendar today is the Feast Day of Laurian of Seville.

On this day **Loriana Ramirez** was born in Barangu in 1899. She is the daughter of **Carmen Ramirez** and **Eustaquia Palacio**. Loriana married **Canuto Zuniga**. **Maria Loreta Palacio** is the aunt of Loriana. **Abraham Zuniga** is the son of Loriana.

On this day **Lauriano Zuniga** was born. He is the son of **Clotildo Zuniga** and **Carmela Arzu**.

Alberto Lorenzo was born on this day in 1925 in Barangu. He is the son of **Timoteo Lorenzo** and **Juana "Jane" Palacio**. **Maria Loreta Palacio** is the aunt of Alberto. He is the great-uncle of **Steven "Junior" Gutierrez**.

5th July

In the Catholic calendar today is the Feast Day of Sts. Philomena and Anthony Mary Zaccaria.

Filomeno Lorenzo was born on this day in 1915 in Barangu. He is the son of **Timoteo Lorenzo** and **Juana "Jane" Palacio**. He married **Benedictina Polonio** in 1939 in Barangu. **Maria Loreta Palacio** is the aunt of Filomeno. **Victoriano "Fada" Lorenzo** is the brother of Filomeno.

On this day **Antonette Zuniga** was born in Belize City. She is the daughter of **Wilbert Zuniga** and **Jacinta Palacio**. Antonette is the first cousin thrice removed of **Maria Loreta Palacio**. Antonette is the niece of **Andy Palacio** and she is also the fourth cousin once removed of **Andy Palacio** with **Juan Pedro Cayetano** as the common ancestor.

6th July

In the Catholic calendar today is the Feast Day of St. Tranquillinus.

Tranquilino Martinez was born on this day in 1909 in Peine. He is the son of **Saturnino "Senerial" Martinez** and **Josefa Paulino**. Tranquilino is the grandson of **Augustin "Big Ease" Paulino**.

On this day **Petrona Cayetano** was born in 1935 in Barangu. She is the daughter of **Pascacio Cayetano** and **Eustaquia Satuye**. Her parents are second cousins with **Juan Pedro Cayetano** as the common ancestor. Petrona is the granddaughter of **Maria Loreta Palacio**.

Clarence "Cally" Coffin died on this day in 2008 in Brooklyn. He was born in 1929 in Belize City. **Sylvia Coffin** is the daughter of "Cally" and **Vilma Petrona Chimilio**.

7th July

Hipolito Palacio and **Josefa Zuniga** were married on this day in 1898 in Barangu. Hipolito is the son of **Anastacio Palacio** and **Magdalena Cesaria**. Hipolito was know as "Puludu" in the village. Josefa is the daughter of **Claro Zuniga** and **Mauricia Cayetano**. **Ruben Palacio** is the son of Hipolito and Josefa.

Karina Arzu was born on this day in Peine. She is the daughter of Surusia **Francis Arzu** and **Zita Alvarez**. **Maria Loreta Palacio** is the great-great-great-aunt of Karina. **Austin Arzu** is the first cousin once removed of Karina.

Felicita Valencio was born on this day in Peine in 1927. She is the daughter of **Eufamio Valencio** and **Beatrice Palacio**. She married **Adriano Nicholas** in 1961 in Belize City. **Maria Loreta Palacio** is the first cousin twice removed of Felicita. **Raymond Valencio** is the brother of Felicita.

Claro Zuniga died on this day in 1915 in Barangu. He is the son of **Mariano Zuniga** and **Juana Paula Celertina**. He was born around 1855. Claro married **Mauricia Cayetano** in 1875 in Barangu. **Lucille "Chilagu" Valencio nee Zuniga** is the granddaughter of Claro.

Anacleto Cayetano died on this day in 1901 in Barangu. He is the son of **Juan Pedro Cayetano** and **Maria Nicolasa Moralez**. He was born around 1833. He was the second generation born in Central America. He married **Dominga Martila Arzu**. **Lucille "Chilagu" Valencio nee Zuniga** is the great-granddaughter of Anacleto.

8th July

Today in the pre-1969 Catholic calendar is the Feast Day of St. Elizabeth of Portugal and St. Procopius of Scythopolis.

Veronica Petillo was born on this day in 1899 in Peine. She is the daughter of **Cosme Petillo** and **Francisca Avilez**. Veronica is the great-grand daughter of **Santiago Avilez**, the founder of Barangu.

On this day **Elizabeth Arzu** was born in 1894 in Peine. She is the daughter of **Sebastian Arzu** and **Luciana Enriquez**. She married **Walter Alfonso Williams** in 1916 in Peine. Her father Sebastian also had children with **Eluteria Cayetano**.

Isabel Nolberto was born on this day in Barangu. He is the son of **Dionisio Nolberto** and **Nicolasa Martinez**. He is known as "Beans." He married **Elodia "Loya" Palacio**. Isabel is the brother of **Paula Nolberto**.

On this day **Procopio Flores** was born in Barangu. He is the son of **Candido Flores** and **Isidora Bermudez**. Procopio is known as "Prook" in the village. "Prook" is the brother of **Mary Casimiro nee Flores**.

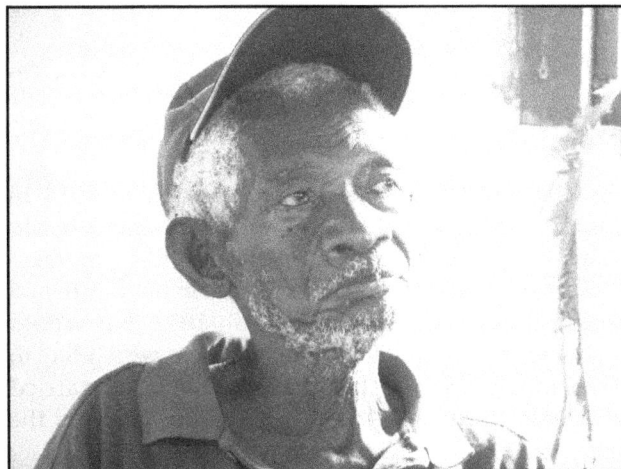

Procopio "Prook" Flores (2009)

Isabel Palacio was born on this day in 1908 in Barangu. He is the son of **Catarino T. Palacio** and **Francisca Sacasa (Ortiz)**. **Maria Loreta Palacio** is the aunt of Isabel.

9th July

Evelyn Enriquez was born on this day in 1938. She is the daughter of **Dionisia Santino**. Evelyn is the mother of **Maria Zuniga nee Casimiro**.

On this day **Sebastian Noralez** was born in 1879 in Peine. He is the son of **Florencio Noralez** and **Gregoria Mena**. Sebastian is the brother of **Venancio Noralez**. **Eugenia "Jean" Zuniga nee Noralez** is the grand niece of Sebastian.

Raymond Valencio was born on this day in Barangu. He is the son of **Eufamio Valencio** and **Beatrice Palacio**. His father, Eufamio is from Limon, Indura. Raymond married **Lucille "Chilagu" Zuniga** in Barangu. **Maria Loreta Palacio** is the first cousin twice removed of Raymond. He is a fisher and a cast net maker.

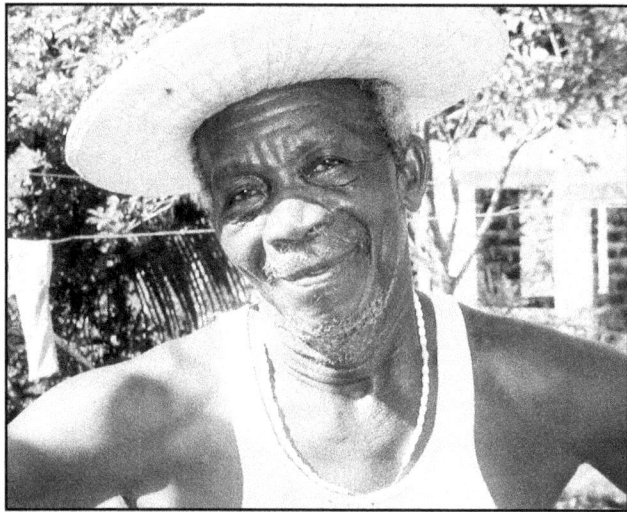

Raymond Valencio

On this day **Cirila Martinez** was born in 1914 in Barangu. She is the daughter of **Pedro Nicasio Martinez** and **Augustina Nunez**. She married **Valentino Castro** in Peine. (In a note in her baptismal record it says she married him in 1924 that would make her ten years old at her marriage which has to be incorrect.) Her husband, Valentino, later married **Michaela Lorenzo** in 1933 in Barangu. Cirila is the sister of **Melvinia "Grandma Mi" Martinez**.

10th July

Trevor Ariola was born on this day in Peine. He is the son of **Francisco "Chico or Paco" Ariola** and **Naomi Colon**. **Maria Loreta Palacio** is the great-great-aunt of Trevor.

On this day **Akeem "Conceto" Loredo** was born in Peine. He is the son of **Alvin Loredo** and **Sharon Nunez**. Akeem's parents are second cousins with **Eulalio Loredo** as the common ancestor and his parents are also third cousins once removed with **Francisco Nolberto** as the common ancestor. **Maria Loreta Palacio** is the first cousin four times removed of Akeem.

Alfanette Ashanti Loredo was born on this day in Belize City. She is the daughter of **Isaac Loredo** and **Myra Moreira**. **Maria Loreta Palacio** is the first cousin thrice removed of Alfanette. **Egbert Valencio** is Alfanette's first cousin.

11th July

In the Catholic calendar today is the Feast Day of Pope St. Pius I.

Pia Magdelano was born on this day in Newtown. She is the daughter of **Joseph Magdelano** and **Camila Contreras**. She is known as "Mamacita." She married **Victor Arana** in 1964 in Barangu. She is the sister of **Cleofa Avilez** and also the sister of **Bartolo Polonio**.

Pia "Mamacita" Magdelano (2009)

12th July

In the Catholic calendar today is the Feast Day of St. John Gualbert.

Felicita Reyes was born on this day in 1886 in Barangu. She is the daughter of **Martin Reyes** and **Luisa Roches**. Martin is from Indura. Felicita married **Saturnino Palacio** in 1906 in Barangu. **Raymond Valencio** is the grandson of Felicita.

On this day **Jane Victoriana Villafranco** was born in 1895 in Peine. She is the daughter of **Luis Majin Villafranco** and **Antonia Zuniga**. Jane married **Andres Patricio Enriquez** in 1912 in Peine. Jane lived in Barangu while her husband taught school in Barangu. She died in 1968 in Belize City.

Juana Ariola was born on this day in 1908 in Barangu. She is the daughter of **Patricio Ariola** and **Vicenta Castillo**. **Francisco "Chico" or "Paco" Ariola** is the nephew of Juana.

On this day **Wilhelmina Loredo** was born in 1902 in Barangu. She is the daughter of **Eulalio Loredo** and **Gregoria Palacio**. She married **Matildo Martinez Leiva** in 1942 in Barangu. **Maria Loreta Palacio** is the first cousin once removed of Wihelmina. She is the great-aunt of **Alvin Loredo**.

Juan Petillo was born on this day in 1904 in Peine. He is the son of **Bonifacio Petillo** and **Carmen Enriquez**. Juan is the brother of **Leonard "Mr. Pete" Petillo**.

Stephen Francis Hecker was born on this day in 1974. He is the son of **Naomi Colon**. Stephen died in 2005. Stephen is the grandson of **Irene Gibbons**.

On this day **Anacleta Nolberto** was born. She is the daughter of **Dionisio Nolberto** and **Nicolasa Martinez**. She is known as "Da" or "Da Cleta" in the village. "Da" led the singing in the church for many years.

13th July

No events.

14th July

Llwelyn Martinez and **Dativa Elizabeth Melendrez** were married on this day in 1979 in Belize City. Llwelyn is the son of **Francis Benedict Martinez** and **Victoria Barcelona**. Dativa is the daughter of **Evaristo Melendrez** and **Lucila "Shuna" Arana**. **Zaira Mierelli Martinez** is the daughter of Llwelyn and Dativa.

Octaviano Paulino was born on this day in 1908 in Barangu. He is the son of **Eusebio Paulino** and **Telesflora Bermudez**. Octaviano's parents are second cousins.

Anacleta Castro was born on this day in 1903 in Peine. She is the daughter of **Leon Castro** and **Victoriana Arana**. She married **Bernard Avilez** in 1924 in Peine. Anacleta died in 1940 in Peine.

On this day **Regina Lorenzo** died in 2006 in Belize City. She is the daughter of **Timoteo Lorenzo** and **Juana "Jane" Palacio**. Regina was born in 1920 Barangu. Regina married **Hipolito Martinez** in 1939 in Barangu. **Maria Loreta Palacio** is the aunt of Regina. **Elliot Martinez** is the son of Regina.

15th July

Carlos Martinez and **Pantaleona Valentine** were married on this day in 1936 in Peine. Carlos is the son of **Victoriano Martinez** and **Isabela Zuniga**. Pantaleona is the daughter of **Martin Valentine** and **Ambrosia Avila**. Carlos is the brother of **Crispino Martinez**. Pantaleona is the first cousin once removed of **Marti Cain nee Arana** with **Victoriano Avila** as the common ancestor.

Bernadine Casimiro was born on this day. She is the daughter of **Erasmo Casimiro** and **Paula Noralez**. Bernadine married **Philip Alvarez**.

16th July

Paul Casimiro and **Margarita Lorenzo** were married on this day in 1933 in Barangu. Paul is the son of **Pablo Casimiro** and **Bernadina Nolberto**. Margarita is the daughter of **Timoteo Lorenzo** and **Juana "Jane" Palacio**. **Jovita Casimiro** is the daughter of Paul and Margarita.

There were two weddings on this day in 1933 in Barangu. The above was one, the following is the other marriage.

On this day in 1933 in Barangu **Cipriano Nicholas** and **Ursula "Usu" Arana** were married. Cipriano is the son of **Sotero Nicholas** and **Paula Nunez**. Ursula is the daughter of **Alejandro Arana** and **Gregoria Bermudez**. **Andres Nicholas** is the son of Cipriano and Ursula.

Paul A.M. Williams and **Cecilia Rhys** were married on this day in 1977 in Dangriga. Paul is the son of **Dionisio Williams** and **Eugenia "Henny" Martinez**. **Kenisha "Kenny" Williams** is the daughter of Paul and Cecilia.

Anastacia Vicenta Santiago was born on this day in 1898 in Peine. She is the daughter of **Raymond Santiago** and **Marcelina Pamfila Servio**. She married **Secundino Joseph Martinez** in 1929 in Peine. Anastacia died in 1966. **Emily Ramirez nee Martinez** is Anastacia's granddaughter.

On this day **Leonard Nunez** was born. He is the son of **Evaristo "Bob Steele" Nunez** and **Alexine Loredo**. **Maria Loreta Palacio** is the first cousin twice removed. **Sharon Nunez** is the daughter of Leonard.

17th July

In the Catholic calendar today is the Feast Day of St. Alexis.

Eldred Roy Cayetano and **Phyllis Miranda** were married on this day in Dangriga in 1971. Roy is the son of **Eugenio Cayetano** and **Manuela Marin**. Both Roy and Phyllis are educators.

Alexis Simeon Arana was born on this day in Barangu. He is the son of **Francisco Bonifacio "Frank" Arana** and **Narcisa Esther Contreras**. Alexis was born in Barangu while his father was a farm demonstrator in the village.

Steven Gregory Gutierrez was born on this day in Peine. He is the son of **Steven Gutierrez** and **Valentina "Flora" Lorenzo**. Maria Loreta Palacio is the great-great-aunt of Steven. Steven is known as "Junior" in the village.

Joseph Margarito Petillo was born on this day in 1915 in Peine. He is the son of **Bonifacio Petillo** and **Carmen Enriquez**. Joseph married **Adriana Lopez** in 1942 in Peine. Joseph is the brother of **Leonard "Mr. Pete" Petillo**.

18th July

In the Catholic calendar today is the Feast Day of Sts. Camillus de Lellis and Frederick of Utrecht.

Liberato Palacio and **Romalda Zuniga** were married on this day in 1903 in Barangu. Liberato is the son of **Anastacio Palacio** and **Magdalena Cesaria**. Romalda is the daughter of **Claro Zuniga** and **Mauricia Cayetano**. Romalda and Liberato had one son, **Demetrio Palacio**. After Liberato's death Romalda married **Andres Sebastian**.

Frederico Martinez and **Cecilia Lopez** were married on this day in 1928 in Peine. Frederico is the son of **Saturnino "Senerial" Martinez** and **Josefa Paulino**.

Frederico Martinez was also born on this day in 1904 on the Sarstoon Bar (where many of the Martinez family lived). He is the son of **Saturnino "Senerial" Martinez** and **Josefa Paulino**.

On this day **Shaynah Ariola** was born in Barangu in 1984. She is the daughter of **Francisco Ariola** and **Naomi Colon**. Shaynah died in 2007 in Peine. **Maria Loreta Palacio** is the great-great-aunt of Shaynah.

Camila Contreras was born on this day in 1897 in Peine. She is the daughter of **Andres Contreras** and **Secundina Colindres**. She married **Cecilio "Dick" Polonio** in 1920 in Peine. She died in 1970 in Barangu. **Bartolo Polonio** is the son of Camila. **Cleofa Avilez** and **Pia "Mamacita" Arana nee Magdelano** are daughters of Camila.

On this day **Frederick Nicholas** was born in Barangu. He is the son of **Tiburcio Nicholas** and **Candida Palacio**. Frederick married **Joyce Lopez**. **Erlinda "Delane" Ogaldez nee Nicholas** is the daughter of Frederick. He is known as "Fred" in the village.

Frederick Nicholas

19th July

Ireneo Martinez and **Bernardina Santino** were married on this day in 1907 in Barangu. Ireneo is the son of **Pedro Martinez** and **Regina Virgen Luis**. Bernardina is the daughter of **Philip Santino** and **Justina Cayetano**. Victoriana **Victoriana "Vicky" Nolberto nee Martinez** is the granddaughter of Eraino and Bernardina.

Lucila "Shuna" Arana died on this day in 1998. She is the daughter of **Concepcion Arana** and **Simeona Flores**. She was born in 1920 in Peine. Lucila married **Evaristo Melendrez** in 1941. Surusia **Peitra Arana** is the grand niece of Lucila.

20th July

On this day in 1903 in Barangu there were two weddings performed. One was between **Luis Palacio** and **Felipa Garcia**. Luis is the son of **Teodoro "Joe Young" Palacio** and **Petrona Cayetano**. Felipa is the daughter of **Apolinario Garcia** and **Marcelina Augustina Martinez**. These families were both founding families of the village. **Emily Ramirez nee Martinez** is the great-granddaughter of Luis and Felipa.

The other marriage on this day in 1903 is the marriage between **Felix Noralez** and **Juana Nolberto**. Felix is the son of **Tomas Noralez** and **Felicita Nunez**. Juana is the daughter of **Pio Nolberto** and **Casimiro Nicholas**. Felix married again to **Silveria Bernardez**. **Teresa "Tandu" Noralez** is the granddaughter of Felix and Juana.

Cornelio Castillo and Lillian Enriquez were married on this day in 1940. Cornelio is the son of Inez Castillo and Martha Fuentes. Lillian is the daughter of Sebastina Arzu and Luciana Enriquez.

On this day Eudora Zuniga was born in 1960 in Barangu. She is the daughter of Clotildo Zuniga and Eugenia "Jean" Noralez. She was born in 1960 in Barangu. She married Benito Martinez in 1986 in Orange Walk. "Dora," as she was known, was a maker of recado, a local spice made from annato.

Dion Trevor Makin died on this day in 2012 on the northern Highway in an automobile accident. Dion is the son of Andres Dion Makin and Emily Williams Ramirez. Dion was born in 1987 in Belize City. Dion was a police constable. Vicenta "Lulu" Sanchez is the grandmother of Dion.

21st July

In the Catholic calendar today is the Feast Day of St. Praxedes.

Bernadette Loredo was born in Barangu. She is the daughter of Henry Loredo and Martina Avilez. She married Candido Arzu in 1938 in Barangu. For many years during the Christmas Season, Bernadette led the children in "Pastora." She was also very involved in the singing in the church. Maria Loreta Palacio is the first cousin twice removed of Bernadette. Austin Arzu is the son of Bernadette.

On this day Apolinaria Mejia was born in 1891 in Barangu. She is the daughter of Simon Mejia and

Bernadette Arzu nee Loredo (2000)

Andrea Nicholas. Apolinaria married Pascacio Cayetano in 1912 in Barangu. Nathaniel "Shorty" Cayetano is the grandson of Apolinaria.

Prajedes Palacio was born on this day in 1900. She is the daughter of Nolberto Palacio and Nieves Juarez. Prajedes married Ernest Bernard in 1928 in Peine. She died in 1997 in Peine. Maria Loreta Palacio is the aunt of Prajedes. Clifford King is the grandson of Prajedes.

Mercedes Enriquez was born on this day in 1914 in Peine. She is the daughter of Lino Enriquez and Nazaria Zuniga. Mercedes is the sister of Bonifacia Ramirez with a different father.

22nd July

In the Catholic calendar today is the Feast Day of St. Mary Magdelene.

Frank Dean Arana died on this day in 1984 in Barangu. He is the son of Alejandro Arana and Gregoria Bermudez. He was born in 1909 in Barangu. He married Bonifacia Ramirez in 1936. Victor "Bobby" Arana is Frank's son.

Felipa Bermudez died on this day in 1970. she is the daughter of Narciso Bermudez and Dominga "Gadu" Marin. Felipa was born in 1883. Felipa is the great-great-aunt of Erlinda "Delane" Ogdalez nee Nicholas.

On this day Vicenta Castillo was born in 1878 in Barangu. She is the daughter of Rafael Castillo and Simona Garcia. She married Patricio Ariola in 1904 in Barangu.

Maria Magdalena Paulino was born on this day in 1894 in Barangu. She is the daughter of Augustin "Big Ease" Paulino and Juana Luis.

Randal James Palacio was born on this day in Belize City. He is the son of Paul Palacio and Ethel Dee Loredo. Maria Loreta Palacio is the great-great-aunt of Randal.

On this day Francisco Palacio and Escolastica Gomez were married in 1936 in Barangu. Francisco is the son of Peter Palacio and Tranquilina Zuniga. Escolastica is the daughter of Cesaria Gomez and Florentina (unknown last name).

23rd July

In the Catholic calendar today is the Feast Day of St. Apollinaris.

Christina Lopez was born on this day in Barangu. She is the daughter of **Yvonne Lopez**. Christina married **Clifford King** in 1999. **Maria Loreta Palacio** is the great-great-great-aunt of Christina.

Apolinaria Ogaldez was born on this day in 1895 in Peine. She is the daughter of **Secundino Ogaldez** and **Alberta Ciego**. Apolinaria married **Martin Bernardez** in 1916 in Peine. Her father, Secundino, taught school in Barangu. Apolinaria's daughter with Martin, **Silveria Bernardez**, married **Felix "Aska" Noralez** in 1943 in Peine.

24th July

In the Catholic calendar and the pre-1969 calendar today is the Feast Day of Sts. Christiana, Christina of Bolsena, Christina of Tyre and Christina the Astonishing.

Domingo Arzu and **Dominica Noralez** were married on this day in 1942 in Belize City. Domingo was from Labuga. Dominica is the daughter of **Venancio Noralez** and **Gumercinda Palacio**. Domingo went to Scotland during WWII and served there cutting timber.

On this day **Christina Nolberto** was born. She is the daughter of **Francisco Nolberto** and **Francisca Serapia**. She was one of the first children born in Barangu. Christina married **Natividad Zuniga**. **Kevin Zuniga** is the great-great-grandson of Christina.

Viviana Palacio was born on this day in 1880. She is the daughter of **Anastacio Palacio** and **Sotera Gutierrez**. Viviana married **Pedro John Avila** in 1898 in Barangu. She died in Peine in 1954. Viviana is the mother of **Reginald Avila** and the grandmother of **Marti Cain nee Arana**.

On this day **Crispino Martinez** was born in Peine in 1913. He is the son of Victoriano and **Isabela Zuniga**. He married **Florencia Avila** in 1996 in Peine.

Santiaga Avilez was born on this day in 1914 in Peine. She is the daughter of **Antonio Avilez** and **Juana Palacio**. She married **Maximino Lino** in 1933 in Peine. **Maria Loreta Palacio** is the first cousin once removed of Santiaga.

On this day **Cristino Cayetano** was born in 1906 in Barangu. He is the son of **Cayetano Amaya** and **Josefa Paulino**. Cristino is the grandson of **Augustin "Big Ease" Paulino**. Cayetano was used as both a first and last name.

Francisco Avilez was born this day in 1907 in Peine. He is the son of **Ambrosio "Sabigi" Avilez** and **Justa Polonio**. Francisco is the grandson of **Santiago "Gaünbü" Avilez**.

25th July

In the Catholic calendar today is the Feast Day of St. James the Greater.

Loreta Palacio died on this day in 1946. She is the daughter **Pascacio Cayetano** and **Eustaquia Satuye**. Loreta was born in 1927. **Maria Loreta Palacio** is the grandmother of Loreta.

On this day **Santiago Martinez** was born in 1893 in Barangu. He is the son of **Florentino Martinez** and **Apolonia Francisca Foster**. Santiago married **Florentina Avila** in 1945 in Peine.

Santiaga Enriquez was born on this day in 1911. She is the daughter of **Anacleto Enriquez** and **Diega Avila**. Santiaga married **John Paulino** in 1929. **John Paulino** was a school teacher in Barangu.

On this day **Dionisio M. Colon** and **Francisca "Chica" Ariola** were married in 1934 in Peine. Dionisio is the son of **John Colon** and **Leonarda Zuniga**. Francisca is the daughter of **Patricio Ariola** and **Vicenta Castillo**.

26th July

No events.

27th July

In the Catholic calendar today is the Feast Day of St. Pantaleon.

Pantaleona Mejia was born on this day in 1917 in Barangu. She is the daughter of **Simon Mejia** and **Nicolasa Palacio**. She married **Feliciano "Felix" Alvarez** in 1937 in Barangu. She died in 1980 in Barangu. **Maria Loreta Palacio** is the first cousin thrice removed of Pantaleona. **Angelina "Angie" Nicholas nee Alvarez** is the daughter of Pantaleona.

On this day **Anita Marin** was born. She is the daughter of **Clarence Marin** and **Dionisia Santino**. **Maria Loreta Palacio** is the first cousin thrice removed of Anita.

Simeona Mejia died on this day in in 1982 in Barangu. She is the daughter of **Simon Mejia** and **Petrona Severia**. Simeona was born in 1905 in Barangu. She married **Augustine Palacio** in 1923 in Peine. **Ludwig Palacio** is the grandson of Simeona.

On this day **Elvira Cris Velasquez** died in 1999 in Barangu. She is the daughter of **Solomon Velasquez** and **Cristobel Loredo**. Elvira was born in 1925 in Barangu. **Maria Loreta Palacio** is the first cousin twice removed of Elvira.

Jahleel Cadle was born on this day in Belize City. He is the son of **Dwight Cadle** and **Kareen Casimiro**. **Maria Loreta Palacio** is the great-great-great-great-aunt of Jahleel. **Alice Casimiro nee Nicholas** is the grandmother of Jahleel.

28th July
In the Catholic calendar today is the Feast Day of Sts. St. Nazarius and Celsus.

Adriano Nicholas and **Felicita Valencio** were married in 1961 in Belize City. Adriano is the son of **Pablo Nicholas** and **Aniceta Blas**. Felicita is the daughter of **Eufamio Valencio** and **Beatrice Palacio**. **Raymond Valencio** is the brother of Felicita.

Nazaria Zuniga was born on this day in 1897 in Labuga. She is the daughter of **Nicholas Zuniga** and **Mariana Rodriguez**. Nazaria married **Lino Enriquez** in 1913 in Peine. She died in 1988 in Barangu. She was an active church member. **Victor "Bobby" Arana** is the grandson of Nazaria.

On this day **Kalin Palacio** was born in Belize City. He is the son of **Timothy Palacio** and **Gaynor Ferguson**. **Maria Loreta Palacio** is the great-great-great-aunt of Kalin.

Rosanna Martinez Rogers was born on this day in New Orleans, Louisiana. She is the daughter of **Leopoldo Rogers** and **Martha Castillo**. **Melvinia "Grandma Mi" Martinez** is the grandmother of Rosanna.

Ifasina Efunyemi was born on this day in Belize City. She is the daughter of **Luke Mariano** and **Jacinta Palacio**. Ifasina is also known as "**Anthea Benita Mariano**." **Maria Loreta Palacio** is the first cousin thrice removed.

Cecilia Flores died on this day in 2005 in Belize City. She is the daughter of **John Sanchez** and **Isidora Bermudez**. Cecilia was born in 1911 in Barangu. She is the sister of **Procopio Flores** and **Mary Casimiro nee Flores**.

29th July
Paulina Lopez was born on this day in 1912 in Seine Bight. She is the daughter of **Santiago Lopez** and **Felicita Bermudez**. She married **Victor Leonard Nicholas**. Paulina died in 1991 in Bridgeport,

Connecticut. **Martin "Game and Gone" or "Tin-Tin" Victor Nicholas** is the son of Paulina.

On this day **Martin Avilez** was born in 1896 in Peine. He is the son of **Ambrosio "Sabigi" Avilez** and **Justa Polonio**. Martin is the grandson of **Santiago "Gaünbü" Avilez**.

Eugenio Cayetano died on this day in 1983 in Peine. He died in a boating accident. He is the son of **Luis Cayetano** and **Paulina Reyes**. Eugenio was born in 1915 in Peine. **Alfonsa Zuniga** and Eugenio were married in Barangu in 1938. Eugenio married a second time to **Manuela Marin** in 1941 in Barangu.

30th July
In the Catholic calendar today is the Feast Day of St. St. Rufinus of Assisi.

Francis Blanco died on this day in 1993 in Belize City. He was born in 1915 in Dangriga. He was known as "Badi." He lived for a period of time with **Elvira Cris Velasquez**.

On this day **Rufina Maxima Avila** was born in 1908 in Barangu. She is the daughter of **Pedro John Avila** and **Viviana Palacio**. **Maria Loreta Palacio** is the first cousin once removed of Rufina.

Adela Cayetano was born on this day in 1923 in Barangu. She is the daughter of **Gregorio Cayetano** and **Teofila Flores**. **Maria Loreta Palacio** is the grandmother of Adela.

31st July
In the Catholic Calendar today is the Feast Day of St Ignatius of Loyola.

Ignacio Nicholas was born on this day in 1899 in Barangu. He is the son of **Leoncio Nicholas** and **Alberta Nolberto**. He married **Perfecta Avilez** in 1925 in Barangu. **Maxie Nicholas** is the son of Ignacio.

On this day **Ignacio Mejia** was born in 1912 in Barangu. He is the son of **Simon Mejia** and **Nicolasa Palacio**. **Maria Loreta Palacio** is the first cousin once removed of Ignacio.

Lynette Valerie Valerio was born on this day in Peine. She is the daughter of **Peter Valerio** and **Hermenehilda "Maria" Lopez**. **Clinton Rodriguez** married Lynette in 1998 in Ladyville. **Maria Loreta Palacio** is the great-great-great-aunt of Lynette.

AUGUST

1st August

Henry Santino and Virginia Nunez were married on this day in 1935 in Peine. Henry is the son of Philip Santino and Nicasia Martinez. Virginia is the daughter of Francisco Nunez and Martina (Obispa) Martinez. Henry is the uncle of Jacinta Trigueno nee Santino.

Recillia Martinez was born on this day. She is the daughter of Gloria Martinez. Maria Loreta Palacio is the first cousin thrice removed of Recillia. Recillia is the granddaughter of Simon Martinez and Ambrosine Mejia.

2nd August

In the pre-1969 Catholic calendar today is the Feast Day of St. Alphonsus Liguori.

Luis Palacio and Pietra Avilez were married on this day in 1969. Luis is the son of Augustine Palacio and Simeona Mejia. Pietra is the daughter of Bernard Avilez.

Alfonso Noralez was born on this day in 1915 in Barangu. He is the son of Felix "Aska" Noralez and Juana Nolberto. Alfonso is the uncle of Teresa "Tandu" Noralez.

Wasany Wellington Ramos was born on this day. He is the son of Wellington Ramos and Rose Maria Arana. Wasany is the grandson of Francisco Bonifacio "Frank" Arana. Frank was a farm demonstrator in Barangu.

On this day Henry Loredo was born in Dangriga in 1897. He is the son of Eulalio Loredo and Gregoria Palacio. He married Martina Avilez in 1920 in Barangu. After Martina's death he married Ursula Polonio. He died in 1982 in Barangu. Henry was a school teacher in the 1920's in Barangu. Maria Loreta Palacio is first cousin once removed of Henry.

Romana Velasquez was born on this day in 1917 in Dangriga. She is the daughter of Domingo Velasquez. She married Frank G. Santino in 1935 in Barangu.

3rd August

Carlson John Tuttle and Valerie Delcy Valencio were married on this day in 1989 in Barangu. Carlson is the son of Farice Tuttle and Marion Elizabeth Lent. Delcy is the daughter of Raymond Valencio and Lucille "Chilagu" Zuniga.

Dominga Marin was born on this day in 1863 in Barangu. She is the daughter of Eulogio Marin and Luisa Cayetano. Dominga is one of the first children born in Barangu. She is known as "Gadu" in the village. She married Narciso Bermudez in 1880 in Barangu. Cecilia "Luncy" Arzu nee Alvarez is the great-great-granddaughter of Dominga. Dominga also had children with Juan Avilez.

On this day Felipa Bermudez was born in 1883. She is the daughter of Narciso Bermudez and Dominga "Gadu" Marin. She died in 1970. Felipa is the great-great-aunt of Erlinda "Delane" Ogaldez nee Nicholas.

Romana Nolberto was born on this day in 1888 in Peine. She is the daughter of Macario Nolberto and Josefa Alvarez.

On this day Daniel Ariola died in 1900 in Barangu. He is the son of Rufino Ariola and Luisa Martinez. He married Alberta Nicholas in 1898 in Barangu. Braulio Ariola is the son of Daniel.

4th August

In the pre-1969 Catholic calendar today is the Feast Day of St. Dominic.

Marcelino H. Johnson and Beatrice Palacio were married on this day in 1941 in Belize City. Marcelino is from Dangriga. Beatrice is the daughter of Saturnino Palacio and Felicita Reyes. Raymond Valencio is the son of Beatrice.

On this day Reginald Avila was born in 1921 in Barangu. He is the son of Pedro John Avila and Viviana Palacio. Reginald married Georgiana Palacio in 1944 in Peine. He died in 1995 in Peine. Maria Loreta Palacio is the first cousin once removed of Reginald. Lynn Zuniga nee Arnold is the granddaughter of Reginald.

Dominica Noralez was born on this day in 1914 in Peine. She is the daughter of Venancio Noralez and Gumercinda Palacio. Dominica married Domingo Arzu in 1942 in Belize City. She died in a fire in 1983 in Barangu. Maria Loreta Palacio is the first cousin twice removed of Dominica.

On this day Cynthia Nicholas was born. She is the daughter of Frederick Nicholas and Joyce Lopez. Maria Loreta Palacio is the first cousin four times removed of Cynthia. Erlinda "Delane" Ogaldez nee Nicholas is the sister of Cynthia.

Bonifacio Zuniga died on this day in 1997 in Labuga. He is the son of Canuto Zuniga and Loriana Ramirez. Bonifacio was a basket maker. Abraham Zuniga is the brother of Bonifacio. **Maria Loreta Palacio** is the great-aunt of Bonifacio.

Jeremiah Cadle was born on this day in Dakar, Senegal. He is the son of **Dwight Cadle** and **Kareen Casimiro**. **Maria Loreta Palacio** is the great-great-aunt of Jeremiah. **Alice Casimiro nee Nicholas** is the grandmother of Jeremiah. Here is an example of a Baranguna being born in an African country. There are Baranguna in Canada, the United States, Mexico, Japan, Scotland, England and many other countries.

5th August

Isaac Velasquez was born on this day in 1928 in Barangu. He is the son of **Solomon Velasquez** and **Cristobel Loredo**. **Maria Loreta Palacio** is the first cousin twice removed of Isaac. **Elvira Cris Velasquez** is the sister of Isaac.

Elfreda Paulino was born on this day in Peine. She is the daughter of **Guadalupe Paulino** and **Rosenda Enriquez**. Elfreda married **James Goree** and then married **Stephen Sideroff**. Elfreda heads up the Garifuna Film Festival.

On this day a set of twins, **Liraine Miranda** and **Miraine Miranda** were born in Belmopan. They are the daughters of **Thomas Miranda** and **Rhoda Alvarez**.

6th August

Oswald Lopez was born on this day. He is the son of **Cleofa Avilez**. Oswald is the brother of **Andy Palacio**.

On this day **Elvira Cris Velasquez** was born in 1925 in Barangu. She is the daughter of **Solomon Velasquez** and **Cristobel Loredo**. She married **Francis "Badi" Blanco**. Elvira died in 1999 in Barangu.

Benjamin Nicholas was born on this day in 1930. He is the son of **Ignacio Nicholas** and **Perfecta Avilez**. Benjamin is a noted painter who lived for years in Dangriga but was from Barangu. He died in 2012 in Dangriga. **Victor Joseph "Master Vic" Nicholas** is the brother of Benjamin.

On this day **Juana Palacio** died in 1937. She is the daughter of **Anastacio Palacio** and **Magdalena Cesaria**. Juana was born in 1883. She married **Antonio Avilez** in 1904 in Peine. Antonio is the grandson of **Santiago "Gaünbü" Avilez**. **Maria Loreta Palacio** is the first cousin of Juana.

7th August

Althea Marie Valerio was born on this day in Monkey River Town. She is the daughter of **Peter Valerio** and **Hermenenehilda "Maria" Lopez**. **Maria Loreta Palacio** is the great-great-great-aunt of Althea.

Paulina Lopez died on this day in 1991 in Bridgeport, Connecticut. She is the daughter of **Santiago Lopez** and **Felicita Bermudez**. Paulina is from Seine Bight. She married **Victor Leonard Nicholas**. **Martin "Game and Gone" "Tin-Tin" Nicholas** is the son of Paulina.

On this day **Telesflora Simeona Mejia** died in 1980 in Peine. She is the daughter of **Abraham Bernard Mejia** and **Victoriana Santino**. Telesflora "Stella" was born in 1919 in Barangu. She married **John Jacob Zuniga** in 1939 in Barangu.

8th August

Santiago Martinez and **Florentina Avila** were married on this day in 1945 in Peine. Santiago is the son of **Florentino Martinez** and **Apolonia Francisca Foster**. Florentina is the daughter of **Alcardio Avila** and **Justa Gonzalez**.

On this day **Feliciano Jimenez** and **Leona Martinez** were married in 1937 in Peine. **Leona Martinez** is the daughter of **Ireneo Martinez** and **Bernardina Santino**. Leona is the aunt of **Victoriana "Vicky" Nolberto nee Martinez**.

Justin Nicholas was born on this day in 1938. He is the son of **Tiburcio Nicholas** and **Candida Palacio**. Justin is the brother of **Frederick Nicholas**.

On this day **Kendra Cayetano** was born in Peine. She is the daughter of **Wallace Cayetano** and **Alfonsa Arana**.

Leonides Sanchez was born on this day. He is the son of **Dorotea Nicholas**. He is known as "Leo." Leo is the great-great-grandson of **Joseph Alexander Nicholas** and **Maria Eugenia Delavez** are both founders of Barangu.

On this day **Stephen Paulino** died in 1996 in Peine. He is the son of **Eusebio Paulino** and **Maria Nolberto**. Stephen was born in 1906 in Barangu. Stephen married **Eulogia Nicholas** in 1942 in Peine. **Elfreda Sideroff nee Paulino** is the granddaughter of Stephen.

Augustine Palacio died on this day in 1980 in Barangu. He is the son of **Nolberto Palacio** and **Ignacia "Glessima" Arana**. He was born in 1899 in Barangu. He married **Simeona Mejia** in 1923 in Peine. **Maria Loreta Palacio** is the aunt of Augustine.

9th August

Augustine Palacio and **Simeona Mejia** were married on this day in 1923 in Peine. Augustine is the son of **Nolberto Palacio** and **Ignacia "Glessima" Arana**. Simeona is the daughter of **Simon Mejia** and **Petrona Severia**. Surusia **Ludwig Palacio** is the grandson of Augustine and Simeona.

Augustine Palacio and Simeona Mejia

Hanjai Gregory Arzu was born on this day. He is the son of **Harold "Greg" Arzu** and **Sheridan Petillo**. **Maria Loreta Palacio** is Hanjai's great-great-great-aunt, first cousin four times removed, and great-great-grandmother.

On this day **Justa Lopez** was born in Seine Bight in 1910. She is the daughter of **Santiago Lopez** and **Felicita Bermudez**. Justa is the sister of **Toribio Joseph Lopez**.

Kahle Austin Arzu was born. He is the son of **Austin Arzu** and **Suzette Staine**. Kahle is the grandson of **Bernadette Arzu nee Loredo** and **Candido Arzu**. **Maria Loreta Palacio** is the great-great-great-aunt, and the first cousin four times removed of Kahle.

Dominga Martila Arzu died on this day in 1904 in Barangu. She married **Anacleto Cayetano**. Dominga was one of the early settlers of Barangu. Dominga is the great-great-grandmother of **Sebastian Cayetano**.

Joseph Orlando Palacio and **Myrtle Cacho** were married on this day in 1969. Joseph is the son of **Joseph Pollard Palacio** and **Hilaria Mejia**. **Arreini Paula Palacio** is the daughter of Joseph and Myrtle.

Luis Marfield and **Marthy "Marti" Arana** were married on this day in 1973. **Marthy** is the daughter of **Cipriano Arana** and **Leonora Avila**.

On this day **Martina Cornelia Palacio** was born in Peine. She is the daughter of **Paul Palacio** and **Ethel Dee Loredo**. Martina married **David Alvarez** in 1983 in Peine. **Maria Loreta Palacio** is the great-great-aunt and the first cousin thrice removed of Martina. Martina is a primary school teacher and is member of the St. Peter Claver Parish Council.

10th August

Gloria Martinez was born on this day in 1942. She is the daughter of **Simon Martinez** and **Ambrosine Mejia**. **Maria Loreta Palacio** is the first cousin twice removed of Gloria.

On this day **Kareem Davon Underwood** was born in Belize City. She is the daughter of **Godfrey Underwood** and **Sharon Loredo**. **Maria Loreta Palacio** is the first cousin four times removed and the first cousin five times removed of Kareem.

11th August

In the Catholic calendar today is the Feast Day of St. Tiburtius.

Viviano Gregorio and **Bernardina Santino** were married on this day. Viviano is the son of **John Gregorio** and **Desideria** Zuniga. Bernardina is the daughter of **Philip Santino** and **Justina Cayetano**. Viviano and Bernardina are the parents of **Petrona "Petu" Gregorio**.

Tiburcio Nicholas was born on this day in 1898 in Barangu. He is the son of **Sotero Nicholas** and **Paula Nunez**. Tiburcio married **Candida Palacio**. **Frederick Nicholas** is the son of Tiburcio.

On this day (there is a question of whether it is today or the 12 August) **Tomasine Loredo** died in 1937 in Barangu. She is the daughter of **Eulalio Loredo** and **Gregoria Palacio**. Tomasine was born in 1908 in Barangu. She married **John Jacob Zuniga** in 1927 in Barangu. **Maria Loreta Palacio** is the first cousin once removed of Tomasine. **Felicita "Cita" Zuniga** is the daughter of Tomasine.

12th August

Darnell Higinio was born. He is the son of **Mike Higinio** and **Anita Marin**. **Maria Loreta Palacio** is the first cousin four times of Higinio. **Angela Palacio** is the first cousin once removed of Darnell with **Aparicio Marin** as the common ancestor and **Angela Palacio** is also the fourth cousin once removed of Darnell with **Juan Pedro Cayetano** as the common ancestor.

13th August

In the Catholic calendar today is the Feast Day of St. Hippolytus.

Lino Enriquez and Nazaria Zuniga were married on this day in 1913 in Peine. Lino is the son of Nolberto Enriquez and Eulalia Zuniga. Nazaria is the daughter of Nicholas Zuniga and Mariana Diego. Nazaria is from Labuga. Nazaria led the "Posada" pageant in Barangu at Christmas time for many years.

Evaristo Melendrez and Lucila "Shuna" Arana were married on this day in 1941. Lucila is the daughter of Concepcion Arana and Simeona Flores. Dativa Elizabeth Martinez nee Melendrez is the daughter of Evaristo and Lucila.

On this day Augustin Paulino and Martina Arzu were married in 1902 in Barangu. Augustin is the son of Diego Paulino and Dominga Cayetano. Martina is the daughter of Augustin Arzu and Cayetana Gonzalez. This was the second marriage for both Augustin and Martina. Augustin first married Juana Luis in 1883. Martina first married Anacleto Garcia in 1890. Augustin was known as "Big Ease."

Ibime Cayetano was born on this day in Dangriga. He is the son of E. Roy Cayetano and Phyllis Miranda. Maria Loreta Palacio is the first cousin four times removed of Ibime.

On this day Albertina Bermudez was born on this day. She is the daughter of Nolasca Avila. Maria Loreta Palacio is the first cousin twice removed of Albertina. Albertina is the granddaughter of Pedro John Avila and Viviana Palacio.

Frances Ramos was born on this day. She is the daughter of Eudora Zuniga. Frances is the granddaughter of Clotildo Zuniga and Eugenia "Jean" Noralez.

On this day Sharon Zuniga was born in Belize City. She is the daughter of John Ray Zuniga and Trinidad Moriera. Sharon is the great-greatgranddaughter of Claro Zuniga.

Afieni Tirhysi Tanigi Cayetano was born on this day in the Bronx. She is the daughter of E. Roy Cayetano. Maria Loreta Palacio is the first cousin five times removed of Afieni.

Hipolito Martinez (*right*) was born on this day in 1920 in Peine. He is the son of Prudencio "Brown" Martinez and Gabina Zuniga. Hipolito married Regina Lorenzo in 1939 in Barangu. Hipolito died in 2003 in Barangu. Martin Martinez is the son of Hipolito.

On this day Arcilia Nicholas was born. She is the daughter of Frederick Nicholas and Joyce Lopez. Maria Loreta Palacio is the first cousin four times removed.

Phyllis Miranda was born on this day in Dangriga. She married Eldred Roy Cayetano in 1971 in Dangriga. Phyllis is an educator. Isani Cayetano is the son of Phyllis.

14th August

Emelia Castillo was born on this day in Dangriga. She is the daughter of Peter "Cadi" Castillo and Anastacia Christina Ramirez. Maria Loreta Palacio is the first cousin four times removed of Emelia.

15th August

On this day in 1973 in Belize City Callistus Cayetano was ordained a Catholic priest. He the son of Francis Benedict Cayetano and Florencia Lucas.

Joseph Pollard Palacio died on this day in 1975 in Peine. He is the son of Nolberto Palacio and Ignacia Arana. He was born in 1902 in Barangu. He married Hilaria Mejia in 1924 in Barangu. After Hilaria died Joseph married Felipa Carlota Marin. Maria Loreta Palacio is the aunt of Joseph. Rita Enriquez nee Avila is the granddaughter of Joseph.

Henrietta Enriquez died on this day in 2001 in Peine. She was born in 1931 in Peine. Martin Petillo is the son of Henrietta.

On this day Jennifer Shireen Arzu was born. She is the daughter of Ellis Henry Arzu and Elma Martinez. Maria Loreta Palacio is the great-great-great-aunt of Jennifer and she is also the first cousin four times removed of Maria Loreta Palacio.

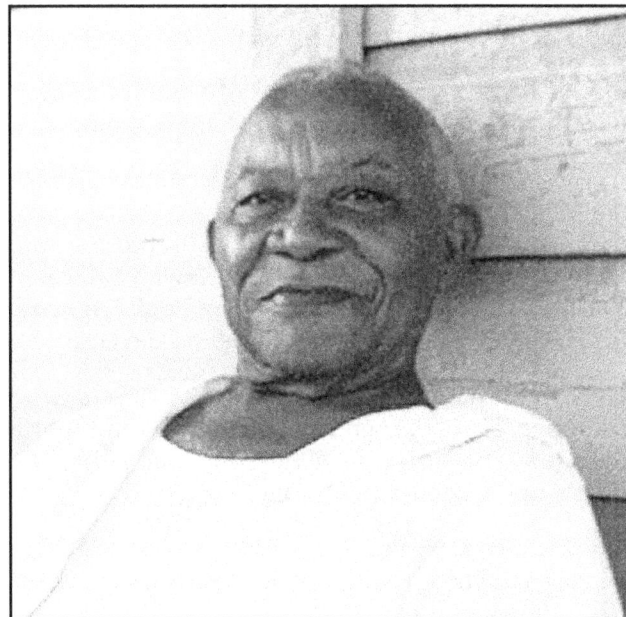

Hipolito Martinez

16th August

Hilaria Palacio nee Mejia died on this day in 1946 in Peine. She is the daughter of **Simon Mejia** and **Andrea Nicholas**. Hilaria was born in 1906 in Barangu. She married **Joseph Pollard Palacio** in 1924 in Barangu.

On this day **Peter Valerio** died in 1993 in Belize City. He is the son of **Santiago Valerio** and **Santiaga** (last name unknown). Peter was born in 1949 in Seine Bight. **Ian Dane Valerio** is the son of Peter.

Clifford King was born on this day in Peine. He is the son of **Julian King** and **Maxie Bernard**. Clifford married **Christine Lopez** in 1999. **Maria Loreta Palacio** is the great-great-aunt of Clifford. **Theodore Palacio** is the first cousin once removed of Clifford.

17th August

In the Catholic calendar today is the Feast Day of St. St. Hyacinth.

Bernard Cain and **Marthy "Marti" Arana** were married on this day in 1995 in Belize City. Bernard is from Belize City and Marthy is the daughter of **Cipriano Arana** and **Leonora Avila**.

Marcelo Cayetano died on this day in 1907 in Barangu. He is the son of **Anacleto Cayetano** and **Dominga Martila Arzu**. Marcelo married **Maria Loreta Palacio** in 1883 in Barangu. **Juan Pedro Cayetano** is the grandfather of Marcelo. **Father Callistus Cayetano** is the great-grandson of Marcelo.

Leandra Blanco was born on this day. She is the daughter of **Cynthia Lavinia Lynn Martinez**. She is the great-granddaughter of **Bernadette Arzu nee Loredo** and **Candido Arzu**. **Maria Loreta Palacio** is the great-great-great-great-aunt of **Leandra Blanco**. Leandra is also the first cousin five times removed of **Maria Loreta Palacio**.

On this day **Jacinta Santino** (*right*) was born in Barangu. She is the daughter of **Eusebio Santino** and **Vicenta Blas**. Jacinta married **Froylan Palacio** in 1965 After his death Jacinta married **Fred Trigueno**. Jacinta is the granddaughter of **Justina Cayetano**.

Patrick Mariano (*right*) was born on this day in Dangriga. He is the son of **Martin Reyes** and **Maria Mariano**. Patrick is an "Ebu" and has led many events in the dabuyaba here in Barangu.

On this day **Haneefa Kerian Valencio** was born n Belize City. She is the daughter of **Rudolph "Rudie" Paul Valencio** and **Caroline Tasher**. **Maria Loreta Palacio** is the first cousin four times removed.

18th August

James Martinez and **Teofila Palacio** were married on this day in 1942. James is from Dangriga and is the son of **Rafael Martinez** and **Margarita Nunez**. Teofila is the daughter of **Luis Palacio** and **Felipa Garcia**.

On this day **John Baptist Palacio** was born in 1868 in Barangu. He is the son of **Anastacio Palacio** and **Sotera Gutierrez**. **Maria Loreta Palacio** is the first cousin of John.

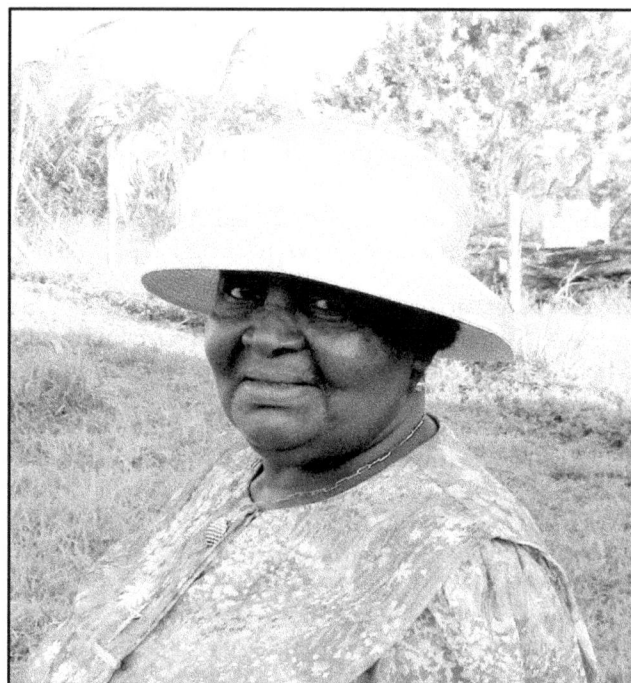
Jacinta Trigueno nee Santino (2006)

Patrick Mariano (2010)

Rufino Ariola died on this day in 1924. He is the son of **Ariola Gonzalez**. Rufino was also known as **Rufino Gonzalez**. He married **Ascenciona Paulino** in 1888 in Peine. Rufino is said to have come from Trujillo. **Francisco "Chico" Ariola** is the great-grandson of Rufino.

Shaynah Ariola died on this day in 2007 in Peine. She is the daughter of **Francisco "Chico" Ariola** and **Naomi Colon**. Shaynah was born in 1984 in Barangu. **Trevor Ariola** is the sister of Shaynah. **Maria Loreta Palacio** is the great-great-aunt of Shaynah.

On this day **Pablo Baltazar** died in 1986 in Los Angeles, California. He is the son of **Augustin "Ding" Baltazar** and **Faustina Mariano**. Pablo was born in 1913 in Labuga. He married **Adriana Lauriano** in 1945 in Dangriga. Pablo is the father of **Valentina Marin nee Baltazar**.

19th August

In the Catholic calendar today is the Feast Day of St. Louis of Toulouse.

Dionisio Nolberto and **Nicolasa Martinez** were married on this day in 1924 in Peine. Dionisio is the son of **Pio Nolberto** and **Casimira Nicholas**. Nicolasa is the daughter of **Liborio Martinez** and **Eluteria Cayetano**. Dionisio had a farm up the Temash River on the right ascension called "Quiripi." Dionisio was elected second alcalde for Barangu in 1927. He was elected first alcalde for Barangu in 1933 and re-elected to the same post in 1934. **Alvin Loredo** is the grandson of Dionisio and Nicolasa.

Bonifacio Ramirez and **Evangelista Nunez** were married on this day in 1925. Bonifacio is the son of **Carmen Ramirez** and **Eustaquia Palacio**. Evangelista is the daughter of **Bonifacio Nunez** and **Marciana Valencio**. Bonifacio was elected second alcalde for Barangu in 1926. In 1933 and 1934 again he was elected second alcalde for Barangu. **Justina Nicholas nee Ramirez** is the daughter of Bonifacio and Evangelista.

On this day **Elena Paulino** was born in 1889 in Barangu. She is the daughter of **Augustin "Big Ease" Paulino** and **Juana Luis**.

Luis Palacio was born on this day in 1945. He is the son of **Augustine Palacio** and **Simeona Mejia**. Luis was a school teacher. He married **Pietra Avilez**. He died in 1974. **Maria Loreta Palacio** is the great-aunt of Luis.

On this day **Amelita Cloudina Daniels** was born in 1927. She is the daughter of **Salvatore Basil "S.B." Daniels** and **Victoria Ogaldez**. Amelita is the daughter of a long time principal teacher in Barangu.

20th August

Today in the Catholic calendar is the Feast Day of both St. Bernard of Clairaux and St. Bernard of Valdeiglesius.

Delia Makin was born on this day. She is the daughter of **Perfecto Makin** and **Vicenta "Lulu" Sanchez**. **Maria Loreta Palacio** is the great-great-aunt of Delia.

On this day **Derrick Zuniga** and **Maria Casimiro** were married in 1988 in Peine. Derrick is the son of **Henry Peter Zuniga** and **Sotera Moriera**. Maria is the daughter of **Francis Casimiro** and **Evelyn Enriquez**. Derrick and Maria are fourth cousins once removed.

Bernard Cayetano was born on this day in Barangu. He is the son of **Francis Benedict Cayetano** and **Florencia Lucas**. **Maria Loreta Palacio** is the great-grandmother of Bernard.

21st August

Francisco Garcia was born on this day in 1915 in Barangu. He is the son of **Margarito Garcia** and **Aurelia Baltazar**. Francisco is the grandson of **Apolinario Garcia** and **Marcelina Augustina Martinez** both early settlers of Barangu.

22nd August

In the Catholic calendar today is the Feast Day of St. Antoninus.

Ezechiel Garcia was born on this day in 1900 in Barangu. He is the son of **Esmith Garcia** and **Cornelia Martinez**.

On this day **Delita Almira Cayetano** was born. She is the daughter of **Eugenio Cayetano** and **Manuela Marin**. **Maria Loreta Palacio** is the first cousin thrice removed of Delita. Delita is the sister of **Judith Cayetano**.

Rudolph Arana was born on this day in 1975 in Dangriga. He is the son of **Rudy Concepcion Arana** and **Mildred Hernandez**. Rudolph died three months later in November of 1975. Surusia **Peitra Arana** is the sister of Rudolph.

On this day **Kayla Georgene Arana** was born in Dangriga. She is the daughter of Rudy **Concepcion Arana** and **Mildred Hernandez**. Kayla married Keith Bassett in 2006. Surusia **Peitra Arana** is the sister of Kayla.

Anthony Phillip Martinez was born on this day. He is the son of **Francis Benedict Martinez** and **Victoria Barcelona**.

23rd August

In the Catholic calendar today is the Feast Day of St. Philip Benizi.

O'Dillan Petillo and **Antonia King** were married on this day in 1944 in Peine. O'Dillan is the son of **Bonifacio Petillo** and **Carmen Enriquez**. **Leonard "Mr. Pete" Petillo** is the brother of O'Dillan.

On this day **Felipe Lambey** was born in 1897. He is the son of **John Lambey** and **Gregoria Nolberto**. Felipe is the first cousin once removed of **Paula Nolberto** with **Francisco Nolberto** as the common ancestor.

Benito Palacio was born on this day in 1929 in Barangu. He is the son of **Jacob Palacio** and **Tomasa Polonio**. **Maria Loreta Palacio** is the first cousin twice removed of Benito. **Ruben Palacio** is the uncle of **Benito Palacio**.

On this day **Luis Jarvis Casimiro** is born in Barangu. He is the son **Gonzalez Casimiro** and **Mary Flores**. Luis is the brother of **Adriana "Tun" Casimiro**.

Luis Franco Martinez was born on this day in 1906 in Peine. He is the son of **Francisco Martinez** and **Estefania Avila**. **Rita Enriquez nee Avila** is the first cousin once removed of Luis.

On this day **Luis Nicholas** was born in Barangu in 1915. He is the son of **Pablo Nicholas** and **Aniceta Blas**. **Frederick Nicholas** is the second cousin of Luis.

Luis Alvarez was born on this day in Peine. He is the son of **Simon Aloysius Alvarez** and **Phyllis Palacio**. Luis is his own fourth cousin because his parents are third cousins. **Maria Loreta Palacio** is the great-great-aunt of Luis. Maria is also the first cousin once removed of Luis and lastly Maria is the great-great-grandmother of Luis.

24th August

In the Catholic calendar today is the Feast Day of St. Bartholomew the Apostle.

Secundino Avilez and **Bonifacia Ramirez** were married on this day in 1922 in Peine. Secundino is the son of **Ambrosio "Sabigi" Avilez** and **Justa Polonio**. Bonifacia is the daughter of **Peter Ramirez** and Juanna Gonzalez.

Bartolo Polonio was born on this day in Peine. He is the son of **Cecilio "Dick" Polonio** and **Camila Contreras**. In his working career Bartolo was a school teacher and a member of the police force. He is also a lay Catholic minister.

Bartolo Martinez was born on this day in 1909 in Peine. He is the son of **Florentino Martinez** and **Apolonia Francisca Foster**.

Luis Alvarez and Maria Loreta Palacio I		
Teodoro Palacio	common ancestor	Teodoro Palacio
Catarino T. Palacio	siblings	Maria Loreta Palacio
Alejandro Palacio	aunt	Maria Loreta Palacio
Phyllis Palacio	grand-aunt	Maria Loreta Palacio
Luis Alvarez	great-grand-aunt	Maria Loreta Palacio
Luis Alvarez and Maria Loreta Palacio II		
Francisco Palacio	common ancestor	Francisco Palacio
Teodoro Palacio	siblings	Anastacio Palacio
Nicholasa Palacio	first cousins	Maria Loreta Palacio
Pantaleona Mejia	first cousins, once removed	Maria Loreta Palacio
Simon Aloysius Alvarez	first cousins, twice removed	Maria Loreta Palacio
Luis Alvarez	first cousins thrice removed	Maria Loreta Palacio
Luis Alvarez and Maria Loreta Palacio III		
		Maria Loreta Palacio
mother		Pascacio Cayetano
grandmother		Sarah Cayetano
great-grand-mother		Phyllis Palacio
great-great-grandmother		Luis Alvarez

25th August

In the Catholic calendar today is the Feast Day of St. Luis IX.

Jesbert Ramirez was born on this day in Peine. He is the son of **Bonifacio Ramirez** and **Irene Nunez**. Jesbert is the grandson of **Eduviges "Auntie Bea" Ramirez**. **Maria Loreta Palacio** is the great-great-great-aunt of Jesbert.

26th August

In the Catholic calendar today is the Feast Day of St. St. Victor.

Victor Arana was born on this day in 1938 in Barangu. He is the son of **Frank Dean Arana** and **Bonifacia Ramirez**. Victor was known as "Bobby" in the village. Bobby married **Pia Magdelano** in 1964 in Barangu.

Victor Garcia died on this day in 1955. He is the son of **Esmith Garcia** and **Blacina Apolonio**. Victor was born in Peine in 1893. Victor immigrated to Wadimalu in the 1920's to work for United Fruit Company. He married **Estanislada Rodriguez** in 1935 in Peine.

Seferino Polonio was born on this day in 1918 in Barangu. He is the son of **Pantaleon Odway Polonio** and **Petrona Paulino**. Seferino is the first cousin of **Bartolo Polonio**.

On this day **Seferino Nicholas** was born in Barangu in 1920. He is the son of **Pablo Nicholas** and **Aniceta Blas**. Seferino is the second cousin once removed of **Erlinda "Delane" Ogaldez nee Nicholas**.

Ambrosio Contreras and **Petrona Leoncio** were married on this day in 1962 in Dangriga. Ambrosio is son of **Andres Contreras** and **Secundina Colindres**. Ambrosio is the uncle of **Bartolo Polonio** and **Pia Arana nee Magdelano**.

27th August

In the pre-1969 Catholic calendar today is the Feast Day of St. Joseph Calasanctius.

Allen Palacio was born on this day in Belize City. He is the son of **Theodore Palacio** and **Briget Marin**. **Maria Loreta Palacio** is the great-great-aunt of Allen and also the first cousin thrice removed of Allen.

Josefa Paulino was born on this day in 1868 in Barangu. She is the daughter of **Diego Paulino** and **Maria Victoria Gamboa**. Josefa's parents were early settlers of Barangu. Josefa is the sister of **Augustin "Big Ease" Paulino** with a different mother. Augustin later had a daughter whose name was also **Josefa Paulino**.

28th August

In the Catholic calendar today is the Feast Day of St. Augustine of Hippo.

Augustine Palacio was born on this day in 1899 in Barangu. He is the son of **Nolberto Palacio** and **Ignacia Arana**. Augustine was known in the village as "Baba Titi." He married **Simeona Mejia** in 1923 in Peine. Augustine died in 1980 in Barangu. **Maria Loreta Palacio** is the aunt of Augustine. **Surusia Ludwig Palacio** is the grandson of Augustine.

On this day **George Hill** was born in 1945. He is the son of **Isabela Mejia**. George died in 1997 in Dangriga. **Leslie Carlton Colon** is the son of George.

Jason Joseph was born on this day in Barangu. He is the son of **Ambrosio Joseph** and **Petrona Palacio**. **Maria Loreta Palacio** is the great-great-aunt of Jason.

On this day **Victoria Fabiana Daniels** was born in 1928. She is the daughter of **Salvatore Basil "S.B." Daniels** and **Victoria Ogaldez**. Fabiana's father was a long time principal teacher at St. Joseph RC Primary School in Barangu.

Peter Casimiro died on this day in 1958 in Barangu. He is the son of **Pablo Casimiro** and **Bernadina Nolberto**. Peter was born in 1916 in Barangu. **Petrona Ariola** married Peter. **Paul Hudson Casimiro** is the son of Peter.

On this day **John Jacob Zuniga** and **Telesfora "Stella" Simeona Mejia** were married in 1939 in Barangu. John is the son of **Ascencion Zuniga** and **Eluteria Cayetano**. Telesflora is the daughter of **Abraham Bernard Mejia** and **Victoriana Santino**. This was John's second marriage. **Delvarene Zuniga** is the daughter of John and Stella.

Augustina Lucas was born on this day in 1918 in Peine. She is the daughter of **John Nipalmson Lucas** and **Benita Nunez**. Augustina was a seamstress and played the banjo. She raised **Fatima Cayetano**.

29th August

No events

30th August

In the pre-1969 Catholic calendar today is the Feast Day of St. Rose of Lima.

Alberta Felipa Labriel and **Morris Castro** were married on this day in 1947 in Peine. Alberta is the granddaughter of **Ambrosio "Sabigi" Avilez**. Alberta is the great-granddaughter of **Santiago "Gaünbü" Avilez**, the founder of Barangu.

Rosita Trigueno was born on this day in Puerto Barrios, Wadimalu. She is the daughter of **Isidro Trigueno** and **Paula Martinez**. "Mammie" is the nickname of Rosita. Rosita is the niece of **Melvinia "Grandma Mi" Martinez**.

On this day **Ligoria Rose Avila** was born. She is the daughter of **Peter Anthony Avila** and **Sotera Nicholas**. **Ligoria Rose Avila** entered the Religious order of the Oblate Sisters of Providence in Baltimore, Maryland in 1959. Ligoria is the sister of **Albertha Magna Gibbs nee Avila**.

On this day **Rose Joseph** was born in Peine. She is the daughter of **Ambrosio Joseph** and **Petrona Palacio**.

Rose lives in Caye Caulker. **Maria Loreta Palacio** is the great-great-aunt of Rose.

31 August

In the pre-1969 Catholic calendar today is the Feast Day of St. Raymond Nonnatus.

Gregoria Paulino died on this day in 1991. She is the daughter of **Eugenio Paulino** and **Nicolasa Zuniga**. Gregoria was known as "Gogo." She was born in 1916 in Barangu. Gregoria married **Presentacion Nunez** in 1938. Gregoria is the mother of **Rudy Concepcion Arana**.

On this day **Ramona Polonio** was born in Barangu in 1914. She is the daughter of **Apolonio Polonio** and **Damiana Garcia**. Ramona is the sister of **Henry Loredo**'s second wife, **Ursula Polonio**.

More Life Events in July and August

_____

_____

_____

_____

_____

_____

_____

_____

_____

_____

_____

_____

_____

_____

_____

_____

_____

SEPTEMBER

1st September

In the Catholic calendar today is the Feast Day of St. Giles the Abbot.

Dwight Cadle and **Kareen Casimiro** were married on this day in 2000 in Roaring Creek. Kareen is the daughter of **Dionisio Casimiro** and **Alice Nicholas**.

Virgen M. Martinez and **Felix Gonzalez** were married on this day in 1920 in Peine. Virgen is the daughter of **Bernardo Martinez** and **Felipa Bermudez**. **Sebastian Gonzalez** is the son of Virgen and Felix. **Lucille Valencio nee Zuniga** is the third cousin of Virgen with **Juan Pedro Cayetano** as the common ancestor.

Victoria Ogaldez was born on this day in 1903 in Peine. She is the daughter of **Secundino Ogaldez** and **Alberta Ciego**. Victoria's father taught school in Barangu in 1897/98. He again taught school in Barangu in 1916 and 1917. Victoria married **Salvatore Basil "S.B." Daniels** in 1922 in Peine. She lived in Barangu for many years as the wife of the principal teacher.

On this day **Cuthbert Joseph Giles Martinez** was born. He is the son of **Francis Benedict Martinez** and **Victoria Barcelona**.

Lorn Miranda was born on this day in Belize City. She is the daughter of **Thomas Miranda** and **Rhoda Alvarez**. Lorn is the granddaughter of **Jerome Alvarez**.

2nd September

In the pre-1969 Catholic calendar today is the Feast Day of St. Stephen, King of Hungary.

Esteban Palacio (*right*) was born on this day. He is the son of **Runulfo "Roman" Palacio** and **Estela Rubio**. "Esti" as he is known has conducted many dugus here in Barangu. His father "Roman" was a noted singer and composer of arumahani songs. "Esti" was recognized by the President of Wadimalu in 2012 as an important traditional healer in the Garifuna Community.

Stephen Martinez was born on this day in 1908 in Barangu. He is the son of **Domingo Martinez** and **Maria Nolberto**. Stephen is the first cousin of **Anacleta "Da" Nolberto**.

On this day **Norma Estefania Martinez** was born. She is the daughter of **Francis Benedict Martinez** and **Victoria Barcelona**.

On this day **Agnes Felicita Palacio** died in 2006. She married **Fabian Cayetano** in 1976. She was born in 1952.

Stephen Paulino was born on this day in 1906 in Barangu. He is the son of **Eusebio Paulino** and **Maria Nolberto**. Stephen married **Eulogia Nicholas** in 1942 in Peine. He died in 1996 in Peine. Stephen is the grandson of **Augustin "Big Ease" Paulino**. **Victor Paulino** is the son of Stephen and Eulogia.

On this day **Malik Zuniga** was born in Barangu. He is the son of **Kevin Zuniga** and **Lynn Arnold**. **Maria Loreta Palacio** is the great-great-great-great-aunt of Malik. **Eugenia "Jean" Zuniga nee Noralez** is the great-grandmother of Malik.

3rd September

In the Catholic calendar today is the Feast Day of Sts. Anthony Ishida and Euphemia.

Francisco Bonifacio "Frank" Arana and **Narcisa Esther Contreras** were married on this day in 1955 in Peine. Francisco known as "Frank" is the son of **Adriano Natividad Arana** and **Basilia Luis**. Narcisa is the daughter of **Marcos Contreras** and **Cornelia Petillo**. Frank was a farm demonstrator in Barangu Narcisa was known as "Es." Frank was instrumental in the marking of the Barangu road.

On this day **Antonia Ariola** was born in 1926 in Barangu. She is the daughter of **Catarino Patricio Ariola** and **Benita Nunez**. Antonia married **Ruben**

Esteban Palacio (2010)

Palacio in 1945. **Jacinta Palacio** is the daughter of Antonia.

Euphemia "Tecki" Ramirez was born on this day in 1929. She is the daughter of **Cecilio Ramirez** and **Matilda Arana**. Euphemia is the older sister of **Mauricio Linford "Linsy" Ramirez**.

Gloria Avila was born on this day in 1938. She is the daughter of **Peter Anthony Avila** and **Sotera Nicholas**. **Frederick Nicholas** is the first cousin of Gloria with **Sotero Nicholas** as the common ancestor.

Theodore Palacio died on this day in 2012. He is the son of **Joseph Pollard Palacio** and **Hilaria Mejia**. He was born in 1930 in Barangu. Theodore married **Bridget Marin**. He has one sister, **Olivia Prudencia Avila nee Palacio** and two brothers, **Aloysius Alan Palacio** and Surusia **Joseph Orlando Palacio**. Theodore was a noted educator. **Maria Loreta Palacio** is the great-aunt of Theodore.

4th September

In the Catholic calendar today is the Feast Day of Saint Rosalia.

Today a set of twins were born. **Rosalia Avilez** and **Rosalio Avilez** were born on this day in 1922 in Peine. They are the children of **Casimiro Avilez** and **Simeona Teo**. Rosalia and Rosalio are the grandchildren of **Ambrosio "Sabigi" Avilez**. **Santiago "Gaünbü" Avilez**, the founder of Barangu, is the great-grandfather of Rosalia and Rosalio.

Rosalio Enriquez was born on this day in 1918 in Peine. He is the son of **Silverio Enriquez** and **Marcelina Avilez**.

On this day **Bonifacio Ramirez** died in 1975 in Barangu. He is the son of **Carmen Ramirez** and **Eustaquia Palacio**. Bonifacio was born in 1892. He married **Evangelista Nunez** in 1925. **Maria Loreta Palacio** is the aunt of Bonifacio. **Justina Nicholas nee Ramirez** is the daughter of Bonifacio.

Shanda Ariola was born on this day in Belize City. She is the daughter of **Avis Ariola**. **Maria Loreta Palacio** is the great-great-great-aunt of Shanda and **Maria Loreta Palacio** is also the first cousin five times removed. **Francisco "Chico" Ariola** is the grandfather of Shanda. Shanda was raised by **Almira "Irma" Gonzalez nee Ariola**.

On this day **John Nipalmson Lucas** was born this day in 1900 in Peine. He is the son of **Joseph Robert Lucas** and **Alfonsa Gabriel**. John married **Clotilda Nunez**. John died in 1961 in Peine. **Nathaniel "Shorty" Cayetano** is the grandson of John.

5th September

In the Catholic calendar today is the Feast Day of St. Lawrence Justinian.

Lorenza Avilez was born on this day in 1897 in Peine. She is the daughter of **John Justo Avilez** and **Paula Noralez**. Lorenza's baptism paper lists her name as Laurentia. Lorenza married **Julio Luis** in 1925. **Antonio Luis** is the son of Lorenza.

On this day **Emeni Cayetano** was born in Dangriga. He is the son of **E. Roy Cayetano** and **Phyllis Miranda**. **Maria Loreta Palacio** is his first cousin four times removed.

Sharron Williams was born on this day. She is the daughter of **Claudio Alonzo Williams** and **Delvarene Zuniga**. Sharron is the granddaughter of **John Jacob Zuniga**.

On this day **Olivia Justiniana Enriquez** was born in 1918 in Peine. She is the daughter of **Andres Patricio Enriquez** and **Jane Victoriana Villafranco**. She married **Henry H. Hartman** in 1956 in Peine. Her father **A.P. Enriquez** taught school for a short period of time in 1916 and 1917 in Barangu.

6th September

In the Catholic calendar today is the Feast Day of St. Eugene of Cappadocia.

John Polonio died on this day in 1901 in Barangu. He is the son of **Eusebio "Hayu" Polonio** and **Lucia Ordonez**. John was born in 1896 in Peine. His father, Eusebio, was the last alcalde in Peine. John is the uncle of **Bartolo Polonio**.

Zacarias Arzu was born on this day in 1898 in Peine. He is the son of **Sebastian Arzu** and **Luciana Enriquez**.

On this day **Zacaria Rose Martinez** was born. She is the daughter of **Francis Benedict Martinez** and **Victoria Barcelona**. Zacaria married **Augustus Palacio**. Surusia **Ludwig Palacio** is the son of Zacaria.

Eugenia "Jean" Noralez (*next page*) was born on this day in Barangu. She is the daughter of **Martin Benjamin Noralez** and **Jane Lino**. Jean married **Clotildo Zuniga** in 1966. **Kevin Zuniga** is grandson of Jean.

On this day **Reginald Avila** and **Georgiana Palacio** were married in 1944 in Peine. Reginald is the son of **Pedro John Avila** and **Viviana Palacio**. Geogiana is the daughter of **Augustine Palacio** and **Simeona Mejia**. Reginald and Georgiana are second cousins once removed with **Francisco Palacio** as the common

Eugenia "Jean" Noralez (2006)

ancestor. **Lynn Zuniga nee Arnold** is the grand-daughter of Reginald and Georgiana.

7th September

In the Catholic calendar today is the Feast Day of St. Regina.

Regina Lorenzo (*right*) was born on this day in 1920 in Barangu. She is the daughter of **Timoteo Lorenzo** and **Juana "Jane" Palacio**. She married **Hipolito Martinez** in 1939 in Barangu. She died in 2006 in Belize City. **Maria Loreta Palacio** is the aunt of Regina. **Martin Martinez** is the son of Regina.

On this day **Marcos Ramirez** was born in 1910 in Barangu. He is the son of **Sebastian Ramirez** and **Manuela Ariola.**

Estefania Avila was born on this day in 1907 in Peine. She is the daughter of **Antonio Albert "Yubu" Avila** and **Alberta Enriquez**. She married Evangelisto (last name unkown) in Corozal in 1944. Estefania is the sister of **Peter Anthony Avila.**

Marcus Garvey Zuniga was born on this day in 1933. He is the son of **Isabela Mejia**. He was probably named after Marcus Garvey, who visited Belize in 1927 and 1929 and had a tremendous impact on the re-awakening of black people in then British Honduras. This naming speaks to the several kinds of infuences on parents in naming their children.

On this day **Cristobel Loredo** died in 1990 in Barangu. She is the daughter of **Eulalia Loredo** and **Gregoria Palacio**. Cristobel was born in 1889 in Barangu. She married **Pablo Jimenez** in Peine in 1922 who died within a few hours of the wedding. She then married **Solomon Velasquez** in 1925 in Peine. **Maria Loreta Palacio** is the first cousin once removed of Cristobel.

8th September

In the Catholic calendar today is the Feast Day of Adrian of Nicomedia.

Victoriano Lorenzo died on this day in 1994. He is the son of **Timoteo Lorenzo** and **Juana "Jane" Palacio**. He was born in 1923 in Barangu. Victoriano was known as "Father" in the village. He married **Virgilia Ariola** in 1947 in Peine. He was noted for his fudge. **Maria Loreta Palacio** is the aunt of Victoriano. Glen Gutierrez is the grandson of Victoriano.

On this day in 1996 **Victor Leonard Nicholas** died in Bridgeport, CT. He is the son of **Philip Nicholas** and **Fabiana Palacio**. Victor was born in 1909 in Barangu. He married **Paulina Lopez** of Seine Bight. Victor was a school teacher and a farmer. **Maria Loreta Palacio** is the first cousin once removed of Victor. Martin Victor "Game and **Gone**" **Nicholas** is the son of Victor.

Jane Victoriana Villafranco died on this day in 1968 in Belize City. She is the daughter of **Luis Majin Villafranco** and **Antonia Zuniga**. Jane was born in 1895 in Peine. She married **Andres Patricio Enriquez** in 1912 in Peine. She was the wife of a rural school teacher and accompanied her husband to remote villages in the Toledo and Cayo districts.

Regina Martinez nee Lorenzo

On this day **Cornelio Nicholas** was born in 1913 in Peine. He is the son of **Pablo Nicholas** and **Aniceta Blas**.

Adriana Casimiro was born on this day in Barangu. She is the daughter of **Gonzalez Casimiro** and **Mary Flores**. Adriana is known as "Tun."

On this day **Petrona Ariola** was born in 1892 in Barangu (the government records have her born on the 8th and the church baptism record have her born on the 9th). She is the daughter of **Rufino Ariola** and **Ascenciona Paulino**. She married **Anastacio Arzu (Noralez)**. **Estanislao Arzu** is the son of Petrona.

Adriano Natividad Arana was born on this day in 1903. He is the son of **Concepcion Arana** and **Simeona Flores**. He married **Basilia Luis** in 1929 in Peine. He died in 1948 in Peine. Adriano is the father of **Francisco Bonifacio "Frank" Arana** who served as a farm demonstrator in Barangu.

On this day **Adriana Lauriano** was born in 1924. She is the daughter of **Thomas Charles Lauriano** and **Concepcion Mejia**. Adriana married **Pablo Baltazar** in 1945 in Dangriga. **Valentina Marin nee Baltazar** is the daughter of Adriana.

Paul Nicholas and **Melvinia Noralez** were married on this day in 1962 in Peine. Paul is the son of **Philip Nicholas** and **Fabiana Palacio**. **Maria Loreta Palacio** is the first cousin once removed of Paul.

9th September

In the Catholic calendar today is the Feast Day of St. Peter Claver who is the Patron Saint of the Peine Roman Catholic Church. Peter Claver was a priest in Cartagena, Columbia who served the slaves coming off the slave ships. The Patron Saint of the Peine Church originally was St. Michael the Archangel. It then became Peter Claver Parish, after Peter Claver was beatified but before he had become a Saint. In 1888 he was canonized and the Peine church became St. Peter Claver Parish.

Bernard Avilez and **Anacleta Castro** were married on this day in 1924 in Peine. Bernard is the son of **Ambrosio "Sabigi" Avilez** and **Justa Polonio**. Anacleta is the daughter of **Leon Castro** and **Victoriana Arana**.

On this day **Petrona Lino** was born in Barangu in 1896. She is the daughter **Obispo Lino** and **Francisca Cayetano**.

Eulalia Arana died on this day in 1996 in Belize City. She is the daughter of **Alejandro Arana** and **Gregoria Bermudez**. Eulalia was born in 1906 in Barangu. She married **Joseph Velasquez** in 1935 in Barangu.

On this day **Petrona Gregorio** was born in 1912 in Barangu. She is the daughter of **Viviano Gregorio** and **Bernardina Santino**. She died in 2002 in Barangu. Petrona, known as "Petu," was the aunt of **Victoriana "Vicky" Nolberto nee Martinez**.

Vilma Petrona Chimilio was born on this day in Barangu. She is the daughter of **Timoteo Chimilio** and **Geronima Martinez**. She married **Victor Enriquez** in 1981. **Maria Loreta Palacio** is the first cousin thrice removed of Vilma. **Jarreen J. Ramos** is the granddaughter of Vilma.

Vilma Petrona Chimilio

Gieri Palacio was born on this day in Peine. He is the son of **Augustus Palacio** and **Alberta Diego**. Gieri is the brother of **Ludwig Palacio**.

On this day **Peter Alvarez** was born in Peine. He is the son of **Simon Aloysius Alvarez** and **Phyllis Palacio**. Peter's parents are cousins in two different ways. Simon and Phyllis are third cousins with **Francisco Palacio** and are also third cousins once removed with Francisco Palacio on a different line.

10th September
Happy 10th of September

In the pre-1969 Catholic calendar today is the Feast Day of Saint Nicholas of Tolentino.

Atanacio Noralez and **Nicasia Lambey** were married on this day in 1938 in Peine. Atanacio is the son of **Martin Benjamin Noralez** and **Modesta Lucas**. Nicasia is the daughter of **Severiano Lambey** and

Romana Arana. Atanacio is the brother of **Eugenia "Jean" Zuniga nee Noralez.**

Tolentina Palacio was born on this day in Barangu. She is the daughter of **Santiago Martinez** and **Carciana Palacio**. Tolentina's father was from Indura. She is the sister of **Vicenta "Lulu" Sanchez.**

On this day **Sindulfo Garcia** was born in 1911 in Barangu. He is the son of **Margarito Garcia** and **Diega Benguche**. Sindulfo is the brother of **Jane Lino.**

Nicholas Ariola was born on this day in 1901 in Barangu. He is the son of **Patricio Ariola** and **Vicenta Castillo**. **Alicia Ariola** is the daughter of Nicholas.

On this day **Lillian Enriquez** was born in 1904 in Peine. She is the daughter of **Sebastian Arzu** and **Luciana Enriquez**. Lillian married **Cornelio Castillo** in 1940.

11th September

In the Catholic calendar today is the Feast Day of St. Hyacinth of Rome.

Jacinta Palacio (*right*) was born on this day in Barangu. She is the daughter of **Gregorio Ruben Palacio** and **Antonia Ariola**. **Maria Loreta Palacio** is the first cousin twice removed of Jacinta. **Beatrice Mariano** is the daughter of Jacinta.

On this day **Karen Nunez** was born. She is the daughter of **Leonard Nunez** and **Carmen Zuniga**. **Maria Loreta Palacio** is the first cousin thrice removed. Karen is the sister of **Nelson Nunez.**

Felipa Castillo was born on this day in 1905 in Barangu. She is the daughter of **Inez Castillo** and **Martha Fuentes**. Felipa is the sister of **Nicodemus Castillo.**

On this day **Felicita Arzu** was born. She is the daughter of **Candido Arzu** and **Irene Gibbons**. She married a Casimiro. She is known as "Cita." **Maria Loreta Palacio** is the great-great-aunt of Felicita. **Naomi Colon** is the sister of Felicita.

Felipa Castillo was born on this day in 1905 in Barangu. She is the daughter of **Inez Castillo** and **Martha Fuentes**. Felipa is the sister of **Nicodemus Castillo** and **Margarita Castillo.**

12th September

Narcisa Esther Contreras died on this day in 2003 in California and was buried in Belmopan. She is the daughter of **Marcos Contreras** and **Cornelia Petillo**.

She was born in 1935 in Peine. Narcisa married **Francisco Bonifacio "Frank" Arana** in 1955 in Peine.

On this day **Inaruni Mohammed Castillo** was born in Barangu. He is the son of **Augusto Castillo** and **Dercy Sandoval**. **Maria Loreta Palacio** is the first cousin four times removed of Inaruni.

13th September

Filomeno Lorenzo and **Benedictina Polonio** were married on this day in 1939 in Barangu. Filomeno is the son of **Timoteo Lorenzo** and **Juana "Jane" Palacio**. Benedictina is the daughter of **Pantaleon Odway Polonio** and **Petrona Paulino**.

On this day **Britney Valencio** was born in Belmopan. She is the daughter of **Egbert Anthony Valencio** and **Salomie Maximo**. **Maria Loreta Palacio** is the first cousin four times removed of Britney.

Celestino Paulino died on this day in 1887. He is the son of **Diego Paulino** and **Dominga "Waganga" Cayetano**. He married **Mercedes Palacio** in Peine in 1886. **Brigida Marin nee Paulino** is the daughter of Celestino who was born after her father's death.

Jacinta Palacio

Conrad Norman Arzu, Jr. was born in Belize City. He is the son of **Conrad Allen Arzu** and **Martina Martinez**. His parents are cousins in two different ways. Conrad and Martina are second cousins once removed with **Teodoro "Joe Young" Palacio** as the common ancestor and also third cousins once removed with **Francisco Palacio** as the common ancestor. **Maria Loreta Palacio** is the great-great-great-aunt of Conrad Jr. She is also the first cousin four times removed of Conrad Jr. with **Francisco Palacio** as the common ancestor. Maria is also great-great-aunt of Conrad. **Ellis Arzu** is the uncle of Conrad Jr.

On this day **Charlotte Underwood** was born in Belize City. She is the daughter of **Agnes "Sista" Alvarez**. **Maria Loreta Palacio** is the first cousin four times removed of Charlotte.

14th September

Today in the Roman Catholic Calendar is the Feast Day of St. Crescentian of Carthage and St. Crescentius of Rome.

Pablo Casimiro and **Bernadina Nolberto** were married on this day in 1907 in Barangu. Pablo is the son of **Ciriaco Casimiro**. Bernadina is the daughter of **Pio Nolberto** and **Casimira Nicholas**. **Bernadina Nolberto** later married **Nolberto Palacio** in 1935 in Barangu.

Isaac Zuniga was born on this day. He is the son of **Clotildo Zuniga** and **Eugenia Jean Noralez**. **Kevin Zuniga** is the son of Isaac.

On this day **Crescencia Zuniga** was born in 1897 in Barangu. She is the daughter of **Claro Zuniga** and **Mauricia Cayetano**. Crescencia married **Ermeterio Romero** in 1924 in San Pedro Columbia. Crescencia is the aunt of **Lucille "Chilagu" Valencio nee Zuniga.**

Rosalia Martinez was born on this day in Barangu. She is the daughter of **Julio Martinez** and **Eulalia Arana**. She is known as "Baby Rose."

Toribio Lopez was born on this day. He is the son of **Toribio Joseph Lopez** and **Emelda Marin**. **Angela Palacio** is the first cousin of Toribio.

On this day **Virginia Nunez** was born in 1911 in Peine. She is the daughter of **Francisco Nunez** and **Martina "Obispa" Martinez**. She married **Henry Santino** in 1935 in Peine.

Crescencia Arzu was born on this day in 1900 in Barangu. She is the daughter of **Sebastian Arzu** and **Luciana Enriquez**.

On this day **Crescencia Arzu** was born in Peine in 1920. She is the daughter of **Fabiano Arzu** and **Eustacia Martinez**. Crescencia married **Vicente Zuniga** in 1944 in Peine.

15th September

In the Catholic calendar today is the Feast Day of St. Nicomedes.

Gabina Zuniga died on this day in 1946 in Barangu. She is the daughter of **Claro Zuniga** and **Mauricia Cayetano**. Gabina was born in 1888 in Barangu. She married **Prudencio Brown Martinez** in 1905 in Peine. **Elliot Martinez** is the grandson of Gabina.

On this day **Apolinaria Garcia** died in 1901 in Barangu. She is the daughter of **Esmith Garcia** aqnd **Blacina Apolonio**. Apolinaria was born in 1897 in Barangu.

Steven Gibbons was born on this day in 1898 in Barangu. He is the son of **Isaac Gibbons** and **Ascenciona Paulino**. Steven married **Estena Blanco** from Labuga in 1922 in Barangu. Steven died in Guatemala City. **Irene Gibbons** is the daughter of **Steven Gibbons** and **Paula Paulino**.

On this day **Shalamar Marcy Loredo** was born in Barangu. She is the daughter of **Alvin Loredo** and **Sharon Nunez**. Shalamar's parents are cousins in two ways. Alvin and Sharon are second cousins with **Eulalio Loredo** as the common ancestor and are also third cousins once removed with **Francisco Nolberto** as the common ancestor. **Maria Loreta Palacio** is the first cousin four times removed of Shalamar.

Thomas Nunez was born on this day in Corozal. He is the son of **Thomas Nunez** and **Maria Roches**. **Maria Loreta Palacio** is the great-great-great-aunt of Thomas. Thomas is the second cousin once removed of **Angela Palacio** with **Nolberto Palacio** as the common ancestor.

Catarino Nicodemus Martinez was born on this day in 1916 in Barangu. There is some confusion to his name and birthday, the government birth records have him born on the 15th and named Catarino but the church baptism records have him born on the 16th and named Nicodemus. He is the son of **Pedro Nicasio Martinez** and **Augustina Nunez**. Catarino is the brother of **Melvinia "Grandma Mi" Martinez**.

Manuel (Nicholas) Lambey was born on this day in 1891 in Barangu. He is the son of **John Lambey** and **Gregoria Nolberto**. This is an example of the early Lambey/Nolberto connection that continues to this day.

On this day **Dominga Avila** was born in 1912 in Peine. She is the daughter of **Pantaleon Avila** and **Juliana Garcia**. Dominga married **William Lucas** in 1937 in Peine.

Dolores Martinez was born on this day in 1916 in Barangu. She is the daughter of **Pedro Nicasio Martinez** and **Augustina Nunez**. Dolores is the sister of **Melvinia "Grandma Mi" Martinez**.

16th September

In the Catholic calendar today is the Feast Day of Pope Saint Cornelius.

Cornelio Castillo was born on this day in 1897 in Labuga. He is the son of **Inez Castillo** and **Martha**

Fuentes. He died in 1979. He married **Lillian Enriquez** in 1940. In Cornelio's baptism record from Labuga there is a note added at a later date that states "Casado en Punta Gorda con Crescencius Arzu." I am not sure about this since I can find no record of this in the Peine sacramental records. Cornelio is the father of **Edward "Hapu" Castillo** with **Melvinia "Grandma Mi" Martinez**.

On this day **Cornelia Petillo** was born in 1897 in Peine. She is the daughter of **Cosme Petillo** and **Francisca Avilez**. Cornelia's great-grandfather is **Santiago "Gaünbü" Avilez**, the founder of Barangu. **Narcisa Esther Contreras** is the daughter of **Cornelia Petillo** and **Marcos Contreras**.

Cornelio Martinez was born on this day in Barangu. He is the son of **Hipolito Martinez** and **Regina Lorenzo**. His parents are second cousins once removed. **Maria Loreta Palacio** is the great-aunt of Cornelio. **Viola Martinez** is the sister of Cornelio.

Michael Joseph was born on this day in Peine. He is the son of **Ambrosio Joseph** and **Petrona Palacio**. **Maria Loreta Palacio** is the great-great-aunt of Michael.

Dolores Paulino was born in 1908 in Barangu. She is the daughter of **Eugenio Paulino** and **Nicolasa Zuniga**. **Gregoria "Gogo" Paulino** is the sister of Dolores.

Shantay Loredo was born on this day in Barangu. She is the daughter of **Alvin Loredo** and **Sharon Nunez**. Her parent's Alvin and Sharon are second cousins with **Eulalio Loredo** as the common ancestor and are also third cousins once removed with **Francisco Nolberto** as the common ancestor. **Maria Loreta Palacio** is the first cousin four times removed of Shantay.

Patience Daniels was born on this day. She is the daughter of **Salvatore Basil "S.B." Daniels** and **Victoria Ogaldez**. Patience's father was a long-time principal teacher in Barangu.

17th September

In the Catholic calendar today is the Feast Day of the Sacred Stigmata of Saint Francis of Assisi.

Manuela Marin died on this day in 1991 in Chicago. She is the daughter of **Aparicio Santiago Marin** and **Brigida Paulino**. Manuela was born in 1922 in Barangu. She married **Eugenio Cayetano** in 1941 in Barangu. **Maria Loreta Palacio** is the first cousin twice removed of Manuela. **Judith Cayetano** is the daughter of Manuela.

Francisco Bonifacio "Frank" Arana was born on this day in 1931 in Peine. He is the son of **Adriano Natividad Arana** and **Basilia Luis**. Francisco married **Narcisa Esther Contreras** in 1955 in Peine. He died in 2005 in Belmopan. Francisco was a farm demonstrator in Barangu. He also worked for the Rural Women's Association and was instrumental in getting the first mechanical cassava grinder in Barangu.

Francisco Bonifacio "Frank" Arana (2002)

On this day **Claudia Avila** was born in Peine. She is the daughter of **Cirilo Avila** and **Olivia Prudencia Palacio**. **Maria Loreta Palacio** is the great-great-aunt of Claudia. **Marsha Margaret Suazo** is the daughter of Claudia.

Francisca Ariola was born on this day in 1914. In the baptism records it says she was born on the 27th of September. She is the daughter of **Patricio Ariola** and **Vicenta Castillo**. She married **Dionisio M. Colon** in 1934 in Peine.

On this day **Francisca Palacio** was born in 1927 in Barangu. She is the daughter of Carlos Palacio and Lousia Nunez. **Maria Loreta Palacio** is the great-aunt of Francisca. **Emily Ramirez nee Martinez**, a former school teacher in Barangu, is the daughter of Francisca.

Cynthia Lavinia Lynn Martinez was born on this day. She is the daughter of **Michael Martinez** and

Hazel Elinor Arzu. **Maria Loreta Palacio** is both the great-great-great-aunt and the first cousin four times removed of Cynthia. **Candido Arzu**, long time principal teacher in Barangu, is the grandfather of Cynthia.

18th September

Adonis Darius Daniels was born on this day. He is the son of **Salvatore Basil "S.B." Daniels** and **Victoria Ogaldez**. He married Gloria Avilez. His father was a principal teacher in Barangu.

On this day **Simon Aloysius Alvarez** was born. He is the son of **Feliciano "Felix" Alvarez** and **Pantaleona Mejia**. He married **Phyllis Palacio**. **Maria Loreta Palacio** is the first cousin twice removed of Simon. **Michelle Alvarez** is the daughter of Simon.

Joseph Zuniga was born on this day in 1908 in Barangu. He is the son of **Viviano Zuniga** and **Filomena Paulino**. Viviano and Filomena are second cousins with **Juan Pedro Cayetano** as the common ancestor.

On this day **Silas Cayetano** died in 2010 in Belize City. He is the son of **Pascacio Cayetano** and **Eustaquia Satuye**. Silas was born in 1925 in Barangu. Silas was a Justice of Peace and received

Silas Cayetano (2005)

a Member of the British Empire (M.B.E.) from the Queen of England. Silas was an educator. **Maria Loreta Palacio** is the grandmother of Silas.

Simeona Teo died on this day in 1922 in Peine. She is the daughter of **Juan Bautista Teo** and **Bonlea Martina Sanchez**. Simeona was born in 1890 in Peine. Simeona married **Casimiro Avilez** in 1919 in Peine.

19th September

John Arzu was born on this day in 1920 in Barangu. He is the son of **Isidro Arzu** and **Maxima Ariola**.

He married **Gladys Palacio** in 1941 in Peine. John is the great-great-grandson of **Juan Pedro Cayetano**.

Illona Lynette Arzu was born in this day in Belize City. She is the daughter of **Ellis Henry Arzu** and **Elma Yvonne Martinez**. Illona is the granddaughter of **Candido Arzu** and **Bernadette Loredo**.

20th September

In the Catholic calendar today is the Feast Day of St Eustachius.

Eustaquia Satuye was born on this day in 1897 in Labuga. She is the daughter of **Clemente Satuye** and **Eluteria Sanchez**. **Sheridan Arzu nee Petillo** is the granddaughter of Eustaquia.

On this day **Silas Cayetano** was born in 1925 in Barangu. He is the son of **Pascacio Cayetano** and **Eustaquia Satuye**. He died in 2010 in Belize City. He was an educator. He was a Justice of the Peace and received a Member of the British Empire (M.B.E.) from Queen Elizabeth. **Maria Loreta Palacio** is the grandmother of Silas. Nurse **Mary Petillo nee Cayetano** is the sister of Silas.

Eustaquio Paulino was born on this day in 1863 in Peine. He is the son of **Diego Paulino** and **Maria Victoria Gamboa**. Eustaquio is the brother of **Augustin "Big Ease" Paulino**.

On this day in 1894 **Santiago Avilez** died in Barangu. Santiago was 90 years old when he died. He was the founder of Barangu. He brought **Desideria** and her two sons, **Teodoro Palacio** and **Anastacio Palacio** to Barangu. He and Desideria had one child, **Ignacia Avilez**. Santiago was the first alcalde to be elected nd appointed to represent Barangu and the second or third alcalde appointed in the whole colony.

21st September
Enjoy your Independence Day!

Allison Steven Palacio was born on this day in Orange Walk. He is the son of **Wilfred Martinez** and **Jacinta Palacio**. **Maria Loreta Palacio** is the first cousin thrice removed.

22nd September

In the Catholic calendar today is the Feast Day of St. Maurice.

Mauricio Roches was born on this day in 1922 in Peine. He is the son of **Elijio Roches** and **Francisca Lucas**. Mauricio is the second cousin of **Hazel Cayetano nee Castro** with **Domingo Labriel** as the common ancestor.

23rd September

In the Catholic calendar today is the Feast Day of St. Thecla.

Filomena Cayetano was born on this day in 1901 in Barangu. She is the daughter of **Marcelo Cayetano** and **Maria Loreta Palacio,** whose 150th birthday we are celebrating this year.

On this day **Tecla Palacio** was born in 1933 in Barangu. She is the daughter of **Jacob Palacio** and **Tomasa Polonio**. **Maria Loreta Palacio** is the first cousin twice removed of Tecla. Tecla is the niece of **Ruben Palacio**.

Cosme Petillo and **Antonia Zuniga** were married on this day in 1914 in Peine. Cosme is the son of **Juan Petillo** and an unknown Luis. Antonia changed her last name from Zuniga to Gabriel. She is the daughter of **Martin Zuniga** and **P. Labriel**. This is Cosme's second marriage. He had married **Francisca Avilez** in 1894 in Peine. Cosme is the great-great-grandfather of **Wasany Wellington Ramos.**

24th September

Sidney Rodrick Arzu was was born on this day. He is the son of **Candido Arzu** and **Bernadette Loredo**. Sidney is related to **Maria Loreta Palacio** on both his mother's side and his father's side. On his father's side Maria is the great-great-aunt of Sidney. On his mother's side Maria is the first cousin thrice removed of Sidney. **Hazel Martinez nee Arzu** is the sister of Sidney.

On this day **Cleofa Avilez** was born in 1930 in Peine. She is the daughter of **Eufamio Avilez** and **Camila Contreras**. She died in 2010 in Barangu. Cleofa is the mother of **Andy Palacio** who was an Ambassador for Peace for the United Nations and noted muscian of Garifuna music.

Maria Mariano died on this day in 2003 in Dangriga. She is the daughter of **Angelina Diego**. Maria was born in 1958 in Dangriga. Maria is the mother of **Patrick Mariano**, the Ebu.

25th September

Luciano Cayetano and **Eretia Nunez** were married on this day in 1870 in Labuga. Luciano is the son of **Juan Pedro Cayetano** and **Maria Nicolasa Moralez**. Eretia is the daughter of **Sebastian Nunez** and **Maria J. Zuniga**. Luciano is the uncle of **Marcelo Cayetano.**

Justina Cayetano was born on this day in 1865 in Barangu. She is the daughter of **Anacleto Cayetano** and **Dominga Martila Arzu**. Justina married **Philip Santino** in 1883 in Barangu. Justina is the grandmother of **Jacinta Trigueno nee Santino.**

Concepcion Arana died on this day in 1925 in Peine. He is the son of Philip Arana and Corona Nunez. **Concepcion Arana** was born in 1871 in Peine. He married **Simeona Flores**. Concepcion owned land up Monkey River where they raised bananas. Concepcion is the great-grandfather of Surusia **Peitra Arana.**

On this day **Calistra Cayetano** died in 1986 in Peine. She is the daughter of **Steven Cayetano** and **Francisca Nunez**. She was born in 1926 in Peine. Calistra is the grandmother of **Patrick Mariano**. Patrick is an Ebu serving the Garifuna community.

26th September

In the Catholic calendar today is the Feast Day of St. Cyprian of Antioch.

Antonio Palacio and **Andrea Palacio** were married on this day in 1934 in Peine. Antonio is the son of **Dionisio Palacio** and **Catarina Nunez**. **Andrea Palacio** is the daughter **Catarino T. Palacio** and **Francisca Sacasa (Ortiz)**. Antonio and Andrea are first cousins once removed with **Francisco Palacio** as the common ancestor. Although we have noted several husbands and wives who are closely related, it is rare that both share the same last name as in this case.

Cornelio Castillo was born on this day in 1897 in Labuga. He is the son of **Inez Castillo** and **Martha Fuentes**. Cornelio married **Lillian Enriquez** in 1940. Cornelio died in 1979. **Edward Castillo** is the son of Cornelio with **Melvinia "Grandma Mi" Martinez**.

On this day **Cipriano Nicholas** was born in 1907 in Barangu. He is the son of **Sotero Nicholas** and **Paula Nunez**. He married **Ursula Arana** in 1933. **Andres Nicholas** is the son of Cipriano.

Cipriano Arana was born on this day in Newton in 1918. He is the son of **Atancio Arana** and **Leona Garcia**. He married **Leonora Avila** in 1937 in Barangu. **Florine Thelma Arana** is the daughter of Cipriano.

Cipriano Nicholas was born on this day in Barangu in 1914. He is the son of **Philip Nicholas** and **Fabiana Palacio**. Cipriano is the brother of **Victor Leonard Nicholas. Maria Loreta Palacio** is the first cousin once removed of Cipriano. **Martin "Game and Gone" or "Tin-Tin" Nicholas** is the nephew of Cipriano.

On this day **Genaro Arzu** was born in 1920 in Barangu. He is the son of **Isidro Arzu** and **Maxima Ariola**.

Arlene Ogaldez was born on this day in Barangu. She is the daughter of **Anthony Alexander Ogaldez** and **Erlinda "Delane" Nicholas**. Her father Anthony was a long time principal teacher in Barangu. **Maria Loreta Palacio** is the first cousin five times removed of Arlene.

Cipriano Avilez was born on this day in Barangu. He is the son of **John Justo Avilez** and **Paula Noralez**. He the brother of **James J. Avilez**. **Calvin Avilez** is the son of Cipriano.

27th September

Matea Paulino was born on this day in 1899 in Barangu. She is the daughter of **Augustin "Big Ease" Paulino** and **Juana Luis**. She died in 1931 in Peine.

George Avila born on this day in Peine in 1901. He is the son of **Pedro John Avila** and **Viviana Palacio**. George is the brother of **Reginald Avila**. **Maria Loreta Palacio** is the first cousin once removed of George.

28th September

Mary Lino was born on this day in Dangriga. She had a son, **Anthony Lino**, with **Paul Hudson Casimiro**.

On this day **Angus Claude Cayetano** died in 2000 in Dangriga. He is the son of **Gregorio Cayetano** and **Teofila Flores**. He was born in Dangriga in 1919. He married **Adela Jaime** in 1949. Angus was a Justice of the Peace. He also was a lay minster in the Methodist Church. He served the British Empire during World War Two working in the "Panama Canal Zone." He received a MBE knighthood from Queen Elizabeth II. **Maria Loreta Palacio** is the grandmother of Angus.

29th September

In the pre-1969 Catholic calendar today is the Feast Day of the Dedication of St. Michael the Archangel.

Viviana Palacio died on this day in 1954 in Peine. She is the daughter of **Anastacio Palacio** and **Sotera Gutierrez**. She married **Pedro John Avila** in 1898 in Barangu. **Maria Loreta Palacio** is the first cousin of Viviana. **Lynn Zuniga nee Arnold** is the great-granddaughter of Viviana and the first cousin four times removed of Viviana.

On this day **Beatrice Sanchez** (*right*) was born in 1963 in Barangu. She is the daughter of **Amanda Zuniga**. She married **Robert Cayetano**. Beatrice died in 2011 in Belize City. Beatrice was an educator, teaching for a few years in Barangu. **Maria Loreta Palacio** is the first cousin thrice removed of Beatrice. **Robert Cayetano** Jr. is the son of Beatrice.

Isani Cayetano was born on this day in Dangriga. He is the son of **E. Roy Cayetano** and **Phyllis Miranda**. **Maria Loreta Palacio** is the first cousin four times removed of Isani.

Michaela Lorenzo was born on this day in 1906 in Peine. She is the daughter of **Timoteo Lorenzo** and **Juana "Jane" Palacio**. She married **Valentino Castro** in 1933 in Barangu. **Dale Gutierrez** is the grand-nephew of Michaela.

Celia Casimiro was born on this day. She is the daughter of **Erasmo Casimiro** and **Paula Noralez**. Celia is the sister of **Muriel Williams nee Casimiro**.

On this day **Charlotte Michael Lorenzo** was born. She is the daughter of **Felix Melendrez** and **Valentina Lorenzo**. **Maria Loreta Palacio** is the great-great-aunt of Charlotte. **Steven "Junior" Gutierrez** is the brother of Charlotte.

Melchisedech Daniels was born on this day. He is the son of **Salvatore Basil "S.B." Daniels** and **Victoria Ogaldez**. Melchisedech's father was a long time principal teacher in Barangu.

Hubert Aloyius Martinez was born on this day. He is the son of **Francis Benedict Martinez** and **Victoria Barcelona**. Hubert is the brother of **Elma Yvonne Arzu nee Martinez**.

On this day **Miguel Daniels** and **Tomasa Martinez** were married in 1906 in Peine. Miguel is the son of **Francis Daniels** and **Fabiana Gutierrez**. Tomasa is the daughter of **Bruno Martinez** and **Luisa Zuniga**. Miguel and Tomasa are the parents of **Salvatore Basil "S.B." Daniels** also known as **Sam Daniels** or SBD, long time principal teacher in Barangu.

Beatrice Cayetano nee Sanchez

96

30th September

Lloyd Enriquez was born on this day. He is the son of **Contestine Enriquez** and **Eugenia Jean Noralez**. Lloyd married **Rita Avila**. He is the grandson of **Andres Patricio Enriquez** who taught school in Barangu for a short time in 1916 and again in 1918.

On this day **Felix Lucas** died in 1940. He is the son of **William Lucas** and **Isabel Nunez**. Felix married **Josefa Paulino** in 1934.

More Life Events in September

OCTOBER

1st October

In the Catholic calendar today is the Feast Day of St. Remigius of Rheims.

Remigio Martinez was born on this day in 1894 in Barangu. He is the son of Peter Reyes and **Cornelia Martinez**. Remigio's mother, Cornelia Martinez, had a number of children with Esmith Garcia.

Remijio Arzu was born on this day in 1911. He is the son of **Isidro Arzu** and **Maxima Ariola**. **Maxima Ariola** is the sister of **Patricio "Mouni" Ariola**.

On this day **Remigio Avilez** was born in 1902. He is the son of **John Justo Avilez** and **Paula Noralez**. Remigio was a student teacher in Barangu in 1916. Remigio is the grandson of **Santiago "Gaünbü" Avilez**, the founder of Barangu. Remigio is the father of **John Napoleon Avilez**, who was a lawyer.

Lucio Avilez and **Losanta Cacho** were married on this day in 1933. Lucio is the son of **Juan Avilez** and **Dominga "Gadu" Marin**. Losanta is the daughter of **Leoncio Cacho** and **Apolinaria Martinez**.

Teresa "Tandu" Noralez was born on this day. She is the daughter of **Leonarda "Leoni" Noralez**. Teresa is the granddaughter of **Felix "Aska" Noralez**.

2nd October

Pablo Casimiro died on this day in 1931 in Barangu. He is the son of **Ciriaco Casimiro**. Pablo married **Bernadina Nolberto** in 1907 in Barangu. Pablo is the grandfather of **Fermin Casimiro** and **Paul Hudson Casimiro**.

On this day **Prudencio Daniels** died in 1946 in Peine. He is the son of **Salvatore Basil "S.B." Daniels** and **Victoria Ogaldez**.

Custodio Sanchez was born on this day in 1909 in Peine. He is the son of **John Sanchez** and **Isidora Bermudez**. Custodio is the grandson of **Dominga "Gadu" Marin**.

On this day **Nelson Leonard Nunez** was born in Dangriga. He is the son of **Leonard Nunez** and **Carmen Zuniga**. **Maria Loreta Palacio** is the first cousin thrice removed of Nelson. Nelson is a police constable.

3rd October

In the Catholic calendar today is the Feast Day of St. Candidus the Martyr.

Nolberto Lopez and **Beatrice Barcelona** were married on this day in 1933 in Peine. Beatrice is the daughter of **Isabel Barcelona** and **Fecunda Gabriel**. Beatrice is the sister of **Victoria Martinez nee Barcelona**.

On this day **Matildo Lino** and **Teresa Zuniga** were married in 1918 in Peine. Matildo is the son of **Nievi Lino** and **Polonia Santino**. Teresa is the daughter of **Nolasco Zuniga** and **Hilaria** (unknown last name). **Joseph Lino** is the son of Matildo and Teresa.

Isaac Loredo was born on this day in 1952. He is the son of **Henry Loredo** and **Ursula Polonio**. **Maria Loreta Palacio** is the first cousin twice removed of Isaac. Isaac is the father of **Alfanette Ashanti Loredo**.

On this day **Candido M. Castro** was born in 1903 in Peine. He is the son of **Leon Castro** and **Victoriana Arana**. Candido married **Sofia Mejia** in 1953 in Peine.

Candido Arzu was born on this day in 1917 in Barangu. He is the son of **Francisco Ellis Arzu** and **Patrocinia Palacio**. Candido married **Bernadette Loredo** in 1938 in Barangu. He died in Belmopan in 1992. Candido was an educator. He was for many years the principal of St. Joseph R.C. School in Barangu. **Maria Loreta Palacio** is the great-aunt of Candido. Surusia **Harriet Scarborough nee Arzu** is the daughter of Candido.

On this day **Candido Flores** was born in Peine. He is the son of **Philip Flores** and **Veronica Avilez**. Candido died in 1943 in Belize City. **Mary Casimiro nee Flores** is the daughter of **Candido Flores**.

Candida Palacio was born on this day in 1902 in Peine. She is the daughter of **Dionisio Palacio** and **Catarina Nunez**. Candida married **Tiburcio Nicholas**. **Maria Loreta Palacio** is the first cousin of Candida. **Frederick Nicholas** is the son of Candida.

Shemar Mariano was born on this day in Belize City. He is the son of **Beatrice Magdalene Mariano** and **Roy Flores**. **Maria Loreta Palacio** is the first cousin four times removed of Shemar. Shemar is the great-grandson of **Antonia Palacio nee Ariola**.

On this day **Estevan Bermudez** was born in 1930. He is the son of **Nolasca Avila**. Estevan is the grandson of **Pedro John Avila**. **Maria Loreta Palacio** is the first cousin twice removed of Estevan.

Francisco Rash was born on this day in Barangu. He is the son of **Alfredo Rash** and **Maria Makin**. Francisco is the first cousin once removed of **Delia Makin**.

Camila Contreras died on this day in 1970 in Barangu. She is the daughter of **Andres Contreras** and **Secundina Colindres**. Camila was born in 1897 in Peine. She married **Cecilio "Dick" Polonio** in 1920 in Peine. She is the mother of **Bartolo Polonio, Cleofa Avilez** and **Pia Arana nee Magdelano**.

4th October

In the Catholic calendar today is the Feast Day of St. Francis of Assisi.

Francisco Lucas was born on this day in 1913 in Peine. He is the son of **Ireneo Lucas** and **Gertrude Labriel**. Francisco is the cousin once removed of **Hazel Cayetano nee Castro**.

On this day **Carla Ramirez** was born in Seine Bight. She is the daughter of **Carlos Ramirez** and **Elizabeth Martinez**. Carla is the great-granddaughter of **Secundina "Kunda" Guzman**. Carla is also the great-great-great-granddaughter of **Martin Reyes**.

Francis Casimiro was born on this day in Barangu. He is the son of **Gonzalez Casimiro** and **Mary Flores**. Francis is the brother of **Fermin "Rama" Casimiro**.

On this day **Francis Blanco** was born in 1915 in Dangriga. He married **Elvira Cris Velasquez**. Sista Blanco is the daughter of Francis.

Charles Francis Joseph was born on this day. He is the son of **Ambrosio Joseph** and **Petrona Palacio**. **Maria Loreta Palacio** is the great-great-aunt of Charles.

On this day **Mauricia Cayetano** died in 1923 in Barangu. She is the daughter of **Anacleto Cayetano** and **Dominga Martila Arzu**. She married **Claro Zuniga** in 1875 in Barangu. Mauricia is the grandmother of **Lucille Valencio nee Zuniga**.

Candido Arzu died on this day in 1992 in Belmopan. He is the son of **Patrocinia Palacio** and **Francisco Ellis Arzu**. He was a principal teacher in Barangu for many years. **Maria Loreta Palacio** is the great-aunt of Candido. **Harold "Greg" Arzu** is the son of Candido.

5th October

John "Shamba" Dominquez died on this day in 1999 in Belize City. He was born in 1936 in Belize City. John is the father of **Nora Arana**.

Pastora Lambey died on this day in 1899 in Barangu. She is the daughter of **John Lambey** and **Gregoria Nolberto**. Pastora was six months old when she died. She is the first cousin twice removed of **Alvin Loredo**.

On this day **Fabiana Palacio** died in 1945 in Barangu. She is the daughter of **Anastacio Palacio** and **Magdalena Cesaria**. Fabiana married **Philip Nicholas** in 1908 in Peine. **Maria Loreta Palacio** is the first cousin of Fabiana. **Paul Nicholas** is the son of Fabiana.

Froylan Palacio was born on this day in 1928 in Barangu. He is the son of **Augustine Palacio** and **Simeona Mejia**. Froylan married **Jacinta Santino** in 1965. **Maria Loreta Palacio** is the great-aunt of Froylan.

On this day **Hector Loredo** was born in 1934. He is the son of **Henry Loredo** and **Ursula Polonio**. He died in 1978 in a drowning accident. Hector is the father of **Mark Loredo**.

6th October

Bruno Nolberto was born on this day in 1885 in Barangu. He is the son of **Macario Nolberto** and **Josefa Alvarez**. Bruno is the first cousin twice removed of **Alvin Loredo**.

On this day **Marva Casimiro** was born in Barangu. She is the daughter of **Gonzalez Casimiro** and **Mary Flores**. Marva is the sister of **Adriana "Tun" Casimiro**.

Brigida Castillo was born on this day in 1916 in Barangu. She is the daughter of **Nicodemus Castillo** and **Ramona Marin**. Brigida is the granddaughter of **Inez Castillo**.

7th October

Brigida Paulino died on this day in 1961 in Belize City. She is the daughter of **Celestino Paulino** and **Mercedes Palacio**. Her father, Celestino, died before she was born in 1887 in Barangu. She married **Aparicio Santiago Marin**. She is the mother of **Bridget Palacio nee Marin**.

Brigida Paulino and Aparicio Santiago Marin

Dionisio M. Colon was born on this day in 1918 in Peine. He is the son of **John Colon** and **Leonarda Zuniga**. Dionisio married **Francisca Ariola** in 1934 in Peine. Francisca is the daughter of **Patricio Ariola**.

8th October

In the pre-1969 Catholic calendar today is the Feast Day of St. Bridget of Sweden.

Brigida Paulino was born on this day in 1887 in Barangu. She is the daughter of **Celestino Paulino** and **Mercedes Palacio**. She died in 1961 in Belize City. **Maria Loreta Palacio** is the first cousin once removed of Brigida. Brigida is the mother of **Clarence Marin**.

Simon Lucas was born on this day in 1924 in Barangu. He is the son of **"Clarinet" Lucas** and **Lamarta Zuniga**. Simon is the nephew of **Inocente "Mafia" Zuniga**.

On this day **Simeon Trigueno** was born in Puerto Barrios. He is the son of **Isidro Trigueno** and **Paula Martinez**. Simeon is the nephew of **Melvinia "Grandma Mi" Martinez**.

9th October

In the Catholic calendar today is the Feast Day of St. Dionysius the Aeropagite.

Dionisia Santino was born on this day in 1922 in Barangu. She is the daughter of **Eusebio Santino** and **Vicenta Blas**. Dionisia married **Clarence Marin** in 1967. **Anita Marin** is the daughter of Dionisia.

On this day **Dionisia Lambey** was born on this day in 1900 in Barangu. She is the daughter of **John Lambey** and **Gregoria Nolberto**. Dionisia is the first cousin once removed of **Paula Nolberto**.

Nelson Lacio was born on this day. He is the son of **Nadeth Martinez**. **Maria Loreta Palacio** is the great-great-great-great-aunt of Nelson. **Maria Loreta Palacio** is also the first cousin five times removed of Nelson.

10th October

In the Catholic calendar today is the Feast Day of St. Francis Borgia.

On this day **Francis Avila** was born in 1906 in Barangu. He is the son of **Pedro John Avila** and **Viviana Palacio**. **Maria Loreta Palacio** is the first cousin once removed of Francis. **Reginald Avila** is the brother of Francis.

Francisco Ariola (*right*) was born on this day in Barangu. He is the son of Catarino **Patricio Ariola** and **Carciana Palacio**. Francisco is known as "Chico."

Vicenta "Lulu" Sanchez is the sister of Francisco. **Trevor Ariola** is the son of Francisco.

11th October

Alan Casimiro was born on this day. He is the son of **Erasmo Casimiro** and **Paula Noralez**. **Etta Casimiro** and **Helen Casimiro** are children of Allan.

Fermina Nicholas was born on this day in 1917 in Barangu. She is the daughter of **Pablo Nicholas** and **Aniceta Blas**. Fermina married **Marcus Lambert Arzu** in 1947 in Potu (Puerto Cortez), Indura.

On this day **Nicasio Santino** was born in 1931 in Barangu. He is the son of **Eusebio Santino** and **Vicenta Blas**. **Jacinta Trigueno nee Santino** is the sister of Nicasio.

Lucas Teo was born on this day in 1909 in Peine. He is the son of **Casimiro Avilez** and **Simeona Teo**. **Santiago "Gaünbü" Avilez** is the great-grandfather of Lucas.

Ainsworth Philip Valerio was born on this day in Orange Walk Town. He is the son of **Peter Valerio** and **Hermenehilda "Maria" Lopez**. Kaya Valerio is the daughter of Ainsworth.

Martin Martinez and **Parlet McFadzean** were married on this day in 1997. Martin is the son of **Martin Martinez** and **Evilia Gonzalez**.

On this day **Ernest Bernard** and **Prajedes Palacio** were married in 1928 in Peine. Prajedes is the daughter of **Nieves Juarez** and **Nolberto Palacio**.

Francisco "Chico" or "Paco" Ariola (2009)

Maximino Lino and Santiaga Avilez were married on this day in Peine in 1933. Maximino is the son of Rosendo Lino and Clemencia Nunez. Santiaga is the daughter of Antonio Avilez and Juana Palacio.

On this day Pascual Cayetano and Dominga Gonzalez were married in 1866 in Labuga. Pascual is the son of Juan Pedro Cayetano and Maria Celestina (unknown last name). Dominga Gonzalez is the daughter of Severiano Gonzalez and Maria Luisa Palma. This is Pascual's second marriage, he married Dominga after his first wife, Juana Nunez, died.

12th October

Naomi Colon was born on this day in 1951. She is the daughter of Antonio Colon and Irene Gibbons. Shaynah Ariola is the daughter of Naomi.

On this day Felicita Zuniga was born in Barangu. She is the daughter of John Jacob Zuniga and Tomasine Loredo. Felicita is known as "Cita" in the village. Maria Loreta Palacio is the first cousin twice removed of Felicita. Dercy Sandoval is the daughter of Felicita.

Felicita "Cita" or "Nitu" Zuniga (2003)

Magdalena Palacio was born on this day in 1902 in Barangu. She is the daughter of Liberato Palacio and Florencia Blas. Magdalena was named after her grandmother Magdalena Cesaria. Maria Loreta Palacio is the first cousin once removed of Magdalena.

Virgilia Lorenzo nee Ariola died on this day in 2012 in Los Angeles, California. She is the daughter of Benita Nunez and Catarino Ariola. She was born in 1929 in Peine. Virgilia married Victoriano "Fada" Lorenzo in 1947 in Peine. Valentina "Flora" Lorenzo is her daughter. For many years Virgilia headed the St. Joseph Credit Union in Barangu.

13th October

Eustacio Alvarez and Toribia Garcia were married on this day in 1961 in Barangu. Eustacio is the son of Jerome Alvarez and Ignacia "Inez" Arana. Toribia is the daughter of Geronima Martinez. Zita Arzu nee Alvarez is the daughter of Eustacio and Toribia.

Rossele Ortilia Zuniga was born on this day in Barangu. She is the daughter of John Ray Zuniga and Vicenta "Lulu" Sanchez. Maria Loreta Palacio is the great-great-aunt of Rossele.

On this day Joy Melanie Cayetano was born in Peine. She is the daughter of Wallace Cayetano and Alfonsa Arana. Joy's father, Wallace, was a principal teacher in Barangu.

On this day Peter Philip Valerio, Jr. was born in 1975. He is the son of Peter Valerio and Hermenehilda "Maria" Lopez. Peter died in 1998 in Belize City. Karon Valerio is the son of Peter with Andrea Middleton.

14th October

In the Catholic calendar today is the Feast Day of Saint Pope Callistus I.

Maura Makin was born on this day in Barangu. She is the daughter of Perfecto Makin and Vicenta "Lulu" Sanchez. She married a Macfarlane. Maria Loreta Palacio is the great-great-aunt of Maura.

Calistra Cayetano was born on this day in 1926 in Peine. She is the daughter of Steven Cayetano and Francisca Nunez. Calistra died in 1986 in Peine. The Ebu, Patrick Mariano, is the grandson of Calistra.

Inocente Zuniga died on this day in 1980 in Barangu. He is the son of Claro Zuniga and Mauricia Cayetano. Inocente was born in 1893 in Barangu. He is known as "Mafia" in the village. He married Luciana Nolberto in 1916 in Peine. Inocente played the transverse flute for the mumming play "Pia Manadi" which the Garifuna Community celebrates during the Christmas Season.

On this day Leonora Avila died in 1981 in Peine. She is the daughter of Pedro John Avila and Viviana Palacio. She was born in 1918 in Barangu. Leonora married Cipriano Arana in 1937 in Barangu. She spent her adult life as a mother and wife of a rural primary school teacher. Her granddaughter, **Nora Arana**, is named after her grandmother, Leonora. **Maria Loreta Palacio** is the first cousin once removed of Leonora.

15th October

Geoffrey Austin Arzu was born on this day. He is the son of **Candido Arzu** and **Bernadette Loredo**. Austin married **Suzette Staine** of Peine in 1988. Austin retired as an associate director of Peace Corps in Belize in 2010 and is now an education officer in Toledo District and a lecturer at the University of Belize. **Maria Loreta Palacio** is the great-great-aunt of Austin. Maria is also the first cousin thrice removed of Austin. Austin and Suzette have two children, **Kahle Austin Arzu** and **Kandese Auzette Arzu**, both students at the University of Arizona.

Edward Castillo was born on this day in 1939. He is the son of **Cornelio Castillo** and **Melvinia Martinez**. He is known as "Hapu" in the village. He died in 1996 in Barangu.

On this day **Kevaan Aranda** was born. He is the son of **Moses Aranda** and **Celestina Enriquez**. **Maria Loreta Palacio** is the first cousin five times removed. Kevaan is the grandson of **Vilma Petrona Chimilio**.

Ursula Arana died on this day in 1983 in Barangu. She is the daughter of **Alejandro Arana** and **Gregoria Bermudez**. She died in a dory on the way to Peine to get medical attention. Ursula was born in 1911 in Barangu. **Evilia Martinez nee Gonzalez** is the daughter of **Ursula Arana** and **Justo Gonzalez**.

On this day **Ascencion Zuniga** died in 1910 in Peine. He was buried in Labuga. Ascencion with **Eluteria Cayetano** fathered **John Jacob Zuniga**. The family say that **Ascencion Zuniga** is from Labuga. Father Lyman S.J. says in Ascencion's Last Rites form that he lived in Labuga but was a Peine "native." This would indicate that Ascencion is likely the brother of **Claro Zuniga** and **Natividad Zuniga** and the son of **Mariano Zuniga**.

16th October

Secundino Joseph Martinez and **Anastacia Vicenta Santiago** were married on this day in 1929 in Peine. Secundino is the son of **Saturnino "Senerial" Martinez** and **Josefa Paulino**. Anastacia is the daughter of **Raymond Santiago** and **Marcelina Pamfila Servio**. Secundino later married **Bonifacio Avilez** in 1969 in Orange Walk.

Magdalena Cesaria died in 1910 in Barangu. She married **Anastacio Palacio**. According to the government death records Magdalena was 65 when she died. In my database I have 350 descendants of Magdalena

and there are many more that I do not have. She is definitely one of the "mothers of Barangu."

Stanislao Reyes died in 1901 in Barangu. He is the son of **Martin Reyes** and **Luisa Roches**. Stanislao was born in 1889. He is the great-great-uncle of **Egbert Anthony Valencio** and the great-uncle of E. **Roy Cayetano**.

17th October

Simon Mejia and **Andrea Nicholas** were married on this day in 1890 in Barangu. Simon is the son of **Nicolas Mejia**. Andrea is the daughter of **Leoncio Nicholas** and **Christina Garcia**. **Angela Palacio** and **Sebastian Cayetano** are the great grandchildren of Simon and Andrea.

On this day **Alejandro Arana** and **Gregoria Bermudez** were married in 1915 in Barangu. Alejandro is the son of **Dioncio Arana** and **Basilia Labriel**. Gregoria is the daughter of **Narciso Bermudez** and **Dominga "Gadu" Marin**. **Eulalia "Lala" Arana** and **Frank Dean Arana** are children of Alejandro and Gregoria.

Pablo Baltazar and **Adriana Lauriano** were married on this day in 1945 in Dangriga. Pablo is the son of **Augustin "Ding" Baltazar** (the famous buyei of Chewecha) and **Faustina Mariano**. Adriana is the daughter of **Thomas Charles Lauriano** and **Concepcion Mejia**. **Valentina Marin nee Baltazar** is the daughter of Pablo and Adriana.

Vicenta Blas was born on this day in 1899 in Barangu. She is the daughter of **Macario Blas** and **Leonarda Nunez**. Vicenta married **Eusebio Santino** in 1922 in Barangu. She died in 1991 in Barangu. **Clifford Marin** is the grandson of Vicenta. **Jacinta Trigueno nee Santino** is the daughter of Vicenta.

On this day in 1899 **Cristobel Loredo** was born in Barangu. She is the daughter of **Eulalio Loredo** and **Gregoria Palacio**. She married **Pablo Jimenez** in 1922 in Peine. She later married **Solomon Velasquez** in 1925 in Peine. **Henry Loredo** is her brother. **Maria Loreta Palacio** is the first cousin once removed of Cristobel. **Elisa Ariola** is the great-granddaughter of Cristobel.

Verona Valerie Arzu was born on this day in Belize City. She is the daughter of **Conrad Allen Arzu** and **Martina Norma Martinez**. Verona's parents are second cousins once removed. **Maria Loreta Palacio** is the great-great-great-aunt of Verona. **Maria Loreta Palacio** is also the great-great-aunt of Verona. **Maria Loreta Palacio** is also the first cousin four times removed of Verona. Verona is related to **Maria Loreta Palacio** two ways on her father's side and one way on her mother's side.

18th October

Eduviges Ramirez was born on this day in 1926 in Barangu. She is the daughter of **Bonifacio Ramirez** and **Evangelista Nunez**. Eduviges is known as "Auntie Bia" in the village. **Maria Loreta Palacio** is the great-aunt of Eduviges. **Catarino Claude Zuniga** is the son of Eduviges.

Eduviges "Auntie Bia" Ramirez

Alejandro Palacio was born on this day in 1938 in Tiquisate, Wadimalu. He is the son of **Alejandro Palacio** and **Sarah Cayetano**. Alejandro's parents are first cousin once removed. **Maria Loreta Palacio** is the great-aunt of Alejandro and also the great-grandmother of Alejandro.

On this day **Lucas Lucas** was born in 1901 in Peine. He is the son of **Joseph Robert Lucas** and **Alfonsa Gabriel**. **John Nipalmson Lucas** is the brother of Lucas. Lucas is the great-uncle of **Father Callistus Cayetano**.

Santos Leon Avila and **Elogia Cacho** were married on this day in 1938 in Peine. Santos is the son of **Pantaleon Avila** and **Juliana Garcia**. Elogia is the daughter of **Mariano Cacho** and **Matilda Gonzalez**.

Peter Egbert Hernandez and **Paula Serano** were married on this day in 1944 in Belize City. Peter and Paula are the maternal grandparents of Surusia **Peitra Arana**.

19th October

Solomon Marin was born on this day in 1926 in Barangu. He is the son of **Aparicio Santiago Marin** and **Brigida Paulino**. He married **Ruth Flowers**. **Maria Loreta Palacio** is the first cousin twice removed of Solomon. **Angela Palacio** is the niece of Solomon.

On this day in 1904 a set of twins, **Pedro Palacio** and **Virgen Palacio**, were born in Barangu. As was often the case with twins in those days soon after they were born they died. They were the children of **Hipolito Palacio** and **Josefa Zuniga**. **Maria Loreta Palacio** is the first cousin once removed of Pedro and Virgen. **Ruben Palacio** is the brother of Pedro and Virgen.

Evangelista Lino, also known as **Bonifacia Ramirez** was born on this day in 1918 in Peine. She is the daughter of **Lino Enriquez** and **Nazaria Zuniga**. Evangelista's mother was very much involved with the church in Barangu and led the "Posada" pageant in the village. Evangelista is the aunt of **Victor "Bobby" Arana**.

Maria Cayetano was born on this day in 1843 in Labuga. She is the daughter of **Juan Pedro Cayetano** and **Maria Nicolasa Moralez**. Maria Cayetano is the great-great-great-aunt of **E. Roy Cayetano**.

20th October

In the Catholic calendar today is the Feast Day of St. Irene of Tomar.

Sotero Arana and **Epifania Loredo** were married on this day in 1917 in Peine. Sotero is the son of **Dionisio Arana** and **Basilia Labriel**. Epifania is the daughter of **Eulalio Loredo** and **Gregoria Palacio**. Epifania is the mother of **Gladys Clarice Lino nee Loredo**.

Luis Tomas Leopoldo Cayetano and **Florencia Lopez** were married on this day in 1868 in Labuga. Luis is the son of **Juan Pedro Cayetano** and **Maria Celestina** (unknown last name). Florencia is the daughter of **Juan Guadalupe Lopez** and **Jacoba Mauricia** (unknown last name). Luis is the great great-great-uncle of Evan Cayetano.

Irene Gibbons (2009)

On this day in 1920 **Irene Gibbons** was born in Barangu. She is the daughter of **Steven Gibbons** and **Paula Paulino**. Irene is the oldest living person in the village. She is the mother of **Naomi Colon** and **Felicia Casimiro nee Arzu**.

Madeline Loredo was born on this day in Barangu. She is the daughter of **Henry Loredo** and **Ursula Polonio**. **Maria Loreta Palacio** is the first cousin twice removed of Madeline. **Bernadette Arzu nee Loredo** is the sister of Madeline.

On this day in 1892 **Francisco Nolberto** was born in Barangu. He is the son of **Macario Nolberto** and **Josefa Alvarez**. **Francisco Nolberto** was named after his grandfather, **Francisco Nolberto**, who was one of the first settlers of Barangu. Francisco is the first cousin once removed of **Paula Nolberto**.

Cancio Avila was born on this day in 1919 in Peine. He is the son of **Alcardio Avila** and **Justa Gonzalez**. Cancio is the uncle of **Rita Enriquez nee Avila**.

21st October

In the Catholic calendar today is the Feast Day of St. Ursula.

Ursula Arana was born on this day in 1911 in Barangu. She is the daughter of **Alejandro Arana** and **Gregoria Bermudez**. Ursula died in 1983 in Barangu. **Evilia Martinez nee Gonzalez** is the daughter of Ursula.

Ursula Arana was born on this day in 1906 in Peine. She is the daughter of **Concepcion Arana** and **Simeona Flores**. Ursula married **Cipriano Nicholas** in 1933. Ursula is the mother of **William "Country" Nicholas** who taught school for a while in Barangu.

On this day in Peine **Cecilia Joseph** was born. She is the daughter of **Ambrosio Joseph** and **Petrona "Peti" Palacio**. **Maria Loreta Palacio** is the great-great-aunt of Cecilia.

Ursulus Polonio was born on this day in 1886 in Peine. He is the son of **Eusebio Polonio** and **Lucia Ordonez**. Ursulus is the uncle of **Bartolo Polonio**.

On this day in 1920 **Ursula Martinez** was born in Peine. She is the daughter of **Victoriano Martinez** and **Isabela Zuniga**. Ursula married **Faustino Zuniga** in 1920 in Peine. **Crispino Martinez** is the brother of Ursula. **Liborio Martinez** is the grandfather of Ursula.

22nd October

Mary Flores (*right*) was born on this day in 1928 in Barangu. She is the daughter of **Candido Flores** and **Isidora Bermudez**. She married **Gonzalez Casimiro** in 1944. They had eleven children. Mary died in 2012 in Barangu. Mary is the sister of **Procopio Flores**. **Julius Casimiro** is the son of Mary.

Ursula Polonio was born on this day in 1909 in Barangu. She is the daughter of **Apolonio Polonio** and **Damiana Garcia**. Ursula married **Henry Loredo** in 1928. She is the mother of **Hector Loredo** (Alvin Loredo's father) and **Margaret Buckley**. **Bartolo Polonio** is the first cousin of Ursula.

Toribia Garcia died on this day in 1994 in Belize City. She is the daughter of **Bonifacio Garcia** and **Geronima Martinez**. Toribia was born in 1934. She was known as "Junic" in the village. She married **Eustacio Alvarez** in 1961. Rhoda, Zita, Sadie and Emily are daughters of Toribia.

23rd October

Petrona Ariola was born on this day in Barangu. She is the daughter of **Catarino Patricio Ariola** and **Virginia Garcia**. Petrona is the mother of **Paul Hudson Casimiro**. **Jacinta Palacio** is the niece of Petrona.

Yvonne Carmen Arana was born on this day in Belize City. She is the daughter of **Francisco Bonifacio "Frank" Arana** and **Narcisa Esther Contreras**. Yvonne married **Johnny Baltazar** in 1982. Her father was a farm demonstrator in Barangu.

24th October

In the Catholic calendar today is the Feast Day of St. Irene of Tomar.

Bernardo Casimiro was born on this day in 1918 in Barangu. He is the son of **Pablo Casimiro** and **Bernadina Nolberto**. Bernardo is the brother of **Gonzalez Casimiro** and the first cousin once removed of **Alvin Loredo**.

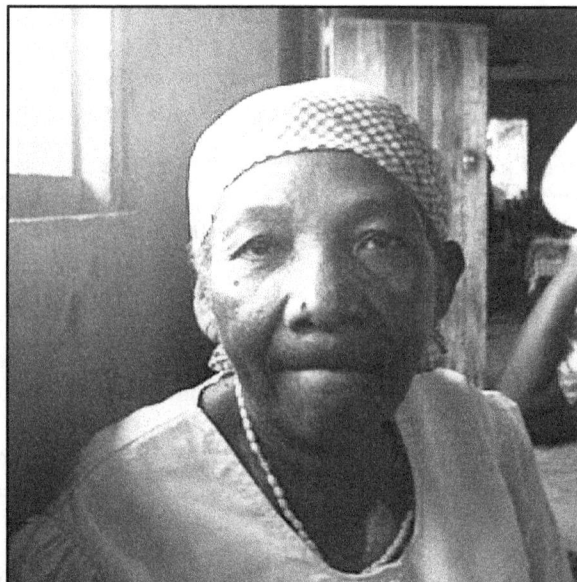

Mary Casimiro nee Flores (2009)

On this day **Nadeth Michelle Martinez** was born in San Ignacio. She is the daughter of **Michael Alejandro Martinez** and **Hazel Elinor Arzu**. **Maria Loreta Palacio** is the great-great-great-aunt and the first cousin four times removed of Nadeth.

Matea Paulino died on this day in 1931 in Peine. She is the daughter of **Augustin "Big Ease" Paulino** and **Juana Luis**. Matea was born in 1899 in Barangu. Merejilda and Henrietta Blanco are daughters of Matea.

25th October

In the Catholic calendar today is the Feast Day of St. Daria.

Evaristo Nunez was born on this day in 1909 in Peine. He is the son of **Francisco Nunez** and **Martina "Obispa" Martinez**. Evaristo married **Alexine Loredo** in 1938 in Barangu. Evaristo is known as "Bob Steele" in Barangu. **Elorine Nunez** is the daughter of Evaristo.

On this day **Darius Avila** was born in Peine. He is the son of **Cirilo Avila** and **Olivia Prudencia Palacio**. He married **Lisa Woodye**. **Maria Loreta Palacio** is the great-great-aunt of Darius. Darius started the Garifuna celebratory event "The Battle of the Drums" held each year in Peine in November.

Raphael Bernardez was born on this day in 1905 in Barangu. He is the son of **Agapito Bernardez** and **Venancia Nolberto**. **Anacleta "Da Cleta" Nolberto** is the first cousin once removed of Raphael.

On this day **Estela Barcelona** was born in 1914 in Peine. She is the daughter of **Isabel Barcelona** and **Fecunda Gabriel**. Estela married **Estevan Bardalez** in 1962 in Peine. Estela is the sister of Victoria Martinez nee Barcelona. **Elma Yvonne Arzu nee Martinez** is the niece of Estela.

26th October

Victor Enriquez and **Vilma Petrona Chimilio** were married on this day in 1981. Victor is from Honduras. Vilma is the daughter of **Timoteo Chimilio** and **Geronima Martinez**. **Celestina Enriquez** is the daughter of Victor and Vilma.

Rafael Zuniga was born on this day in 1891 in Peine. He is the son of **Claro Zuniga** and **Mauricia Cayetano**. Rafael married **Catarina Paulino** in 1916 in Peine. Inocente "Mafia" Zuniga is the brother of Rafael. **Felix Zuniga** and **Marcelo Zuniga** are children of Rafael.

On this day **Bernice Norma Arzu** was born in Barangu. She is the daughter of **Conrad Allen Arzu** and **Martina Norma Martinez**. **Maria Loreta Palacio** is the great-great-great-aunt and the first cousin four times removed of Bernice.

Cynthia Leanne Cayetano was born on this day in Barangu. She is the daughter of **Wallace Secundino Cayetano** and **Martina Lorraine Arzu**. **Maria Loreta Palacio** is the great-great-great-aunt and the first cousin four times removed of Cynthia.

27th October

Sabina Benguche was born on this day in Peine in 1910. She is the daughter of **Gregorio Benguche** and **Sabina Gonzalez**. Sabina is the sister of **Diega Benguche** with a different mother.

28th October

Cirilo Avila was born on this day in 1928 in Peine. He is the son of **Alcardio Avila** and **Justa Gonzalez**. Cirilo married **Olivia Prudencia Palacio** in 1995 in Peine. He died in 1997 in Peine. **Rita Enriquez nee Avila** is the daughter of Cirilo.

Cleon Castillo was born on this day in Dangriga. He is the son of **Peter Castillo** and **Anastacia Christina Ramirez**. **Maria Loreta Palacio** is the first cousin four times removed of Cleon.

Marco Trigueno was born on this day in Puerto Barrios. He is the son of **Isidro Trigueno** and **Paula Martinez**. **Melvinia "Grandma Mi" Martinez** is the aunt of Marco.

On this day **Serafina Alvarez** was born. She is the daughter of **Feliciano "Felix" Alvarez** and **Pantaleona Mejia**. Serafina is the sister of **Angelina "Angie" Nicholas nee Alvarez**.

29th October

In the Catholic calendar today is the Feast Day of Saint Narcissus of Jerusalem.

Narciso Arana was born on this day in 1917 in Barangu. He is the son of **Alejandro Arana** and **Gregoria Bermudez**. Narciso is the brother of **Eulalia Arana**.

Narcisa Esther Contreras was born on this day in 1935. She is the daughter of **Marcos Contreras** and **Cornelia Petillo**. Narcisa married **Francisco Bonifacio "Frank" Arana** in Peine in 1955. Narcisa died in 2005 in California. **Pia Arana nee Magdelano** is the first cousin of Narcisa.

On this day **Alfonsa Arana** was born in Peine. She is the daughter of **Adriano Natividad Arana** and **Basilia Luis**. **Joy Melanie Cayetano** and **Kendra Cayetano** are children of Alfonsa.

Elia Chimilio was born on this day in 1928 in Barangu. She is the daughter of **Marcial Chimilio** and **Inocenta Nicholas**. Surusia **Bertie Chimilio** is the nephew of Elia.

Prajedes Palacio died on this day in 1997 in Peine. She is the daughter of **Nolberto Palacio** and **Nieves Juarez**. Prajedes was born in 1900 in Barangu. She married **Ernest Bernard** in Peine in 1928. **Maria Loreta Palacio** is the aunt of Prajedes. **Clifford King** is the grandson of Prajedes.

Braulio Ariola died on this day in 1899 in Barangu. He is the son of **Daniel Ariola** and **Alberta Nicholas**. Seven months earlier he was born in Barangu. **Francisco "Chico" Ariola** is the first cousin once removed of Braulio.

30th October

In the Catholic calendar today is the Feast Day of Saint Claudius of Leon.

Claudio Martinez was born on this day in 1904 in Barangu. He is the son of **Ireneo Martinez** and Bernardina Santino. He died in 1940 in Quiriguá. His body was transported to Peine and then the "Heron H" brought it to Barangu to be buried. Claudio is the father of **Victoriana "Vicky" Martinez nee Nolberto**.

On this day **Claudio Ariola** was born in 1890 in Barangu. He is the son of **Rufino Ariola** and **Ascenciona Paulino**. Ascenciona's parents are **Dominga "Waganga" Cayetano** and **Diego Paulino**, who were among the pioneers of Barangu. Claudio died 15 months later in Jan of 1892 in Barangu. Claudio is the great-uncle of **Francisco "Chico" Ariola**.

Claudio Lambey was born on this day in 1912 in Peine. He is the son of **Severiano Lambey** and **Romana Arana**. **Gregoria Nolberto** is the grandmother of Claudio. **Paula Nolberto** is the second cousin of Claudio.

Lisani Emmuel Davimar Alvarez was born on this day in Peine. She is the daughter of **David Alvarez** and **Martina "Mamita" Cordella Palacio**. **Maria Loreta Palacio** is the great-great-great-aunt of Lisani. **Maria Loreta Palacio** is also the first cousin six times removed of Lisani.

31st October

Lucille Luciana Zuniga was born on this day in Barangu. She is the daughter of Inocente Zuniga and Luciana Nolberto. She is know as "Chilagu" in the village. She married **Raymond Valencio** in Barangu. **Egbert Anthony Valencio** is the son of Lucille.

Lucille "Chilagu" Valencio nee Zuniga (2004)

Lucila Arana was born on this day in 1920 in Peine. She is the daughter of **Concepcion Arana** and **Simeona Flores**. Lucila is know as "Shuna." She married **Evaristo Melendrez** in 1941. **Dative Elizabeth Martinez nee Melendrez** is the daughter of Lucila.

On this day **Luciana Nolberto** died in 1961 in Barangu. She is the daughter of **Pio Nolberto** and **Casimira Nicholas**. Luciana was born in 1896 in Barangu. She married **Inocente Zuniga** in 1916 in Barangu. **Valerie Delcy Tuttle nee Valencio** is the granddaughter of Luciana.

Isidora Bermudez died on this day in 1950 in Barangu. She is the daughter of **Narciso Bermudez** and **Dominga "Gadu" Marin**. Isidora was born in 1887 in Barangu. **Procopio "Prook" Flores** is the son of Isidora.

Marcos Oliver Casimiro died on this day in 1983. He is the son of **Gonzalez Casimiro** and **Mary Flores**. He was born in 1945 in Barangu. Marcos is the father of **Melquiades Julius "Jimbo" Loredo**.

Timoteo Lorenzo died on this day in 1961 in Barangu. Timoteo is the son of **Manuel Lorenzo** and **Rubeajia Fuentes**. Timoteo married **Juana "Jane" Palacio** in 1903 in Barangu. **Victoriano "Fada" Lorenzo** is the son of Timoteo.

Rasheed Hassan Palacio was born on the 31 October. He is the son of **Clifford Joseph Marin** and Beth Palacio. **Maria Loreta Palacio** is the first cousin four times removed of Rasheed.

NOVEMBER

1st November

Rudy Concepcion Arana and **Mildred Hernandez** were married in 1969 in Belize City. Rudy is the son of **Eulalio "Bidun" Arana** and **Gregoria "Gogo" Paulino**. Mildred is the daughter of **Peter Egbert Hernandez** and **Paula Serano**. Surusia **Peitra Arana** is the daughter of Rudy and Mildred.

On this day **Justina Casimiro** was born. She is the daughter of **Erasmo Casimiro** and **Paula Noralez**. Justina is the older sister of **Ricorda Geraldine Casimiro**.

Santos Arzu was born on this day in 1904 in Peine. He is the son of **Juan Bautista Arzu** and **Obispa Florentina Paulino**. Santos taught school in Barangu for a time.

Eustaquia Palacio was born on this day in 1871 in Barangu. She is the daughter of **Teodoro "Joe Young" Palacio** and **Tomasa Martinez**. Eustaquia married **Carmen Ramirez** in 1889 in Barangu. **Maria Loreta Palacio** is the sister of Eustaquia. **Catarino "Claudi" Zuniga** is the great-grandson of Eustaquia. **Erick "Moon" Moreira** is the great-great-grandson of Eustaquia.

Ricardo Ramirez was born on this day in 1931. He is the son of **Bonifacio Ramirez** and **Evangelista Nunez**. He died in Guatemala City and was buried in Labuga. Ricardo is the brother of **Eduviges "Auntie Bea" Ramirez**.

2nd November

On this day **Angus Claude Cayetano** and **Adela Jaime** were married in Dangriga in 1949. Angus is the son of **Gregorio Cayetano** and **Teofila Flores**. Adela is from Dangriga. Angus was a bookkeeper, accountant and a lay minister in the Methodist church. During WWII he served in the Panama Canal Zone. He was appointed a Justice of the Peace in 1992. Angus and Adela had ten children.

Teofila Palacio was born on this day in 1905. She is the daughter of **Luis Palacio** and **Felipa Garcia**. Teofila married **James Martinez** of Dangriga in 1942. **Maria Loreta Palacio** is the aunt of Teofila.

On this day **Daisy Mae Valencio** was born in Barangu. She is the daughter of **Raymond Valencio** and **Luciana Zuniga**. **Maria Loreta Palacio** is the first cousin thrice removed of Mae. **Alvin Zuniga** is the sister of Mae.

3rd November

Leonard Petillo's granddaughter **Shay Petillo** was born on this day in Los Angeles. Shay is the daughter of **Martin Petillo** and **Marge Avila**. She is the granddaughter of **Olivia Prudencia Avila nee Palacio** and the third cousin twice removed of **Egbert Valencio**.

On this day in 1930 **Dominga Cayetano** died at the age of 81. She is the daughter of **Juan Pedro Cayetano**. **Irene Gibbons** is her great-granddaughter. Dominga was known as "Waganga" in the village.

Salvatore Basil "S.B." Daniels was born on this day in 1898. He is the son of **Miguel Daniels** and **Tomasa Martinez**. S.B. died in Belize City in 1963. He was the principal teacher at St Joseph RC Primary School in Barangu from the mid-1930's until 1950. Mr. Daniels and his wife had 14 children. Maestro Daniels was named after Salvatore DiPietre, S.J., an Italian Jesuit who served in Belize after being expelled from Guatemala. This explains the Italian form of his first name.

Pascual Paulino was born on this day in 1904 in Barangu. He is the son of **Eugenio Paulino** and **Nicolasa Zuniga**. **Natividad Zuniga** is the grandfather of Pascual. **Clotildo Zuniga** is the first cousin of Pascual.

Denzel Miller died on this day in 1989 in Belize City. He is the father of **Joycelyn Miller**.

4th November

In the Catholic calendar today is the Feast Day of St. Charles (Carlo) Borromeo.

Felipa Carlota Marin died on this day in 1995 in Belize City. She is the daughter of **Aparicio Santiago Marin** and **Brigida Paulino**. Carlota was born in 1916 in Barangu. She married **Joseph Pollard Palacio**. **Maria Loreta Palacio** is the first cousin twice removed of Carlota. **Bridget Palacio nee Marin** is the sister of Carlota. **Linda Arana nee Lopez** is the daughter of Carlota. Carlota is the second cousin once removed of **Alvin Loredo**

Pedro Nicasio Martinez and **Augustina Nunez** were married on this day in 1907. Pedro is the son of **Pedro Martinez** and **Regina Virgen Luis**. Augustina is the daughter of **Martin Nunez** and **Ascenciona "Da Sola" Paulino**. "Da Sola" got her nickname from her great voice and her quick ability to sing "do re me fa so la ti do." Pedro and Augustina are the parents of **Melvinia "Grandma Mi" Martinez**.

Carlos Palacio was born on this day in 1902 in Barangu. He is the son of **Luis Palacio** and **Felipa Garcia**. **Maria Loreta Palacio** is the aunt of Carlos.

Emily Ramirez nee Martinez who taught school in Barangu for a time. She is the granddaughter of Carlos.

Carlos Martinez was born on this day in 1911 in Peine. He is the son of **Victoriano Martinez** and **Isabela Zuniga**. Carlos married **Pantaleona Valentine** in 1936 in Peine. Carlos is the brother of **Crispino Martinez**.

5th November

Govel Morgan, Sr., died on this day in 1999 in Peine. He is the son of **Modesto Morgan** and **Anastacia Figueroa**. Grovel was born in 1922 in Commerce Bight. Govel was a school teacher and one of the first group of Garifuna school teachers to attend St. John's College. His son Govel operates "Wamalali Radio" in Peine.

Mary Martha Cayetano was born on this day in 1921 in Barangu. She is the daughter of **Pascacio Cayetano** and **Eustaquia Satuye**. Mary was known as "Nurse Petillo." She was the first trained nurse from Barangu. She was married to **Leonard Petillo** in 1959 in Crique Sarco. **Maria Loreta Palacio** is the grandmother of Mary. She is the mother of **Sheridan Arzu nee Petillo**.

Simon Martinez and Ambrosine Mejia were married on this day in 1938 in Barangu. Simon is the son of **Francisco Martinez** and **Estefania Avila**. Ambrosine is the daughter of **Simon Mejia** and **Nicolasa Palacio**. Simon went to Scotland to work cutting lumber to support the war effort. Simon is the brother of **Francis Benedict Martinez**.

Valentino Castro and Michaela Lorenzo were married on this day in 1933 in Barangu. Valentino is the son of **Leon Castro** and **Victoriana Arana**. Michaela is the daughter of **Timoteo Lorenzo** and **Juana "Jane" Palacio**.

On this day **Pio Nolberto** and **Florencia Blas** were married in 1903 in Barangu. Pio is the son of **Francisco Nolberto** and **Francisca Serapia** (unknown last name). Florencia is the daughter of **John Blas**. This was Pio's second marriage. His first was to **Casimira Nicholas** in 1883 in Barangu. Pio also married a third time to **Cipriana Gregorio** in 1921 in Peine.

Benito Chimilio and Saturnina Palacio were married on this day in 1903 in Barangu. Benito is the son of **Antonio Chimilio**. Saturnina is the daughter of **Anastacio Palacio** and **Sotera Gutierrez**. **Marcial Chimilio** is the son of Benito and Saturnina. **Elia Chimilio** is the granddaughter of Benito and Saturnina.

On this day **Diega Benguche** was born in 1893 in Peine. She is the daughter of **Gregorio Benguche** and **Teofila "Wana" Martinez**. At one point in her life Diega immigrated to Wadimalu though we see later her returning to the Colony. Diega, like so many other women of that period, also moved to a few mahogany banks in Belize with her spouse. Diega is the grandmother of **Eugenia "Jean" Zuniga nee Noralez**.

Diega Benguche

Conrad Allen Arzu was born on this day. He is the son of **Candido Arzu** and **Bernadette Loredo**. Conrad married **Martina Norma Martinez**. Conrad retired from the Customs Department. **Bernice Norma Arzu** is the child of Conrad.

Perfecta Avilez was born on this day in 1907. She is the daughter of **John Justo Avilez** and **Paula Noralez**. Perfecta married **Ignacio Nicholas** in 1925 in Barangu. Perfecta is the great-granddaughter of **Santiago "Gaünbü" Avilez**, who is the founder of Barangu.

On this day **Lacaria Casimiro** was born in Barangu in 1925. She is the daughter of **Pablo Casimiro** and **Bernadina Nolberto**. Lacaria is the sister of **Gonzalez Casimiro**.

6th November

In the Catholic calendar today is the Feast Day of Sts. Leonard of Limoges and Leonard Reresby.

On this day in 1997 **Margarita Lorenzo** died in Peine at the age of 88. She is the daughter of **Timoteo Lorenzo** and **Juana "Jane" Palacio**. Margarita married **Paul Casimiro** in 1933 in Barangu. **Maria Loreta**

Palacio is the aunt of Margarita. Margarita is the mother of **Jovita Casimiro**.

On this day in 1924 **Leonard Petillo** was born in Peine. He was the son of **Bonifacio Petillo** and **Carmen Enriquez**. He was known as "Mr. Pete." Leonard married **Mary Martha Cayetano** in 1959 in Crique Sarco. He captained a boat in the late 1980's that transported Baranguna between Barangu and Peine before the all-weather road was completed. **Sheridan Petillo** Arzu is his daughter.

Arieni Arzu was born on this day in New York City. She is the daughter of **Stephen Arzu** and **Elida Palacio**. Arieni's parents are fourth cousins once removed. **Maria Loreta Palacio** is the great great-great-grandmother of Arieni. **Maria Loreta Palacio** is also the first cousin five times removed of Arieni. **Vilma Petrona Chimilio** is the grandmother of Arieni.

7th November

In the Catholic calendar today is the Feast Day of Saint Florentius of Strasburg.

Cosme Petillo and **Francisca Avilez** were married on this day in 1894 in Peine. Cosme is the son of **Juan Petillo** and (unknown first name) **Luis**. Francisca is the daughter of **Justo Avilez**. Francisca is the granddaughter of **Santiago "Gaünbü" Avilez**, the founder of Barangu. **Narcisa Esther Contreras** is the granddaughter of Cosme and Francisca.

Florentina Avila was born on this day in 1920 in Peine. She is the daughter of **Alcardio Avila** and **Justa Gonzalez**. She married **Santiago Martinez** in 1945 in Peine. She married **Crispino Martinez** in 1996 in Peine. Florentina is the aunt of **Rita Enriquez nee Avila**

Florentina "Flora" Avila

Alicia Ariola was born on this day. She is the daughter of **Nicholas Ariola**. Alicia is the first cousin of **Francisco "Chico" Ariola**.

On this day **Lloyd Casimiro** was born in Barangu. He is the son of **Gonzalez Casimiro** and **Mary Flores**. Lloyd is the brother of Fermin "The Millionaire" Casimiro.

Nerisa Marla Gutierrez was born on this day in Belize City. She is the daughter of **Steven Gutierrez** and **Valentina "Flora" Lorenzo**. Maria Loreta Palacio is the great-great-aunt of Nerisa. **Steven "Junior" Gutierrez** is the brother of Nerisa.

Alfonsa Zuniga died on this in 1939 in Belize City. She is the daughter of **Inocente Zuniga** and **Luciana Nolberto**. She was born in 1920 in Peine. She married **Eugenio Cayetano** in 1938 in Barangu.

Juslin Nunez died on this day in 1996 in Belize City. He is the son of **Mackie Nunez** and **Joycelyn Miller**. He was born in 1991 in Belize City. **Maria Loreta Palacio** is the great-great-great-aunt of Juslin.

8th November

Merline Alvarez was born on this day in Peine. She is the daughter of **Simon Aloysius Alvarez** and **Phyllis Palacio**. Merline's parents are related two ways. Simon and Phyllis are third cousins and third cousins once removed. **Maria Loreta Palacio** is the great-great-aunt of Merline and the first cousin once removed of Merline and the great-great-grandmother of Merline.

Kevin York Marin was born on this day in Los Angeles. He is the son of **Gilbert Marin** and **Valentina Baltazar**. Maria Loreta Palacio is the first cousin four times removed of Kevin. **Clifford Marin** is the uncle of Kevin.

On this day **Severiano Nicholas** was born in 1925 in Barangu. He is the son of **Philip Nicholas** and **Fabiana Palacio**. Maria Loreta Palacio is the first cousin once removed of Severiano.

9th November

In the Catholic calendar today is the Feast day of St. Theodor Tiro of Euchaita.

Macario Blas and **Leonarda Nunez** were married on this day in 1910 in Barangu. Leonarda is the daughter of **Thomas Nunez** and **Francisca** (unknown last name). **Clifford Marin** is the great-grandson of Macario and Leonarda. **Jarreen J. Ramos** is the great-great-great-granddaughter of Macario and Leonarda. Macario returned to Honduras and died in Travesia in 1948.

Teodora Nicholas was born on this day in 1904 in Barangu. She is the daughter of **Sotero Nicholas** and **Paula Nunez**. Teodora married **Joseph Givera** in 1933 in Barangu. Teodora is the aunt of **Frederick Nicholas** and the great-aunt of **Erlinda "Delane" Ogaldez nee Nicholas**.

Nahyil Arana was born on this day. He is the son of **Francis Arana** and **Helen Reynolds**. Nahyil is the grandson of **Francisco Bonifacio "Frank" Arana**.

On this day **Karlon Evin Guerra** was born in Belmopan. He is the son of **Carlos Guerra** and **Opal Arzu**. Karlon is the grandson of **Candido Arzu** and **Bernadette Loredo**.

10th November

In the Catholic calendar today is the Feast Day of St. Andrew Avellino.

Alice Nicholas was born on this day in Barangu. She is the daughter of **Ignacio Nicholas** and **Josephine Palacio**. Alice married **Dionisio Casimiro**. **Maria Loreta Palacio** is the great-great-aunt of Alice.

Andres Patricio Enriquez was born on this day in 1886 in Peine. He is the son **Joseph Victoriano Enriquez** and **Maria Genera Colindres**. He was known as "A.P." Andres married **Jane Victoriana Villafranco** in 1912 in Peine. **A.P. Enriquez** taught primary school for many years in San Antonio. **Jerry Enriquez** is the grandson of Andres.

11th November

In the Catholic calendar today is the Feast Day of St. Martin of Tours.

Marthy "Marti" Arana was born on this day in Barangu. She is the daughter of **Cipriano Arana** and **Leonarda Avila**. Marthy is the daughter of a rural primary school teacher so she grew up in a number of rural villages. She married **Bernard Cain** in 1995 in Belize City. **Maria Loreta Palacio** is the first cousin twice removed of Marthy.

Martina Castillo was born on this day in 1948. She is the daughter of **Cornelio Castillo** and **Melvinia Martinez**.

On this day **Martina Nunez** was born in 1932 in Barangu. She is the daughter of **Evaristo "Bob Steele" Nunez** and **Alexine Loredo**. **Elorine Nunez** is the sister of Martina.

Luis Tomas Leopoldo Cayetano was born in 1843. He was baptised in Santo Tomas. He is the son of **Juan Pedro Cayetano** and **Maria Celestina**. Luis Tomas was named Leopoldo after the king of Belgium. There had recently been a Belgian Colony in Santo Tomas. He married **Florencia Lopez** in 1868 in Labuga. Luis Tomas is the brother of **Anacleto Cayetano**.

12th November

In the pre-1969 Catholic calendar today is the Feast Day of Pope St. Martin.

Martin Martinez was born on this day in Barangu. He is the son of **Hipolito Martinez** and **Regina Lorenzo**. He married **Evilia Gonzalez** in 1970 in Belize City. **Maria Loreta Palacio** is the great-aunt of Martin.

Martina Norma Martinez was born on this day in 1941 in Barangu. She is the daughter of **Hipolito Martinez** and **Regina Lorenzo**. She married **Conrad Allen Arzu**. She died in 1980 in Belize City. **Maria Loreta Palacio** is the great-aunt of Martina.

Martin Victor Nicholas was born on this day in 1934 in Barangu. He is the son of **Victor Leonard Nicholas** and **Paulina Lopez**. He died in 2006 in Barangu. Martin, known as "Game and Gone," was a basket maker who spent a good bit of his life living in Seine Bight (his mother's home village) before returning to his home village of Barangu. **Maria Loreta Palacio** is the first cousin twice removed of Martin.

Martin Victor "Game and Gone" Nicholas (2005)

Martina Arzu was born on this day in 1870 in Peine. She is the daughter of **Augustin Arzu** and **Cayetana Gonzalez**. Martina first married **Anacleto Garcia** in 1890 in Peine. She then married **Augustin "Big Ease" Paulino** in 1902 in Peine. **John Paulino** is the son of Martina and Augustin.

On this day **Thomas Santino** was born in 1892 in Barangu. He is the son of **Philip Santino** and **Justina Cayetano**. Thomas is the brother of **Eusebio Santino** and **Escolastica "Ka" Martinez nee Santino**.

13th November

In the pre-1969 Catholic calendar today is the Feast Day of St. Stanislaus Kostka.

Derrick Zuniga was born on this day in Seine Bight. He is the son of **Henry Peter Zuniga** and **Sotera Moriera**. He married **Maria Casimiro** in 1988 in Peine. **Maria Loreta Palacio** is the first cousin thrice removed of Derrick.

Sotero Nicholas died on this day in 1943 in Barangu. He is the son of **Joseph Alexander Nicholas** and **Eugenia Delavez**. Sotero married **Paula Nunez**. He is the great-grandfather of **Erlinda "Delane" Ogaldez nee Nicholas**. Sotero had a large dory called the "Recuerdo" which travelled as far as Belize City carrying goods and passengers. **Sotero Nicholas** farmed up Boyo Creek.

Narciso Bermudez died on this day in 1888. He is the son of **Santiago Bermudez** and **Rosa Angela** (unknown last name). He was only 38 when died. He is one of the early unsung founders of Barangu. He had six daughters with **Dominga "Gadu" Marin**, his wife. **Erlinda "Delane" Ogaldez nee Nicholas** is the great-great-granddaughter of **Narciso**.

Pablo Nicholas and **Aniceta Blas** were married on this day in 1912 in Barangu. Pablo is the son of **Leoncio Nicholas** and **Christina Garcia**. Aniceta is the daughter of **Macario Blas** and **Leonarda Nunez**. **Alice Casimiro nee Nicholas** is the granddaughter of Pablo and Aniceta.

Pascacio Cayetano and **Apolinaria Mejia** were married on this day in 1912. Pascacio is the son of **Marcelo Cayetano** and **Maria Loreta Palacio**. Apolinaria is the daughter of **Simon Mejia** and **Andrea Nicholas**. This was Pascacio's first marriage, he also married **Eustaquia Satuye** in 1920 and **Ignacia "Inez" Arana** in 1939. Pascacio and Apoinaria had two children, **Francis Benedict Cayetano** and **Victoria Cayetano**. They were twins, Victoria died as an infant in a boating accident. **Joseph Cayetano**, former area representative for Toledo East, is the grandson of Pascacio and Apolinaria.

Godswell Casimiro was born on this day in Corozal. He is the son of **Dionisio Casimiro** and **Alice Nicholas**. **Maria Loreta Palacio** is the great-great-great-aunt of Godswell.

On this day **Estanislada Rodriguez** was born in 1910 in Barangu. She is the daughter of **Benjamin Rodriguez** and **Victoriana Santino**. She married **Victor Garcia** in 1935 in Peine. **Clifford Marin** is the first cousin once removed of Estanislada.

14th November

In the Catholic calendar today is the Feast Day of St. Serapion.

Victor Ramirez, the son of **Olga "Lettie" Ramirez** was born on this day in Puerto Barrios, Guatemala. **Maria Loreta Palacio** is the great-great-great-aunt of Victor.

Sylvia Coffin, the daughter of **Clarence "Cally" Coffin** and **Vilma Petrona Chimilio** was born on this day in Barangu. **Maria Loreta Palacio** is the first cousin four times removed of Sylvia. **Jarreen J. Ramos** is the daughter of Sylvia.

Serapia Cayetano was born on this day in 1923 in Barangu. She is the daughter of **Pascacio Cayetano** and **Eustaquia Satuye**. **Maria Loreta Palacio** is the grandmother of Serapia. She was the younger sister of **Mary Petillo nee Cayetano**.

On this day **Serapia Martinez** was born in 1916 in Peine. She is the daughter of **Victoriano Martinez** and **Isabela Zuniga**. Serapia is the sister of **Crispino Martinez**.

15th November

In the Catholic calendar today is the Feast Day of St. Eugene.

Eugenio Cayetano was born on this day in 1915 in Peine. He is the son of **Luis Cayetano** and **Paulina Reyes**. He married **Alfonsa Zuniga**, the daughter of **Inocente Zuniga**, in 1938 in Barangu. She died in childbirth and he then married **Manuela Marin** in 1941 in Barangu. Eugenio died in 1983 in Peine. Eugenio was a rural primary school teacher. **Evan Stephen Cayetano** is a son of Eugenio.

On this day **Tomasa Polonio** was born in 1907 in Monkey River. She is the daughter of **Pantaleon Odway Polonio** and Gertrude Lambey. She married **Jacob Palacio**, brother of **Ruben Palacio**. **Bartolo Polonio** is the first cousin of Tomasa.

Solomon Gibbons was born on this day in 1896 in Barangu. He is the son of **Isaac Gibbons** and **Ascenciona Paulino**. Solomon is the uncle of **Irene Gibbons**.

On this day **Clinton Martinez** was born in 1939. He is the son of **Simon Martinez** and **Ambrosine Mejia**. **Maria Loreta Palacio** is the first cousin twice removed of Clinton.

16th November

Maxima Ariola was born on this day in 1888. She is the daughter of Rufino Ariola and Ascenciona Paulino. Maxima married Isidro Arzu in 1903 in Barangu.

On this day in 1870 Martina Arzu was baptised in Peine. The Belgian priest, Father Jean Genon, the founder of the Peine Catholic Mission baptized her. Martina is the daughter of Augustin Arzu and Cayetana Gonzalez. She married her first husband, Anacleto Garcia on 27 February 1890 in Peine. She then married Augustin "Big Ease" Paulino on the 13th of August 1892 in Peine. This was his second marriage also. After his marriage to Martina, Augustin left Barangu with all his children to live in Peine with his new wife.

17th November

Aloysius Alan Palacio was born in 1932 in Barangu. He is the son of Joseph Pollard Palacio and Hilaria Mejia. He died when he was young. Maria Loreta Palacio is the great-aunt of Aloyius. Aloyius is the brother of Theodore Palacio.

Gertrude Petillo was born on this day in 1910 in Peine. She is the daughter of Bonifacio Petillo and Carmen Enriquez. Gertrude was known as "Babo." She married Luis "Butter" Zuniga in 1942 in Belize City.

18th November

In the Catholic calendar today is the Feast Day of St. Maximus.

Paula Paulino was born on this day in 1899 in Barangu. She is the daughter of Liborio Martinez and Francisca Cayetano. Paula is the mother of Irene Gibbons and the grandmother of Anthony "Tony" Alexander Ogaldez.

Cecilia Cayetano was born on this day in Hopkins. She is the daughter of E. Roy Cayetano and Judith Nunez. Maria Loreta Palacio is the first cousin four times removed of Celicia.

On this day Basilia Paulino was born in 1923 in Barangu. She is the daughter of Eugenio Paulino and Nicolasa Zuniga. Clotildo Zuniga is the first cousin of Basilia.

Maxima Lucas was born on this day in 1904 in Peine. She is the daughter of Ireneo Lucas and Gertrude Labriel.

19th November
Happy Garifuna Settlement Day!

Anastacio Reyes and Basilia Lucas were married on this day in 1944 in Barangu. Anastacio is the son of Martin Reyes and Luisa Roches. Basilia is the daughter of Fernando Lucas and Diega Benguche.

Serapia Avilez was born on this day in 1892 in Peine. She is the daughter of Ambrosio "Sabigi" Avilez and Justa Polonio. Santiago "Gaünbü" Avilez, the founder of Barangu, is the grandfather of Serapia. Serapia married Santiago Labriel in 1920 in Peine. Santiago taught school in Barangu.

Justo Gonzalez died on this day in 1964 in Labuga. He is the father-in-law of Irma Gonzalez nee Ariola. Justo was the father of Macario Gonzalez, Pablo Gonzalez and Evilia Martinez nee Gonzalez. Justo's wife was Ursula Arana.

Catalina Castillo died on this day in 1997 in Labuga. She married Procopio Arzu. Catalina is the mother of Surusia Francis Arzu.

Dionisia Marin nee Santino died on this day in Barangu. She is the daughter of Eusebio Santino and Vicenta Blas. Dionisia was born in 1922 in Barangu. She married Clarence Marin in 1967 in Barangu. She was known as "Nicha" and was known for making boola, a large ginger cookie. Anita Edwards nee Marin is the daughter of Dionisia.

20th November

Raynor Verne Valencio was born on this day in Belize City. He is the son of Leroy Bradley and Leolin Elma Valencio. Maria Loreta Palacio is the first cousin four times removed of Verne. Raymond Valencio is the grandfather of Verne.

Felix Zuniga was born on this day in 1915 in Barangu. He is the son of Rafael Zuniga and Catarina Paulino. Felix is the nephew of Inocente "Mafia" Zuniga.

On this day Casimiro Ariola died in 1901. He is the son of Patricio Ariola and Florencia Lambey. He was born in 1899. Casimiro is the great-great-uncle of Antonette Zuniga.

21st November

Leonarda Nicholas was born on this day in 1888 in Barangu. She is the daughter of Leoncio Nicholas and Cristina Garcia. Leonarda is the second cousin twice removed of Erlinda "Delane" Ogaldez nee Nicholas.

Randy Marfield was born on this day in Belize City. He is the son of Dalton Franklin and Marthy "Marti"

Arana. **Maria Loreta Palacio** is the first cousin thrice removed of Randy.

Presentacion Avila was born on this day in 1900 in Peine. She is the daughter of **Pantaleon Avila** and Nolasca Colindres. Presentacion is the first cousin of **Reginald Avila**.

Callistus Cayetano was born on this day in Orange Walk Town. He is the son of **Francis Benedict Cayetano** and **Florencia Lucas**. Callistus is an ordained Roman Catholic Diocesan priest, the first from Barangu. **Maria Loreta Palacio** is the great-grandmother of Callistus.

Callistus "Father Cal" Cayetano (2003)

22nd November

In the Catholic calendar today is the Feast Day of St. Cecilia.

Cecilio "Dick" Polonio was born in 1893 in Peine. He is the son of **Eusebio Polonio** and **Lucia Ordonez**. Cecilio married **Camila Contreras** in 1920 in Peine. He died in 1926 in Peine. Cecilio is the father of **Bartolo Polonio**.

On this day in Peine **Cecilio Ramirez** was born in 1901. He is the son of **Peter Ramirez** and **Juana Gonzalez**. Cecilio married **Matilda Arana** in 1928 in Peine. **Mauricio Linford "Linsy" Ramirez** is the son of Cecilio.

Cecilio Ramirez was born on this day in Newtown. He is the son of **Christino Ramirez** and **Perfecta Luis**. Cecilio married **Natividad Palacio** in 1969 in Hopkins Village. **Anastacia Christina Castillo nee Ramirez** is the daughter of Cecilio.

Cecilia Alvarez was born on this day in Barangu. She is the daughter of **Eustacio Alvarez** and **Lucille "Chilagu" Zuniga**. Cecilia is known as "Luncy" in the village. Cecilia married **Peter "Jack" Arzu**. **Alina Alvarez** is the daughter of Cecilia.

Cecilio Casimiro was born on this day in 1931 in Barangu. He is the son of **Paul Casimiro** and **Margarita Lorenzo**. **Maria Loreta Palacio** is the great-aunt of Cecilio. **Jovita Casimiro** is the sister of Cecilio.

Cecilia Flores was born on this day in 1887 in Barangu. She is the daughter of **Candido Flores** and **Isidora Bermudez**. Cecilia married **Estanislao Arzu** in 1934 in Barangu. She died in Belize City in 2005.

Clemencia was born on this day in 1931 in Barangu. She is the daughter of **Basilia Lucas**. Clemencia is the granddaughter of **Diega Benguche**.

Sotera Gutierrez died on this day in 1919 in Barangu. She is the mother of **Luisa Rochez** and also the mother of **Viviana Avila nee Palacio**. Sotera is the great-grandmother of **Marti Cain nee Arana**.

Apolonia Cayetano died on this day in Barangu in 2011. She is the daughter of **Zacarias Cayetano** and **Serapia Bonilla**. Apolonia was born in 1923 in Rio Tinto, Honduras. Apolonia is the great-grandmother of **Victor Ramirez**.

Yanira Cayetano was born on this day. She is the daughter of **Robert Cayetano** and **Beatrice Sanchez**. Yanira's parents are fourth cousins. **Maria Loreta Palacio** is the great-great-grandmother of Yanira. **Maria Loreta Palacio** is also the first cousin four times removed of Yanira.

23rd November

On this day in 2002 **Paul Casimiro** died in Barangu. He was the son of **Peter Casimiro** and **Petrona Ariola**. He was born in 1945 in Barangu. Paul was a fisherman in Barangu.

Allen Ariola was born on this day in 1977. He is the son of **Thelma Ariola**. Allan died in 2012 in Belize City. **Maria Loreta Palacio** is the great-great-great-aunt of Allan.

Jacqueline Regina Martinez was born on this day. She is the daughter of **Martin Martinez** and **Evilia Gonzalez**. In 1997 she married **Anthony Lopez** in Belize City. **Maria Loreta Palacio** is the great-great-aunt of Jacqueline.

24th November

Alvin Zuniga was born on this day in Barangu. He is the son of **Eustacio Alvarez** and **Lucille "Chilagu" Zuniga.** Alvin works for the Belize Customs Department.

Carmen Zuniga was born on this day in Barangu. She is the daughter of **Eugenia Jean Noralez** and **Clotildo Zuniga**. **Sharon Nunez** is the daughter of Carmen. Carmen now lives in Peine.

Timoteo Lorenzo and **Juana "Jane" Palacio** were married on this day in 1903 in Barangu. Timoteo is the son of **Manuel Lorenzo** and **Maria Rovidia Fuentes**. Juana is the daughter of **Teodoro "Joe Young" Palacio** and **Petrona Cayetano**. **Steven Gutierrez** is the great-grandson of Timoteo and Juana.

Silverio Enriquez and **Marcelina Avilez** were married on this day in 1910 in Peine. Silverio is the son of **Victoriano Enriquez** and **Maria Genera Colindres**. Marcelina is the daughter of **Justo "Bangi" Avilez** and **Suzanna Arana**. Marcelina was known as "Dada Gial." Marcelina is the granddaughter of **Santiago "Gaünbü" Avilez**, the founder of Barangu.

Pedro Juan Avila was born on this day in 1903 in Barangu. He is the son of **Pedro John Avila** and **Viviana Palacio**. Pedro married **Julia Petillo** in 1926. Pedro was a pupil teacher in Barangu in 1917.

Michael A. Martinez, Jr., was born on this day in San Ignacio. He is the son of **Michael Alejandro Martinez** and **Hazel Arzu**. His parents are working in Cayo as a police constable and a school teacher. Michael is known as "Chavo." **Maria Loreta Palacio** is the great-great-great-aunt and the first cousin four times removed of Michael.

Michael A. Martinez, Jr. and Maria Loreta Palacio I

Teodoro Palacio	common ancestor	Teodoro Palacio
Nolberto Palacio	siblings	Maria Loreta Palacio
Patrocinia Palacio	aunt	Maria Loreta Palacio
Candido Arzu	grand-aunt	Maria Loreta Palacio
Hazel ElinorArzu	great-grand-aunt	Maria Loreta Palacio
Michael A. Martinez, Jr.	great-great-grand-aunt	Maria Loreta Palacio

Michael A. Martinez, Jr. and Maria Loreta Palacio II

Francisco Palacio	common ancestor	Francisco Palacio
Teodoro Palacio	siblings	Anastacio Palacio
Gregoria Palacio	first cousins	Maria Loreta Palacio
Henry Loredo	first cousins, once removed	Maria Loreta Palacio
Bernadette Loredo	first cousins, twice removed	Maria Loreta Palacio
Hazel Elinor Arzu	first cousins, thrice removed	Maria Loreta Palacio
Michael A. Martinez, Jr.	first cousins four times removed	Maria Loreta Palacio

25th November

On this day **Catarino Claude Zuniga** was born in Barangu. He is the son of **Clotildo Zuniga** and **Eduviges Ramirez**. **Maria Loreta Palacio** is the great-great-aunt of Claude. Claude is the postal carrier in Barangu. He is the fourth cousin of **Xavier "Harvey" Sandoval**.

Fermin Casimiro was born on this day in Barangu. He is the son of **Mary Flores** and **Gonzalez Casimiro**. Fermin is the fourth cousin of **Steven Gutierrez** with **Juan Pedro Cayetano** as the common ancestor.

Catarino Patricio Ariola and **Benita Nunez** were married on this day in Peine in 1929. Catarino is the son of **Patricio Ariola** and **Florencia Lambey**. Benita is the daughter of **Carmelo Nunez** and **Genevieve Martinez**. **Raheem Mariano** is the great-great-grandson of Catarino and Benita.

Erasmo Casimiro was born on this day in 1913 in Barangu. He is the son of **Pablo Casimiro** and **Bernadina Nolberto**. Erasmo married **Paula Noralez** in 1962 in Barangu. **Muriel Williams nee Casimiro** is the daughter of Erasmo.

Frederick Mervin Nicholas was born on this day in Barangu. He is the son of **Frederick Nicholas** and **Joyce Lopez**. Frederick married **Karen Nerissa Arzu**. **Maria Loreta Palacio** is the first cousin four times removed. **Egbert Valencio** is Frederick Mervin's third cousin once removed and his fourth cousin once removed and his third cousin.

Anastacio Arzu (Noralez) and **Petrona Ariola** were married on this day in 1914 in Barangu. Anastacio is the son of **Bruno Noralez** and **Viviana Arzu**. Petrona is the daughter of **Rufino Ariola** and **Ascenciona Paulino**.

On this day **Stephen Paulino** and **Eulogia Nicholas** were married. Stephen is the son of **Eusebio Paulino** and **Maria Nolberto**. Eulogia is the daughter of **Philip Nicholas** and **Fabiana Palacio**. **Victor Paulino** is the son of Stephen and Eulogia.

Saturnino Jaime and **Casimira Labriel** were married on this day in 1908 in Peine. Saturnino is the son of **Filiberto Jaime** and **Ambrosia Bernardez** and he was from Labuga. Casimira is the daughter of **Domingo Labriel** and **Fernanda Cruz**.

26th November

Juslin Nunez was born on this day in 1991 in Belize City. He is the son of **Mackie Nunez** and **Joycelyn Miller**. Juslin died just before his fifth birthday in 1996.

On this day in 1963 **Concepcion Mejia** died in Dangriga. She is the daughter of **Petrona Johnson**. Concepcion was born in 1902 in Dangriga. Concepcion is the grandmother of **Valentina Marin nee Baltazar**.

David Alvarez and **Martina Cornelia Palacio** were married on this day in 1983 in Peine. David is the son of **John Alvarez** and **Ameliana Avilez**. Martina is the daughter of **Paul Palacio** and **Ethel Dee Loredo**.

Victor Arana died on this day in 2010 in Peine. He is the son of **Frank Dean Arana** and **Bonifacia Ramirez**. Victor was born in 1938 in Barangu. Victor is known as "Bobby" in the village. He married **Pia Magdelano** in 1964 in Barangu.

On this day **Dionisia Arana** was born in 1925. She is the daughter of **Concepcion Arana** and **Simeona Flores**. Dionisia died in 1969. **Antonia Velda "Reds" Colon** is the daughter of Dionisia.

27th November

Patrick Alvarez was born on this day in Barangu. He is the son of **Eustacio Alvarez** and **Lucille "Chilagu" Zuniga**.

Virgilia Ariola was born on this day in 1927 in Peine. She is the daughter of **Catarino Ariola** and **Benita Nunez**. She was known as "Behe" in the village. Virgilia married **Victoriano "Fada" Lorenzo** in 1947 in Peine. Virgilia died 2012 in Los Angeles. **Steven Gutierrez** is the grandson of Virgilia. She was the treasurer of the St. Joseph Credit Union for many years.

Martina Avilez died on this day in Barangu in 1927. She is the daughter of **John Justo Avilez** and **Paula Noralez**. Martina was born in Barangu in 1900. Martina married **Henry Loredo** in 1920 in Barangu. She is the grandmother of **Harriet Scarborough nee Arzu**.

Viviano Zuniga and **Filomena Paulino** were married in Barangu in 1907. Viviano is the son of **Claro Zuniga** and **Mauricia Cayetano**. Filomena is the daughter of **Obispo Lino** and **Francisca Cayetano**. **Orson Lucious Nicholas** is the great-great-grandson of Viviano and Filomena.

Shane Martinez was born on this day. He is the son of **Benito Martinez** and **Eudora Zuniga**. Shane is the grandson of **Eugenia "Jean" Zuniga nee Noralez**.

28th November

Paul Casimiro died in 1977 in Puerto Barrios. He is the son of **Pablo Casimiro** and **Bernadina Nolberto**. Paul married **Margarita Lorenzo**. **Jovita Casimiro** is the daughter of Paul.

Gregorio Palacio was born on this day in Barangu in 1900. He is the son of **Hipolito Palacio** and **Josefa Zuniga**. He is the uncle of **Andy Palacio**. Gregorio died when he was young and his parents had another son and named him also Gregorio. The second Gregorio is **Andy Palacio**'s father, **Gregorio Ruben Palacio**. **Maria Loreta Palacio** is the first cousin once removed of Gregorio.

Isidro Arzu and **Maxima Ariola** were married in 1903 in Barangu on this day. Isidoro is the son of **Augustin Arzu** and **Cayetana Gonzalez**. Maxima is the daughter of **Rufino Ariola** and **Ascenciona Paulino**.

Gregorio Cayetano was born on this day in Barangu in 1884. He is the son of **Marcelo Cayetano** and **Maria Loreta Palacio**. Gregorio married **Teofila Flores** in 1908 in Peine. Gregorio is the grandson of **Anacleto Cayetano** one of the founding families of Barangu. Gregorio is the great-grandson of **Juan Pedro Cayetano**. Gregorio is the fourth generation of Cayetanos born in Central America after the exile. Gregorio is the great-uncle of **Fabian Cayetano**. **Angus Cayetano** is Gregorio's son.

John Herbert Earl Arana died on this day in 2003 in Peine. He is the son of **Eulalio "Bidun" Arana** and **Gregoria "Gogo" Paulino**. Earl was born in 1950 in Peine.

On this day **Quinton Paul Rodriguez** was born in New York, New York. He is the son of **Clinton Rodriguez** and **Lynette Valerie Valerio**. **Maria Loreta Palacio** is the great-great-great-great-aunt of Quinton.

29th November

In the Catholic calendar today is the Feast Day of St. Saturninus.

Kareem King was born on this day in Dangriga. He is the son of **Clifford King** and **Beverly Flowers**. Kareem is the great-great-grandson of **Nolberto Palacio**. **Maria Lorea Palacio** is the great-great-great-aunt of Kareem.

Carol Garcia was born on this day in 1967 in Barangu. She is the daughter of **Silvan Joseph Chimilio** and **Josephine Garcia**. Carol died in 2012 in Peine. Carol was raised by **Felicita Zuniga**. **Maria Loreta Palacio** is the first cousin thrice removed of Carol.

Harriet Arzu was born on this day. She is the daughter of **Candido Arzu** and **Bernadette Loredo**. She is an educator in the States. Five of Harriet's great-great-grandparents were early settlers of Barangu: **Theodore Palacio, Maria Tomasa Martinez, Anastacio Palacio, Magdalena Cesaria** and **Santiago Avilez**. She is the first cousin of Surusia **Francis Arzu**. **Maria Loreta Palacio** is the first cousin thrice removed of Harriet and also the great-great-aunt of Harriet.

Alejandro Castillo and **Victoriana Cayetano** were married on this day in 1877 in Barangu. Alejandro is the son of **Jose Castillo** and **Santiaga Avila**. Victoriana is the daughter of **Anacleto Cayetano** and **Dominga Martila Arzu**. Victoriana is the first cousin thrice removed of **Roy Cayetano**.

Saturnina Baltazar was born and baptized on this day in 1895 in Barangu. She is the daughter of Eusebio Baltzar and **Venancia Nolberto**. Saturnina is the first cousin once removed of **Paula Nolberto**. Saturnina is the granddaughter of **Francisco Nolberto**, one of Barangu's founding families.

Victor Saturnino Arana was born on this day in Barangu. He is the son of **Cipriano Arana** and **Leonora Avila**. **Maria Loreta Palacio** is the first cousin twice removed of Victor. Victor is the brother of **Marti Cain nee Arana**.

Stanislao Satuye was born in Labuga in 1895. He is the son of **Clemente Satuye** and **Eluteria Cayetano**. Stanislao is the uncle of Nurse **Mary Petillo nee Cayetano** and also the second cousin once removed of Nurse **Mary Petillo nee Cayetano**.

30th November

In the Catholic calendar today is the Feast Day of St. Andrew, Apostle.

Andrea Martinez was born in 1921 in Barangu. She is the daughter of **Pedro Nicasio Martinez** and **Augustina Nunez**. Andrea is the sister of **Melvinia "Grandma Mi" Martinez**.

Geraldine Arana was born on this day in Belize City. She is the daughter of **John Arana** and **Alberta** (last name unknown). Geraldine is the third cousin of **Raheem Mariano** with **Benita Nunez** as the common ancestor.

More Life Events in October and November

DECEMBER

1st December

Clarence Marin was born on this day in 1910 in Peine. He is the son of **Aparicio Santiago Marin** and **Brigida Paulino**. **Clarence Marin** married **Dionisia Santino** in 1967 in Barangu. Clarence died in 2006 in Barangu. **Maria Loreta Palacio** is his first cousin twice removed.

Clarence Marin (2003)

Amenigi Sandoval was born in Barangu on this day. He is the son of **Augusto Castillo** and **Dercy Sandoval** (*right*). Amenigi is the fifth cousin once removed of **Gary Zuniga** with **Francisco Palacio** being the common ancestor. Amenigi and Gary Zuniga are also fourth cousins with **Anastacio Palacio,** known as "Bai-Bai," as the common ancestor. **Maria Loreta Palacio** is the first cousin four times removed of Amenigi.

Rachel Cayetano was born on this day in New York City. She is the daughter of **Dorla Bradley** and **E. Roy Cayetano**. She is the first cousin twice removed of **Andy Palacio**. She the great-great-great-great-granddaughter of **Juan Pedro Cayetano** and **Francisco Palacio**. **Maria Loreta Palacio** is the first cousin four times removed of Rachel.

Delfina Blas died on this day in 1956 in Barangu. She is the daughter of **Macario Blas** and **Leonarda Nunez**. Delfina was born in Tela in 1889 and was baptised in Peine four months later in April of 1890. Delfina married **John Chimilio** in 1908 in Barangu. **Crispulo Chimilio** is the son of Delfina.

Leonarda Noralez was born on this day in Barangu in 1917. She is the daughter of **Felix Noralez** and **Juana Nolberto**. **Teresa "Tandu" Noralez** is the daughter of Leonarda.

Fulgencio Ramirez was born in 1894 on this day in Barangu. He is the son of **Carmen Ramirez** and **Eustaquia Palacio**. His parents show an example of a recurring pattern in Barangu that being Baranguna woman attracting men from other communities to Barangu. Eustaquia is from Barangu and Carmen is from Labuga. Fulgencio is the great-uncle of **Claude Zuniga**.

2nd December

In the Catholic calendar today is the Feast Day **of St. Bibiana (Vivian).**

Genaro Paulino and Viviano Paulino, a set of twins, were born in Barangu on this day in 1909. They are the sons of **Eugenio Paulino** known as "Megu" and **Nicolasa Zuniga**.

Alexis Adrian Arana, Jr. was born. He is the son of **Alexis Simeon Arana** and **Charlotte Rhaburn**. Alexis is the grandson of **Francisco Bonifacio "Frank" Arana**. Alexis is also the first cousin twice removed of **Bartolo Polonio** with **Andres Contreras** being the common ancestor.

On this day Asili Thair Lambert was born in Belize City. He is the son of **Russell Stephen Lambert** and **Daphne Denise Arana**.

Dercy Sandoval and Augusto Castillo (2006) parents of Amenigi Sandoval

Aurelio Lambey was born on this day in 1906 in Monkey River. His parents are **John Lambey** and **Gregoria Nolberto** who were living in Monkey River at the time of his birth. Aurelio is the first cousin twice removed of **Alvin Loredo** with **Francisco Nolberto** being the common ancestor.

Jameel Nunez was born on this day. His parents are **Neil Nunez** and **Elvira Arana**. Through Jameel's mother, Elvira, **Steven Gutierrez** is the second cousin twice removed of Jameel with **Benita Nunez** being the common ancestor.

On this day in 1896 **Viviana Nunez** was born in Peine. She is the daughter of **Thomas Nunez** and **Tomasa Ortiz**.

Martires Coronado Palacio was born on this day in 1881. He is the son of **Anastacio Palacio** and **Magdalena Cesaria**. He died as a young man in 1904 in Barangu. **Maria Loreta Palacio** is the first cousin of Martires Coronado.

Concepcion Mejia was born on this day in 1902 in Dangriga. She is the daughter of **Petrona Johnson**. Concepcion married **Thomas Charles Lauriano**. Concepcion died in 1963 in Dangriga. **Valentina Marin nee Baltazar** is the granddaughter of Concepcion.

Andy Vivien Palacio was born on this day in 1960. He is the son of **Gregorio Ruben Palacio** and **Cleofa Avilez**. Andy died in 2008. **Maria Loreta Palacio** is the first cousin twice removed of Andy. Andy was a noted musician and government civil servant. Andy had also been appointed an Ambassador for Peace by the United Nations.

3rd December

In the Catholic calendar today is the Feast Day of St. Francis Xavier.

Beatrice Magdalene Mariano was born on this day in Belize City, Belize. She is the daughter of **Jacinta Palacio** and **Luke Mariano**. She is known as "Tricia" in the village. She is the great-great-granddaughter of **Anastacio Palacio**, one of the early settlers of Barangu. **Maria Loreta Palacio** is the first cousin thrice removed of Beatrice.

On this day **Andres Makin** was born in Orange Walk. He is the son of **Perfecto Makin** and **Vicenta "Lulu" Sanchez**. **Maria Loreta Palacio** is the great-great-aunt of **Andres Makin**. He is the nephew of **Paul Palacio**.

Eulalia Avila was born in 1905 in Barangu on this day. She is the daughter of **Juliana Garcia** and **Pantaleon Avila**. Eulalia married **Joseph Colon**. Eulalia is the granddaughter of **Apolinario Garcia**, one of the original settlers of Barangu. Apolinario's descendants have extended within and beyond the village, some of whom include the late **Clotildo Zuniga** as well as Justice **Adolph Lucas**, a judge in our Supreme Court.

Francisco Xavier Martinez was born in Peine in 1906. He is the son of **Ireneo Martinez** and **Bernardina Santino**. Francisco is **Victoriana "Vicky" Nolberto nee Martinez**'s uncle. He is also the first cousin of **Jacinta Trigueno nee Santino**.

On this day **Kent Franklin** was born in Belize City. He is the son of **Dalton Franklin** and **Marthy "Marti" Arana**. **Maria Loreta Palacio** is the first cousin thrice removed.

Leoncio Nicholas died on this day in 1921 in Barangu. He is the son of **Joseph Alexander Nicholas** and **Maria Eugenia Delavez**. Leoncio first married **Christina Garcia** in 1877 in Peine. After his first wife's death he married **Alberta Nolberto** in 1899 in Barangu. Leoncio was a "Mayordomo" of St. Joseph's Roman Catholic church in Barangu for many years. **Victor Joseph Nicholas** is the grandson of Leoncio.

4th December

In the Catholic calendar today is the Feast Day of St. Barbara.

Barbarin Lino was born in 1920 in Peine on this day. His parents are **Rosendo Lino** and **Clemencia Nunez**. Barbarin married **Faith Daniels**, daughter of **S.B. Daniels**, Barangu's school principal of the 1930s and 1940s.

On this day **Luis Arzu** was born. He is the son of **Catarino "Man and a Half" Arzu**, and **Santiaga Mejia**. Luis enrolled in the St. Joseph Primary School on the 15 of January 1945. Luis's parents lived at Cow Shade along the Sarstoon River where other families from Barangu and Peine lived and farmed.

Petrona Arzu was born on this day in 1898 in Peine. She is the daughter of **Sebastian Arzu** and **Eluteria Cayetano**. She is the granddaughter of **Vinciona "Beltrana" Cayetano** and grandniece of **Dominga "Waganga" Cayetano**, both through the patriarch **Juan Pedro Cayetano**. **Petrona Arzu**, **John Jacob Zuniga**, **Nicolasa Martinez** and **Isabela Mejia** have the same mother, Eluteria.

Peter Anthony Avila, Jr. was born on this day in 1934. He is the son of **Peter Anthony Avila** and **Sotera Nicholas**. Peter married **Petrona "Pansy" Apolonio**. **Albertha Magna Avila** is the sister of Peter.

5th December

Marlet Martinez was born in Doublehead Cabbage on this day. She is the daughter of **Martin Martinez** and **Parlet McFadzean**. Marlet is related to **Juan Pedro Cayetano** three different ways, through her great-grandfather **Hipolito Martinez**, through her great-grandmother **Regina Martinez nee Lorenzo** and through her great-grandmother **Ursula Arana**. Marlet is the second cousin once removed of **Steven Gutierrez** through **Regina Martinez nee Lorenzo** with their common ancestor being **Timoteo Lorenzo**. **Maria Loreta Palacio** is the great-great-great-aunt of Marlet (*next page*).

Marlet Martinez and Juan Pedro Cayetano		
Juan Pedro Cayetano	Juan Pedro Cayetano	Juan Pedro Cayetano
Anacleto Cayetano	Petrona Cayetano	Luisa "Ludovica" Cayetano
Mauricia Cayetano	Juana "Jane" Palacio	Dominga Marin
Gabina Zuniga	Regina Lorenzo	Georgia Bermudez
Hipolito Martinez	Martin A. Martinez	Ursula Arana
Martin A. Martinez	Michael A. Martinez, Jr.	Evilia Gonzalez
Michael A. Martinez, Jr.	Marlet Martinez	Martin A. Martinez
Marlet Martinez		Michael A. Martinez, Jr.
		Marlet Martinez
Marlet Martinez and Steven Gregory Gutierrez		
Timoteo Lorenzo	common ancestor	Timoteo Lorenzo
Regina Lorenzo	siblings	Victoriano Lorenzo
Martin A. Martinez	first cousins	Valentina Lorenzo
Michael A. Martinez, Jr.	second cousins	Steven Gregory Gutierrez
Marlet Martinez	second cousins once removed	Steven Gregory Gutierrez
Marlet Martinez and Maria Loreta Palacio		
Teodoro Palacio	common ancestor	Teodoro Palacio
Juana "Jane" Palacio	siblings	Maria Loreta Palacio
Regina Lorenzo	aunt	Maria Loreta Palacio
Martin A. Martinez	grand-aunt	Maria Loreta Palacio
Michael A. Martinez, Jr.	great-grand-aunt	Maria Loreta Palacio
Marlet Martinez	great-greaat-grand-aunt	Maria Loreta Palacio

John Arana was born on this day in 1926 in Peine. He is the son of **Adriano Natividad Arana** and **Basilia**. John died in 1990 in Belize City. John is the older brother of **Francisco Bonifacio "Frank" Arana**.

Christine Nicholas was born on this day in Barangu in 1944. She is the daughter of **Ignacio Nicholas** and **Perfecta Avilez**. Christine is the great-granddaughter of **Joseph Alexander Nicholas**, one of the first settlers of Barangu. She is the sister of **Victor Nicholas** and **David Nicholas**.

Geronimo Avilez was born on this day in 1908 in Peine. He is the son of **Ambrocio Avilez**, known as "Sabigi," and **Justa Polonio**. Geronimo married **Pastora Villafranco** in 1934 in Peine. Geronimo's grandfather is **Santiago Avilez**, one of the original settlers in Barangu.

Tiburcio Baltazar and **Saturnina Baltazar** were married on this day in 1942 in Barangu. **Francisco Nolberto** is the the grandfather of Saturnina through her mother, **Venancia Nolberto**. **Almira "Irma" Gonzalez nee Ariola** is the first cousin twice removed of Saturnina through her mother **Paula Nolberto** with their common ancestor being **Francisco Nolberto**.

6th December

Victor Enriquez died in Belize City on this day in 1981. He was born in Honduras and was married to **Vilma Petrona Chimilio**. He and Vilma had a daughter, **Celestina Enriquez**.

In Peine on this day **Dativa Elizabeth Melendrez** was born. She is the daughter of **Evaristo Melendrez** and **Lucila "Shuna" Arana**. She is an educator. The Aranas are a typical transborder Garifuna family traditionally extending from Dangriga to Labuga. The Arana family had property in Monkey River.

Apolonio Polonio and **Damiana Garcia** were married on this day in 1908 in Barangu. **Ursula Polonio**, Henry Loredo's wife, is their daughter. **Melquiades Julius "Jimbo" Loredo** is the great-grandson of Apolonio and Damiana through his mother, **Isolene Loredo**.

Francisco Xavier Sanchez was born on this day in Barangu in 1865. His parents are **Sebastian Sanchez** and **Vinciona Cayetano**. Vinciona, his mother also known as "Venderana" is sister of **Anacleto Cayetano** from whom descend the twins **Fabian Cayetano** and **Sebastian Cayetano** and their siblings. Francisco

119

is nephew of **Anacleto Cayetano**. **Egbert Valencio** is the first cousin thrice removed of Francisco with **Juan Pedro Cayetano** being their common ancestor.

Delia Gloria Martinez was born on this day. She is the daughter of **Gloria Martinez**. She married **Mark Loredo**. Gloria is the granddaughter of **Simon Martinez** and **Ambrosine Mejia**.

7th December

Geronima Martinez died on this day in 1986 in Belize City. Her parents are **Brown Prudencio Martinez** and **Gabina Zuniga**. Geronima was born in 1911 in Barangu. Geronima is the mother of **Vilma Petrona Chimilio**. Geronima is an older sister of **Hipolito Martinez**. She is the aunt of **Viola Martinez**. Geronima is the first cousin of **Lucille "Chilagu" Valencio nee Zuniga.**

On this day **Gilbert Marin** was born in Barangu. He is the son of **Clarence Marin** and **Dionisia Santino**. He married **Valentina Baltazar**. He is the great-great-grandson of both **Anacleto Cayetano** and **Dominga "Waganga" Cayetano** who are both children of **Juan Pedro Cayetano**. Gilbert is also the great-great-grandson of **Anastacio Palacio**. **Maria Loreta Palacio** is the first cousin thrice removed of Gilbert.

Constantine Enriquez was born on this day in 1931. He is the son of **Andres Patricio Enriquez** and **Jane Victoriana Villafranco**. **Constantine** and **Eugenia Jean Noralez** are the parents of **Lloyd Enriquez**. Lloyd is the husband of **Rita Avila**, who developed the museum in our village.

8th December

Today there are two children born who were named "Ambrose," but today is not the Feast Day of St. Ambrose. In the source I am using, yesterday was the Feast Day of **St. Ambrose.**

Ambrosio Avila was born on this day in 1918 in Barangu. His mother was **Virginia Garcia**, known as "Misi." He is the brother of **Petrona Ariola**. Petrona married **Peter Casimiro** and had two children, **Fidelis Casimiro** and **Paul "Boy" Casimiro**.

Ambrosia Garcia and **Maria Garcia**, a set of twins, were born in 1900 in Barangu. They are the daughters of **Margarito Garcia** and **Augustina Nunez**. They are the sisters of **Melvinia "Grandma Mi" Martinez** with a different father.

Gregoria Noralez was born and baptized on this day in 1912 in Peine. She is the daughter of **Felix "Aska" Noralez** and **Juana Nolberto**. Gregoria was in Barangu's confirmation class of 1922. She is the aunt of **Teresa "Tandu" Noralez**.

9th December

Lucy Martinez was born on this day in Barangu. She is the daughter of **Hipolito Martinez** and **Regina Lorenzo**. **Maria Loreta Palacio** is the great-aunt of Lucy. Lucy is the older sister of **Elliot Martinez**. Lucy is the first cousin once removed of **Dale Gutierrez**.

On this day in 1905 **Beatrice Palacio** was born in Barangu. She is the daughter of **Saturnino Palacio** and **Felicita Reyes**. She married **Marcelino H. Johnson** in 1941. **Maria Loreta Palacio** is the first cousin once removed of Beatrice. **Raymond Valencio**, fisherman, is the son of Beatrice and **Eufamio Valencio**.

Amenigi Castillo was born on this day in Barangu. He is the son of **Augusto Castillo** and **Dercy Sandoval**. **Maria Loreta Palacio** is the first cousin four times removed of Amenigi. **Felicita "Cita" Zuniga** is the grandmother of Amenigi.

10th December

In the Catholic calendar today is the Feast Day of Pope St. Melchiades, but in 1969 his Feast Day was moved to 10 January. This makes my trying to ascribe names chosen to Saint's Feast Days all the more difficult.

Maria Loreta Palacio was born on this day in 1862 in Barangu. She is the daughter of **Teodoro "Joe Young" Palacio** and **Maria Tomasa Martinez**. Maria Loreta was the first recorded birth in Barangu. Obviously people were living in Barangu and there may have even been earlier births but we know nothing of them. Today is the 150th anniversary of the birth of **Maria Loreta Palacio** and by extension it is also the 150th anniversary of the village of Barangu that we celebrate today. Maria Loreta married **Marcelo Cayetano** in 1883 in Barangu. **Maria Loreta Palacio** died in 1925 in Barangu.

On this day in 1948 **Macario Blas** died in Travesia, Honduras. He is the son of **Joanis Blas** and **Clementina** (last name unknown). Macario was born in Jonathan Point as were many other early settlers of Barangu. He married **Leonarda Nunez** in Barangu in 1910. Macario was an early leader of Barangu. In 1911 he and two others obtained a 200 acre parcel of land known as "Section 10" for the use of the entire village. This was done when the colonial government was dispossessing Baranguna of lands they had already owned. Blas is not a name now found in the village but many are descended from Macario, for example **Clifford Marin**, **Jacinta Trigueno nee Santino**, and **Crispulo Chimilio.**

Philip Casimiro was born on this day in Barangu. His parents are **Gonzalez Casimiro** and **Mary Casimiro nee Flores**. He is the brother of **Fermin Casimiro**.

Leon Palacio was born on this day in Georgeville. He is the son of **Augustus Palacio** and **Olga McKoy**. **Surusia Ludwig Palacio** is Leon's brother by a different mother. **Maria Loreta Palacio** is the great-great-aunt of Leon.

On this day **Melquiades Julius Loredo** was born in Barangu. He is the son of **Marcos Oliver Martinez** and **Isolene Loredo**. Melquiades is known as "Jimbo" in the village. **Maria Loreta Palacio** is the first cousin thrice removed of "Jimbo." **Cindy Nicole Martinez** is the daughter of Melquiades.

11th December

In the Catholic calendar today is the Feast Day of Pope St. Damasus I.

Ishmael Sanchez was born on this day in Barangu. He is the son of **Vicenta "Lulu" Sanchez** and **John Ray Zuniga**. **Rodney Zuniga** is Ishmael's older brother. **Paul Palacio** is his uncle. **Maria Loreta Palacio** is the great-great-aunt of Ishmael.

Damasio Joseph Palacio was born in Barangu in 1896. He is the son of **Ignacia Palacio nee Arana** and **Nolberto Palacio**. Damasio is the uncle of **Vicenta "Lulu" Sanchez**. He is the uncle of **Olivia Prudencia Avila nee Palacio**. **Maria Loreta Palacio** is the aunt of Damasio.

Demasia Luis was born on this day in 1918. Her parents are **Basilio Luis** and **Canuta Lucas**. Demasia married **Joseph Benguche** in Peine in 1938. She is the granddaughter of **Benita Nunez**. Demasia is the first cousin once removed of **Antonette "Neti" Zuniga**.

Martina Ariola was born in Barangu on this day in 1917. She is the daughter of **Vicenta Castillo** and **Patricio Ariola**. She is the aunt of **Francisco "Chico" Ariola**.

On this day in 1896 **Thomas Joseph Martinez** was born in Barangu. He is the son of **Romalda Avila** and **Liborio Martinez**. Thomas is the great-uncle of **Alvin Loredo** and the uncle of **Irene Gibbons**.

Augustin Cayetano was born on this day in 1844 "en la Costa" in Guatemala. He is the son of **Juan**

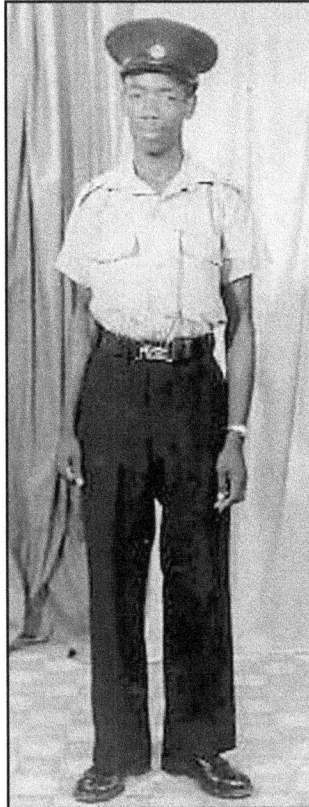

Police Constable Augustus Palacio

Pedro Cayetano and **Maria Nicolasa Moralez**. Augustin is the brother of **Anacleto Cayetano**. **Sebastian Cayetano** is the great-great-great-nephew of Augustin.

Carmen Ramirez died on this day in 1926 in Barangu. He is the son of **Joseph Ramirez** and **Maria Candelaria**. Carmen was from Labuga. Carmen married **Eustaquia Palacio** in 1889 in Barangu. Carmen is the great-grandfather of Catrarino Claude Zuniga.

12th December

In the Catholic calendar today is the Feast Day of Our Lady of Guadalupe.

Isolene Loredo was born in Barangu. She is the daughter of **Henry Loredo** and **Ursula Polonio**. **Maria Loreta Palacio** is the first cousin twice removed of Isolene. She is the mother of **Melquiades Julius Loredo** better know as "Jimbo."

Victoriano Colindres and **Pasquala Ramirez** were married in Barangu in 1908 on this day. Victoriano is the son of **Justo Colindres** and **Petrona Santino**. Pasquala is the daughter of **Carmen Ramirez** and **Eustaquia Palacio**. Pasquala is the aunt of **Eduviges Ramirez** better known as "Auntie Bia." **Dominica Baltazar nee Colindres** is the daughter of Victoriano and Pasquala.

On this day **Ambrosio Noralez** was born in 1912 in Peine. He is the son of **Venancio Noralez** and **Juliana Colindres**. **Eugenia "Jean" Zuniga nee Noralez** is the niece of Ambrosio.

Guadalupe Paulino was born on this day. He is the son of **Stephen Paulino** and **Eulogia Nicholas**. **Maria Loreta Palacio** is the first cousin twice removed of Guadalupe.

13th December

In the Catholic calendar today is the Feast Day of St. Lucy.

Henrietta Blanco was born on this day in 1929. Her parents are **Ciriaco Blanco** and **Matea Paulino**. Here is another example of Baranguna women attracting men to the village. Matea is the daughter of **Augustin "Big Ease" Paulino** and **Juana Paulino nee Luis** of Barangu. Matea's husband, Ciriaco, immigrated to the village.

Joseph Lucy Ogaldez was born on this day in 1918 in Peine. Joseph is the son of **Secundino Ogaldez** and **Alberta Ciego**. Secundino was an early school teacher in Barangu.

Otilia Lucia Martinez was born in 1916 in Peine on this day. Otilda is the daughter of **Secundino Joseph Martinez** and **Anastacia Vicenta Santiago**. Otilda married **Eranio Frazer Francisco** in 1934 in Barangu. Her grandfather is **Saturnino Martinez** and her great-grandfather is **Augustin "Big Ease" Paulino**.

Clinton Rodriguez and Lynette Valerie Valerio were married on this day in 1998 in Ladyville. Lynette is the daughter of **Peter Valerio** and **Heremenhilda "Maria" Lopez**. **Dwayne Rodriguez** and **Quinton Rodriguez** are children of Clinton and Lynette.

On this day **Nicolasa Martinez** died in 1991 in Barangu. She is the daughter of **Liborio Martinez** and **Eluteria Cayetano**. Nicolasa was born in 1907 in Peine. She married **Dionisio Nolberto** in 1924 in Peine. **Alvin Loredo** is the grandson of Nicolasa.

14th December

Eufemio Gutierrez and Juliana Lambey were married in 1940 in Peine on this day. An example of Baranguna leaving Barangu and moving to Peine. Some of both Eufemio's and Juliana's grandparents have Barangu roots, **Narciso Bermudez** and **Dominga "Gadu" Marin** on Eufemio's side and **John Lambey** and **Gregoria Nolberto** on Juliana's side. **Alvin Loredo** is Eufemio's third cousin once removed and Alvin is Juliana's second cousin once removed.

Eulalia Arana was born on this day in 1906 in Barangu. She is the daughter of **Alejandro Arana** and **Gregoria Bermudez**. She married **Joseph Velasquez**. Eulalia was known as "Lala" in the village. **Rosalia "Baby Rose" Martinez** is the daughter of Eulalia.

Elton Tyron Lopez was born on this day in Belize City. He is the son of **Roman Lopez** and **Germaine Martinez**. **Maria Loreta Palacio** is the first cousin four times removed of Elton. **Kaya Lopez** is the sister of Elton.

15th December

Eusebio Polonio was born on this day in Peine in 1863. He is the son of **Francisco Apolonio** and **Leonarda Nunez**. He married **Lucia Ordonez**. He is the grandfather of **Bartolo Polonio**. Eusebio was a Garifuna "mover and shaker" in the region. He was a merchant in Peine. Eusebio had business relations with D. S. Wells of Monkey River and with the German landowner Mr. Cramer. Besides holding three front lots in Barangu he owned a caye and property up Sunday Wood Creek.

Eusebio Lorenzo was born on this day in 1904 in Barangu. He is the son of **Timoteo Lorenzo** and **Juana (Jane) Palacio**. Eusebio died five months later in April 1905 in Barangu. **Maria Loreta Palacio** is the aunt of Eusebio. **Victoriano "Fada" Lorenzo** is the brother of Eusebio.

Monico Santino was married in 1959 on this day in Peine to **Christina Moreria**. Monico's parents are **Philip Santino** and **Nicasia Martinez**. Christina is the daughter of **Marcelino Moreira** and **Luisa Gonzalez**. Monico is uncle to **Jacinta Trigueno nee Santino**.

Rosita Miller and Edward Tingling were married on this day in 1984 in Dangriga. Rosita is the daughter of **Denzel Miller** and **Josephine Palacio**.

Aurelia Enriquez was born on this day in 1920 in Peine. She is the daughter of **Lino Enriquez** and **Nazaria Zuniga**. Aurelia married **Emmanuel Arzu** in 1966 in Peine. Aurelia's mother, Nazaria, led the celebration of "Posada" in the village.

16th December

Before 1969 today in the Catholic calendar today was the Feast Day of St. Eusebio. Yesterday was the Feast Day of St. Christiana, which is reflected in the naming of Christina Zuniga today. To add to the confusion, we have Lazaro Santino born today but the Feast Day of St. Lazarus is tomorrow the 17th of December.

Lazaro Santino was born on this day in 1924 in Barangu. His parents are **Eusebio Santino** and **Vicenta Blas**. **Jacinta Trigueno nee Santino** is Lazaro's sister.

Marcelo Cayetano was born on this day in Barangu in 1930. He is the son of **Pascacio Cayetano** and **Eustaquia Satuye**. Marcelo was named after his grandfather **Marcelo Cayetano**. **Maria Loreta Palacio** is the grandmother of Marcelo. "Nurse" **Mary Petillo nee Cayetano** is his sister.

Christina Zuniga was born on this day in Barangu in 1934. **Loriana Ramirez** and **Canutu Zuniga** are her parents. She is **Abraham Zuniga**'s sister. Christina was named after her grandmother **Christina Zuniga nee Nolberto**. **Maria Loreta Palacio** is the great-aunt of Christina.

On this day in 1884 **Eusebio Paulino** was born in Barangu. He is the son of **Augustin "Big Ease" Paulino** and **Juana Luis**. **Victor Paulino** of Peine is Eusebio's grandson.

Michelle Alvarez was born on this day in Corozal. She is the daughter of **Simon Aloysius Alvarez** and

Phyllis Palacio. **Michelle Alvarez** is a school teacher. **Victor Alvarez** is uncle of Michelle. **Maria Loreta Palacio** is related to Michelle three different ways. Maria Loreta is the great-great-aunt; Maria Loreta is the first cousin thrice removed of Michelle; and Maria Loreta is the great-great-grandmother of Michelle.

On this day **Valentino Castro** was born in 1900 in Peine. He is the son of **Leon Castro** and **Victoriana Arana**. Valentino married **Cirila Martinez** in 1914 in Peine. After her death he then married **Michaela Lorenzo** in 1933 in Barangu.

Mark Rayshawn Loredo was born on this day in Belize City. He is the son of **Mark Loredo** and **Delia Gloria Martinez**. Mark is the grandson of **Anacleta "Da" Nolberto**. **Maria Loreta Palacio** is the first cousin four times removed of Mark.

17th December

In the Catholic calendar today is the Feast Day of St. Lazarus.

Froylan Palacio and Jacinta Santino

On this day in 1965 **Froylan Palacio** and **Jacinta Santino** were married. Froylan is the son of **Augustine Palacio** and **Simeona Mejia**. Jacinta is the daughter of **Eusebio Santino** and **Vicenta Blas**. Jacinta and her second husband **Fred Trigueno** operate a shop in the village.

Cayetano Amaya and **Josefa Paulino** were married on this day in 1908 in Barangu. Cayetano is the son of Thomas Amaya and Benita Martinez. Josefa is the daughter of **Augustin "Big Ease" Paulino** and **Juana Luis**. They had two children, **Peter Amaya** and **Cristino Cayetano**. Josefa was also married to **Felix Lucas** and had children with **Saturnino "Senerial" Martinez**.

On this day **Lazarus Zuniga** was born. His parents are **Canuto Zuniga** and **Loriana Ramirez**. Lazarus is the brother of **Abraham Zuniga**.

Pascacio Cayetano and **Ignacia "Inez" Arana** were married on this day in 1939 in Barangu. Pascacio is the son of **Marcelo Cayetano** and **Maria Loreta Palacio**. Ignacia is the daughter of **Alejandro Arana** and **Gregoria Bermudez**. This was Pascacio's third marriage. His first marriage was to **Apolinaria Mejia** in 1912 in Barangu. His second marriage was to **Eustaquia Satuye** in 1920 in Barangu.

18th December

Karen Nerissa Arzu was born in Belize City on this day. She is the daughter of **Conrad Allen Arzu** and **Martina Norma Arzu nee Martinez**. **Maria Loreta Palacio** is the great-great-great-aunt, the first cousin four times removed and the great-great-aunt of Karen.

Timoteo Chimilio died on this day in 1982 in Barangu. He is the son of **John Chimilio** and **Delfina Blas**. Timoteo was born in Barangu in 1911. Timoteo died in a drowning accident. **Maria Loreta Palacio** is the first cousin twice removed of Timoteo. **Vilma Petrona Chimilio** is his daughter.

On this day in 1907 **Graciano Castillo** was born in Barangu. He is the son of **Victoriano Castillo** and **Carmen Ramirez**. Graciano is **Clotildo Zuniga's** uncle.

Peter Castillo and **Anastacia Christina Ramirez** were married on this day in 1982 in Belize City. Peter, better known as "Caddi," is a school teacher and spiritual worker. They operate a guest house in Hopkins.

On this day in 1910 in Barangu **Dominica Colindres** was born. She is the daughter of **Victoriano Colindres** and **Pasquala Ramirez**. Dominica married **Bernardo Baltazar** in 1929 in Barangu. **Maria Loreta Palacio** is the great-aunt of Dominica.

Lazara Arzu was born in Peine in 1919. She is the daughter of **Evangelisto "16" Reyes** and **Ascenciona Arzu**. Lazara is **Raymond Valencio's** first cousin once removed.

On this day **Dominica Colindres** was born in 1910 in Barangu. She is the daughter of **Victoriano Colindres** and **Pasquala Ramirez**. Dominica married **Bernardo Baltazar** in 1929 in Barangu. **Maria Loreta Palacio** is the great-aunt of Dominica.

Gianne Cayetano and **Janine Jewel Cayetano** were a set of twins born on this day. They are the daughters of **Robert Cayetano** and **Beatrice Sanchez**. **Maria Loreta Palacio** is the great-great-grandmother and also the first cousin four times removed of Gianne and Janine. Janine Jewel married **Eugene Lizama**.

123

19th December

Ethleen Arzu and **Jacob Arzu**, a set of twins, were born on this day in 1917 in Peine. Their parents are **Obispa Florentina Paulino** and **Juan Bautista Arzu**. Ethleen and Jacob are the grandchildren of **Augustin "Big Ease" Paulino**. Ethleen married **Bonifacio Augustin** in 1937. Jacob married **Aniceta Petillo** in 1945. Jacob died the day after his wedding in January of 1945 in Peine.

On this day **Francis Benedict Martinez, Jr.** was born. He is the son of **Francis Benedict Martinez** and **Victoria Barcelona**. Francis is the brother of **Elma Yvonne Arzu nee Martinez**.

20th December

Fermin Jimenez and **Petrona Cayetano** were married on this day in 1887 in Peine. This is a classic example of a traditional Garifuna practice known as "cross-cousin marriage" when children of sisters and brothers marry. This practice of cross-cousin marriage is often used by indigenous peoples to keep power within the family. In this circumstance we have two children of **Juan Pedro Cayetano**, **Rafaela Cayetano** and **Anacleto Cayetano**, who each have a child. Rafaela has **Fermin Jimenez** with **Marcelino Jimenez** and Anacleto has **Petrona Cayetano** with **Dominga Martila Arzu**. The marriage of Fermin and

Cross Cousin Marriage		
Juan Pedro Cayetano	common ancestor	Juan Pedro Cayetano
Rafaela Cayetano	siblings	Anacleto Cayetano
Fermin Jimenez	cross cousins	Petrona Cayetano

Petrona is a cross-cousin marriage because Fermin is the son of a sister, Rafaela, with the daughter, Petrona, of a brother, Anacleto. The Jesuits preached long and hard against this practice. Reminiscence of this practice can be seen in the large number of second cousin marriages within the Garifuna Community.

John Chimilio and **Delfina Blas** were married on this day in Barangu in 1908. John is the son of **Benito Chimilio** and **Saturnina Palacio**. Delfina is the daughter of **Macario Blas** and **Leonarda Nunez**. John and Delfina are **Crispulo Chimilio's** parents.

On this day **Marty Leroy Alvarez** was born in Belmopan. Marty is the son of **David Alvarez** and **Martina Cornelia Palacio**. **Maria Loreta Palacio** is the great-great-great-aunt, also the first cousin four times removed and the first cousin six times removed of Marty. **Paul Palacio** is the grandfather of Marty.

Jason Paul Williams was born on this day in Belize City. He is the son of **Paul Williams** and **Cecilia Rhys**. Jason is the great-grandson of **Prudencio Martinez** and **Gabina Zuniga**.

21st December

On this day in 1907 in Barangu **Desideria "Maga Gidei"** died. This lady went by many names. You may know her as **"Quiteria."** As to a last name, some think it was Lambey; others think it was Alvarez. We are not sure. She was 98 when she died. Many would call her the "Mother of Barangu" as she came along with **Santiago Avilez** as the first pioneers of the village. Santiago was her husband, while also being her uncle, according to oral tradition. For that reason they had to get a church dispensation to get married. While living in Dangriga before her union with Santiago, she had a relationship with **Francisco Palacio**; and together they had **Teodoro "Joe Young" Palacio** and **Anastacio "Baibai" Palacio**. From these two sons all the Palacios in Barangu originated. **Maria Loreta Palacio** is the granddaughter of Maga Gadei.

Victor Paulino and **Berta Petillo** were married on this day in 1985 in Peine. Victor lives in Peine, but all four of his grandparents are from Barangu: Paulino, Palacio, Nolberto, and Nicholas. **Maria Loreta Palacio** is the first cousin twice removed of Victor.

22nd December

In the Catholic calendar today is the Feast Day of St. St. Demetrius.

Soledad Noralez was born on this day in 1924 in Barangu. She is the daughter of **Juana Nolberto** and **Felix Noralez**. Solada is the aunt of **Teresa "Tandu" Noralez**. **Paula Nolberto** is Soledad's first cousin.

Macario Gonzalez and **Almira "Irma" Ariola** were married on this day in Barangu in 1970. Macario is the son of **Justo Gonzalez** and **Ursula Arana**. Almira is daughter of **Francisco "Chico" Ariola** and **Paula Nolberto**.

Demetrio Palacio was born on this day in 1902 in Barangu. Demetrio is the son of **Romalda Zuniga** and **Liberato Palacio**. Demetrio is the first cousin of **Ruben Palacio**, which is a case of two closely related Palacio men marrying two Zuniga sisters: Josefa, the mother of Ruben, and Romalda, the mother of Demetrio. **Maria Loreta Palacio** is the first cousin once removed of Demetrio.

Sean Palacio was born on this day in Belize City. He is the son of **Clarence Adolphus** and **Jermaine**

Palacio. Sean is the grandson of **Theodore Palacio**. **Maria Loreta Palacio** is the great-great-great-aunt and also the first cousin four times removed of Sean.

On this day **Florine Thelma Arana** was born in Barangu. She is the daughter of **Cipriano Arana** and **Leonora Avila**. Thelma is the sister of **Marti Cain nee Arana**. **Maria Loreta Palacio** is the first cousin twice removed of Thelma.

Martin Victor Nicholas died on this day in 2006 in Barangu. He is the son of **Victor Leonard Nicholas** and **Paulina Lopez**. He was born in Barangu in 1934. Martin was a basketmaker. Martin was known as "Game and Gone" in the village.

23rd December

Victor Joseph Nicholas was born in 1932 in Barangu. Victor is the son of **Ignacio Nicholas** and **Perfecta Avilez**. **Victor Nicholas** was the principal teacher for a few years at the St. Joseph R.C. School in Barangu. He also held the position of principal of the Belize Teacher Training College. He retired to Barangu and with his second wife **Angelina Alvarez** founded the farm "Vinland." Victor died in 2006 in Barangu.

Sindulfo Garcia was baptized on this day in 1911 in Peine. He was born earlier in Barangu. Sindulfo is the son of **Margarito Garcia** and **Diega "Cocona" Benguche**. Sindulfo is most remembered for his tremendous sense of humour. During the Christmas church services he would do a dance as he went to pay respects to the image of Baby of Jesus. Sindulfo is the great-great-uncle of **Kevin Zuniga**.

On this day in Barangu in 1922 **Manuela Marin** (*right*) was born. She is the daughter of **Aparicio Marin** and **Brigida Paulino**. **Manuela Marin** married **Eugenio Cayetano** in 1941. Manuela died in 1991 in the States. **Roy Cayetano** is Manuela's son.

Russell Stephen Lambert and **Daphne Denise Arana** were married on this day in 1995 in Belize City. Daphne is the daughter of **Rudy Concepcion Arana** and **Mildred Hernandez**. Daphne is the granddaughter of **Eulalio "Bidun" Arana** and **Gregoria "Gogo" Paulino**.

Tomas Martinez was born on this day in 1924 in Peine. He is the son of **Francisco Martinez** and **Estefania Avila**. Tomas is the brother of **Simon Martinez** (presently living in Scotland) and **Francis Benedict Martinez**.

24th December

In the Catholic calendar today is the Feast Day of Saint Delphinus of Bordeaux.

Jermaine "Lily" Palacio was born on this day in Barangu. She is the daughter of **Bridget Marin** and **Theodore Palacio**. Jermaine married Keith Francis. **Maria Loreta Palacio** is the great-great-aunt and the first cousin thrice removed of Jermaine. She is the sister of **Angela Palacio**.

On this day in 1950 **Martina Lorraine "Deidei" Arzu** was born. She is the daughter of **Bernadette Arzu nee Loredo** and **Candido Arzu**. She died in 1973. **Maria Loreta Palacio** is the great-great-aunt and the first cousin thrice removed of Lorraine. Lorraine is the sister of **Harold "Greg" Arzu**.

Georgiana Palacio was born on this day in 1925 in Barangu. Georgiana is the daughter of **Augustine Palacio** and **Simeona Palacio nee Mejia**. She married **Reginald Avila** in 1944. **Maria Loreta Palacio** is the great-aunt of Georgiana. **Urban Paul Avila** is her son. **Lynn Zuniga nee Arnold** is Georgiana's granddaughter.

Delfina Paulino was born on this day in Barangu in 1865. She is the daughter of **Diego Paulino** and **Maria Victoria Gamboa**. Delfina is half sister to **Augustin "Big Ease" Paulino** and a distant relative to **Irene Gibbons**.

A set of twins was born born on this day in Barangu in 1895, **Gregorio Avilez** and **Gregoria Avilez**. They are the children of **Juan Avilez** and **Dominga "Gadu" Marin**. Gregorio and Gregoria are the great-uncle and great-aunt of **Andy Palacio** through his mother **Cleofa Avilez**.

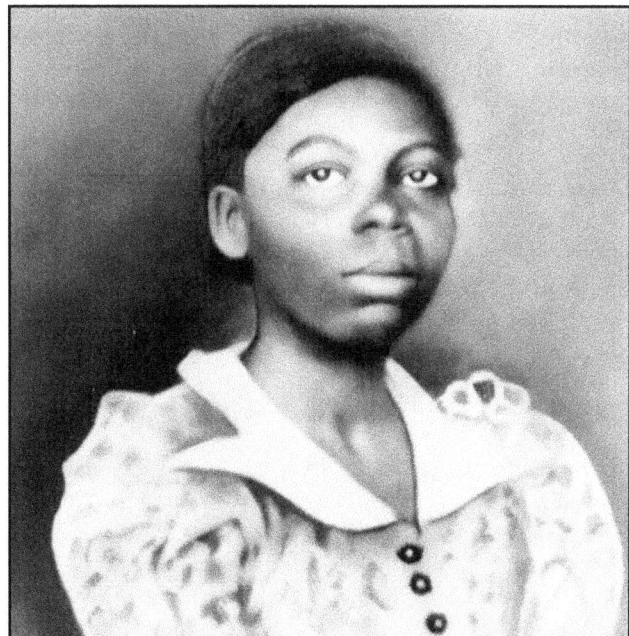

Manuela Marin

December

Francis Harold Arzu was born on this day in Labuga. He is the son of **Procopio Arzu** and **Catalina Castillo**. Francis married **Zita Alvarez**. Francis received a Doctor of Veternarian Medicine from a Mexican University. Surusia Arzu also has spent many years as an educator in the Toledo District. Francis is one of the few Baranguna to have a logging concession. **Maria Loreta Palacio** is the great-great-aunt of Francis.

Delfina Blas was born on this day in 1889 in Tela, Honduras and then baptized in Peine four months later. She is the daughter of **Macario Blas** and **Leonarda Nunez**. Delfina married **John Chimilio** in 1908 in Barangu. Delfina died in 1956 in Barangu. She was known as a seamstress in the village. **Vilma Petrona Chimilio** is the granddaughter of Delfina.

On this day **Cecilio "Dick" Polonio** died in 1926 in Peine. He is the son of **Eusebio Polonio** and **Lucia Ordonez**. Cecilio was born in 1893 in Peine. He married **Camila Contreras** in 1920 in Peine. Anthony Polonio is the grandson of Cecilio.

25th December

Cornelio Castillo died on this day in 1979. He was born in 1897 in Labuga, Guatemala. Cornelio had children with **Melvinia "Grandma Mi" Martinez**. The father of Cornelio was Ines and his father was **Rafael Castillo**. Together with his wife **Simona Garcia**, Rafael was among the early pioneers of Barangu forging links in the village between persons coming from Labuga and the Dangriga-Jonathan Point area. The late **Clotildo Zuniga** derives from this Castillo line.

On this day in Barangu **Gricelda Joseph** was born. She is the daughter of **Petrona Palacio** and **Ambrosio Joseph**. **Maria Loreta Palacio** is the great-great-aunt of Gricelda.

Alfredo Rash was born on this day in El Estor, Guatemala. He is the son of **Juan Rash** and **Candelaria**. He is the grandfather of **Lumar Valencio**. El Estor is located on the shore of Lake Isabel; it is named for one of the company stores that was found along the lake. Alfredo's migration to Barangu follows the footsteps of several non-Garifuna who had become established in our village early in its history.

In Barangu on this day in 1931 **Natividad Palacio** was born. She is the daughter of **Jacob Palacio** and **Tomasa Polonio**. Natividad married **Cecilio "Nudi" Ramirez** in 1969 in Hopkins. **Maria Loreta Palacio** is the first cousin twice removed of Natividad. Natividad is the mother of **Anastacia Christina Castillo nee Ramirez**. **Andy Palacio** is the first cousin of Natividad.

Inocenta Nolberto was born on this day in Barangu in 1915. She is the daughter of **Ireno Nolberto** and Ambrosia Martinez. She is the sister of "Thunder."

On this day in 1892 **Francisco Nolberto** was baptized in Peine. He is the son of **Macario Nolberto** and **Josefa Alvarez**. Francisco was named after his grandfather **Francisco Nolberto**, an early settler of Barangu. **Lucille Valencio nee Zuniga** is the first cousin once removed of Francisco.

Henry Loredo and **Ursula Polonio** were married on this day in 1928. Henry is the son of **Eulalio Loredo** and **Gregoria Palacio**. Ursula is the daughter of **Apolonio Polonio** and **Damiana Garcia**. This was Henry's second marriage. **Madeline Loredo** is the daughter of Henry and Ursula.

26th December

Victor "Bobby" Arana and Pia Magdelano were married on this day in Barangu in 1964. Bobby is an example of a Baranguna leaving the village in search of employment. He worked for many years up north in the sugar industry, making occasional short visits to Barangu over the years. Upon retirement he returned permanently with his wife to Barangu. He lived there until his death, raising two of his grandchildren with his wife Pia.

Victor "Bobby" Arana and Pia "Mamacita" Magdelano (2006)

On this day in 1934 in Peine **James Avilez** and **Margarita Castillo** married. James was a storekeeper in Barangu. He was also thought by many to be an "innovative farmer." Around 1950 James served as first alcalde for Barangu.

Tomasa Polonio was baptized on this day in 1907 in Monkey River. **Pantaleon Odway Polonio** and Gertrude Lambey are the parents of Tomasa. Many of the early Lambeys of Barangu also lived in Monkey River or had relationships there. Tomasa married **Jacob Palacio**.

On this day **Estefania Avila** was born in 1885 in Peine. She is the daughter of **Victoriano Avila** and **Cesaria Zuniga**. Estefania married **Francisco Martinez** in 1914 in Peine. Estefania is the mother of **Simon Martinez** and **Francis Benedict Martinez**. **Elma Arzu nee Martinez** is the granddaughter of Estefania.

Primrose Augustine was born on this day in Belize City. She is the daughter of **Sadie Nolasca Alvarez**. Primrose is the great-granddaughter of **Geronima Martinez**.

Frank G. Santino and **Romana Velasquez** were married on this day in 1935 in Peine. Frank is the son of **Augustin Santino** and **Pauline Palacio**. Frank was baptized in Seine Bight, but confirmed in Barangu in 1924.

27th December

On this day in 1960 in Barangu **Eudora "Dora" Zuniga** was born She is the daughter of **Eugenia Jean Noralez** and **Clotildo Zuniga**. She married **Benito Martinez** in 1986. Dora died in Orange Walk in 2007. Eudora is **Kevin Zuniga's** aunt.

Valentino Castro and **Michaela Lorenzo** were married on this day in Barangu in 1933. Valentino was from Peine. Michaela was from Barangu, her parents are **Timoteo Lorenzo** and **Juana Palacio**. **Steven "Junior" Gutierrez** is Michaela's grand nephew.

On this day in 1918 **Evangelista Martinez** was born on the Sarstoon Bar. She is the daughter of **Victoriano Martinez** and **Isabela Zuniga**. One of the satellite communities of Barangu was "Cow Shade" on the Guatemala side of the Sarstoon River. "Cow Shade" along with San Martin (also on the Guatemala side) were the realm of the Martinez family. Evangelista is the granddaughter of **Liborio Martinez**.

Francisco Nunez was born on this day. He is the son of **Evaristo "Bob Steele" Nunez** and **Alexine Loredo**. Francisco is **Elorine Nunez's** brother.

Pascacio Cayetano and **Eustaquia Satuye** were married on this day in 1920 in Barangu. Pascacio is the son of **Marcelo Cayetano** and **Maria Loreta Palacio**. Eustaquia is the daughter of **Clemente Satuye** and **Eluteria Cayetano**. This was the second of three marriages for Pascacio. **Sheridan Arzu nee Petillo** is the granddaughter of Pascacio.

Briana Gentle was born on this day in Belize City. She is the daughter of **Don Gentle** and **Dorla Marian Casimiro**. Briana is the granddaughter of **Ricorda Geraldine Casimiro**.

28th December

In the Catholic calendar today is the Feast Day of the Holy Innocents.

Inocente Zuniga was born on this day in Barangu in 1893. He is the son of **Claro Zuniga** and Mauricia Zuniga nee Cayetano. Inocente married **Luciana Nolberto**. Inocente was a well known flute player and led the music for Pia Manadi. He died in 1980 in Barangu. **Lucille Valencio nee Zuniga** is the daughter of Inocente.

Inocente Lopez was born on this day in Barangu in 1920. He is the son of **Santiago Lopez** and **Felicita Bermudez**. Felicita's mother was **Dominga "Gadu" Marin**, the second person to be born in the village according to church records. Gadu was a midwife.

On this day in Barangu in 1900 **Inocenta Nicholas** was born. She is the daughter of **Sotero Nicholas** and **Paula Nunez**. She married **Marcial Chimilio** in 1923 and married **Facundo Martinez** in 1939. Inocenta is Surusia **Bertie Chimilio's** grandmother.

Cyrilo Avila and **Olivia Prudencia Palacio** were married on this day in Peine in 1995. They are the parents of **Rita Enriquez nee Avila** and **Darius Avila**.

Toribio Joseph Lopez and **Emelda Marin** were married on this day in 1937. **Erlinda "Delane" Ogaldez nee Nicholas** is the granddaughter of Toribio and Emelda

Inocenta Avila was born on this day in Peine in 1915. She is the daughter of **Pantaleon Avila** and **Juliana Garcia**. Juliana's parents are **Apolinario Garcia** and **Marcelina "Magiri" Garcia nee Martinez**, who were among the pioneering settler families of the village. Inocenta moved from the village to live in Peine and one of her descendants is Justice **Adolph Lucas** of the Belize Supreme Court.

On this day in Barangu in 1903 **Inocente Lambey** was born. His parents are **John Lambey** and **Gregoria Nolberto**. **Paula Nolberto** is Inocente's first cousin once removed.

Joseph Guevara and **Teodora Nicholas** were married on this day in 1933 in Barangu. Joseph is the son of **Esteban Guevara** and **Marcelina Mejia**. Theodora is the daughter of **Sotero Nicholas** and **Paula Nunez**. Theodora had **Ben Arzu** from a different relationship.

29th December

Venancio "Ben" Noralez died on this day in Barangu in 1926. He is the son of **Florencio Noralez** and

Gregoria Mena. He was 67 when he died. Venancio was brother to the mother of **James "Jim" Avilez**, **Paula Noralez**. Venancio married **Gumercinda Palacio** in 1894. Venancio is the grandfather of Eugenia "Jean" Zuniga nee Noralez.

On this day in 1973 **Sebastian Cayetano** and **Isabel Nunez** were married. Sebastian is a retired school teacher. He is active in the Belize City Branch of the National Garifuna Council and is also involved with the Garifuna Choir at St. Martin de Porres. He is the great-grandson of **Maria Loreta Palacio**.

Procopio "Tito" Arzu and **Encarnacion Martinez** were married in Barangu in 1941. Procopio is the son of **Francisco Ellis Arzu** and Patrocinia Palacio and is also the brother of **Candido Arzu**. Encarnacion is the daughter of **Macario Martinez** and **Escolastica "Ka" Santino**. **Maria Loreta Palacio** is the great-aunt of Procopio.

30th December

Bonifacia Francois died on this day in Dangriga in 1970. She is the daughter of **Francisco Francois** and **Ambrosia Servio**. Bonifacia is the mother of **Victoriana "Vicky" Nolberto nee Martinez**.

Dickson Castro was born on this day in Dangriga. He is the son of **Vicenta "Lulu" Sanchez** and Francis Castro. **Maria Loreta Palacio** is the great-great-aunt of Dickson.

On this day in 1943 in Peine **Felix "Aska" Noralez** and **Silveria Bernardez** were married. This was a second marriage for Felix. **Silveria Bernardez** is the daughter of **Martin Bernardez** and **Apolinaria Ogaldez**. He was married earlier to **Juana "Gubida" Nolberto**, who was a well known midwife in the village.

Gregoria Noralez and **Valentine Baltazar** were married on this day in Peine in 1940. Gregoria is the daughter of **Felix "Aska" Noralez** and **Juana "Gubida" Nolberto**. Valentine is the son of **Eusebio Baltazar** and **Cayetana Rivas**. Gregoria is the aunt of **Teresa "Tandu" Noralez**.

31st December

Candido Arzu and **Bernadette Loredo** were married on this day in 1938 in Barangu. Candido was the principal teacher in Barangu for over 20 years. After retiring Candido remained in the village doing farming and fishing and sharing his strong leadership skills in village affairs. Among other qualities, he was very knowledgeable about village history.

Hilario Nolberto and Victoriana "Vicky" Martinez

On this day **Hilario Nolberto** and **Victoriana "Vicky" Martinez** were married. Hilario is the son of **Dionisio Nolberto** and **Nicolasa Martinez**. "Vicky" is the daughter of **Claudio Martinez** and **Bonifacia Francois**. Hilario was a carpenter; one of the last buildings he constructed was the dubuyaba in Barangu. "Vicky" was a noted craft lady in the village. She was the Community Health Worker in the village for a number of years.

Maria Loreta Palacio died on this day in 1925 in Barangu. She is the daughter of **Teodoro "Joe Young" Palacio** and **Maria Tomasa Martinez**. She was born in 1862 in Barangu (this birth was the first recorded birth in Barangu). Maria Loreta was also baptized on this day in 1862. This baptism was the first recorded baptism in the village. Maria Loreta married **Marcelo Cayetano** in 1883 in Barangu.

More Life Events in December

_____

_____

_____

_____

_____

_____

_____

_____

_____

_____

Family Charts

Descendants of Desideria

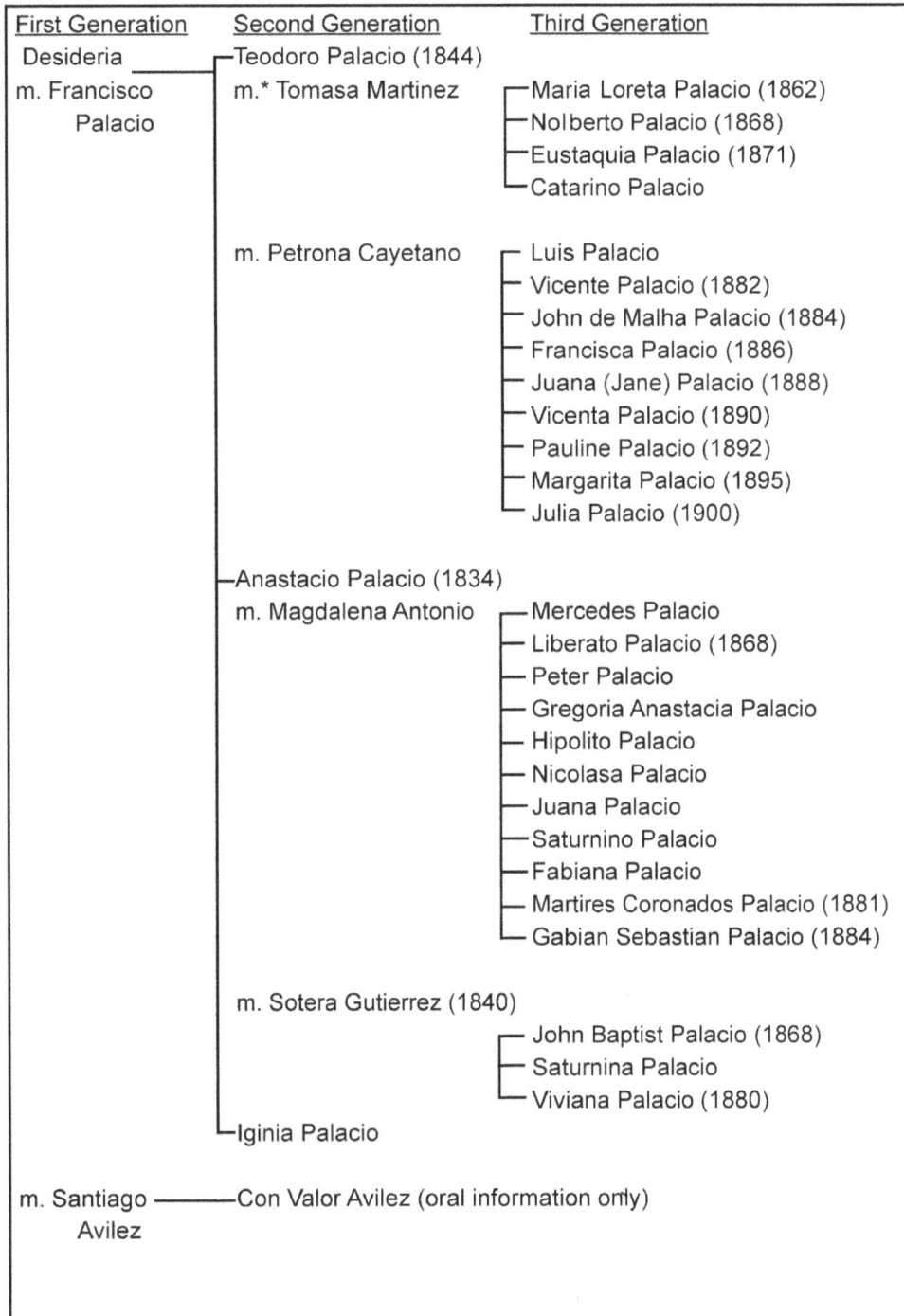

First Generation	Second Generation	Third Generation
Desideria	┌Teodoro Palacio (1844)	
m. Francisco Palacio	m.* Tomasa Martinez	┌Maria Loreta Palacio (1862)
		├Nolberto Palacio (1868)
		├Eustaquia Palacio (1871)
		└Catarino Palacio
	m. Petrona Cayetano	┌ Luis Palacio
		├ Vicente Palacio (1882)
		├ John de Malha Palacio (1884)
		├ Francisca Palacio (1886)
		├ Juana (Jane) Palacio (1888)
		├ Vicenta Palacio (1890)
		├ Pauline Palacio (1892)
		├ Margarita Palacio (1895)
		└ Julia Palacio (1900)
	─Anastacio Palacio (1834)	
	m. Magdalena Antonio	┌─Mercedes Palacio
		├ Liberato Palacio (1868)
		├ Peter Palacio
		├ Gregoria Anastacia Palacio
		├ Hipolito Palacio
		├ Nicolasa Palacio
		├ Juana Palacio
		├ Saturnino Palacio
		├ Fabiana Palacio
		├ Martires Coronados Palacio (1881)
		└ Gabian Sebastian Palacio (1884)
	m. Sotera Gutierrez (1840)	
		┌ John Baptist Palacio (1868)
		├ Saturnina Palacio
		└ Viviana Palacio (1880)
	└Iginia Palacio	
m. Santiago Avilez	──Con Valor Avilez (oral information only)	

*m means "married," but throughout we mean a relationship that resulted in children, not necessarily that they went through a ceremony. The years in parentheses are approximate birth dates or birth-death dates. Some were calculated from age given in marriage or death records, which is not as accurate as birth dates.

Descendants of Juan Pedro Cayetano and Nicolasa Moralez

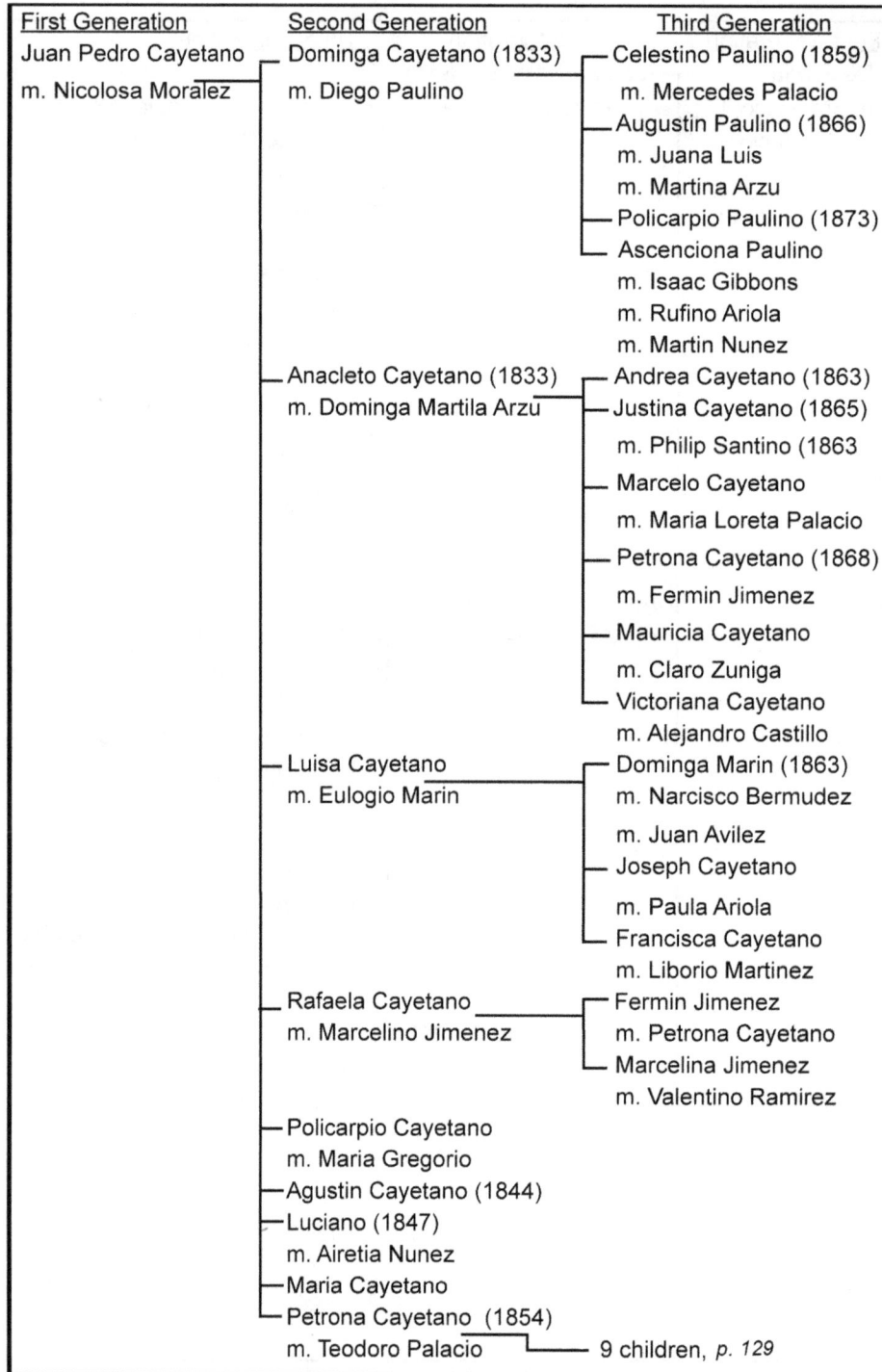

First Generation	Second Generation	Third Generation
Juan Pedro Cayetano	Dominga Cayetano (1833)	Celestino Paulino (1859)
m. Nicolosa Moralez	m. Diego Paulino	m. Mercedes Palacio
		Augustin Paulino (1866)
		m. Juana Luis
		m. Martina Arzu
		Policarpio Paulino (1873)
		Ascenciona Paulino
		m. Isaac Gibbons
		m. Rufino Ariola
		m. Martin Nunez
	Anacleto Cayetano (1833)	Andrea Cayetano (1863)
	m. Dominga Martila Arzu	Justina Cayetano (1865)
		m. Philip Santino (1863
		Marcelo Cayetano
		m. Maria Loreta Palacio
		Petrona Cayetano (1868)
		m. Fermin Jimenez
		Mauricia Cayetano
		m. Claro Zuniga
		Victoriana Cayetano
		m. Alejandro Castillo
	Luisa Cayetano	Dominga Marin (1863)
	m. Eulogio Marin	m. Narcisco Bermudez
		m. Juan Avilez
		Joseph Cayetano
		m. Paula Ariola
		Francisca Cayetano
		m. Liborio Martinez
	Rafaela Cayetano	Fermin Jimenez
	m. Marcelino Jimenez	m. Petrona Cayetano
		Marcelina Jimenez
		m. Valentino Ramirez
	Policarpio Cayetano	
	m. Maria Gregorio	
	Agustin Cayetano (1844)	
	Luciano (1847)	
	m. Airetia Nunez	
	Maria Cayetano	
	Petrona Cayetano (1854)	
	m. Teodoro Palacio	9 children, *p. 129*

Descendants of Alexander Nicholas and Eugenia Delavez

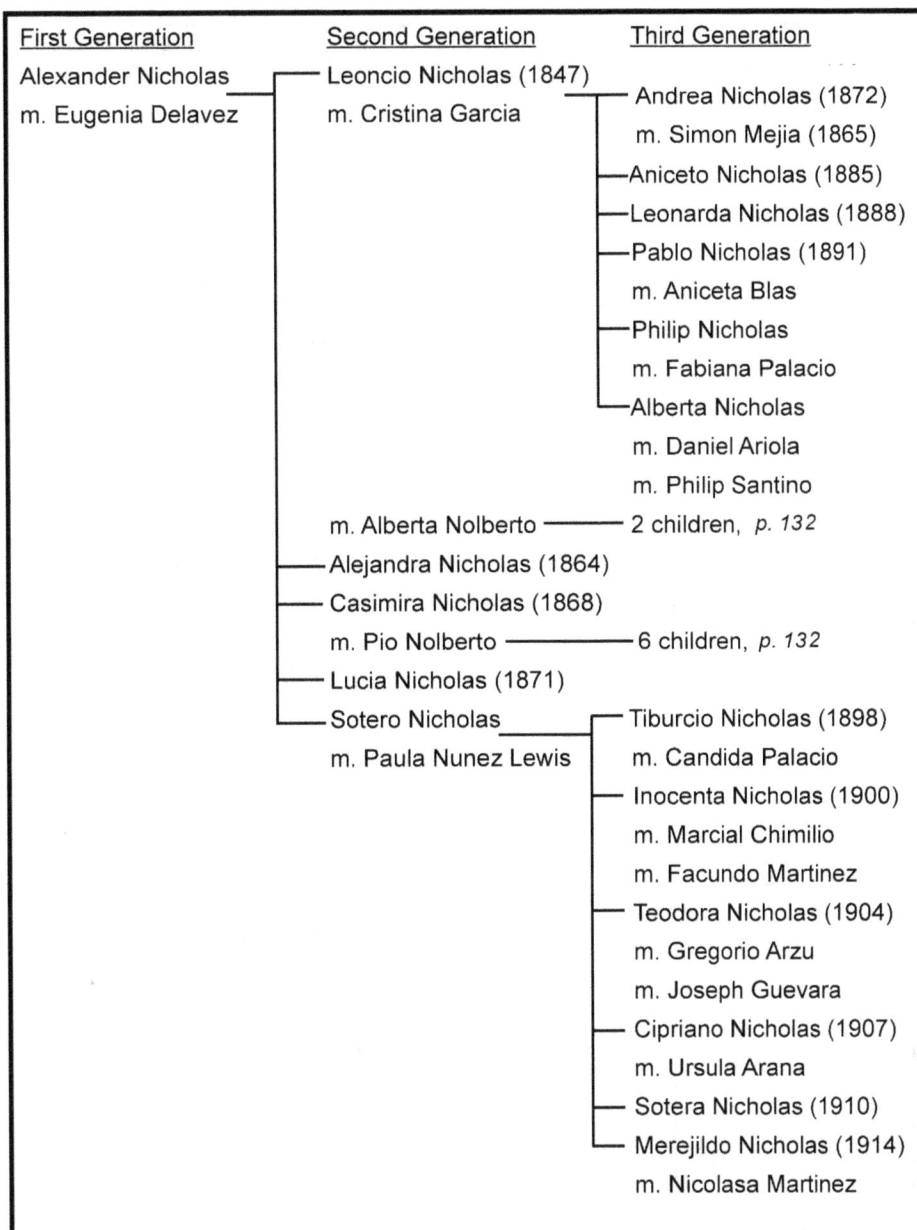

First Generation	Second Generation	Third Generation
Alexander Nicholas	Leoncio Nicholas (1847)	
m. Eugenia Delavez	m. Cristina Garcia	Andrea Nicholas (1872)
		m. Simon Mejia (1865)
		Aniceto Nicholas (1885)
		Leonarda Nicholas (1888)
		Pablo Nicholas (1891)
		m. Aniceta Blas
		Philip Nicholas
		m. Fabiana Palacio
		Alberta Nicholas
		m. Daniel Ariola
		m. Philip Santino
	m. Alberta Nolberto ——	2 children, *p. 132*
	Alejandra Nicholas (1864)	
	Casimira Nicholas (1868)	
	m. Pio Nolberto ——	6 children, *p. 132*
	Lucia Nicholas (1871)	
	Sotero Nicholas	Tiburcio Nicholas (1898)
	m. Paula Nunez Lewis	m. Candida Palacio
		Inocenta Nicholas (1900)
		m. Marcial Chimilio
		m. Facundo Martinez
		Teodora Nicholas (1904)
		m. Gregorio Arzu
		m. Joseph Guevara
		Cipriano Nicholas (1907)
		m. Ursula Arana
		Sotera Nicholas (1910)
		Merejildo Nicholas (1914)
		m. Nicolasa Martinez

131

Descendants of Francisco Nolberto and Serapia Alvarez

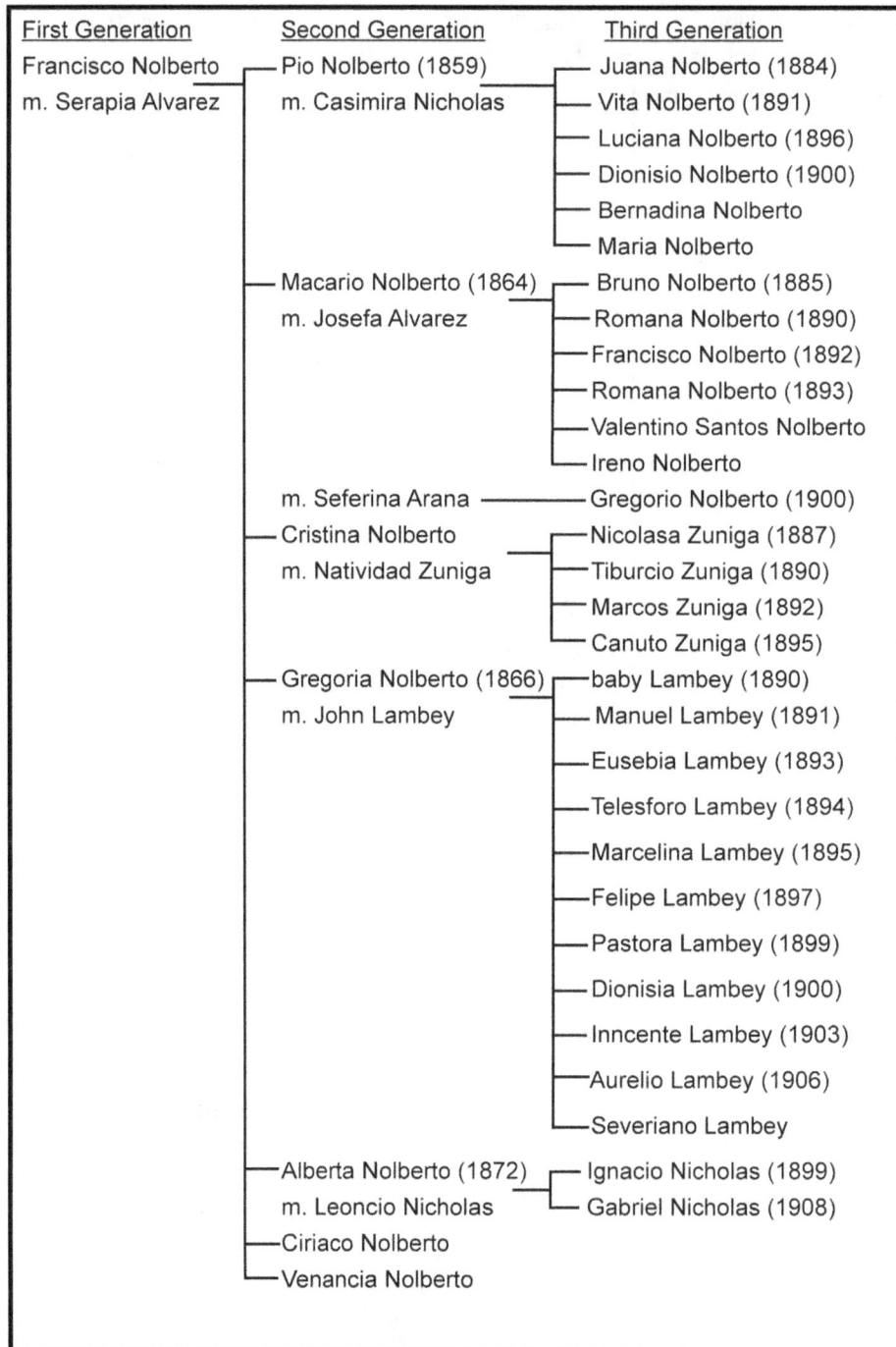

First Generation	Second Generation	Third Generation
Francisco Nolberto	Pio Nolberto (1859)	Juana Nolberto (1884)
m. Serapia Alvarez	m. Casimira Nicholas	Vita Nolberto (1891)
		Luciana Nolberto (1896)
		Dionisio Nolberto (1900)
		Bernadina Nolberto
		Maria Nolberto
	Macario Nolberto (1864)	Bruno Nolberto (1885)
	m. Josefa Alvarez	Romana Nolberto (1890)
		Francisco Nolberto (1892)
		Romana Nolberto (1893)
		Valentino Santos Nolberto
		Ireno Nolberto
	m. Seferina Arana	Gregorio Nolberto (1900)
	Cristina Nolberto	Nicolasa Zuniga (1887)
	m. Natividad Zuniga	Tiburcio Zuniga (1890)
		Marcos Zuniga (1892)
		Canuto Zuniga (1895)
	Gregoria Nolberto (1866)	baby Lambey (1890)
	m. John Lambey	Manuel Lambey (1891)
		Eusebia Lambey (1893)
		Telesforo Lambey (1894)
		Marcelina Lambey (1895)
		Felipe Lambey (1897)
		Pastora Lambey (1899)
		Dionisia Lambey (1900)
		Inncente Lambey (1903)
		Aurelio Lambey (1906)
		Severiano Lambey
	Alberta Nolberto (1872)	Ignacio Nicholas (1899)
	m. Leoncio Nicholas	Gabriel Nicholas (1908)
	Ciriaco Nolberto	
	Venancia Nolberto	

Descendants of Apolinario Garcia and Marcelina Martinez

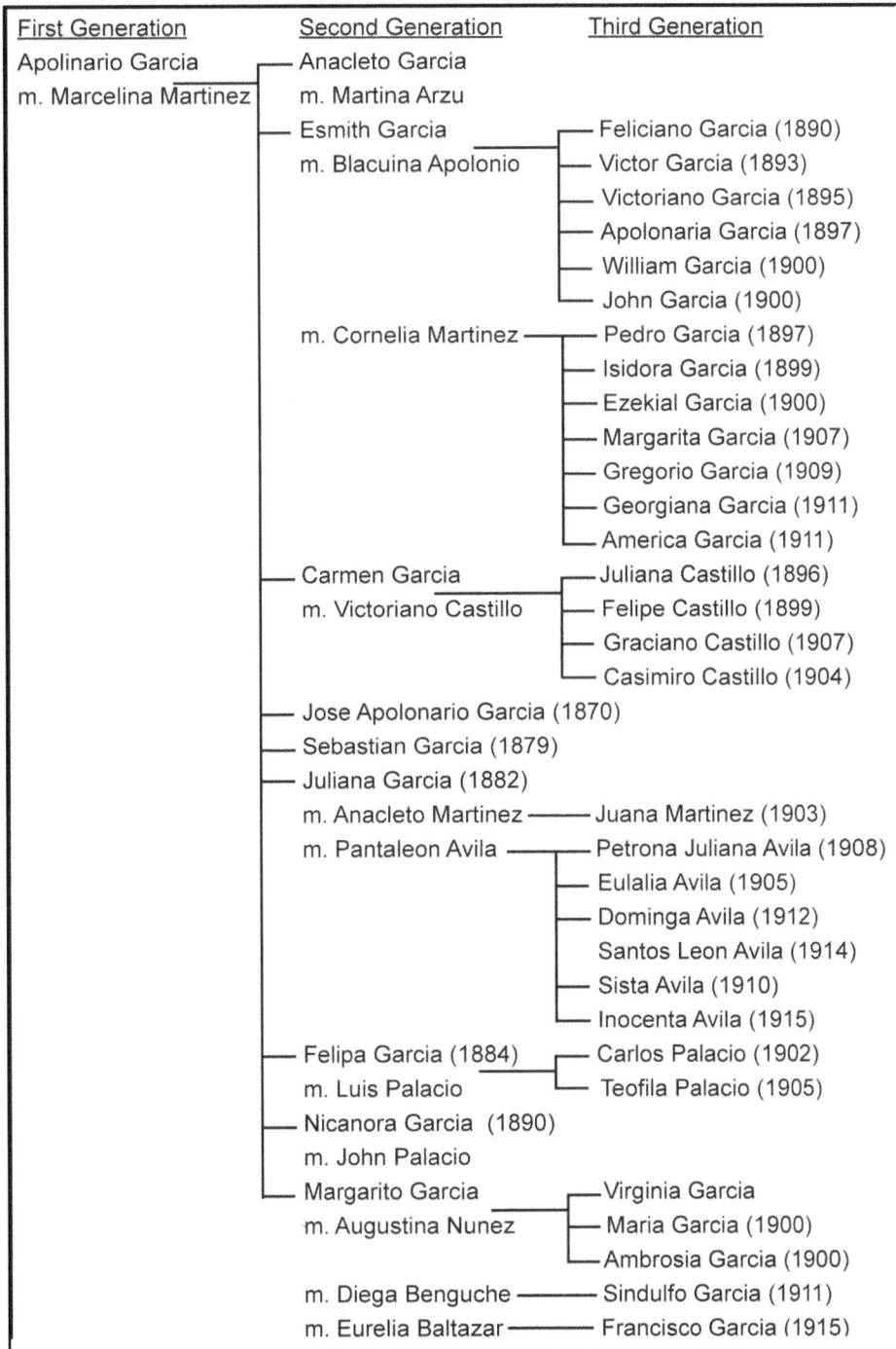

First Generation	Second Generation	Third Generation
Apolinario Garcia m. Marcelina Martinez	Anacleto Garcia m. Martina Arzu	
	Esmith Garcia m. Blacuina Apolonio	Feliciano Garcia (1890) Victor Garcia (1893) Victoriano Garcia (1895) Apolonaria Garcia (1897) William Garcia (1900) John Garcia (1900)
	m. Cornelia Martinez	Pedro Garcia (1897) Isidora Garcia (1899) Ezekial Garcia (1900) Margarita Garcia (1907) Gregorio Garcia (1909) Georgiana Garcia (1911) America Garcia (1911)
	Carmen Garcia m. Victoriano Castillo	Juliana Castillo (1896) Felipe Castillo (1899) Graciano Castillo (1907) Casimiro Castillo (1904)
	Jose Apolonario Garcia (1870)	
	Sebastian Garcia (1879)	
	Juliana Garcia (1882)	
	m. Anacleto Martinez	Juana Martinez (1903)
	m. Pantaleon Avila	Petrona Juliana Avila (1908) Eulalia Avila (1905) Dominga Avila (1912) Santos Leon Avila (1914) Sista Avila (1910) Inocenta Avila (1915)
	Felipa Garcia (1884) m. Luis Palacio	Carlos Palacio (1902) Teofila Palacio (1905)
	Nicanora Garcia (1890) m. John Palacio	
	Margarito Garcia m. Augustina Nunez	Virginia Garcia Maria Garcia (1900) Ambrosia Garcia (1900)
	m. Diega Benguche	Sindulfo Garcia (1911)
	m. Eurelia Baltazar	Francisco Garcia (1915)

Descendants of Rufino Ariola

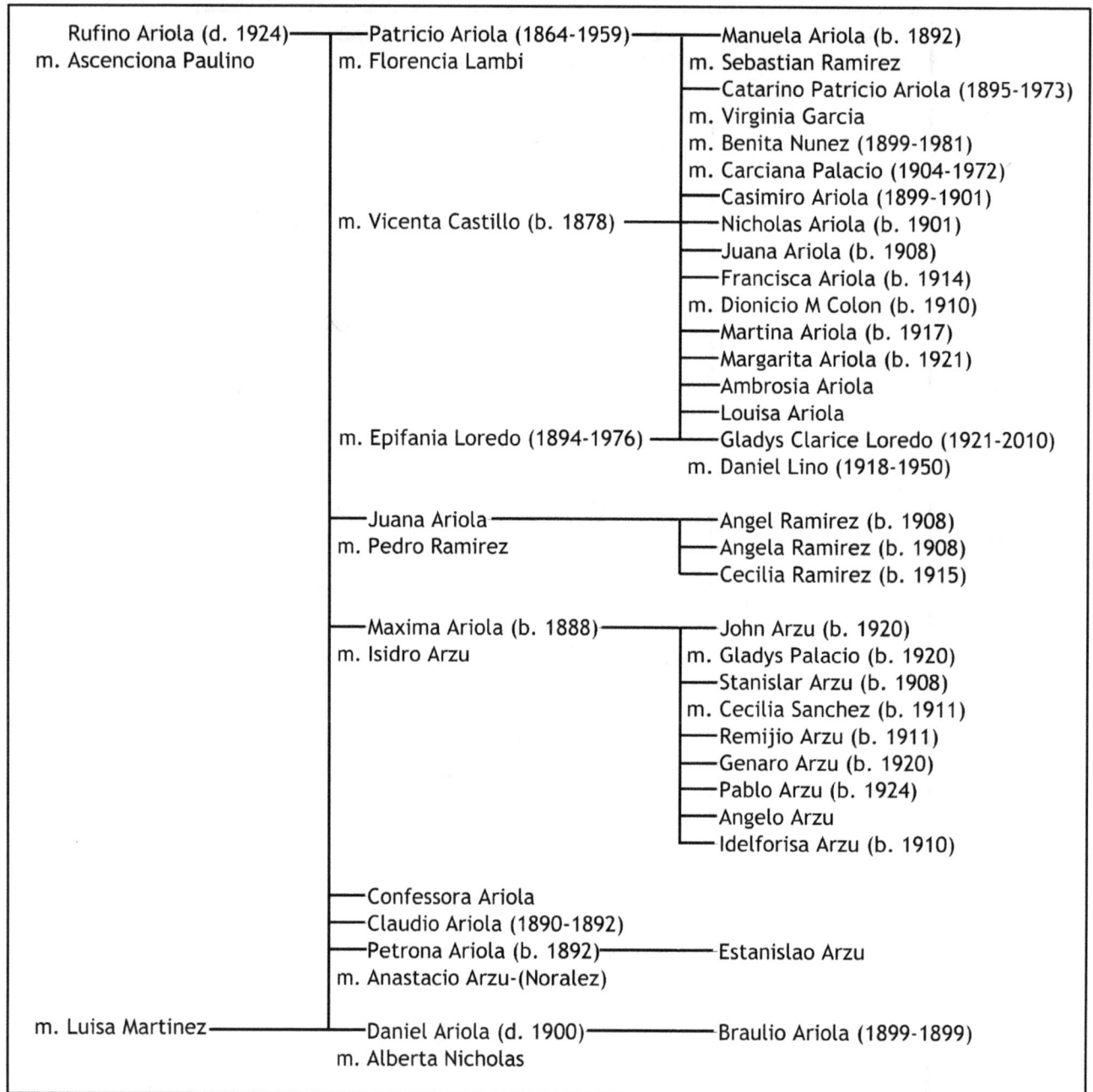

```
Rufino Ariola (d. 1924)──────Patricio Ariola (1864-1959)──────Manuela Ariola (b. 1892)
m. Ascenciona Paulino        m. Florencia Lambi                m. Sebastian Ramirez
                                                               ──Catarino Patricio Ariola (1895-1973)
                                                               m. Virginia Garcia
                                                               m. Benita Nunez (1899-1981)
                                                               m. Carciana Palacio (1904-1972)
                                                               ──Casimiro Ariola (1899-1901)
                             m. Vicenta Castillo (b. 1878)────Nicholas Ariola (b. 1901)
                                                               ──Juana Ariola (b. 1908)
                                                               ──Francisca Ariola (b. 1914)
                                                               m. Dionicio M Colon (b. 1910)
                                                               ──Martina Ariola (b. 1917)
                                                               ──Margarita Ariola (b. 1921)
                                                               ──Ambrosia Ariola
                                                               ──Louisa Ariola
                             m. Epifania Loredo (1894-1976)───Gladys Clarice Loredo (1921-2010)
                                                               m. Daniel Lino (1918-1950)

                             ──Juana Ariola───────────────────Angel Ramirez (b. 1908)
                             m. Pedro Ramirez                  ──Angela Ramirez (b. 1908)
                                                               ──Cecilia Ramirez (b. 1915)

                             ──Maxima Ariola (b. 1888)────────John Arzu (b. 1920)
                             m. Isidro Arzu                    m. Gladys Palacio (b. 1920)
                                                               ──Stanislar Arzu (b. 1908)
                                                               m. Cecilia Sanchez (b. 1911)
                                                               ──Remijio Arzu (b. 1911)
                                                               ──Genaro Arzu (b. 1920)
                                                               ──Pablo Arzu (b. 1924)
                                                               ──Angelo Arzu
                                                               ──Idelforisa Arzu (b. 1910)

                             ──Confessora Ariola
                             ──Claudio Ariola (1890-1892)
                             ──Petrona Ariola (b. 1892)────────Estanislao Arzu
                             m. Anastacio Arzu-(Noralez)

m. Luisa Martinez────────────Daniel Ariola (d. 1900)──────────Braulio Ariola (1899-1899)
                             m. Alberta Nicholas
```

Descendants of Diego Paulino

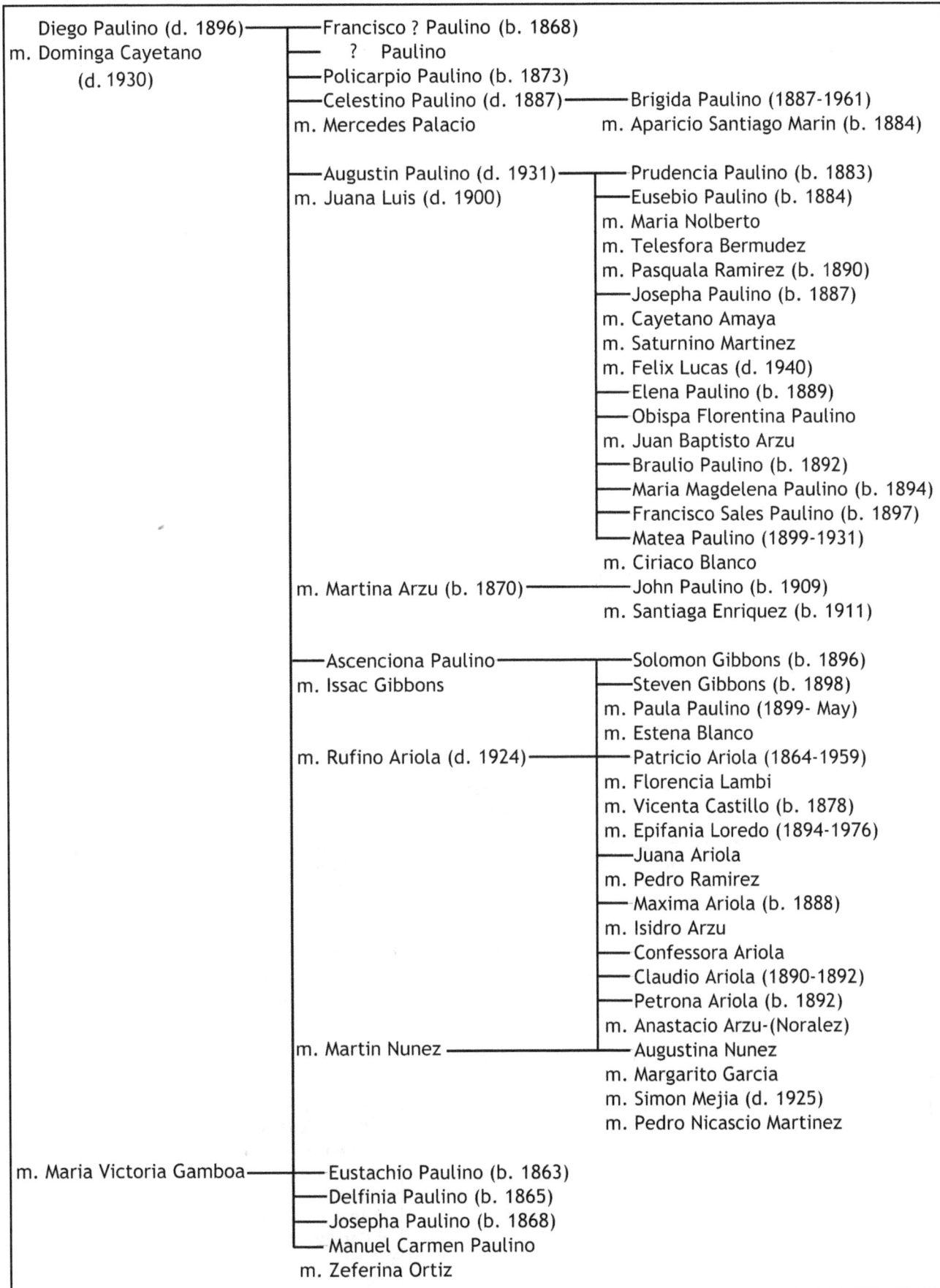

Diego Paulino (d. 1896)———— Francisco ? Paulino (b. 1868)
m. Dominga Cayetano   —   ?   Paulino
      (d. 1930)   ——Policarpio Paulino (b. 1873)
    ——Celestino Paulino (d. 1887)———— Brigida Paulino (1887-1961)
    m. Mercedes Palacio   m. Aparicio Santiago Marin (b. 1884)

    ——Augustin Paulino (d. 1931)———— Prudencia Paulino (b. 1883)
    m. Juana Luis (d. 1900)   ——Eusebio Paulino (b. 1884)
                                      m. Maria Nolberto
                                      m. Telesfora Bermudez
                                      m. Pasquala Ramirez (b. 1890)
                                  ——Josepha Paulino (b. 1887)
                                      m. Cayetano Amaya
                                      m. Saturnino Martinez
                                      m. Felix Lucas (d. 1940)
                                  ——Elena Paulino (b. 1889)
                                  ——Obispa Florentina Paulino
                                      m. Juan Baptisto Arzu
                                  ——Braulio Paulino (b. 1892)
                                  ——Maria Magdelena Paulino (b. 1894)
                                  ——Francisco Sales Paulino (b. 1897)
                                  ——Matea Paulino (1899-1931)
                                    m. Ciriaco Blanco
    m. Martina Arzu (b. 1870)———— John Paulino (b. 1909)
                                    m. Santiaga Enriquez (b. 1911)

    ——Ascenciona Paulino———— Solomon Gibbons (b. 1896)
    m. Issac Gibbons   ——Steven Gibbons (b. 1898)
                                    m. Paula Paulino (1899- May)
                                    m. Estena Blanco
    m. Rufino Ariola (d. 1924)———— Patricio Ariola (1864-1959)
                                    m. Florencia Lambi
                                    m. Vicenta Castillo (b. 1878)
                                    m. Epifania Loredo (1894-1976)
                                ——Juana Ariola
                                    m. Pedro Ramirez
                                ——Maxima Ariola (b. 1888)
                                    m. Isidro Arzu
                                ——Confessora Ariola
                                ——Claudio Ariola (1890-1892)
                                ——Petrona Ariola (b. 1892)
                                    m. Anastacio Arzu-(Noralez)
    m. Martin Nunez ———— Augustina Nunez
                                    m. Margarito Garcia
                                    m. Simon Mejia (d. 1925)
                                    m. Pedro Nicascio Martinez

m. Maria Victoria Gamboa———— Eustachio Paulino (b. 1863)
                     ——Delfinia Paulino (b. 1865)
                     ——Josepha Paulino (b. 1868)
                     —— Manuel Carmen Paulino
                     m. Zeferina Ortiz

Descendants of Ascenciona Paulino

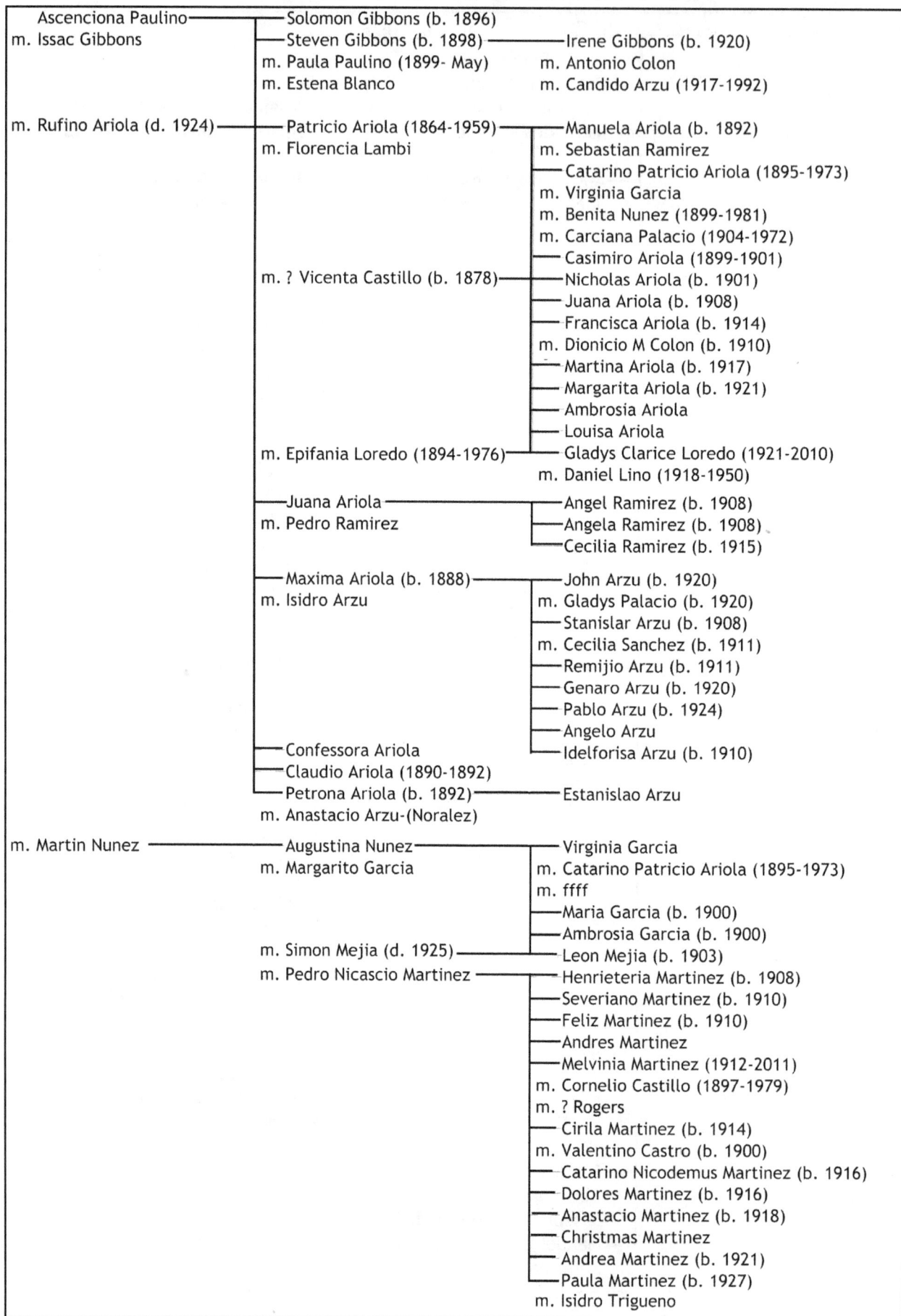

```
Ascenciona Paulino ──────────── Solomon Gibbons (b. 1896)
m. Issac Gibbons                 Steven Gibbons (b. 1898) ──────── Irene Gibbons (b. 1920)
                                 m. Paula Paulino (1899- May)      m. Antonio Colon
                                 m. Estena Blanco                  m. Candido Arzu (1917-1992)

m. Rufino Ariola (d. 1924) ───── Patricio Ariola (1864-1959) ───── Manuela Ariola (b. 1892)
                                 m. Florencia Lambi                m. Sebastian Ramirez
                                                                   Catarino Patricio Ariola (1895-1973)
                                                                   m. Virginia Garcia
                                                                   m. Benita Nunez (1899-1981)
                                                                   m. Carciana Palacio (1904-1972)
                                                                   Casimiro Ariola (1899-1901)
                                 m. ? Vicenta Castillo (b. 1878)── Nicholas Ariola (b. 1901)
                                                                   Juana Ariola (b. 1908)
                                                                   Francisca Ariola (b. 1914)
                                                                   m. Dionicio M Colon (b. 1910)
                                                                   Martina Ariola (b. 1917)
                                                                   Margarita Ariola (b. 1921)
                                                                   Ambrosia Ariola
                                                                   Louisa Ariola
                                 m. Epifania Loredo (1894-1976)─── Gladys Clarice Loredo (1921-2010)
                                                                   m. Daniel Lino (1918-1950)

                                 Juana Ariola ──────────────────── Angel Ramirez (b. 1908)
                                 m. Pedro Ramirez                   Angela Ramirez (b. 1908)
                                                                    Cecilia Ramirez (b. 1915)

                                 Maxima Ariola (b. 1888) ───────── John Arzu (b. 1920)
                                 m. Isidro Arzu                     m. Gladys Palacio (b. 1920)
                                                                    Stanislar Arzu (b. 1908)
                                                                    m. Cecilia Sanchez (b. 1911)
                                                                    Remijio Arzu (b. 1911)
                                                                    Genaro Arzu (b. 1920)
                                                                    Pablo Arzu (b. 1924)
                                                                    Angelo Arzu
                                 Confessora Ariola                  Idelforisa Arzu (b. 1910)
                                 Claudio Ariola (1890-1892)
                                 Petrona Ariola (b. 1892) ───────── Estanislao Arzu
                                 m. Anastacio Arzu-(Noralez)

m. Martin Nunez ──────────────── Augustina Nunez ──────────────── Virginia Garcia
                                 m. Margarito Garcia                m. Catarino Patricio Ariola (1895-1973)
                                                                    m. ffff
                                                                    Maria Garcia (b. 1900)
                                                                    Ambrosia Garcia (b. 1900)
                                 m. Simon Mejia (d. 1925) ───────── Leon Mejia (b. 1903)
                                 m. Pedro Nicascio Martinez ─────── Henrieteria Martinez (b. 1908)
                                                                    Severiano Martinez (b. 1910)
                                                                    Feliz Martinez (b. 1910)
                                                                    Andres Martinez
                                                                    Melvinia Martinez (1912-2011)
                                                                    m. Cornelio Castillo (1897-1979)
                                                                    m. ? Rogers
                                                                    Cirila Martinez (b. 1914)
                                                                    m. Valentino Castro (b. 1900)
                                                                    Catarino Nicodemus Martinez (b. 1916)
                                                                    Dolores Martinez (b. 1916)
                                                                    Anastacio Martinez (b. 1918)
                                                                    Christmas Martinez
                                                                    Andrea Martinez (b. 1921)
                                                                    Paula Martinez (b. 1927)
                                                                    m. Isidro Trigueno
```

Descendants of Eulalio Loredo

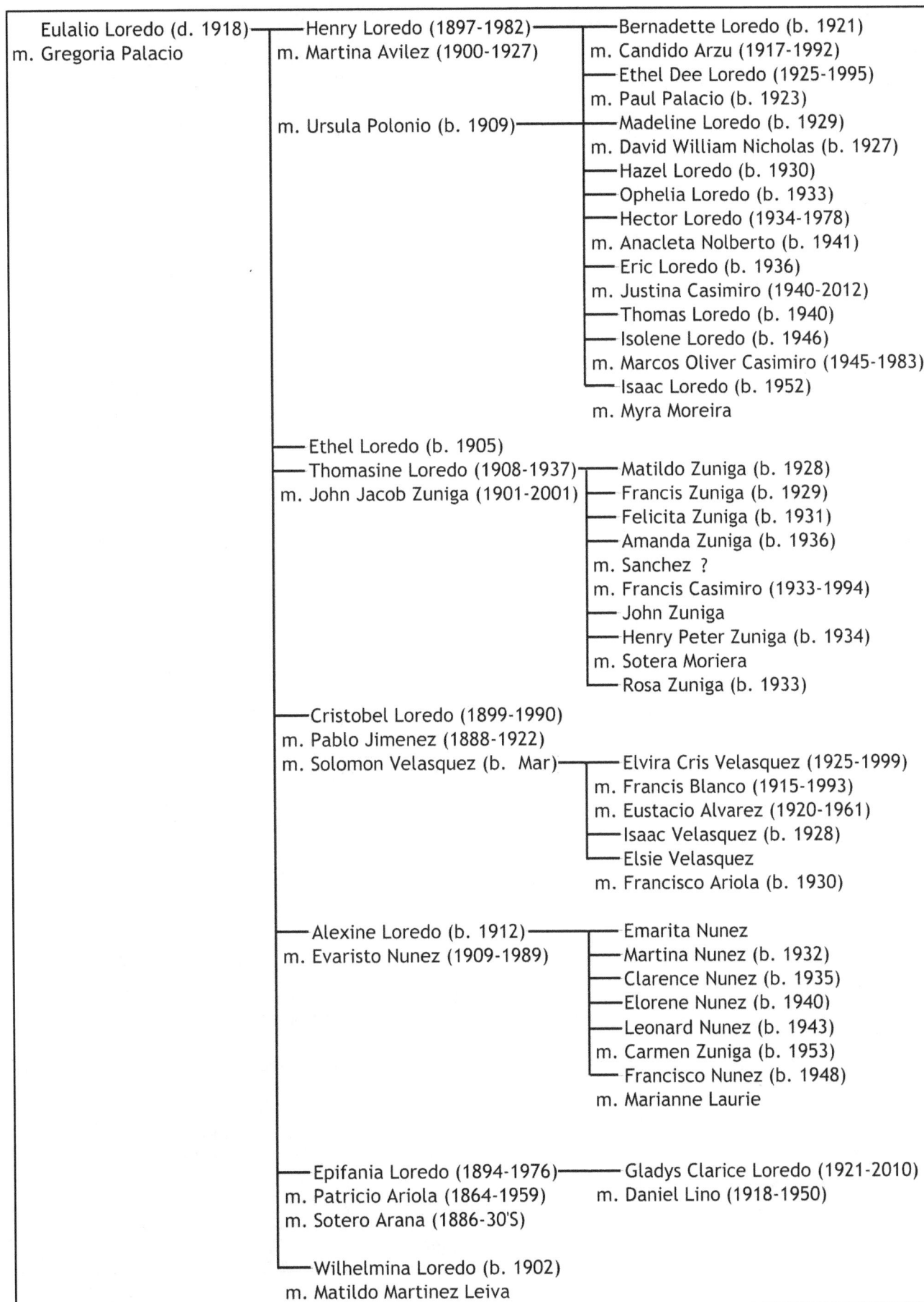

Eulalio Loredo (d. 1918)
m. Gregoria Palacio

— Henry Loredo (1897-1982)
m. Martina Avilez (1900-1927)

  — Bernadette Loredo (b. 1921)
  m. Candido Arzu (1917-1992)
  — Ethel Dee Loredo (1925-1995)
  m. Paul Palacio (b. 1923)

m. Ursula Polonio (b. 1909)

  — Madeline Loredo (b. 1929)
  m. David William Nicholas (b. 1927)
  — Hazel Loredo (b. 1930)
  — Ophelia Loredo (b. 1933)
  — Hector Loredo (1934-1978)
  m. Anacleta Nolberto (b. 1941)
  — Eric Loredo (b. 1936)
  m. Justina Casimiro (1940-2012)
  — Thomas Loredo (b. 1940)
  — Isolene Loredo (b. 1946)
  m. Marcos Oliver Casimiro (1945-1983)
  — Isaac Loredo (b. 1952)
  m. Myra Moreira

— Ethel Loredo (b. 1905)
— Thomasine Loredo (1908-1937)
m. John Jacob Zuniga (1901-2001)

  — Matildo Zuniga (b. 1928)
  — Francis Zuniga (b. 1929)
  — Felicita Zuniga (b. 1931)
  — Amanda Zuniga (b. 1936)
  m. Sanchez ?
  m. Francis Casimiro (1933-1994)
  — John Zuniga
  — Henry Peter Zuniga (b. 1934)
  m. Sotera Moriera
  — Rosa Zuniga (b. 1933)

— Cristobel Loredo (1899-1990)
m. Pablo Jimenez (1888-1922)
m. Solomon Velasquez (b. Mar)

  — Elvira Cris Velasquez (1925-1999)
  m. Francis Blanco (1915-1993)
  m. Eustacio Alvarez (1920-1961)
  — Isaac Velasquez (b. 1928)
  — Elsie Velasquez
  m. Francisco Ariola (b. 1930)

— Alexine Loredo (b. 1912)
m. Evaristo Nunez (1909-1989)

  — Emarita Nunez
  — Martina Nunez (b. 1932)
  — Clarence Nunez (b. 1935)
  — Elorene Nunez (b. 1940)
  — Leonard Nunez (b. 1943)
  m. Carmen Zuniga (b. 1953)
  — Francisco Nunez (b. 1948)
  m. Marianne Laurie

— Epifania Loredo (1894-1976)
m. Patricio Ariola (1864-1959)
m. Sotero Arana (1886-30'S)

  — Gladys Clarice Loredo (1921-2010)
  m. Daniel Lino (1918-1950)

— Wilhelmina Loredo (b. 1902)
m. Matildo Martinez Leiva

Descendants of Narciso Bermudez

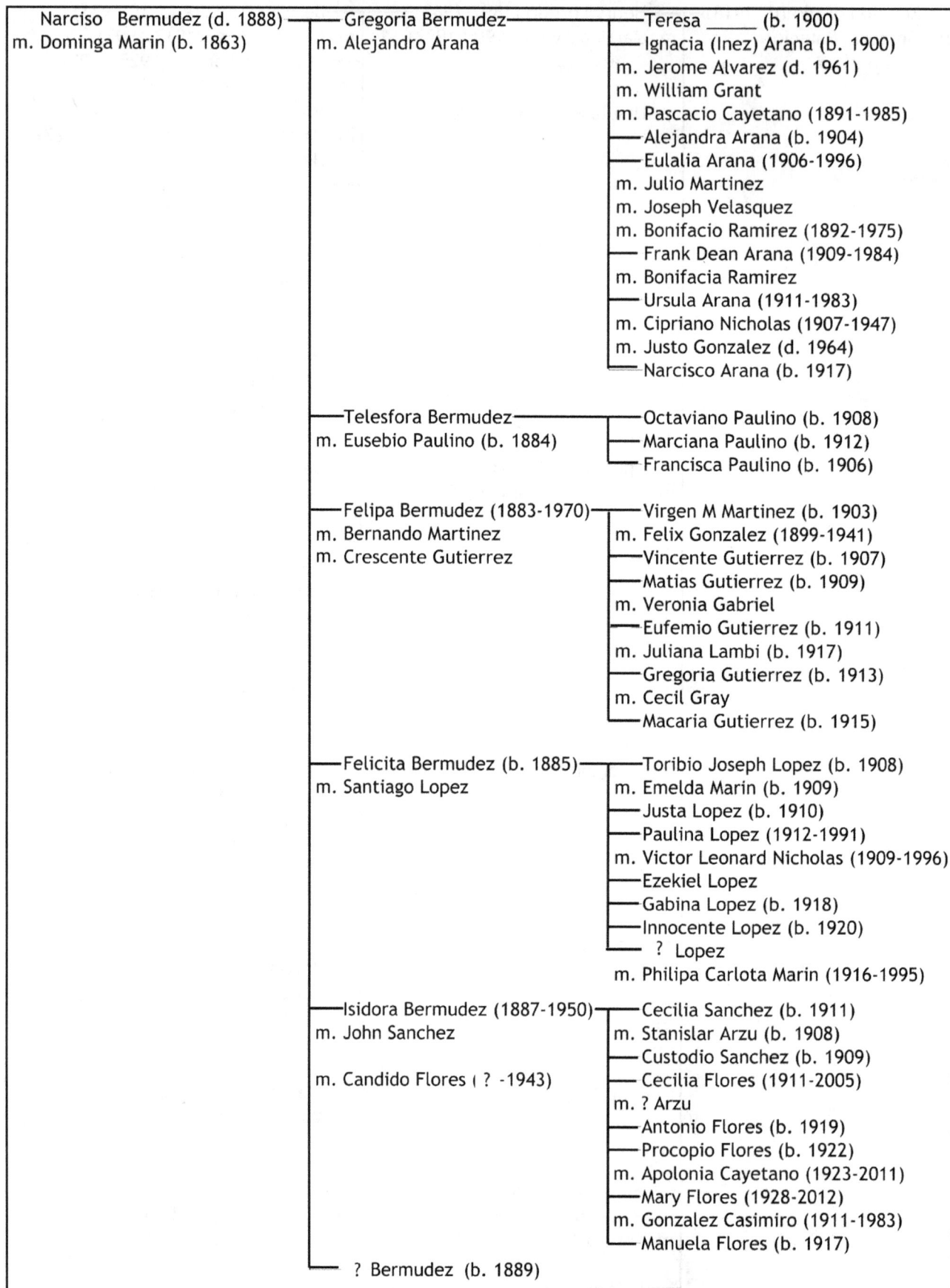

Narciso Bermudez (d. 1888) —— Gregoria Bermudez —————— Teresa _____ (b. 1900)
m. Dominga Marin (b. 1863)   m. Alejandro Arana   — Ignacia (Inez) Arana (b. 1900)
                                                                  m. Jerome Alvarez (d. 1961)
                                                                  m. William Grant
                                                                  m. Pascacio Cayetano (1891-1985)
                                                                — Alejandra Arana (b. 1904)
                                                                — Eulalia Arana (1906-1996)
                                                                  m. Julio Martinez
                                                                  m. Joseph Velasquez
                                                                  m. Bonifacio Ramirez (1892-1975)
                                                                — Frank Dean Arana (1909-1984)
                                                                  m. Bonifacia Ramirez
                                                                — Ursula Arana (1911-1983)
                                                                  m. Cipriano Nicholas (1907-1947)
                                                                  m. Justo Gonzalez (d. 1964)
                                                                — Narcisco Arana (b. 1917)

                                —Telesfora Bermudez—————————Octaviano Paulino (b. 1908)
                                 m. Eusebio Paulino (b. 1884)   —Marciana Paulino (b. 1912)
                                                                —Francisca Paulino (b. 1906)

                                —Felipa Bermudez (1883-1970)—— Virgen M Martinez (b. 1903)
                                 m. Bernando Martinez   m. Felix Gonzalez (1899-1941)
                                 m. Crescente Gutierrez   —Vincente Gutierrez (b. 1907)
                                                               —Matias Gutierrez (b. 1909)
                                                                 m. Veronia Gabriel
                                                               —Eufemio Gutierrez (b. 1911)
                                                                 m. Juliana Lambi (b. 1917)
                                                               —Gregoria Gutierrez (b. 1913)
                                                                 m. Cecil Gray
                                                               —Macaria Gutierrez (b. 1915)

                                —Felicita Bermudez (b. 1885)——Toribio Joseph Lopez (b. 1908)
                                 m. Santiago Lopez   m. Emelda Marin (b. 1909)
                                                               —Justa Lopez (b. 1910)
                                                               —Paulina Lopez (1912-1991)
                                                                 m. Victor Leonard Nicholas (1909-1996)
                                                               —Ezekiel Lopez
                                                               —Gabina Lopez (b. 1918)
                                                               —Innocente Lopez (b. 1920)
                                                               — ? Lopez
                                                                 m. Philipa Carlota Marin (1916-1995)

                                —Isidora Bermudez (1887-1950)—Cecilia Sanchez (b. 1911)
                                 m. John Sanchez   m. Stanislar Arzu (b. 1908)
                                                               — Custodio Sanchez (b. 1909)
                                 m. Candido Flores (? -1943) —Cecilia Flores (1911-2005)
                                                                 m. ? Arzu
                                                               —Antonio Flores (b. 1919)
                                                               —Procopio Flores (b. 1922)
                                                                 m. Apolonia Cayetano (1923-2011)
                                                               —Mary Flores (1928-2012)
                                                                 m. Gonzalez Casimiro (1911-1983)
                                                               —Manuela Flores (b. 1917)

                                — ? Bermudez (b. 1889)

Descendants of Philip Santino

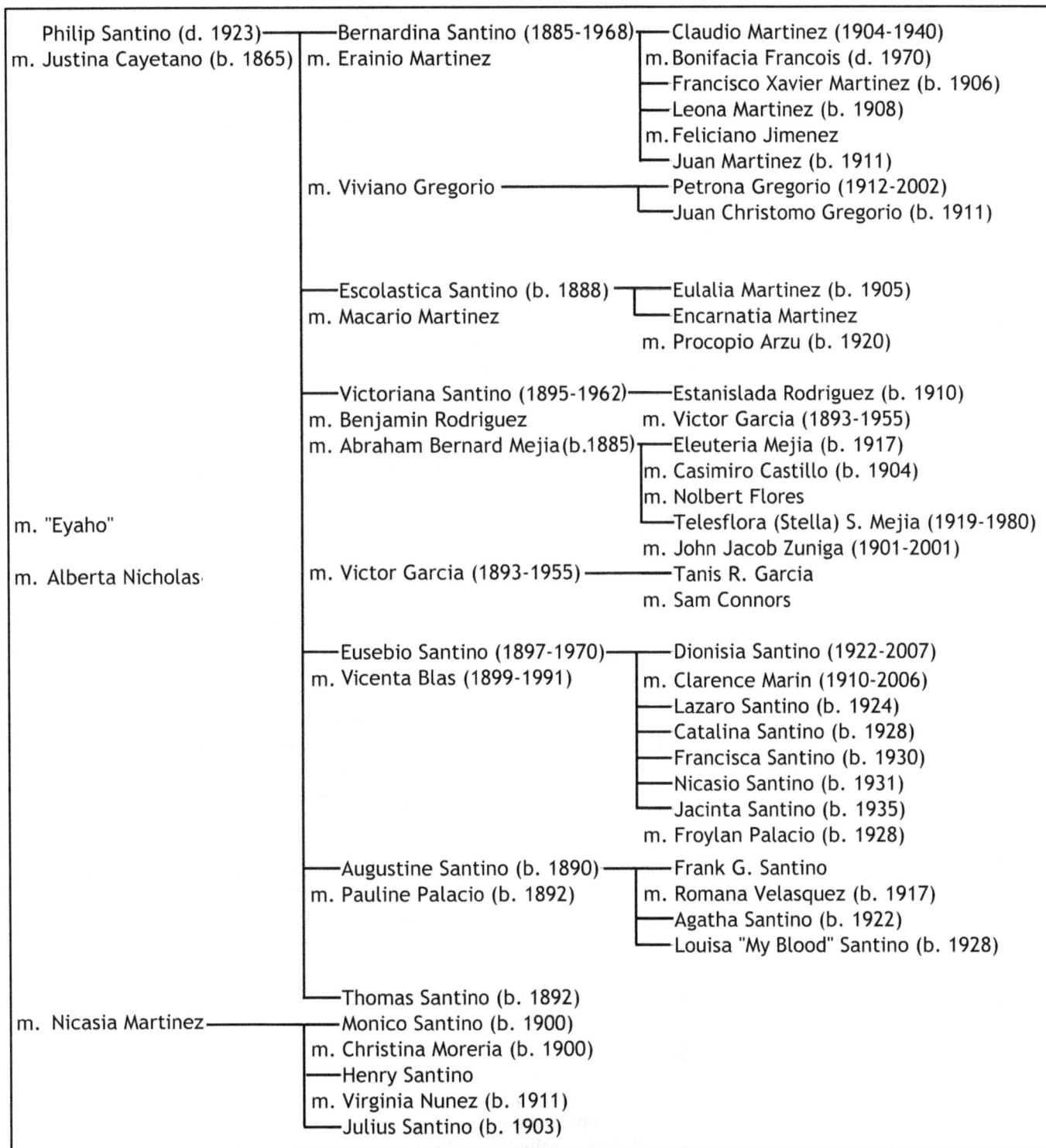

```
Philip Santino (d. 1923)──────┬──Bernardina Santino (1885-1968)─┬──Claudio Martinez (1904-1940)
m. Justina Cayetano (b. 1865) │  m. Erainio Martinez            │  m. Bonifacia Francois (d. 1970)
                              │                                 ├──Francisco Xavier Martinez (b. 1906)
                              │                                 ├──Leona Martinez (b. 1908)
                              │                                 │  m. Feliciano Jimenez
                              │                                 └──Juan Martinez (b. 1911)
                              │  m. Viviano Gregorio ───────────┬──Petrona Gregorio (1912-2002)
                              │                                 └──Juan Christomo Gregorio (b. 1911)
                              │
                              │
                              ├──Escolastica Santino (b. 1888)──┬──Eulalia Martinez (b. 1905)
                              │  m. Macario Martinez            └──Encarnatia Martinez
                              │                                    m. Procopio Arzu (b. 1920)
                              │
                              │
                              ├──Victoriana Santino (1895-1962)────Estanislada Rodriguez (b. 1910)
                              │  m. Benjamin Rodriguez             m. Victor Garcia (1893-1955)
                              │  m. Abraham Bernard Mejia(b.1885)┬──Eleuteria Mejia (b. 1917)
                              │                                  │  m. Casimiro Castillo (b. 1904)
                              │                                  │  m. Nolbert Flores
                              │                                  └──Telesflora (Stella) S. Mejia (1919-1980)
m. "Eyaho"                    │                                     m. John Jacob Zuniga (1901-2001)
                              │  m. Victor Garcia (1893-1955) ─────Tanis R. Garcia
m. Alberta Nicholas·          │                                    m. Sam Connors
                              │
                              │
                              ├──Eusebio Santino (1897-1970)────┬──Dionisia Santino (1922-2007)
                              │  m. Vicenta Blas (1899-1991)    │  m. Clarence Marin (1910-2006)
                              │                                 ├──Lazaro Santino (b. 1924)
                              │                                 ├──Catalina Santino (b. 1928)
                              │                                 ├──Francisca Santino (b. 1930)
                              │                                 ├──Nicasio Santino (b. 1931)
                              │                                 └──Jacinta Santino (b. 1935)
                              │                                    m. Froylan Palacio (b. 1928)
                              │
                              ├──Augustine Santino (b. 1890)────┬──Frank G. Santino
                              │  m. Pauline Palacio (b. 1892)   │  m. Romana Velasquez (b. 1917)
                              │                                 ├──Agatha Santino (b. 1922)
                              │                                 └──Louisa "My Blood" Santino (b. 1928)
                              │
                              │
                              ├──Thomas Santino (b. 1892)
m. Nicasia Martinez──────────┼──Monico Santino (b. 1900)
                              │  m. Christina Moreria (b. 1900)
                              ├──Henry Santino
                              │  m. Virginia Nunez (b. 1911)
                              └──Julius Santino (b. 1903)
```

Descendants of Paula Noralez

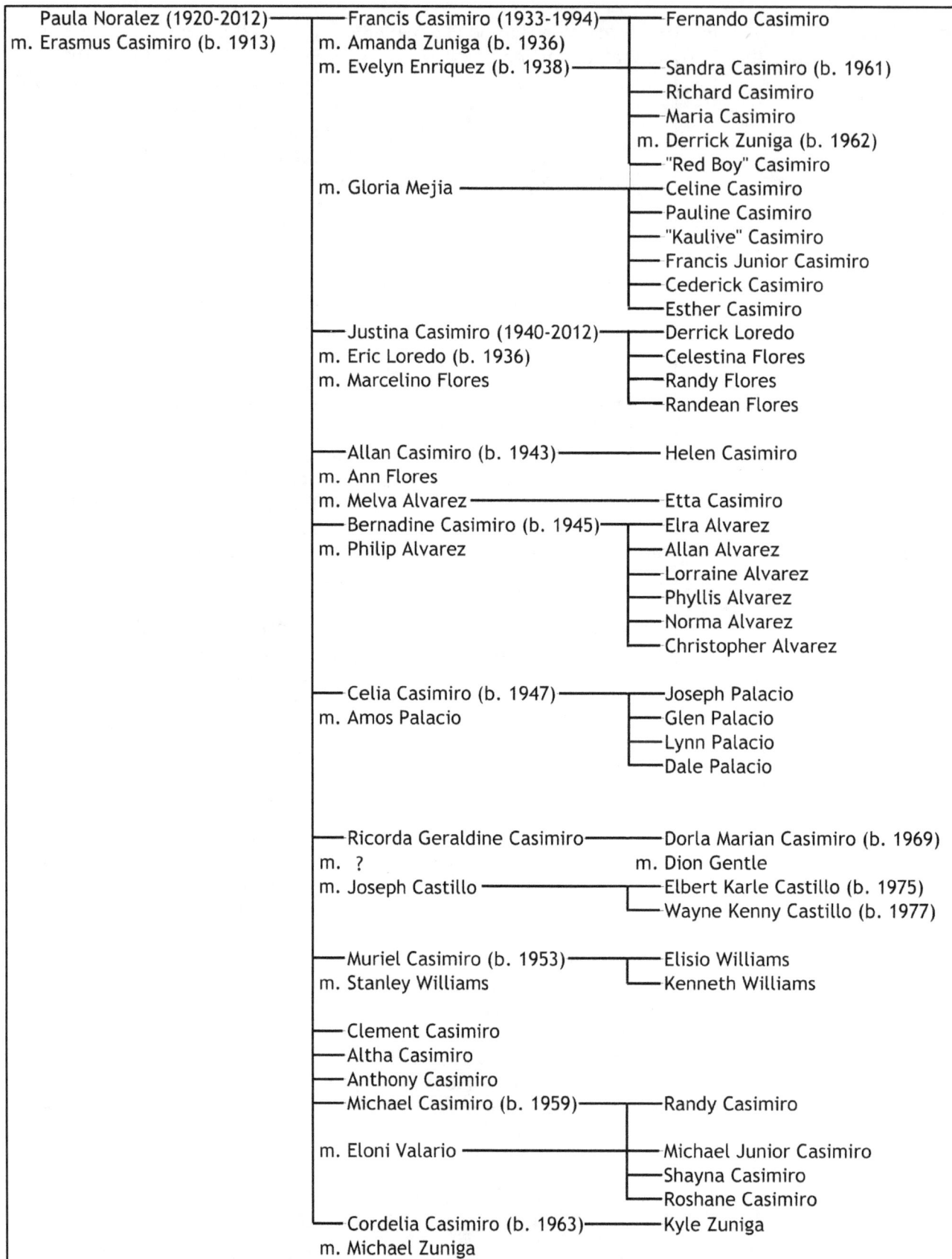

```
Paula Noralez (1920-2012)──────┬── Francis Casimiro (1933-1994)──────── Fernando Casimiro
m. Erasmus Casimiro (b. 1913)  │   m. Amanda Zuniga (b. 1936)
                               │   m. Evelyn Enriquez (b. 1938)────┬── Sandra Casimiro (b. 1961)
                               │                                   ├── Richard Casimiro
                               │                                   ├── Maria Casimiro
                               │                                   │   m. Derrick Zuniga (b. 1962)
                               │                                   ├── "Red Boy" Casimiro
                               │   m. Gloria Mejia ────────────────┼── Celine Casimiro
                               │                                   ├── Pauline Casimiro
                               │                                   ├── "Kaulive" Casimiro
                               │                                   ├── Francis Junior Casimiro
                               │                                   ├── Cederick Casimiro
                               │                                   └── Esther Casimiro
                               │
                               ├── Justina Casimiro (1940-2012)──┬── Derrick Loredo
                               │   m. Eric Loredo (b. 1936)      ├── Celestina Flores
                               │   m. Marcelino Flores           ├── Randy Flores
                               │                                 └── Randean Flores
                               │
                               ├── Allan Casimiro (b. 1943)───────── Helen Casimiro
                               │   m. Ann Flores
                               │   m. Melva Alvarez ─────────────── Etta Casimiro
                               ├── Bernadine Casimiro (b. 1945)──┬── Elra Alvarez
                               │   m. Philip Alvarez             ├── Allan Alvarez
                               │                                 ├── Lorraine Alvarez
                               │                                 ├── Phyllis Alvarez
                               │                                 ├── Norma Alvarez
                               │                                 └── Christopher Alvarez
                               │
                               ├── Celia Casimiro (b. 1947)──────┬── Joseph Palacio
                               │   m. Amos Palacio               ├── Glen Palacio
                               │                                 ├── Lynn Palacio
                               │                                 └── Dale Palacio
                               │
                               ├── Ricorda Geraldine Casimiro──────── Dorla Marian Casimiro (b. 1969)
                               │   m. ?                               m. Dion Gentle
                               │   m. Joseph Castillo ────────────┬── Elbert Karle Castillo (b. 1975)
                               │                                   └── Wayne Kenny Castillo (b. 1977)
                               │
                               ├── Muriel Casimiro (b. 1953)─────┬── Elisio Williams
                               │   m. Stanley Williams           └── Kenneth Williams
                               │
                               ├── Clement Casimiro
                               ├── Altha Casimiro
                               ├── Anthony Casimiro
                               ├── Michael Casimiro (b. 1959)────┬── Randy Casimiro
                               │                                 │
                               │   m. Eloni Valario ─────────────┼── Michael Junior Casimiro
                               │                                 ├── Shayna Casimiro
                               │                                 └── Roshane Casimiro
                               │
                               └── Cordelia Casimiro (b. 1963)─────── Kyle Zuniga
                                   m. Michael Zuniga
```

Descendants of Simon Mejia

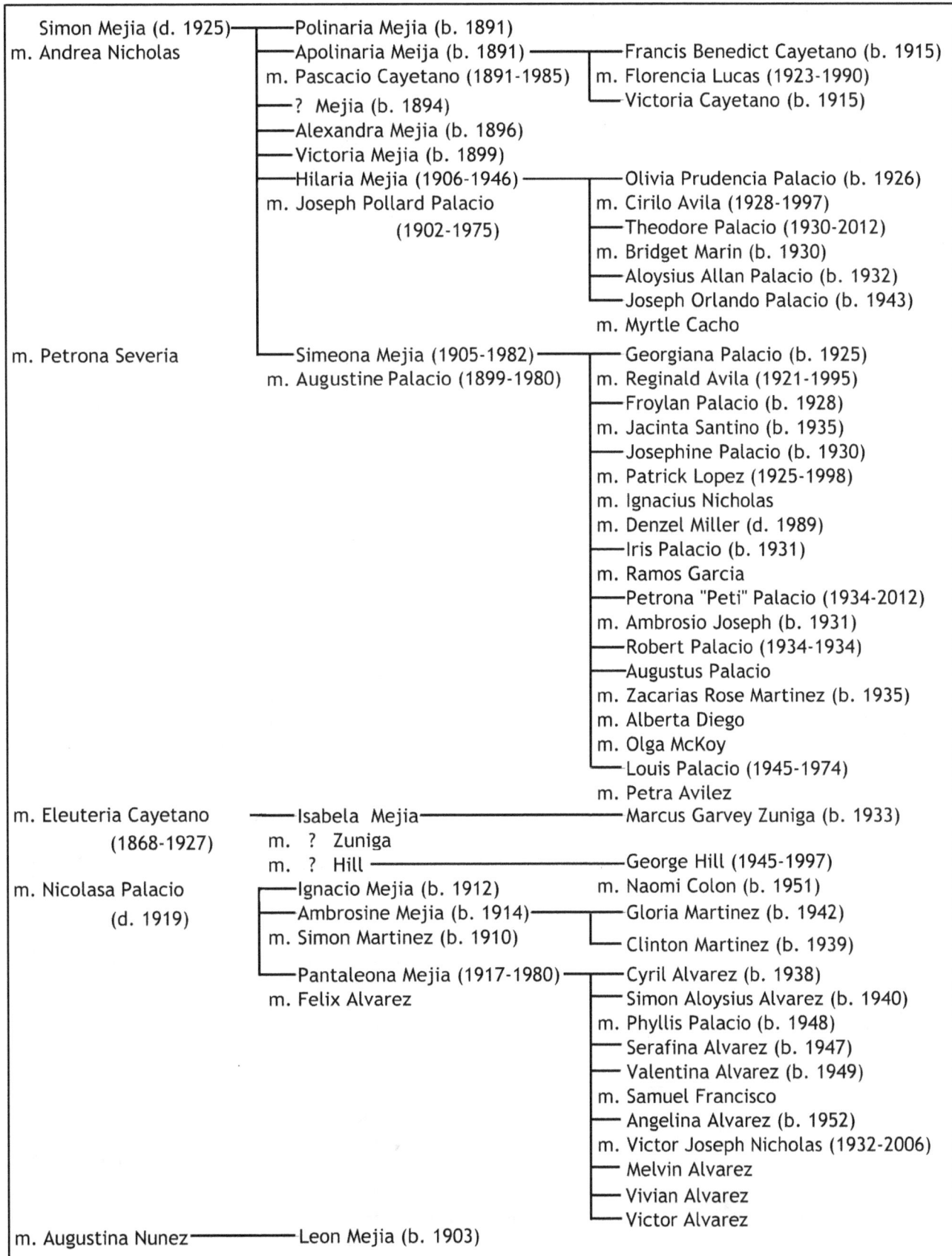

Simon Mejia (d. 1925) — Polinaria Mejia (b. 1891)
m. Andrea Nicholas

— Apolinaria Mejia (b. 1891) —— Francis Benedict Cayetano (b. 1915)
m. Pascacio Cayetano (1891-1985)   m. Florencia Lucas (1923-1990)
                                    — Victoria Cayetano (b. 1915)

— ? Mejia (b. 1894)

— Alexandra Mejia (b. 1896)

— Victoria Mejia (b. 1899)

— Hilaria Mejia (1906-1946) —— Olivia Prudencia Palacio (b. 1926)
m. Joseph Pollard Palacio   m. Cirilo Avila (1928-1997)
         (1902-1975)   — Theodore Palacio (1930-2012)
                               m. Bridget Marin (b. 1930)
                               — Aloysius Allan Palacio (b. 1932)
                               — Joseph Orlando Palacio (b. 1943)
                               m. Myrtle Cacho

m. Petrona Severia

— Simeona Mejia (1905-1982) —— Georgiana Palacio (b. 1925)
m. Augustine Palacio (1899-1980) m. Reginald Avila (1921-1995)
                               — Froylan Palacio (b. 1928)
                               m. Jacinta Santino (b. 1935)
                               — Josephine Palacio (b. 1930)
                               m. Patrick Lopez (1925-1998)
                               m. Ignacius Nicholas
                               m. Denzel Miller (d. 1989)
                               — Iris Palacio (b. 1931)
                               m. Ramos Garcia
                               — Petrona "Peti" Palacio (1934-2012)
                               m. Ambrosio Joseph (b. 1931)
                               — Robert Palacio (1934-1934)
                               — Augustus Palacio
                               m. Zacarias Rose Martinez (b. 1935)
                               m. Alberta Diego
                               m. Olga McKoy
                               — Louis Palacio (1945-1974)
                               m. Petra Avilez

m. Eleuteria Cayetano ——— Isabela Mejia ——————— Marcus Garvey Zuniga (b. 1933)
      (1868-1927)   m. ? Zuniga
                        m. ? Hill ——————————— George Hill (1945-1997)
m. Nicolasa Palacio   — Ignacio Mejia (b. 1912)   m. Naomi Colon (b. 1951)
      (d. 1919)   — Ambrosine Mejia (b. 1914) —— Gloria Martinez (b. 1942)
                        m. Simon Martinez (b. 1910)   — Clinton Martinez (b. 1939)

                        — Pantaleona Mejia (1917-1980) —— Cyril Alvarez (b. 1938)
                        m. Felix Alvarez   — Simon Aloysius Alvarez (b. 1940)
                                                      m. Phyllis Palacio (b. 1948)
                                                      — Serafina Alvarez (b. 1947)
                                                      — Valentina Alvarez (b. 1949)
                                                      m. Samuel Francisco
                                                      — Angelina Alvarez (b. 1952)
                                                      m. Victor Joseph Nicholas (1932-2006)
                                                      — Melvin Alvarez
                                                      — Vivian Alvarez
                                                      — Victor Alvarez

m. Augustina Nunez ——————— Leon Mejia (b. 1903)

Descendants of Concepcion Arana

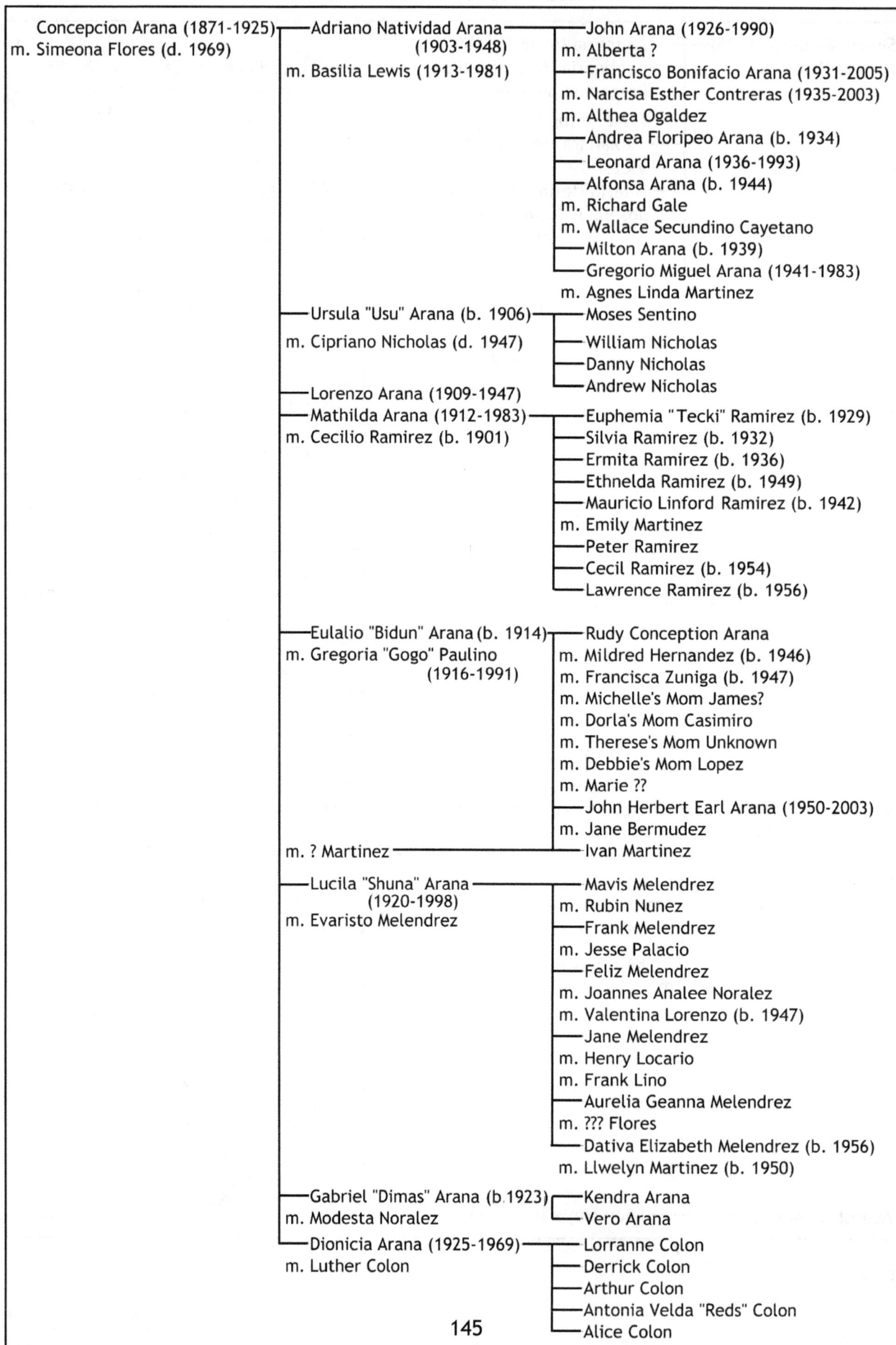

Concepcion Arana (1871-1925)
m. Simeona Flores (d. 1969)

— Adriano Natividad Arana (1903-1948)
m. Basilia Lewis (1913-1981)
- John Arana (1926-1990)
  m. Alberta ?
- Francisco Bonifacio Arana (1931-2005)
  m. Narcisa Esther Contreras (1935-2003)
  m. Althea Ogaldez
- Andrea Floripeo Arana (b. 1934)
- Leonard Arana (1936-1993)
- Alfonsa Arana (b. 1944)
  m. Richard Gale
  m. Wallace Secundino Cayetano
- Milton Arana (b. 1939)
- Gregorio Miguel Arana (1941-1983)
  m. Agnes Linda Martinez

— Ursula "Usu" Arana (b. 1906)
m. Cipriano Nicholas (d. 1947)
- Moses Sentino
- William Nicholas
- Danny Nicholas
- Andrew Nicholas

— Lorenzo Arana (1909-1947)

— Mathilda Arana (1912-1983)
m. Cecilio Ramirez (b. 1901)
- Euphemia "Tecki" Ramirez (b. 1929)
- Silvia Ramirez (b. 1932)
- Ermita Ramirez (b. 1936)
- Ethnelda Ramirez (b. 1949)
- Mauricio Linford Ramirez (b. 1942)
  m. Emily Martinez
- Peter Ramirez
- Cecil Ramirez (b. 1954)
- Lawrence Ramirez (b. 1956)

— Eulalio "Bidun" Arana (b. 1914)
m. Gregoria "Gogo" Paulino (1916-1991)
- Rudy Conception Arana
  m. Mildred Hernandez (b. 1946)
  m. Francisca Zuniga (b. 1947)
  m. Michelle's Mom James?
  m. Dorla's Mom Casimiro
  m. Therese's Mom Unknown
  m. Debbie's Mom Lopez
  m. Marie ??
- John Herbert Earl Arana (1950-2003)
  m. Jane Bermudez
m. ? Martinez
- Ivan Martinez

— Lucila "Shuna" Arana (1920-1998)
m. Evaristo Melendrez
- Mavis Melendrez
  m. Rubin Nunez
- Frank Melendrez
  m. Jesse Palacio
- Feliz Melendrez
  m. Joannes Analee Noralez
  m. Valentina Lorenzo (b. 1947)
- Jane Melendrez
  m. Henry Locario
  m. Frank Lino
- Aurelia Geanna Melendrez
  m. ??? Flores
- Dativa Elizabeth Melendrez (b. 1956)
  m. Llwelyn Martinez (b. 1950)

— Gabriel "Dimas" Arana (b.1923)
m. Modesta Noralez
- Kendra Arana
- Vero Arana

— Dionicia Arana (1925-1969)
m. Luther Colon
- Lorranne Colon
- Derrick Colon
- Arthur Colon
- Antonia Velda "Reds" Colon
- Alice Colon

145

Descendants of Pedro John Avila

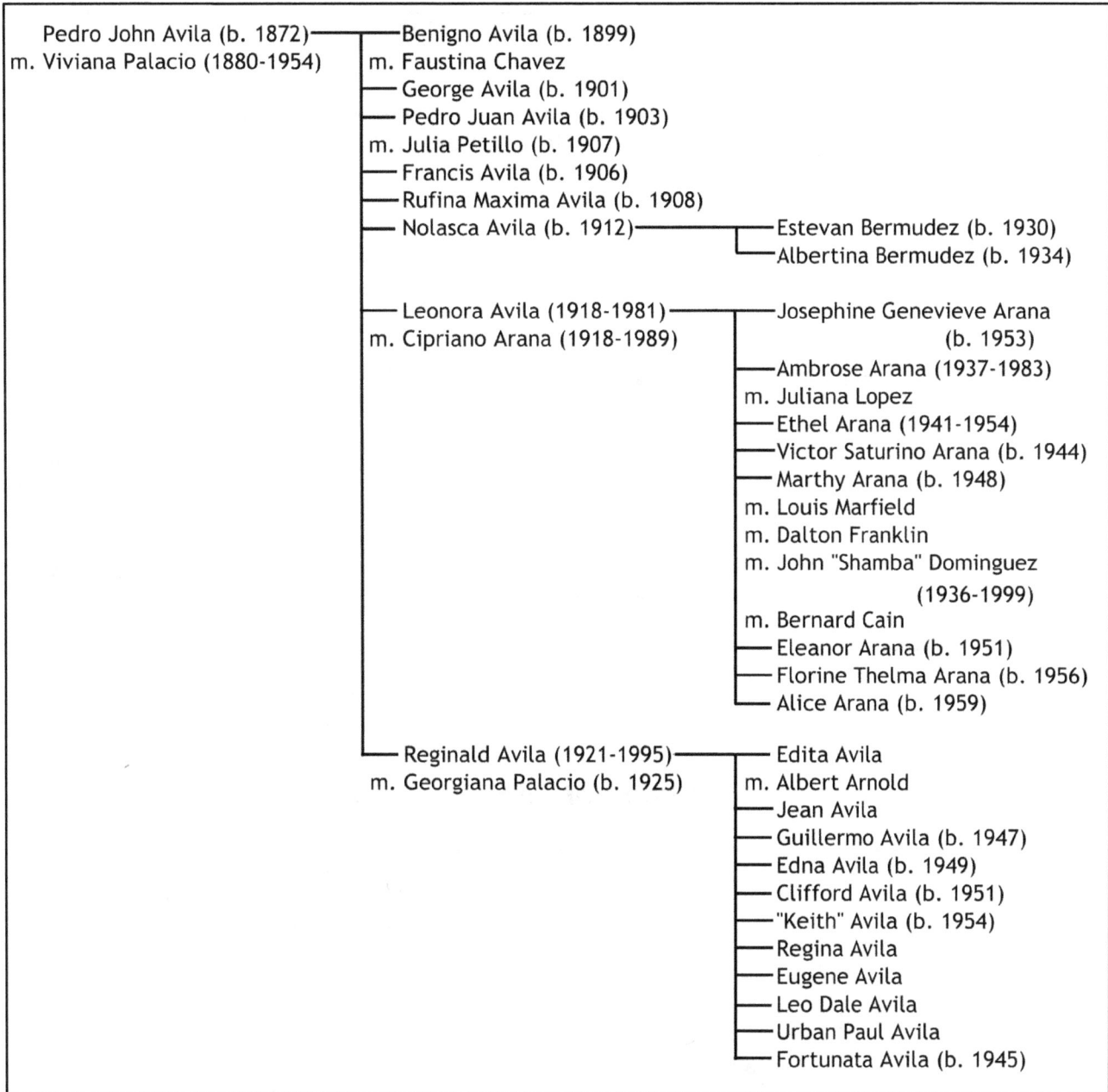

Pedro John Avila (b. 1872)
m. Viviana Palacio (1880-1954)

- Benigno Avila (b. 1899)
  m. Faustina Chavez
- George Avila (b. 1901)
- Pedro Juan Avila (b. 1903)
  m. Julia Petillo (b. 1907)
- Francis Avila (b. 1906)
- Rufina Maxima Avila (b. 1908)
- Nolasca Avila (b. 1912)
  - Estevan Bermudez (b. 1930)
  - Albertina Bermudez (b. 1934)

- Leonora Avila (1918-1981)
  m. Cipriano Arana (1918-1989)
  - Josephine Genevieve Arana (b. 1953)
  - Ambrose Arana (1937-1983)
    m. Juliana Lopez
  - Ethel Arana (1941-1954)
  - Victor Saturino Arana (b. 1944)
  - Marthy Arana (b. 1948)
    m. Louis Marfield
    m. Dalton Franklin
    m. John "Shamba" Dominguez (1936-1999)
    m. Bernard Cain
  - Eleanor Arana (b. 1951)
  - Florine Thelma Arana (b. 1956)
  - Alice Arana (b. 1959)

- Reginald Avila (1921-1995)
  m. Georgiana Palacio (b. 1925)
  - Edita Avila
    m. Albert Arnold
  - Jean Avila
  - Guillermo Avila (b. 1947)
  - Edna Avila (b. 1949)
  - Clifford Avila (b. 1951)
  - "Keith" Avila (b. 1954)
  - Regina Avila
  - Eugene Avila
  - Leo Dale Avila
  - Urban Paul Avila
  - Fortunata Avila (b. 1945)

Descendants of Martin Benjamin Noralez

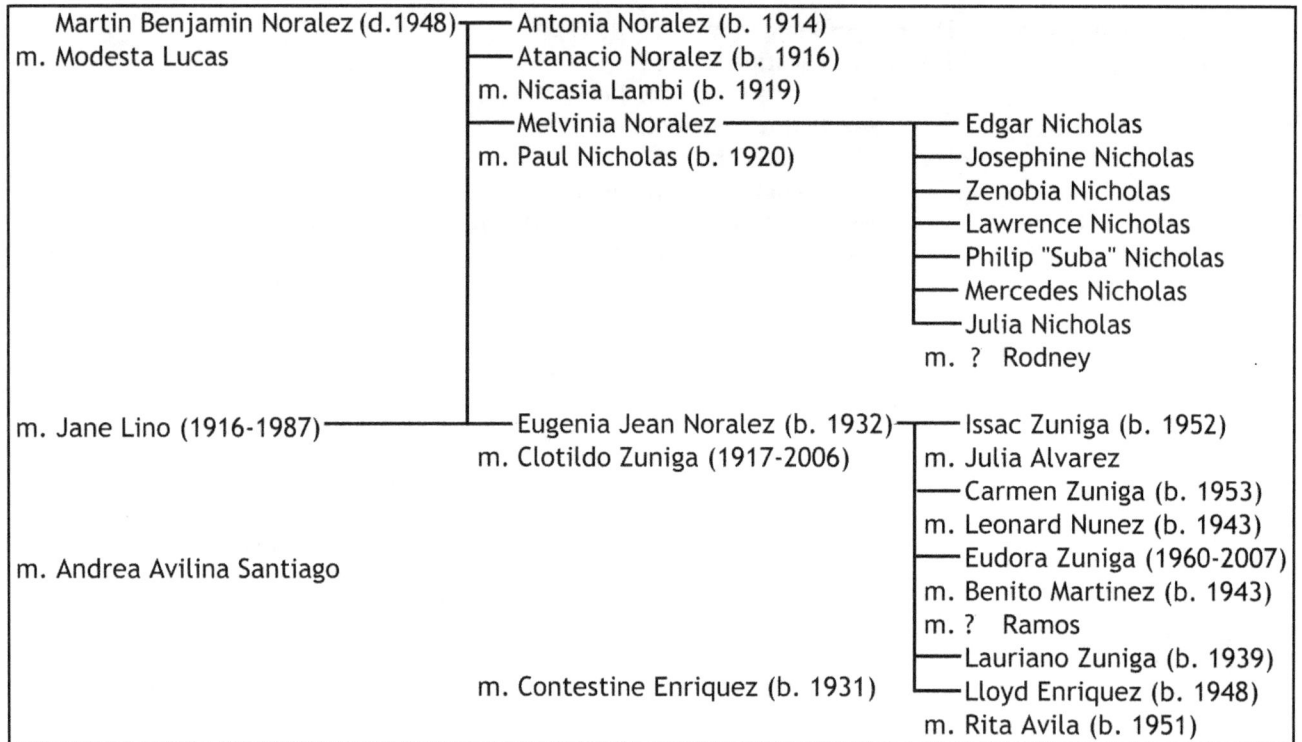

```
Martin Benjamin Noralez (d.1948)─┬─ Antonia Noralez (b. 1914)
m. Modesta Lucas                 ├─ Atanacio Noralez (b. 1916)
                                 │  m. Nicasia Lambi (b. 1919)
                                 ├─ Melvinia Noralez ──────────┬─ Edgar Nicholas
                                 │  m. Paul Nicholas (b. 1920)  ├─ Josephine Nicholas
                                 │                              ├─ Zenobia Nicholas
                                 │                              ├─ Lawrence Nicholas
                                 │                              ├─ Philip "Suba" Nicholas
                                 │                              ├─ Mercedes Nicholas
                                 │                              └─ Julia Nicholas
                                 │                                 m. ? Rodney
m. Jane Lino (1916-1987)─────────┼─ Eugenia Jean Noralez (b. 1932)─┬─ Issac Zuniga (b. 1952)
                                 │  m. Clotildo Zuniga (1917-2006) │  m. Julia Alvarez
                                 │                                 ├─ Carmen Zuniga (b. 1953)
m. Andrea Avilina Santiago       │                                 │  m. Leonard Nunez (b. 1943)
                                 │                                 ├─ Eudora Zuniga (1960-2007)
                                 │                                 │  m. Benito Martinez (b. 1943)
                                 │                                 │  m. ? Ramos
                                 │                                 ├─ Lauriano Zuniga (b. 1939)
                                 │  m. Contestine Enriquez (b. 1931)└─ Lloyd Enriquez (b. 1948)
                                 │                                    m. Rita Avila (b. 1951)
```

Descendants of Santiago Lopez

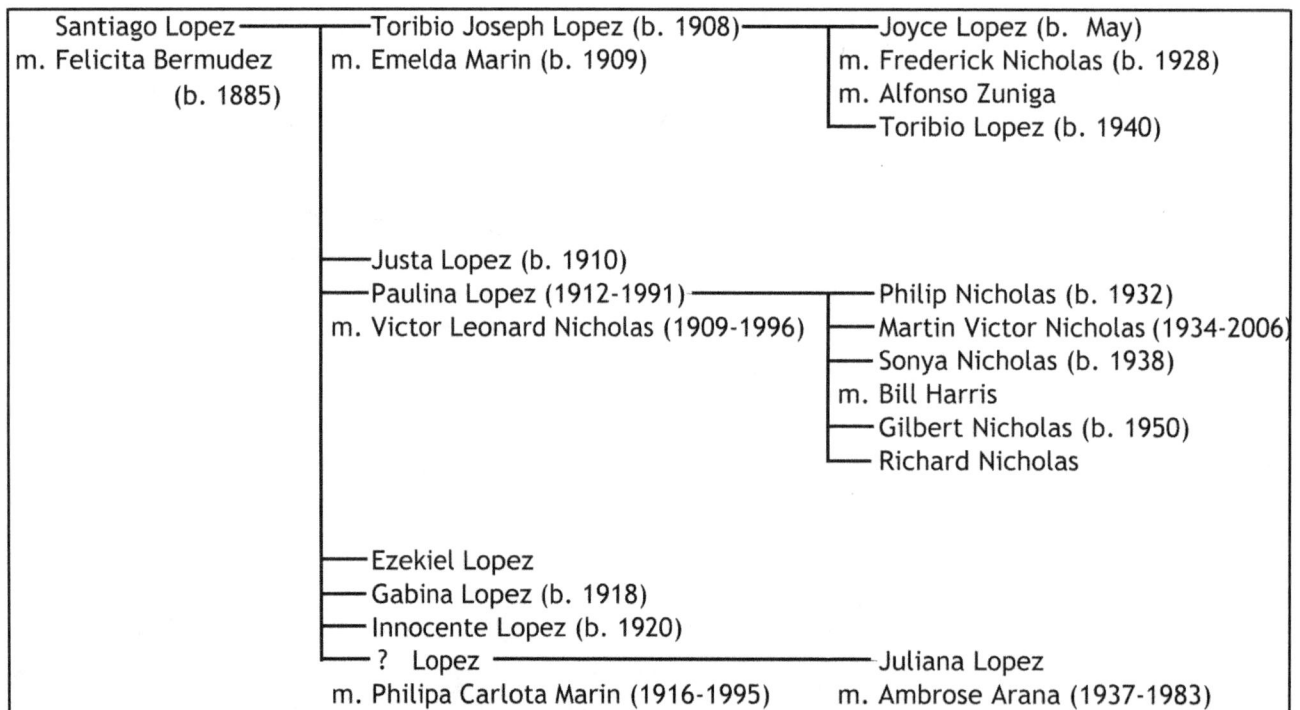

```
Santiago Lopez──────┬─ Toribio Joseph Lopez (b. 1908)──────┬─ Joyce Lopez (b. May)
m. Felicita Bermudez│  m. Emelda Marin (b. 1909)            │  m. Frederick Nicholas (b. 1928)
      (b. 1885)     │                                       │  m. Alfonso Zuniga
                    │                                       └─ Toribio Lopez (b. 1940)
                    │
                    ├─ Justa Lopez (b. 1910)
                    ├─ Paulina Lopez (1912-1991)────────────┬─ Philip Nicholas (b. 1932)
                    │  m. Victor Leonard Nicholas (1909-1996)├─ Martin Victor Nicholas (1934-2006)
                    │                                        ├─ Sonya Nicholas (b. 1938)
                    │                                        │  m. Bill Harris
                    │                                        ├─ Gilbert Nicholas (b. 1950)
                    │                                        └─ Richard Nicholas
                    │
                    ├─ Ezekiel Lopez
                    ├─ Gabina Lopez (b. 1918)
                    ├─ Innocente Lopez (b. 1920)
                    └─ ? Lopez ──────────────────── Juliana Lopez
                       m. Philipa Carlota Marin (1916-1995)  m. Ambrose Arana (1937-1983)
```

Descendants of Eulogio Marin

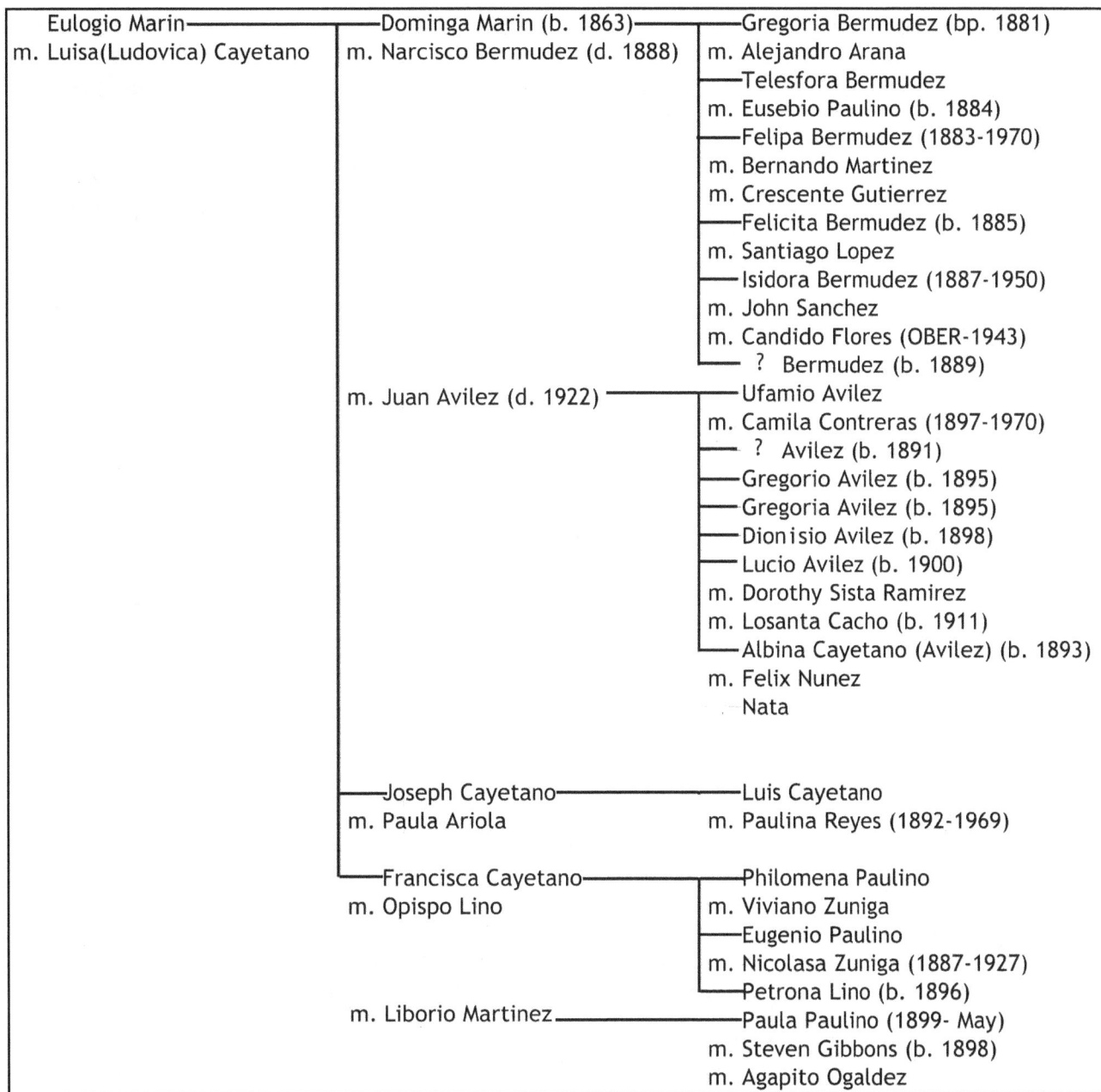

```
Eulogio Marin───────────Dominga Marin (b. 1863)────Gregoria Bermudez (bp. 1881)
m. Luisa(Ludovica) Cayetano  m. Narcisco Bermudez (d. 1888)  m. Alejandro Arana
                                                          ──Telesfora Bermudez
                                                          m. Eusebio Paulino (b. 1884)
                                                          ──Felipa Bermudez (1883-1970)
                                                          m. Bernando Martinez
                                                          m. Crescente Gutierrez
                                                          ──Felicita Bermudez (b. 1885)
                                                          m. Santiago Lopez
                                                          ──Isidora Bermudez (1887-1950)
                                                          m. John Sanchez
                                                          m. Candido Flores (OBER-1943)
                                                          ── ?  Bermudez (b. 1889)
                             m. Juan Avilez (d. 1922)─────Ufamio Avilez
                                                          m. Camila Contreras (1897-1970)
                                                          ── ?  Avilez (b. 1891)
                                                          ──Gregorio Avilez (b. 1895)
                                                          ──Gregoria Avilez (b. 1895)
                                                          ──Dionisio Avilez (b. 1898)
                                                          ──Lucio Avilez (b. 1900)
                                                          m. Dorothy Sista Ramirez
                                                          m. Losanta Cacho (b. 1911)
                                                          ──Albina Cayetano (Avilez) (b. 1893)
                                                          m. Felix Nunez
                                                           Nata

                             ─Joseph Cayetano────────────Luis Cayetano
                             m. Paula Ariola             m. Paulina Reyes (1892-1969)

                             ─Francisca Cayetano─────────Philomena Paulino
                             m. Opispo Lino              m. Viviano Zuniga
                                                          ──Eugenio Paulino
                                                          m. Nicolasa Zuniga (1887-1927)
                                                          ──Petrona Lino (b. 1896)
                             m. Liborio Martinez─────────Paula Paulino (1899- May)
                                                          m. Steven Gibbons (b. 1898)
                                                          m. Agapito Ogaldez
```

Descendants of Joseph Ramirez

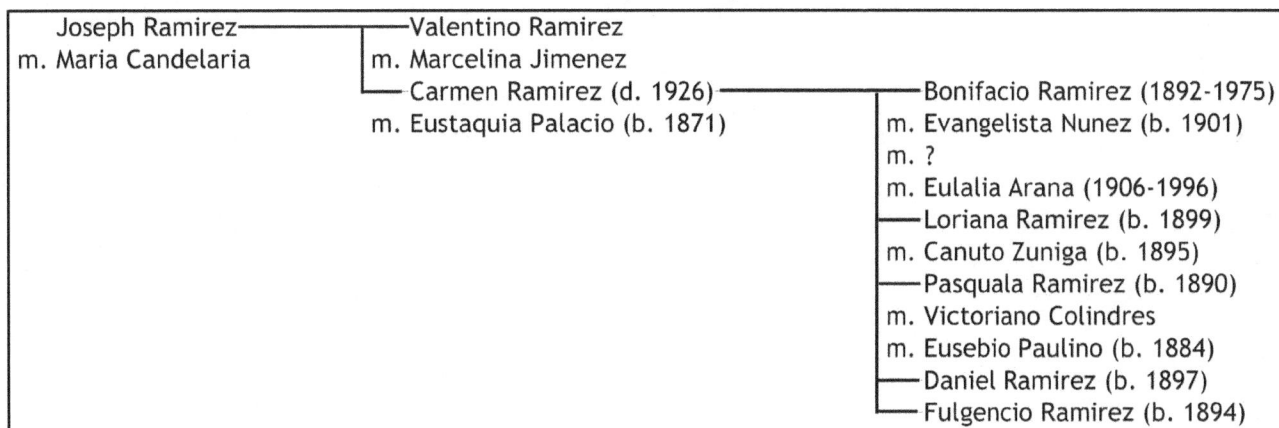

```
Joseph Ramirez──────────Valentino Ramirez
m. Maria Candelaria     m. Marcelina Jimenez
                        ──Carmen Ramirez (d. 1926)────────Bonifacio Ramirez (1892-1975)
                        m. Eustaquia Palacio (b. 1871)    m. Evangelista Nunez (b. 1901)
                                                          m. ?
                                                          m. Eulalia Arana (1906-1996)
                                                          ──Loriana Ramirez (b. 1899)
                                                          m. Canuto Zuniga (b. 1895)
                                                          ──Pasquala Ramirez (b. 1890)
                                                          m. Victoriano Colindres
                                                          m. Eusebio Paulino (b. 1884)
                                                          ──Daniel Ramirez (b. 1897)
                                                          ──Fulgencio Ramirez (b. 1894)
```

Descendants of Francisco Nunez

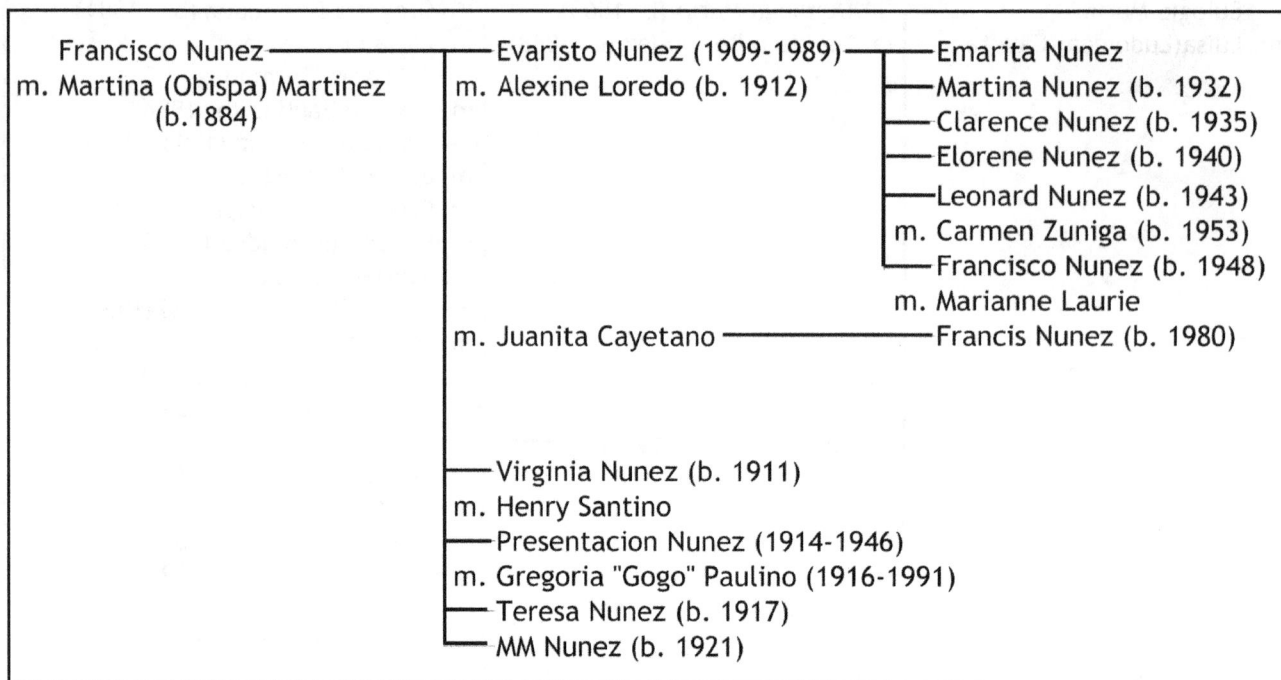

```
Francisco Nunez ─────────── Evaristo Nunez (1909-1989) ─────── Emarita Nunez
m. Martina (Obispa) Martinez     m. Alexine Loredo (b. 1912)       ── Martina Nunez (b. 1932)
         (b.1884)                                                   ── Clarence Nunez (b. 1935)
                                                                    ── Elorene Nunez (b. 1940)
                                                                    ── Leonard Nunez (b. 1943)
                                                                    m. Carmen Zuniga (b. 1953)
                                                                    ── Francisco Nunez (b. 1948)
                                                                    m. Marianne Laurie
                                 m. Juanita Cayetano ───────────── Francis Nunez (b. 1980)


                                 ── Virginia Nunez (b. 1911)
                                 m. Henry Santino
                                 ── Presentacion Nunez (1914-1946)
                                 m. Gregoria "Gogo" Paulino (1916-1991)
                                 ── Teresa Nunez (b. 1917)
                                 ── MM Nunez (b. 1921)
```

Descendants of Juan Avilez

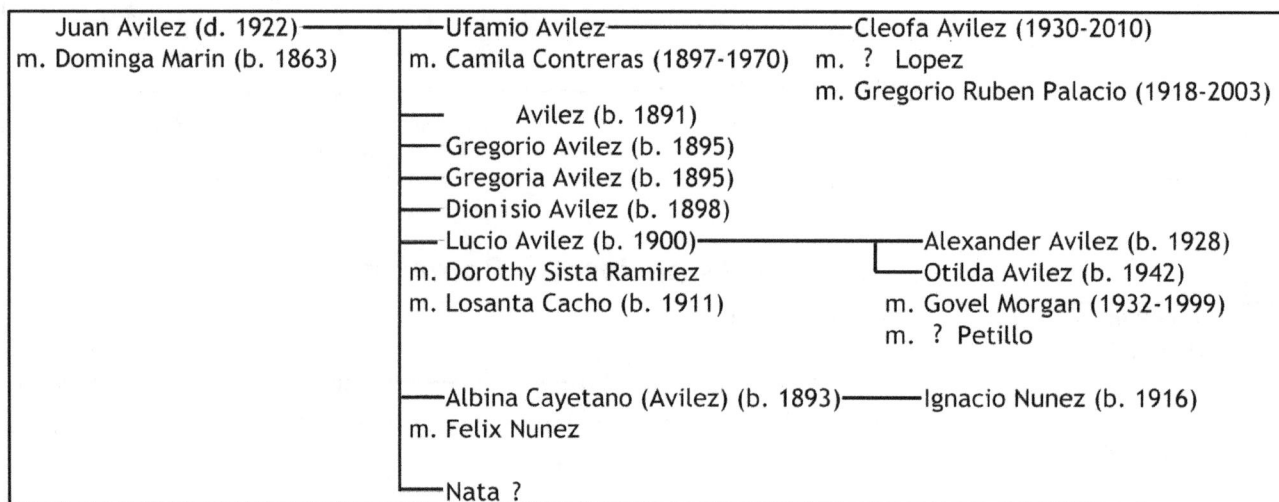

```
Juan Avilez (d. 1922) ─────── Ufamio Avilez ──────────── Cleofa Avilez (1930-2010)
m. Dominga Marin (b. 1863)    m. Camila Contreras (1897-1970)   m. ? Lopez
                                                                m. Gregorio Ruben Palacio (1918-2003)
                              ──        Avilez (b. 1891)
                              ── Gregorio Avilez (b. 1895)
                              ── Gregoria Avilez (b. 1895)
                              ── Dionisio Avilez (b. 1898)
                              ── Lucio Avilez (b. 1900) ──────── Alexander Avilez (b. 1928)
                              m. Dorothy Sista Ramirez           ── Otilda Avilez (b. 1942)
                              m. Losanta Cacho (b. 1911)         m. Govel Morgan (1932-1999)
                                                                 m. ? Petillo

                              ── Albina Cayetano (Avilez) (b. 1893) ──── Ignacio Nunez (b. 1916)
                              m. Felix Nunez

                              ── Nata ?
```

Descendants of Francisco Ellis Arzu

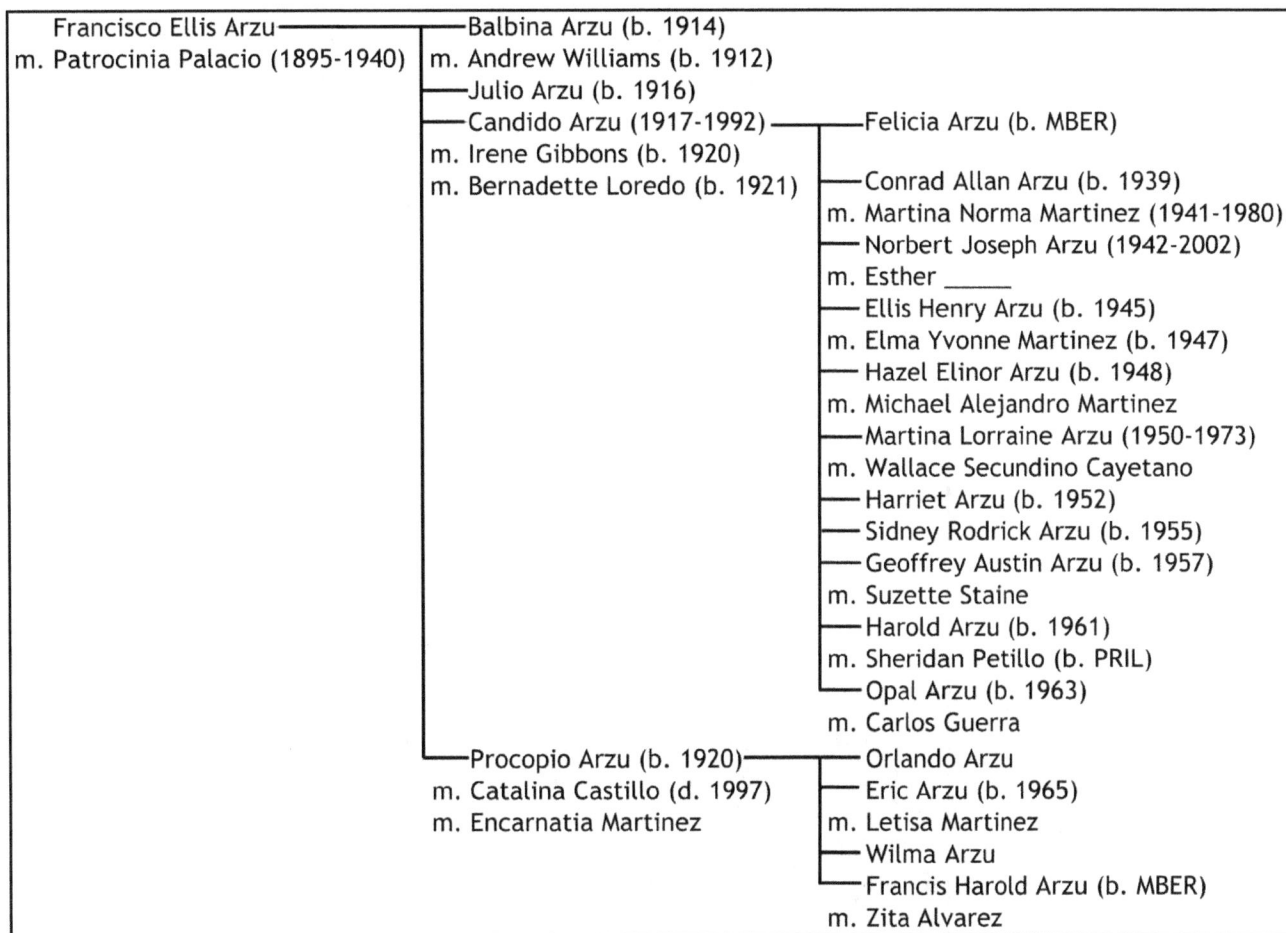

```
Francisco Ellis Arzu ─────────── ┌─Balbina Arzu (b. 1914)
m. Patrocinia Palacio (1895-1940) │ m. Andrew Williams (b. 1912)
                                   ├─Julio Arzu (b. 1916)
                                   ├─Candido Arzu (1917-1992) ──── ┌─Felicia Arzu (b. MBER)
                                   │ m. Irene Gibbons (b. 1920)     │
                                   │ m. Bernadette Loredo (b. 1921) ├─Conrad Allan Arzu (b. 1939)
                                   │                                │ m. Martina Norma Martinez (1941-1980)
                                   │                                ├─Norbert Joseph Arzu (1942-2002)
                                   │                                │ m. Esther _____
                                   │                                ├─Ellis Henry Arzu (b. 1945)
                                   │                                │ m. Elma Yvonne Martinez (b. 1947)
                                   │                                ├─Hazel Elinor Arzu (b. 1948)
                                   │                                │ m. Michael Alejandro Martinez
                                   │                                ├─Martina Lorraine Arzu (1950-1973)
                                   │                                │ m. Wallace Secundino Cayetano
                                   │                                ├─Harriet Arzu (b. 1952)
                                   │                                ├─Sidney Rodrick Arzu (b. 1955)
                                   │                                ├─Geoffrey Austin Arzu (b. 1957)
                                   │                                │ m. Suzette Staine
                                   │                                ├─Harold Arzu (b. 1961)
                                   │                                │ m. Sheridan Petillo (b. PRIL)
                                   │                                └─Opal Arzu (b. 1963)
                                   │                                  m. Carlos Guerra
                                   └─Procopio Arzu (b. 1920) ────── ┌─Orlando Arzu
                                     m. Catalina Castillo (d. 1997)  ├─Eric Arzu (b. 1965)
                                     m. Encarnatia Martinez          │ m. Letisa Martinez
                                                                     ├─Wilma Arzu
                                                                     └─Francis Harold Arzu (b. MBER)
                                                                       m. Zita Alvarez
```

Descendants of Victoriano Castillo

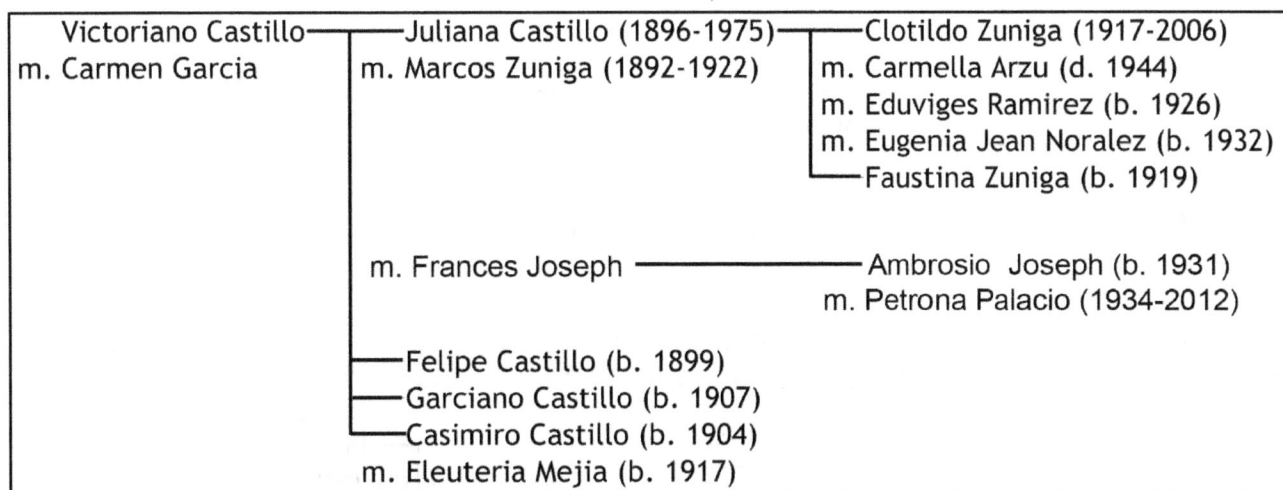

```
Victoriano Castillo ───── ┌─Juliana Castillo (1896-1975) ──── ┌─Clotildo Zuniga (1917-2006)
m. Carmen Garcia          │ m. Marcos Zuniga (1892-1922)       │ m. Carmella Arzu (d. 1944)
                          │                                    │ m. Eduviges Ramirez (b. 1926)
                          │                                    │ m. Eugenia Jean Noralez (b. 1932)
                          │                                    └─Faustina Zuniga (b. 1919)
                          │
                          │ m. Frances Joseph ──────────────── ┌─Ambrosio Joseph (b. 1931)
                          │                                       m. Petrona Palacio (1934-2012)
                          ├─Felipe Castillo (b. 1899)
                          ├─Garciano Castillo (b. 1907)
                          └─Casimiro Castillo (b. 1904)
                            m. Eleuteria Mejia (b. 1917)
```

Descendants of Mariano Zuniga

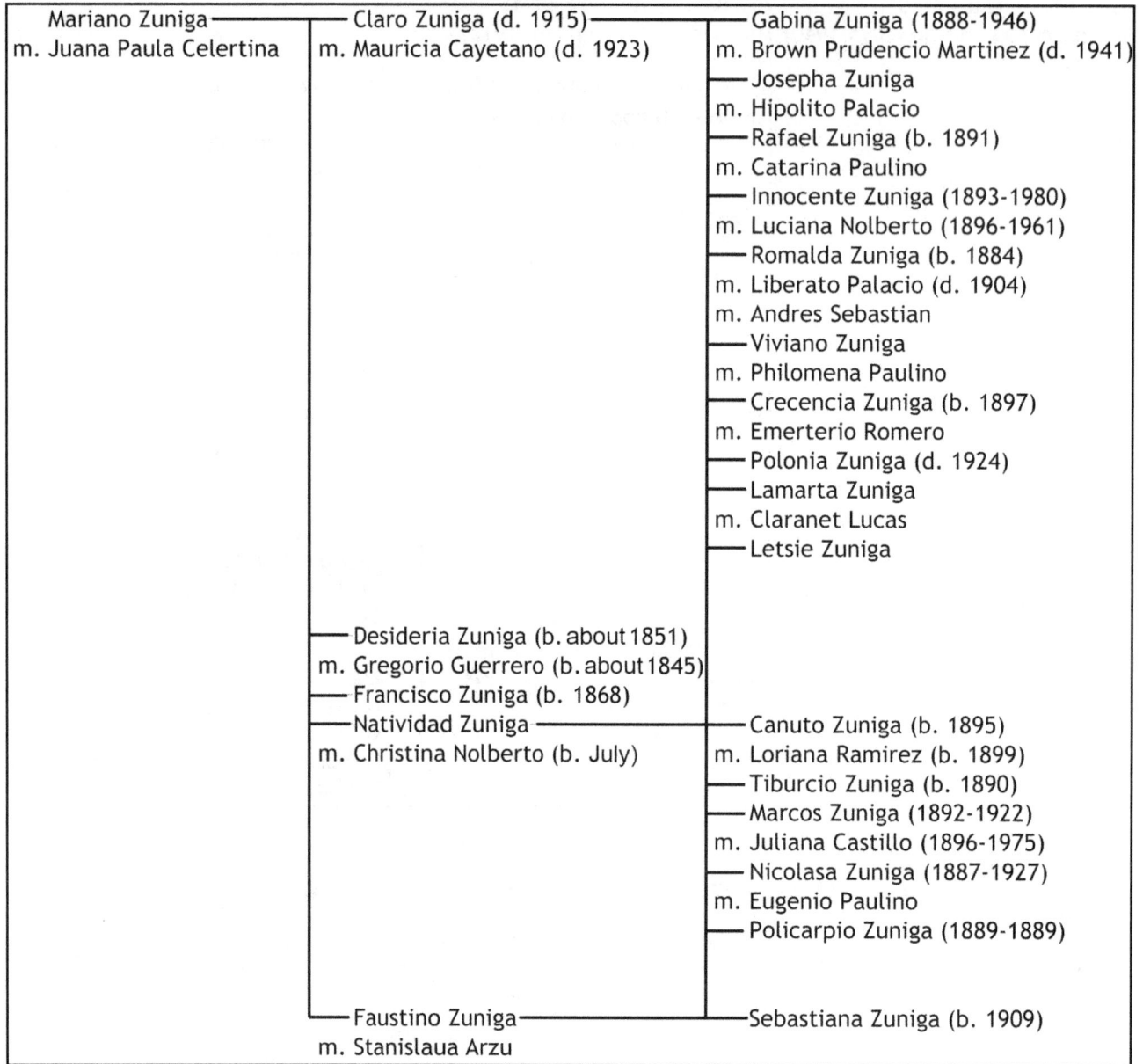

```
Mariano Zuniga──────────── Claro Zuniga (d. 1915)──────── Gabina Zuniga (1888-1946)
m. Juana Paula Celertina    m. Mauricia Cayetano (d. 1923)  m. Brown Prudencio Martinez (d. 1941)
                                                            ─Josepha Zuniga
                                                             m. Hipolito Palacio
                                                            ─Rafael Zuniga (b. 1891)
                                                             m. Catarina Paulino
                                                            ─Innocente Zuniga (1893-1980)
                                                             m. Luciana Nolberto (1896-1961)
                                                            ─Romalda Zuniga (b. 1884)
                                                             m. Liberato Palacio (d. 1904)
                                                             m. Andres Sebastian
                                                            ─Viviano Zuniga
                                                             m. Philomena Paulino
                                                            ─Crecencia Zuniga (b. 1897)
                                                             m. Emerterio Romero
                                                            ─Polonia Zuniga (d. 1924)
                                                            ─Lamarta Zuniga
                                                             m. Claranet Lucas
                                                            ─Letsie Zuniga

                            ─ Desideria Zuniga (b. about 1851)
                            m. Gregorio Guerrero (b. about 1845)
                            ─Francisco Zuniga (b. 1868)
                            ─Natividad Zuniga ──────────── Canuto Zuniga (b. 1895)
                            m. Christina Nolberto (b. July)  m. Loriana Ramirez (b. 1899)
                                                            ─Tiburcio Zuniga (b. 1890)
                                                            ─Marcos Zuniga (1892-1922)
                                                             m. Juliana Castillo (1896-1975)
                                                            ─Nicolasa Zuniga (1887-1927)
                                                             m. Eugenio Paulino
                                                            ─Policarpio Zuniga (1889-1889)

                            ─Faustino Zuniga──────────────Sebastiana Zuniga (b. 1909)
                            m. Stanislaua Arzu
```

Descendants of Joanis Blas

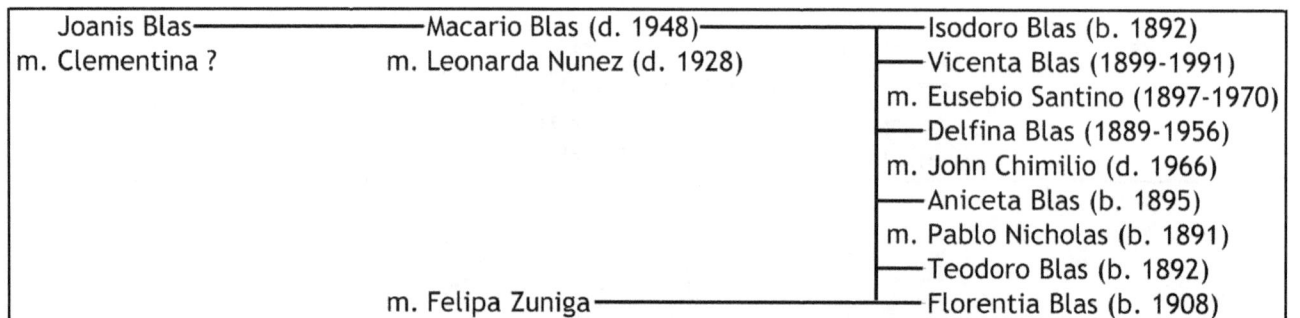

```
Joanis Blas──────────────Macario Blas (d. 1948)─────────Isodoro Blas (b. 1892)
m. Clementina ?           m. Leonarda Nunez (d. 1928)     ─Vicenta Blas (1899-1991)
                                                           m. Eusebio Santino (1897-1970)
                                                           ─Delfina Blas (1889-1956)
                                                           m. John Chimilio (d. 1966)
                                                           ─Aniceta Blas (b. 1895)
                                                           m. Pablo Nicholas (b. 1891)
                                                           ─Teodoro Blas (b. 1892)
                          m. Felipa Zuniga───────────────Florentia Blas (b. 1908)
```

Afterword

The detailed intricate web of family ties that Carlson Tuttle has demonstrated for the small Garifuna village of Barangu in this book is based on *iduheguo*. The closest translation in English for *iduheguo* is kinship, the blood and marital bonds that are formed within a population. But to the Garifuna *iduheguo* is more a way of referring to the people who live within a community; to the Garifuna people within a country; and even to the larger Garifuna nation wherever it is found. Inclusivity is what determines *iduheguo*; and the limit is determined by the scale of reference that one wants to apply. This harks back to the tribal social structure that still underlies Garifuna culture.

People adjust the *iduheguo* as they see fit within its primary characteristic of being initiated and maintained to their convenience. So, while two persons who are first cousins might be extremely helpful to each other, it may not be so between another set who are also first cousins. One activates a bond with another, depending on a variety of situations and ultimately how useful they are to each other. In other words, kinship does not always function on sets of prescribed values. Ultimately, it designates how persons should interrelate with each other and the cultural sanctions may vary.

To the Garifuna, kinship status is like a business card that one shows to another as a way of initiating a relationship. Of course, originating from the same neigbouring community; or being a Garifuna among non-Garifuna are all potentially useful to push forward a bonding at any given moment. Within the long and narrow coastal strip from Nicaragua to Belize where the Garifuna from the early 1800s have been a black ethnic minority, being one people became a much needed asset among themselves for survival. In an earlier volume entitled *Garifuna Continuity in Land: Barranco Settlement and Land Use 1862 to 2000*, Palacio, Tuttle, and Lumb have shown how usufruct rights to land had been transmitted from one generation to another. This principle remains not only in memory but also in the way the present generation envisages receiving land rights from its parents. It is vital social capital that can continue to be transformed for the economic well-being of generations not yet born.

It is tempting to ask how at the dawn of the 21st century the Garifuna can use their extensive kinship bonds strategically for their overall survival, given the scourge of exclusion that they still face. The ample overlaps that Tuttle has documented give us much hope. In starting with the small, we can begin to appreciate better what the macro-scale is and will be. No doubt this 21st century will see our planet earth shrink at an incredible pace as persons originating from different regions form wide ranging inter-personal relations through trade, religious affiliation, joining tour groups, and so on. As such relations are formed, the family ties to which we have grown accustomed will carry us through. Tuttle has shown us how these relations have been cultivated within a small village for generations.

Joseph Orlando Palacio

Index

A

Clarence Adolphus 124
Agnes "Sista" Alvarez 8, 31, 92
Angelina "Angie" Nicholas nee
    Alvarez 2, 55, 64, 65, 76, 105,
    125
Carlette Alvarez 65
Cecilia "Luncy" Arzu nee Alvarez 78,
    113
Cyril Alvarez 41
David Alvarez 2, 19, 80, 106, 115,
    124
David Alvarez, Jr. 19
Emma Alvarez 12
Eustacio Alvarez 8, 12, 20, 36, 101,
    104, 113, 115
Feliciano "Felix" Alvarez 2, 20, 41,
    55, 76, 94, 105
Jane "Wana" Alvarez 20
Jerome Alvarez 12, 22, 36, 47, 87, 101
John Alvarez 115
John Paul Alvarez 2
Josefa Alvarez 4, 21, 29, 65, 78, 99,
    104, 126
Julia Alvarez 44
Lascelle Alvarez 20
Lisani Emmuel Davimar Alvarez 106
Luis Alvarez 84
Martina Cornelia "Mamita" Alvarez
    nee Palacio 2, 19, 27, 68, 80, 106,
    115, 124
Marty Leroy Alvarez 124
Max Alvarez 31
Merline Alvarez 58, 109
Michelle Alvarez 65, 94, 122, 123
Patrick Alvarez 115
Peter Alvarez 90
Philip Alvarez 73
Rhoda Alvarez 22, 26, 37, 79, 87
Sadie Nolasca Alvarez 12, 47, 127
Serafina Alvarez 105
Simon Aloysius Alvarez 65, 84, 90,
    94, 109, 122
Tim Alvarez 12, 63, 64
Tom Alvarez 30
Valentina Alvarez 20
Victor Alvarez 41, 70, 123
Zita Arzu nee Alvarez 10, 20, 31, 71
    101, 126
Cayetano Amaya 33, 66, 76, 123
Peter Amaya 66, 123
Barbara Andrews 16
Blacina Apolonio 4, 5, 13, 34, 45, 53,
    85, 92

Francisco Apolonio 4, 122
Macario Apolonio 12, 68
Petrona "Pansy" Apolonio 118
Vicente Apolonio 12, 68
Adriano Natividad Arana 3, 5, 33,
    55, 87, 90, 93, 106, 119
Alejandra Arana 49
Alejandro Arana 8, 10, 19, 39, 49, 73,
    75, 90, 102, 104, 105, 122, 123
Alexis Adrian Arana, Jr. 117
Alexis Simeon Arana 74, 117
Alfonsa Arana 79, 101, 106
Alice Arana 67
Ambrose Arana 11
Andrea Arana 6
Atanacio Arana 25, 40, 51, 67
Benedictina Arana 42
Cayetana Arana 49
Cipriano Arana 11, 29, 41, 51, 55, 56,
    66, 67, 80, 82, 95, 101, 110, 116,
    125
Concepcion Arana 16, 20, 33, 35,
    51, 66, 74, 81, 83, 86, 90, 95, 104,
    106, 107, 115, 125
Daniel Arana 6
Daphne Denise Arana 117, 125
Dionisia Arana 115
Dionisio Arana 16, 18, 46, 102, 103
Earl Adrian Arana 53
Eleanor Arana 41
Elvira Arana 117
Ethel Arana 66
Eulalia Arana 8, 18, 90, 92, 105, 122
Eulalia "Lala" Arana 102
Eulalio Arana 20
Eulalio "Bidun" Arana 20, 51, 66,
    107, 115, 125
Florine Thelma Arana 95, 125
Francis Arana 51, 110
Francisco Bonifacio "Frank" Arana
    3, 5, 9, 29, 33, 51, 53, 55, 74, 78,
    87, 90, 91, 93, 104, 105, 110, 117,
    119
Frank Dean Arana 19, 39, 42, 75, 84,
    102, 115
Gabriel "Dimas" Arana 35, 66
Geraldine Arana 116
Gilbert Arana 52
Ignacia Palacio nee Arana 7, 13, 16,
    18, 20, 30, 33, 40, 42, 46, 54, 55,
    57, 58, 68, 80, 81, 85
Ignacia "Inez" "Grandma Dadi"
    Arana 10, 24, 36, 37, 101, 111,
    121, 123
Isidora "Manu" Arana 25, 40
Jerroll Giovani Arana 53
John Arana 52, 116, 119
John Herbert Earl Arana 63, 115
Josephine Genevieve Arana 29

Juliana "Linda" Arana nee Lopez 57
Kayla Georgene Arana 83
Lauriano Arana 37
Leoncio Arana 102
Lloyd Arana 31
Lorenzo Arana 66
Lucila "Shuna" Arana 73, 74, 81, 106.
    119
Marthy "Marti" Cain nee Arana 6, 9,
    16, 21, 25, 29, 32, 41, 43, 51, 52,
    66, 76, 80, 82, 110, 112, 118
Matilda Arana 24, 61, 88, 113
Michael Anthony Arana 9
Nahyil Arana 110
Narciso Arana 105
Nora Arana 43, 66, 99, 102
Peitra Arana 10, 16, 51, 63, 74, 83,
    95, 103, 107
Pia "Mamacita" Arana nee
    Magdelano 72, 74, 85, 99, 105,
    115, 126
Romana Arana 11, 35, 66, 91, 106
Rose Maria Arana 29, 78
Rudolph Arana 83
Rudy Concepcion Arana 16, 20, 51,
    83, 86, 107, 125
Seferina Arana 46
Sotero Arana 2, 41, 46, 103
Suzanna Arana 61, 114
Teresa Arana 10
Ursula "Usu" Arana 2, 36, 58, 70, 73,
    95, 102, 104, 112, 118, 124
Victor "Bobby" Arana 19, 39, 42, 72,
    75, 77, 84, 103, 115, 126
Victoriana Arana 73, 90, 98, 108, 123
Victor Saturnino Arana 116
Yvonne Carmen Arana 104
Austin Aranda 57
Kevaan Aranda 102
Moses Aranda 66, 102
Alicia Ariola 91, 109
Allen Ariola 113
Almira Ariola 23
Almira "Irma" Gonzalez nee Ariola
    2, 9, 3, 37, 42, 112, 119, 124
Antonia Palacio nee Ariola 1, 2, 4, 5,
    6, 22, 31, 39, 46, 67, 87, 91, 98
Avis Ariola 88
Benita Ariola nee Nunez 52
Braulio Ariola 35, 78, 106
Casimiro Ariola 28, 112
Catarino Patricio Ariola 1, 17, 20, 60,
    87, 100, 104, 114
Claudio Ariola 10, 106
Daniel Ariola 12, 35, 62, 78, 106
Elisa Ariola 28, 61, 102
Elswith Frances Ariola 28, 54, 61
Eugene Alexander Ariola 50
Francisca "Chica" Ariola 76, 93, 100

Francisco "Chico" or "Paco" Ariola 10, 12, 17, 23, 27, 28, 36, 46, 50, 51, 54, 61, 63, 72, 73, 74, 83, 88, 100, 106, 109, 121, 124

Irma Gonzalez nee Ariola 2, 9, 42, 112

Juana Ariola 13, 16, 27, 73

Manuela Ariola 4, 12, 46, 54, 63, 89

Margarita Ariola 63

Martina Ariola 121

Maxima Ariola 11, 27, 39, 51, 53, 70, 94, 95, 98, 112, 115

Nicholas Ariola 91, 109

Patricio "Mouni" Ariola 1, 2, 4, 10, 17, 20, 21, 28, 32, 36, 37, 54, 60, 63, 73, 75, 76, 91, 93, 98, 100, 112, 114, 121

Petrona Ariola 16, 43, 85, 90, 104, 113, 114, 120

Rufino Ariola 10, 12, 13, 27, 32, 36, 51, 78, 83, 90, 106, 112, 114, 115

Shanda Ariola 88

Shaynah Ariola 74, 83, 101

Thelma Ariola 113

Tremaine Ariola 61

Trevor Ariola 10, 72, 83, 100

Valerie Dawn Ariola 61

Virgilia Lorenzo nee Ariola 20, 34, 60, 89, 115

Lynn Zuniga nee Arnold 5, 39, 44, 52, 60, 63, 78, 87, 89, 96, 125

Arnold Nicholas 46

Alejandro Arzu 22

Amenigi Arzu 42

Anastacio Arzu (Noralez) 90, 114

Angel Arzu 27

Arieni Arzu 109

Ascenciona Arzu 34, 123

Augustin Arzu 25, 53, 81, 110, 112, 115

Austin Arzu 63, 71, 75, 80, 102

Averill Arzu 16

Balbina Arzu 38, 40

Ben Arzu 127

Benito Arzu 22, 27, 30, 68

Bernadette Arzu nee Loredo 1, 6, 8, 80

Bernardina Arzu 33, 56

Bernice Norma Arzu 105, 108

Bima Arzu 56

Candido Arzu 1, 6, 8, 10, 19, 20, 27, 42, 63, 64, 75, 80, 82, 91, 94, 95, 98, 99, 102, 108, 110, 116, 125, 128

Carmela Arzu 9, 25, 70

Catarino "Man and a Half" Arzu 118

Catrino Arzu 68

Cecilia "Luncy" Arzu nee Alvarez 78

Conrad Allen Arzu 91, 102, 105, 108, 110, 123

Conrad Norman Arzu, Jr. 91

Crescencia Arzu 92

Dominga Martila Arzu 7, 17, 18, 39, 71, 80, 82, 95, 99, 116, 124

Domingo Arzu 31, 32, 76, 78

Dominica Arzu nee Noralez 62

Elizabeth Arzu 71

Ellis Henry Arzu 94

Elma Arzu nee Martinez 27, 127

Emmanuel Arzu 1, 122

Eric Arzu 41

Estanislada Arzu 26, 39

Estanislao Arzu 39, 51, 90, 113

Ethleen Arzu 124

Eusebio Arzu 7

Fabiano Arzu 30, 31, 37, 65, 92

Felicia Casimiro nee Arzu 103

Felicita Arzu 91

Fernando Arzu 59

Francis Arzu 54, 71, 112, 116

Francisco Ellis Arzu 3, 7, 13, 19, 38, 54, 98, 99, 128

Francis Harold Arzu 126

Genaro Arzu 95

Gregoria Arzu 31, 37

Gregorio Arzu 30

Hanjai Arzu 66

Hanjai Gregory Arzu 58, 80

Harold "Greg" Arzu 10, 27, 37, 42, 46, 58, 63, 80, 99, 125, 126

Harriet Scarborough nee Arzu 54, 98, 115. 116

Hazel Elinor Martinez nee Arzu 1, 8, 20, 41, 94, 95, 105, 114

Ildefonsa Arzu 11

Illona Lynette Arzu 94

Isidro Arzu 11, 27, 39, 51, 53, 70, 94, 95, 98, 112, 115

Ivan Arzu 16

Jacob Arzu 124

James Alfred Arzu 28

Jennifer Shireen Arzu 81

Jerry Patrickjean Arzu 8

John Arzu 70, 94

Josefa Arzu 18

Juan Bautista Arzu 33, 56, 59, 67, 107, 124

Julian Arzu 16

Julio Arzu 19

Kahle Austin Arzu 80, 102

Kandese Auzette Arzu 102

Karen Nerissa Arzu 114, 123

Karina Arzu 71

Lazara Arzu 123

Luciano Arzu 13, 30

Luis Arzu 118

Marcus Lambert Arzu 51, 100

Martina Lorraine "Deidei" Arzu 14, 20, 31, 67, 81, 105, 110, 112, 125

Martina Norma Arzu nee Martinez 91, 102, 105, 108, 110, 123

Nolbert Joseph Arzu 27, 64

Opal Arzu 6, 42, 110

Pablo Arzu 27, 68

Peter "Jack" Arzu 68. 113

Petrona Arzu 118

Procopio "Tito" Arzu 3, 41, 112, 126, 128

Remijio Arzu 98

Santos Arzu 56, 59, 67, 107

Sarah Arzu 64, 68

Sebastiana Arzu 31

Sebastian Arzu 17, 25, 37, 65, 71, 88, 91, 92, 118

Sheridan Arzu nee Petillo 6, 9, 10, 20, 24, 25, 27, 37, 46, 54, 65, 67, 80, 94, 108, 109, 127

Sidney Rodrick Arzu 95

Silvan Arzu 28

Stephen Arzu 16, 42, 109

Thelma Arzu 56

Verona Valerie Arzu 102

Viviana Arzu 114

Zacaria Arzu 88

Zita Arzu nee Alvarez 10, 20, 101

Zoila Arzu 67

Zoilo Arzu 67

Zuleesa Mireya Arzu 37

Bonifacio Augustine 124

Primrose Augustine 127

Albertha Magna Gibbs nee Avila 60, 85, 118

Alcardio Avila 27, 41, 56, 79, 104, 105, 109

Ambrosia Avila 73

Ambrosio Avila 120

Antonio Albert "Yuboo" Avila 48, 60, 61, 89

Benigno Avila 21, 32, 52

Bonifacia Avila 61

Cancio Avila 104

Cirilo Avila 13, 41, 47, 93, 105, 127

Claudia Avila 36, 93

Daril Avila 25

Darius Avila 25, 33, 47, 62, 105, 127

Diega Avila 76

Estefania Avila 3, 22, 50, 54, 65, 70, 84, 89, 108, 125, 127

Eulalia Avila 118

Florencia Avila 31, 76

Florentina Avila 60, 76, 79, 109

Fortunata Avila 60

Francis Avila 100

George Avila 96

Gloria Avila 46, 88

Guillermo Avila 5

Inocenta Avila 127
Leonarda Avila 110
Leonora Avila 11, 29, 41, 51, 54, 56, 66, 67, 80, 82, 95, 101, 116, 125
Ligoria Rose Avila 85
Marge Avila 47, 107
Marvin Avila 46
Mary Avila 46
Nolasca Avila 21, 81, 98
Nolberta Avila 61
Olivia Prudencia "Aunti Olive" Avila nee Palacio 13, 30, 41, 47, 88, 93, 105, 107, 121, 127
Pantaleon Avila 9, 13, 16, 21, 24, 36, 42, 92, 103, 113, 118, 127
Paul Avila 27, 125
Pedro John Avila 6, 21, 32, 39, 49, 52, 55, 56, 67, 76, 77, 78, 81, 88, 96, 98, 100, 101, 114
Pedro Juan Avila 32, 49, 114
Peter Anthony Avila 46, 48, 60, 61, 85, 88, 89, 118
Petrona Juliana Avila 9
Presentacion Avila 113
Reginald Avila 5, 6, 39, 52, 44, 60, 76, 78, 88, 96, 100, 113, 125
Rita Enriquez nee Avila 3, 13, 27, 41, 46, 56, 60, 63, 81, 84, 97, 104, 105, 109, 120, 127
Romalda Avila 3, 9, 40, 45, 46, 50, 121
Rufina Maxima Avila 77
Santiaga Avila 116
Santos Leon Avila 42, 103
Sista Avila 36
Urban Paul Avila 125
Victoriano Avila 6, 9, 24, 52, 56, 73, 127
Alexander Avilez 22
Ambrosio "Sabigi" Avilez 5, 7, 11, 23, 28, 29, 39, 47, 49, 55, 58, 60, 76, 77, 84, 85, 88, 90, 112, 119
Ameliana Avilez 115
Anastasia Avilez 47
Antonio Avilez 16, 76, 79, 101
Bernard Avilez 11, 55, 73, 78, 90
Bonifacia Avilez 17, 70
Bonifacio Avilez 102
Calvin Avilez 96
Casimiro Avilez 1, 2, 4, 22, 23, 28, 88, 94, 100
Cherry-Mae Avilez 13, 14, 22, 32
Cipriano Avilez 96
Cleofa Avilez 6, 13, 22, 31, 41, 66, 72, 74, 79, 95, 99, 118, 125
Cruz Avilez 49
Dionisio Avilez 41, 44
Epifania Avilez 7, 50, 60
Eufamio Avilez 95

Eulogia Avilez 30
Francisca Avilez 53, 61, 71, 93, 95, 109
Francisco Avilez 76
Fulgencia Avilez 1, 3
Fulgencio Avilez 1, 4
Geronimo Avilez 37, 58, 119
Gloria Avilez 94
Gregoria Avilez 125
Gregorio Avilez 125
Ivan Avilez 11
James Avilez 4, 13, 30, 126
James J. Avilez 30, 32, 33, 49, 96
James "Jim" Avilez 128
John Justo Avilez 11, 13, 30, 33, 43, 49, 52, 58, 60, 63, 65, 88, 96, 98, 108, 115
John Napoleon Avilez 98
Joseph Avilez 33
Juan Avilez 10, 22, 27, 32, 41, 66, 78, 98, 125
Justina Avilez 1, 2
Justo "Bangi" Avilez 11, 13, 30, 33, 43, 49, 52, 53, 58, 60, 61, 63, 65, 88, 96, 98, 108, 109, 115
Leonie Avilez 30
Lorenza Avilez 60, 63, 88, 90, 91, 94
Lucio Avilez 13, 22, 27, 98
Mamerta Avilez 52
Marcelina Avilez 88, 114
Martina Avilez 27, 49, 58, 65, 70, 75, 78, 115
Martin Avilez 77
Maximo Avilez 49, 58
Otilda Avilez 13, 14, 32
Perfecta Avilez 21, 41, 43, 64, 67, 77, 79, 108, 119, 125
Pietra Avilez 78, 83
Remigio Avilez 98
Rosalia Avilez 88
Rosalio Avilez 88
Santiaga Avilez 16, 58, 76, 101
Santiago "Gaünbü" Avilez 1, 7, 11, 28, 29, 33, 39, 50, 52, 58, 60, 61, 63, 65, 66, 71, 76, 77, 79, 85, 88, 93, 94, 98, 100, 108, 109, 112, 114, 116, 119, 124,
Secundino Avilez 29, 55, 84
Serapia Avilez 5, 28, 49, 50, 112
Veronica Avilez 98

B

Joannem Avila Baker 46
Angel Baltazar 57
Augustin "Ding" Baltazar 47, 62, 83, 102
Aurelia Baltazar 83
Bernardo Baltazar 7, 123

Dominica Baltazar nee Colindres 121
Eusebio Baltazar 128
Johnny Baltazar 104
Luis Baltazar 60
Pablo Baltazar 20, 62, 83, 90, 102
Saturnina Baltazar 116, 119
Tiburcio Baltazar 119
Valentina Marin nee Baltazar 20, 35, 46, 47, 62, 83, 90, 102, 109, 115, 118, 120
Valentine Baltazar 57, 128
Beatrice Barcelona 49, 98
Estela Barcelona 105
Isabel Barcelona 14, 49, 50, 98, 105
Victoria Martinez nee Barcelona 8, 14, 27, 50, 53, 54, 70, 73, 83, 87, 88, 96, 98, 105 124
Estevan Bardalez 105
Beatrice Palacio 47
Diega Benguche 23, 37, 45, 52, 53, 91, 105, 108, 112, 113
Diega "Cocona" Benguche 8, 41, 125
Gregorio Benguche 23, 105, 108
Joseph Benguche 121
Sabina Benguche 105
Sotera Franzria Benguche 68
Asia Benjamin 39
Albertina Bermudez 81
Estevan Bermudez 98
Felicita Bermudez 22, 23, 44, 77, 79, 80, 127
Felipa Bermudez 11, 16, 18, 25, 31, 33, 75, 78, 87
Gregoria Bermudez 8, 10, 19, 39, 49, 73, 75, 90, 102, 104, 105, 122, 123
Isidora Bermudez 39, 40, 49, 52, 65, 71, 77, 98, 104, 106, 113
Narciso Bermudez 10, 13, 22, 23, 33, 35, 40, 75, 78, 102, 106, 111, 122
Santiago Bermudez 13, 111
Telesflora Bermudez 27, 35, 52, 73
Ernest Bernard 75, 100, 106
Maxie Bernard 82
Agapito Bernardez 12, 105
Ambrosia Bernardez 114
Felicita Bernardez 12, 68
Francisco Bernardez 12
Marta Bernardez 3, 39, 62
Martin Bernardez 8, 66, 76, 128
Raphael Bernardez 105
Silveria Bernardez 8, 66, 74, 76, 128
Ciriaco Blanco 43, 121
Estena Blanco 6, 92
Felipa Blanco 16
Francis "Badi" Blanco 79. 99
Henrietta Blanco 105, 121
Leandra Blanco 82
Merjilda Blanco 43

Aniceta Blas 28, 45, 48, 51, 62, 77, 84, 85, 90, 100, 111
Delfina Blas 11, 23, 26, 28, 33, 40, 63, 70, 123
Florencia Blas 6, 22, 25, 55, 60, 101, 108
Joanis Blas 120
John Blas 108
Macario Blas 4, 25, 45, 63, 102, 109, 111, 117, 120, 124, 126
Vicenta Blas 4, 5, 20, 28, 30, 70, 82, 100, 102, 112, 122, 123
Bonafacia "Banje" Ramirez 42
Serapia Bonilla 113
Dorla Bradley 117
Leroy Bradley 34, 112
Loreta Brown 33, 37
Margaret Buckley 63, 104

C
Nicolas Caballero 2
Daniel Cacho 5, 32, 66, 68
Devon Cacho 68
Elogia Cacho 103
Eulogia Cacho 42
Keron Cacho 5
Leon Cacho 32
Leoncio Cacho 98
Losanta Cacho 27, 98
Mariano Cacho 103
Myrtle Cacho 19, 25, 53, 80
Dwight Cadle 6, 77, 79, 87
Jahleel Cadle 77
Jeremiah Cadle 79
Bernard Cain 82, 110
Marthy "Marti" Cain nee Arana 6, 9, 16, 21, 25, 29, 32, 41, 51, 52, 66, 76
Candelaria 126
Maria Candelaria 64, 121
Maria Leondre Carmen 41
Adriana "Tun" Casimiro 5, 16, 46, 49, 84, 90, 99
Alan Casimiro 100
Alice Casimiro nee Nicholas 45, 48, 63, 77, 79, 111
Bernadina Casimiro nee Nolberto 18, 62, 73
Bernardo Casimiro 104
Cecilio Casimiro 113
Celia Casimiro 96
Ciriaco Casimiro 92, 98
Claudia Casimiro 23
Cordelia Casimiro 44
Dionisio Casimiro 6, 16, 66, 87, 110, 111
Dorla Marian Casimiro 32, 127
Emry Casimiro 16

Erasmo Casimiro 1, 14, 18, 35, 44, 56, 62, 73, 96, 100, 107, 114
Etta Casimiro 100
Felicia Casimiro nee Arzu 103
Fermin "Rama" Casimiro 12, 17, 18, 20, 46, 98, 99, 114, 121
Fidelis Casimiro 120
Francis Casimiro 1, 30, 83, 99
Gonzalez Casimiro 5, 12, 17, 20, 46, 47, 49, 84, 90, 99, 104, 106, 108, 109, 114, 121
Helen Casimiro 100
Jovita Casimiro 20, 24, 67, 73, 109, 113, 115
Julius Casimiro 47, 104
Justina Casimiro 107
Kareen Casimiro 6, 77, 79, 87
Kelvin Casimiro 12
Lacaria Casimiro 108
Lloyd Casimiro 109
Louis Jarvis Casimiro 84
Marcos Oliver Casimiro 46, 106
Maria "Mari" Zuniga nee Casimiro 1, 2, 18, 30, 71, 83, 111
Marva Casimiro 99
Mary Casimiro nee Flores 40, 52, 65, 71, 77, 98, 121
Muriel Williams nee Casimiro 18, 62, 96, 114
Odelma Casimiro 66
Pablo Casimiro 5, 18, 20, 43, 46, 49, 67, 73, 85, 92, 98, 104, 108, 114, 115
Paula Casimiro nee Noralez 32
Paul Casimiro 16, 20, 24, 67, 73, 108, 113, 115
Paul Hudson "Boy" Casimiro 43, 50, 85, 96, 98, 104, 120
Peter Casimiro 16, 43, 85, 113, 120
Philip Casimiro 18, 46, 121
Rashad Casimiro 16
Ricorda Geraldine Casimiro 14, 19, 32, 35, 56, 62, 107, 127
Sandra Casimiro 30
Tom Andrew Casimiro 17
Valentina Jovita Casimiro 20, 24
Agnus Castillo 24
Alejandro Castillo 47, 116
Amenigi Castillo 120
Anastacia Christina Castillo nee Ramirez 50, 113, 126
Anastacio Castillo 40
Augusto Castillo 14, 91, 117, 120
Aurelio Castillo 53
Brigida Castillo 99
Casimiro Castillo 23, 30
Catalina Castillo 41, 112, 126
Cleon Castillo 105

Cornelio Castillo 40, 75, 91, 92, 95, 102, 110, 126
Dolores Castillo 34
Edward Castillo 95, 102
Edward "Hapu" Castillo 93
Elbert Karle Castillo 56
Emelia Castillo 81
Felipa Castillo 91
Felipe Castillo 18
Graciano Castillo 123
Hermogenes Castillo 44
Inaruni Mohammed Castillo 91
Inez Castillo 4, 32, 34, 40, 75, 91, 92, 95, 99
John Castillo 30, 63
Jose Castillo 116
Joseph Castillo 19, 35, 56
Juana Castillo 6
Juan Fernando Castillo 64
Juliana Castillo 7, 21, 24, 45, 46, 61
Marcelino Castillo 47
Margarita Castillo 4, 32, 49, 91, 126
Martha Castillo 77
Martina Castillo 110
Nicodemus Castillo 34, 40, 44, 91, 99
Peter "Cadi" Castillo 43, 53, 81, 105, 123
Rafael Castillo 10, 24, 75, 126
Seferina Castillo 4
"Showno" Castillo 34
Vicenta Castillo 10, 32, 36, 63, 73, 75, 76, 91, 93, 121
Victoriano "Weibayua" Castillo 18, 21, 24, 30, 48, 123
Wayne Kenny Castillo 19
Anacleta Castro 11, 55, 73, 90
Candido M. Castro 98
Dickson Castro 128
Francisca Castro 61
Hazel Cayetano nee Castro 14, 49, 94, 99
Leon Castro 73, 90, 98, 108, 123
Morris Castro 49, 85
Valentino Castro 72, 96, 108, 123, 127
Catarino Ariola 4, 34, 101, 115
Adela Cayetano 77
Afieni Tirhysi Tanigi Cayetano 81
Albina Cayetano (Avilez) 16, 66
Almira Cayetano 50
Anacleto Cayetano 7, 17, 18, 39, 47, 71, 80, 82, 95, 99, 110, 115, 116, 119, 120, 121, 124
Andrea Cayetano 17
Angus Claude Cayetano 54, 60, 96, 107, 115
Apolonia Cayetano 113
Augustin Cayetano 121
Beatrice Cayetano nee Sanchez 36

Index

Bernard Cayetano 83
Brigid Cayetano 21
Calistra Cayetano 95, 101
Callistus Cayetano 81, 82, 103, 113
Carmela Cayetano 60
Castro Cayetano 35
Cecilia Cayetano 112
Cristino Cayetano 76, 123
Cynthia Leanne Cayetano 20, 105
Delita Almira Cayetano 83
Delita Cayetano 83
Dominga "Waganga" Cayetano 10, 20, 37, 51, 58, 61, 62, 67, 81, 91, 106, 107, 118, 120
Eluteria Cayetano 6, 9, 16, 17, 23, 25, 29, 44, 71, 83, 85, 102, 116, 118, 122, 127
Emeni Cayetano 88
E. Roy Cayetano 2, 23, 25, 29, 34, 36, 43, 46, 55, 67, 74, 81, 88, 96, 102, 103, 112, 116, 117, 125
Eugenio Cayetano 2, 11, 21, 23, 55, 58, 61, 74, 77, 83, 93, 109, 111, 125
Evan Stephen Cayetano 2, 46, 54, 111
Fabian Cayetano 6, 9, 45, 63, 87, 115
Fatima Cayetano 17, 85
Filomena Cayetano 95, 96
Francis Benedict Cayetano 1, 2, 6, 9, 14, 24, 30, 57, 81, 83, 111, 113
Francisca Cayetano 50, 90, 112, 115
Gianne Cayetano 123
Gregorio Cayetano 54, 60, 77, 96, 107, 115
Hazel Cayetano nee Castro 14, 49, 94, 99
Ibime Cayetano 81
Ignacia Cayetano 2
Isani Cayetano 81, 96
Janine Jewel Cayetano 123
Joseph Cayetano 14, 24, 111
Joy Melanie Cayetano 101, 106
Juanita Cayetano 14
Juan Pedro Cayetano 2, 10, 13, 19, 23, 25, 34, 36, 40, 47, 50, 52, 55, 57, 60, 61, 62, 63, 64, 65, 66, 70, 71, 80, 82, 87, 94, 95, 101, 103, 107, 110, 114, 115, 117, 118, 120, 121, 124
Judith Cayetano 58, 83, 93
Justina Cayetano 5, 12, 19, 27, 28, 37, 39, 50, 51, 54, 62, 74, 80, 82, 95, 111
Kendra Cayetano 79, 106
Loreta Cayetano 36, 54, 58, 88
Luciano Cayetano 95
Luisa Cayetano 78
Luis Cayetano 25, 55, 58, 77, 111

Luis Tomas Leopoldo Cayetano 103, 110
Luwani Frances Cayetano 29
Marcelo Cayetano 18, 24, 35, 36, 37, 58, 82, 95, 111, 115, 120, 122, 123, 127, 128
Maria Cayetano 103
Marina Egzine Cayetano 53
Marion Cayetano 29, 55, 61
Martila Cayetano 34
Mary Martha Cayetano 1, 27, 46, 108, 109
Mary Petillo nee Cayetano 94, 111, 116, 122
Mauricia Cayetano 4, 7, 18, 19, 21, 22, 29, 71, 74, 92, 99, 101, 105, 115
Nathaniel "Shorty" Cayetano 1, 57, 75, 88
Pascacio Cayetano 1, 10, 20, 24, 27, 30, 34, 35, 37, 54, 58, 65, 71, 75, 76, 94, 108, 111, 122, 123, 127
Pascual Cayetano 63, 101
Paula Cayetano 64
Pedro Nolasco Cayetano 55
Petrona Cayetano 7, 12, 13, 18, 19, 21, 27, 29, 36, 40, 41, 42, 44, 50, 59, 62, 63, 70, 71, 74, 114, 124
Policarpio Cayetano 19
Rachel Cayetano 117
Rafaela Cayetano 64, 124
Richard Cayetano 58
Robert Cayetano 36, 58, 96, 113, 123
Sarah Cayetano 20, 23, 42, 103
Sebastian Cayetano 6, 9, 18, 58, 80, 102, 121, 128
Serapia Cayetano 111
Silas Cayetano 94
Sixta Cayetano 36
Solomon Cayetano 58
StephAnn Cayetano 46
Steven Cayetano 95, 101
Victoria Cayetano 30, 111
Victoriana Cayetano 47, 116
Vinciona "Beltrana" Cayetano 2, 6, 17, 25, 36, 44, 118, 119
Wallace Cayetano 79, 101
Wallace Secundino Cayetano 105
Yanira Cayetano 113
Zacarias Cayetano 113
Juana Paula Celertina 7, 39, 65, 71
Maria Celestina 25, 63, 101, 103, 110
Magdalena Cesaria 10, 11, 23, 31, 44, 49, 55, 60, 61, 62, 71, 74, 79, 99, 101, 102, 116, 118
Clayton Chavez 8
Faustina Chavez 21, 32, 52
Gilroy Chavez 8
Amelia Chimilio 28

Antonio Chimilio 108
Benito Chimilio 65, 108, 124
Bertie Chimilio 35, 65, 106, 127
Crispulo Chimilio 2, 11, 28, 63, 70, 117, 120, 124
Crispulo "Polo" Chimilio 33, 40
Elia Chimilio 106, 108
Filomena Chimilio 33
Guillerma Chimilio 67
Isidoro Chimilio 40
John Chimilio 11, 23, 26, 28, 33, 40, 63, 70, 117, 123, 124, 126
Macaria Chimilio 26
Macario Chimilio 2
Marcial Chimilio 34, 49, 65, 67, 106, 108, 127
Saturnina Chimilio 70
Silvan Joseph Chimilio 23, 54, 115
Simeon Chimilio 34, 35
Timoteo Chimilio 11, 90, 105, 123
Vilma Chimilio 16
Vilma Petrona Chimilio 11, 16, 24, 32, 34, 52, 62, 66, 68, 71, 90, 102, 105, 109, 111, 119, 120, 123, 126
Alberta Ciego 44, 68, 76, 87, 122
Clarence "Cally" Coffin 24, 71, 111
Sylvia Coffin 24, 62, 71, 111
Dominica Baltazar nee Colindres 121
Dominica Colindres 7, 123
Juliana Colindres 27, 52, 68, 70, 121
Justo Colindres 121
Marcelo Colindres 8
Maria Genera Colindres 12, 110, 114
Pasqualo Colindres 53
Patrocino Colindres 51
Secundina Colindres 18, 74, 85, 98
Victoriano Colindres 8, 51, 53, 64, 121, 123
Antonia Velda "Reds" Colon 115
Antonio Colon 101
Dionisio M. Colon 76, 100
John Colon 76, 100
Joseph Colon 118
Leslie Carlton Colon 44, 85
Leslie Colon 5
Naomi Colon 6, 25, 44, 67, 72, 73, 74, 83, 91, 101, 103
Victoria Colon 45
Vinton Colon 25
Ambrosio Contreras 85
Andres Contreras 18, 74, 85, 98, 117
Camila Contreras 10, 14, 18, 24, 32, 72, 74, 84, 95, 98, 113, 126
Marcos Contreras 87, 91, 93, 105
Narcisa Esther Contreras 9, 29, 51, 55, 74, 87, 91, 93, 104, 105, 109
Ferdinanda Cruz 5, 18, 28, 50
Fernanda Cruz 114

D

Adonis Darius Daniels 94
Amelita Cloudina Daniels 83
Fabiana Sebastiana Daniels 45
Faith Daniels 55, 58, 118
Francis Daniels 96
Herman Tenk Daniels 53
Melchisedech Daniels 96
Michael Angelo Daniels 58
Miguel Daniels 44, 68, 96, 107
Patience Daniels 93
Prudencio Daniels 98
Salvatore Basil "S.B." Daniels 44, 45, 53, 55, 58, 68, 83, 85, 87, 93, 94, 96, 98, 107, 118
Sam Daniels 96
Victoria Fabiana Daniels 85
Dawn Joseph 55, 56
Maria Eugenia Delavez 2, 10, 28, 50, 60, 65, 79, 118
Desideria 13, 31, 63, 80
Desideria "Maga Gidei" 63, 124
Alberta Diego 90
Angelina Diego 35, 95
Mariana Diego 64, 81
John "Shamba" Dominguez 43, 66, 99

E

Anita Edwards nee Marin 112
Ifasina Efunyemi 77
Claudina Elington 29, 61
Alberta Enriquez 48, 60, 61, 89
Anacleto Enriquez 76
Andres "A.P." Patricio Enriquez 61
Andres Patricio Enriquez 12, 58, 72, 88, 89, 97, 110, 120
A.P. Enriquez 43, 47, 88, 110
Aurelia Enriquez 1, 122
Carmen Enriquez 1, 9, 21, 27, 32, 49, 65, 67, 73, 74, 84, 109, 112
Catarina Enriquez 48
Celestina Enriquez 5, 32, 66, 68, 102, 105, 119
Clotildo Enriquez 48
Colin Marlon Enriquez 3
Constantine Enriquez 120
Contestine Enriquez 97
Evelyn Enriquez 30, 71, 83
Henrietta Enriquez 63, 81
Jerry Enriquez 13, 58, 110
Joseph Victoriano Enriquez 12, 110
Lillian Enriquez 75, 91, 93, 95
Lino Enriquez 1, 64, 75, 77, 81, 103, 122
Lloyd Enriquez 3, 13, 97, 120
Luciana Enriquez 25, 37, 65, 71, 75, 88, 91, 92
Mercedes Enriquez 75

Nazaria Enriquez nee Zuniga 1, 19, 48, 64, 75, 77, 81, 103, 122
Nolberto Enriquez 81
Olivia Justiniana Enriquez 61, 88
Rita Enriquez nee Avila 3, 27, 36, 41, 46, 56, 60, 63, 81, 84, 104, 105, 109, 127
Rosalio Enriquez 88
Rosenda Enriquez 79
Santiaga Enriquez 14, 76
Silverio Enriquez 88, 114
Victor Enriquez 34, 66, 105, 119
Victoriano Enriquez 114
Zenobia Enriquez 30, 43, 47

F

Douglas Fairweather 62
Gaynor Ferguson 6, 77
Anastacia Figueroa 108
Antonio Flores 52
Candido Flores 40, 49, 52, 65, 71, 98, 104, 113
Cecilia Flores 16, 77, 113
Felicita Flores 58
Manuela Flores 65
Mary Casimiro nee Flores 5, 12, 17, 20, 40, 46, 47, 49, 52, 65, 71, 77, 84, 90, 98, 99, 104, 106, 109, 114, 121
Nolberto Flores 23
Philip Flores 98
Procopio "Prook" Flores 16, 40, 49, 52, 65, 71, 77, 104, 106
Roy Flores 98
Simeona Flores 20, 33, 35, 66, 74, 81, 90, 95, 104, 106, 115
Teofila Flores 54, 60, 77, 96, 107, 115
Beverly Flowers 115
Ruth Flowers 103
Apolonia Francisca Foster 76, 79, 84
Ireneo Frazer Francisco 122
Bonifacia Francois 43, 52, 128
Francisco Francois 128
Dalton Franklin 112, 118
Kent Franklin 118
Maria Rovidia Fuentes 114
Martha Fuentes 4, 32, 34, 40, 75, 91, 92, 95
Rubeajia Fuentes 106

G

Alfonsa Gabriel 17, 31, 88, 103
Fecunda Gabriel 14, 49, 50, 98, 105
Veronia Gabriel 25
Antonio Gamboa 56
Ashley Gamboa 56
Maria Victoria Gamboa 15, 20, 85, 94, 125

Ambrosia Garcia 120
America Garcia 29, 67
Anacleto Garcia 81, 110, 112
Apolinaria Garcia 45, 92
Apolinario Garcia 4, 5, 7, 21, 24, 36, 49, 53, 55, 58, 74, 83, 118, 127
Bonifacio Garcia 20, 104
Carmen Garcia 18, 21, 24, 30, 48
Carol Garcia 23, 54, 115
Christina Garcia 12, 44, 49, 51, 55, 60, 62, 102, 111, 118
Damiana Garcia 3, 61, 86, 104, 119, 126
Esmith Garcia 4, 5, 13, 24, 29, 30, 34, 40, 45, 53, 67, 68, 83, 85, 92
Ezechiel Garcia 83
Feliciano Garcia 5
Felipa Garcia 49, 74, 82, 107
Felix Garcia 45
Francisco Garcia 83
Georgiana Garcia 29, 67
Gregorio Garcia 30
Isidora Garcia 40, 60
Isidora "Mama Daguwasi" Garcia 34
Jeronima Garcia 5
John Garcia 13
Jose Apolinario Garcia 58
Josephine Garcia 23, 54, 115
Juliana Garcia 9, 13, 21, 24, 36, 42, 92, 103, 118, 127
Leona Garcia 25, 40, 51, 67, 95
Marcelina Augustina "Magiri" Garcia nee Martinez 4, 5, 7, 21, 24, 49, 53, 55, 58, 74, 83, 127
Margarito Garcia 24, 83, 91, 120, 125
Maria Garcia 120
Nicanora Palacio nee Garcia 7, 18, 58
Patrocinia Marcelina Garcia 45
Pedro Garcia 68
Sebastian Garcia 55
Simona Garcia 24, 75, 126
Sindulfo Garcia 91, 125
Toribia Garcia 12, 20, 36, 101, 104
Venturo Garcia 60
Victor Garcia 45, 85, 111
Victoriano Garcia 34
Virginia Garcia 104, 120
William Garcia 13
Sharron Gelobter nee Williams 29, 34, 43, 88
Briana Gentle 127
Don Gentle 127
Irene Gibbons 19, 24, 50, 63, 66, 73, 91, 92, 101, 103, 107, 111, 112, 121, 125
Isaac Gibbons 6, 92, 111
Solomon Gibbons 111
Steven Gibbons 92, 103

Index

Albertha Magna Gibbs nee Avila 60, 85

Magna Avila Gibbs 46

Joseph Givera 110

Alfonsa Gomez 25

Cesaria Gomez 75

Escolastica Gomez 39, 75

Almira "Irma" Gonzalez nee Ariola 2, 9, 3, 37, 42, 112, 119, 124

Ariola Gonzalez 51, 83

Cayetana Gonzalez 25, 53, 81, 110, 112, 115

Dominga Gonzalez 101

Evilia Gonzalez 2, 5, 58, 66, 100, 110, 113

Evilia "Ivy" Martinez nee Gonzalez 36

Evilia Martinez nee Gonzalez 16, 104, 112

Felix Gonzalez 18, 25, 87

Francisca Gonzalez 39

Juana Gonzalez 24, 113

Justa Gonzalez 27, 41, 56, 79, 104, 105, 109

Justo Gonzalez 2, 36, 58, 102, 112, 124

Luisa Gonzalez 122

Macario Gonzalez 112

Matilda Gonzalez 103

Pablo Gonzalez 36, 112

Rufino Gonzalez 83

Sabina Gonzalez 105

Sebastian Gonzalez 25, 87

Severino Gonzalez 101

James Goree 79

William Grant 10

Cipriana Gregorio 20, 22, 55, 108

John Gregorio 80

Juan Christomo Gregorio 13

Justin Vivian Gregorio 69

Maria Gregorio 19

Petrona Gregorio 17, 90

Viviano Gregorio 13, 17, 54, 80, 90

Carlos Guerra 6, 110

Karlon Evin Guerra 110

Esteban Guevara 127

Joseph Guevara 9, 127

Juliana Guevara 9

Cirilo Gutierrez 4

Crescente Gutierrez 11, 16, 25, 31, 33

Dale Gutierrez 10, 31, 34, 39, 51, 60, 96, 120

Eufemio Gutierrez 33, 66, 122

Fabiana Gutierrez 96

Glen Garrett Gutierrez 51

Gregoria Gutierrez 31

Matias Gutierrez 25

Nerisa Marla Gutierrez 109

Sotera Gutierrez 6, 31, 37, 76, 82, 96, 108, 113

Steven Gutierrez 10, 33, 51, 74, 109, 114, 115, 117, 118

Steven Gregory "Junior" Gutierrez 20, 21, 29, 39, 40, 57, 70, 74, 96, 109, 127

Vicente Gutierrez 11

Secundina "Kunda" Guzman 99

H

Henry H. Hartman 61, 88

Stephen Francis Hecker 67, 73

Gloria Avila Hernandez 46

Mildred Hernandez 16, 83, 107, 125

Peter Egbert Hernandez 16, 103, 107

Darnell Higinio 80

Mike Higinio 80

George Hill 5, 44, 85

Sharon Humes 62

J

Jacoba Mauricia 103

Adela Jaime 54, 96, 107

Filiberto Jaime 114

Saturnino Jaime 114

Alejandro Jimenez 50

Angel Jimenez 44, 59

Feliciano Jimenez 42, 79

Fermin Jimenez 44, 50, 59, 62, 63, 124

Marcelina Jimenez 64

Marcelino Jimenez 64, 124

Pablo Jimenez 62, 63, 89, 102

Marcelino H. Johnson 78, 80, 82, 120

Petrona Johnson 115, 118

Ambrosio Joseph 2, 8, 10, 34, 46, 52, 55, 85, 93, 99, 104, 126

Catherine Joseph 34

Cecilia Joseph 104

Charles Francis Joseph 99

Dawn Joseph 55

Edgar Wayne Joseph 10

Francis Joseph 8, 46

Gricelda Joseph 126

Jason Joseph 85

Lambert Joseph 2

Michael Joseph 46, 93

Petrona "Peti" Joseph nee Palacio 2, 8, 10, 34, 46, 52, 55, 85, 93, 99, 104, 126

Rose Joseph 85

Nieves Juarez 75, 100, 106

K

Antonia King 1, 84

Clifford King 5, 75, 76, 82, 106, 115

Julian King 82

Kareem King 115

Shevaughn King 5

L

Alberta Felipa Labriel 49, 85, 86

Apolonia Virginia Labriel 25

Basilia Labriel 16, 18, 46, 102, 103

Casimira Labriel 114

Domingo Labriel 5, 18, 28, 50, 94, 114

Doroteo Labriel 18

Gertrude Labriel 45, 99, 112

Maria Petrona Labriel 13

P. Labriel 95

Santiago Labriel 5, 25, 28, 49, 50, 112

Nelson Lacio 100

Asili Thair Lambert 117

Russell Stephen Lambert 117, 125

Aurelio Lambey 117

Celestina Lambey 68

Claudio Lambey 106

Dionisia Lambey 68, 100

Eusebia (Toribia) Lambey 43

Florencia Lambey 4, 17, 20, 28, 32, 36, 63, 112, 114

Inocente Lambey 127

John Lambey 2, 3, 35, 37, 43, 56, 60, 66, 84, 92, 99, 100, 117, 122, 127

Joseph Antonio Lambey 2, 68

Juliana Lambey 33, 66, 122

Manuel (Nicholas) Lambey 92

Marcellina Lambey 60

Nicasia Lambey 49, 90

Pastora Lambey 37, 99

Severiano Lambey 11, 35, 66, 90, 106

Telesforo Lambey 3

Felipe Lambi 84

Adriana Lauriano 20, 62, 83, 90, 102

Thomas Charles Lauriano 90, 102, 118

Matildo Martinez Leiva 47, 73

Marion Elizabeth Lent 68, 78

Petrona Leoncio 85

Basilia Lewis 3, 5, 55, 87, 90, 93, 106

Basilio Lewis 3, 5, 121

Agnes Lino 5

Anthony Lino 50, 96

Barbarin Lino 58, 118

Daniel Lino 21, 37, 52

Evangelista Lino 103

Gladys Clarice Lino nee Loredo 103

Gladys Lino 2, 51, 52

Hazel Lino 51

Jane Lino 11, 45, 53, 88, 91

Jose Lino Sebastian 41

Joseph Lino 98

Mary Lino 50, 96

Matildo Lino 98

Maximino Lino 58, 76, 101

Nievi Lino 55, 98

Obispo Lino 37, 41, 45, 52, 53, 90, 115

Petrona Lino 90
Rosendo Lino 55, 58, 101, 118
Wilfred Harold Lino 41
Eugene Lizama 123
Adriana Lopez 67, 74
Agnes Lopez 10
Anthony Lopez 66, 113
Antonio Lopez 33, 37
Barbara Lopez 2
Brigina Lopez 34
Cecilia Lopez 74
Christina Lopez 76
Christine Lopez 82
Damiana Lopez 2, 53
David Lopez 67
Elaysia Lopez 39
Elton Tyron Lopez 39, 122
Eugenio Lopez 12
Feliciano Lopez 12, 41
Florencia Lopez 103, 110
Gabina Lopez 22
Hermenehilda "Maria" Lopez 1, 3, 43, 77, 79, 100, 101, 122
Inocente Lopez 127
Joyce Lopez 34, 57, 74, 78, 81, 114
Juan Guadalupe Lopez 103
Juliana "Linda" Arana nee Lopez 57
Juliana "Linda" Lopez 11
Justa Lopez 80
Kaya Lopez 122
Kayla Gloria Lopez 20
Linda Arana nee Lopez 107
Nolberto Lopez 98
Oswald Lopez 79
Patrick Lopez 1, 10, 33, 37, 43
Paula Lopez 12
Paulina Lopez 18, 30, 36, 77, 79, 89, 110, 125
Prudencia Lopez 18
Raymond Lopez 20, 34
Roman Lopez 122
Santiago Lopez 22, 44, 77, 79, 80, 127
Toribio Joseph Lopez 16, 44, 57, 80, 92, 127
Toribio Lopez 92
Yvonne Lopez 1, 26, 33, 37, 52, 76
Akeem "Conceto" Loredo 72
Alexine Loredo 5, 14, 33, 47, 58, 73, 105, 110, 127
Alexine Nunez nee Loredo 51
Alfanette Ashanti Loredo 72, 98
Alvin Loredo 2, 3, 5, 6, 12, 18, 23, 28, 36, 43, 45, 60, 63, 65, 66, 72, 73, 83, 92, 93, 99, 104, 107, 117, 121, 122
Bernadette Arzu nee Loredo 1, 6, 8, 10, 20, 27, 30, 42, 52, 64, 65, 70, 75, 80, 82, 94, 95, 98, 102, 104, 108, 110, 116, 125, 128

Cristobel Loredo 31, 54, 62, 63, 77, 79, 89, 102
Epifania Loredo 2, 21, 32, 36, 37, 41, 46, 103
Eric Loredo 6
Ethel Dee Loredo 3, 27, 34, 70, 75, 80, 115
Eulalia Loredo 49, 89
Eulalio Loredo 2, 3, 10, 14, 25, 28, 41, 47, 58, 63, 72, 73, 78, 80, 92, 93, 102, 103, 126
Gladys Clarice Lino nee Loredo 2, 21, 37, 51, 103
Hazel Loredo 32
Hector Loredo 11, 18, 28, 46, 49, 99, 104
Henry Loredo 5, 6, 14, 18, 27, 32, 36, 49, 54, 58, 65, 70, 75, 78, 86, 98, 99, 102, 104, 115, 119, 121, 126
Isaac Loredo 72, 98
Isolene Loredo 36, 119, 121
Lavern Bernice Loredo 46
Madeline Loredo 3, 46, 61, 104, 126
Mark Loredo 49, 99, 120, 123
Mark Rayshawn Loredo 123
Melquiades Julius "Jimbo" Loredo 10, 23, 54, 106, 121
Michael Luke Loredo 11, 49
Ophelia Loredo 36
Shalamar Marcy Loredo 92
Shantay Loredo 93
Sharday Loredo 43
Sharon Loredo nee Nunez 28, 43, 72, 73, 80, 92, 93, 114
Tomasine Loredo 14, 22, 25, 28, 29, 31, 33, 65, 80
Thomas Loredo 54
Tomasine Loredo 101
Wilhelmina Loredo 73
Wilhemina "Mina" Loredo 47
Alberto Lorenzo 70
Asenciona Lorenzo 31
Charlotte Michael Lorenzo 63, 96
Eusebio Lorenzo 39, 122
Filomeno Lorenzo 33, 70, 91
Francisco Lorenzo 39
Manuel Lorenzo 106, 114
Margarita Lorenzo 20, 24, 67, 73, 108, 113, 115
Michaela Lorenzo 72, 96, 108, 123, 127
Regina Martinez nee Lorenzo 18, 34, 41, 58, 66, 73, 81, 89, 93, 110, 118, 120
Timoteo Lorenzo 21, 24, 29, 31, 34, 39, 41, 60, 70, 73, 89, 91, 96, 106, 108, 114, 118, 122, 127
Valentina "Flora" Lorenzo 10, 20, 34, 51, 74, 96, 101, 109

Victoriano "Fada" Lorenzo 20, 29, 34, 39, 60, 70, 89, 101, 106, 115, 122
Virgilia Lorenzo nee Ariola 20, 34, 60, 89, 101, 115
Lorenzo "Thunder" Nolberto 4, 29, 65
Julio Louis 60, 63, 88
Erlett Lozano 26
Adolph Lucas 118, 127
Augustina Lucas 85
Basilia Lucas 8, 43, 112, 113
Canuta Lucas 3, 5, 121
Ciriaca Lucas 31
"Clarinet" Lucas 100
Felix Lucas 33, 35, 66, 97, 123
Fernando Lucas 8, 112
Florencia Cayetano nee Lucas 1, 2, 6, 9, 14, 24, 30, 57, 81, 83, 113
Francisca Lucas 67, 94
Francisco Lucas 99
Ines Lucas 45
Ireneo Lucas 45, 99, 112
John Nipalmson "Hepu" Lucas 9, 17, 24, 29, 31, 34, 51, 60, 85, 88, 103
Joseph Robert Lucas 17, 31, 88, 103
Lucas Lucas 103
Maxima Lucas 112
Modesta Lucas 9, 49, 90
Robert Lucas 17, 29, 103
Simon Lucas 100
William Lucas 35, 92, 97
Antonio Luis 88
Basilia Luis 3, 5, 55, 87, 90, 93, 106
Demasia Luis 121
Juana Paulino nee Luis 13, 26, 33, 35, 37, 47, 56, 67, 75, 81, 83, 96, 105, 121, 122, 123
Pedro Luis 26
Perfecta Luis 113
Regina Virgen Luis 16, 22, 56, 74, 107

M
Joseph Magdelano 72
Pia "Mamacita" Arana nee Magdelano 72, 74, 85, 99, 105, 115, 126
Andres Dion Makin 67, 75
Andres Makin 118
Delia Makin 83, 98
Dion Trevor Makin 75
Maria Makin 4, 32, 40, 98
Matildo Makin 4
Maura Makin 101
Maxwell Makin 42
Perfecto Makin 37, 42, 83, 101, 118
Miriam Maldonado 60
Louis Marfield 80

Randy Marfield 112
Anthea Benita Mariano 77
Beatrice Magdalene "Tricia" Mariano 20, 50, 52, 57, 91, 98, 118
Faustina Mariano 62, 83, 102
Genevieve Mariano 55
Luke Mariano 77, 118
Maria Mariano 35, 82, 95
Patrick Mariano 34, 35, 82, 95, 101
Raheem Mariano 57, 114, 116
Shemar Mariano 98
Anita Edwards nee Marin 112
Anita Marin 13, 76, 80, 100
Aparicio Santiago Marin 13, 16, 46, 47, 53, 56, 57, 58, 70, 80, 93, 99, 103, 107, 117, 125
Bridget Palacio nee Marin 6, 35, 40, 47, 53, 56, 60, 85, 88, 99, 107, 125
Brigida Marin nee Paulino 91
Carlotta Marin 33
Charles Marin 25
Cirila Marin 46
Clarence Marin 7, 35, 46, 47, 53, 63, 70, 76, 100, 112, 117, 120
Clifford Marin 5, 13, 20, 28, 51, 62, 63, 102, 106, 109, 111, 120
Delia Gloria Martinez 120
Dionisia Marin nee Santino 20, 35, 47, 63, 70, 71, 76, 100, 112, 117, 120
Dominga "Gadu" Marin 10, 11, 13, 16, 22, 23, 25, 27, 31, 32, 33, 35, 40, 41, 66, 75, 78, 98, 102, 106, 111, 122, 125
Emelda Marin 16, 44, 57, 92, 127
Eulogio Marin 78
Felipa Carlota Marin 57, 81, 107
Gilbert Marin 7, 20, 35, 46, 47, 70, 109, 120
Gilbert Michael Marin 46
Godfrey Marin 7, 10
James Marin 7
Kenrick Gilbert Marin 7
Kevin York Marin 109
Leroy Owen Marin 47
Manuela Cayetano nee Marin 2, 21, 23, 55, 58, 61, 74, 77, 83, 93, 111, 125
Ramona Marin 44, 99
Seferino Marin 60
Solomon Marin 103
Anacleto Martinez 13
Anastacio Martinez 50
Andrea Martinez 116, 121
Anthony Phillip Martinez 83
Apolonaria Martinez 98
Bartolo Martinez 84
Benedicto Martinez 33

Benito Martinez 37, 60, 75, 115, 127
Bernardo Martinez 18, 87
Brown Prudencio Martinez 3, 120
Bruno Martinez 96
Canuta Martinez 9
Carlos Martinez 73, 108
Catarino Nicodemus Martinez 92
Cindy Nichole Martinez 23, 121
Cirila Martinez 72, 123
Clara Martinez 13, 26
Claudio Martinez 14, 43, 52, 106, 128
Clinton Martinez 22, 111
Cornelia Martinez 12, 24, 29, 30, 31, 40, 67, 68, 83, 98
Cornelio Martinez 93
Crescencio Martinez 50, 60
Crispino Martinez 31, 46, 73, 76, 104, 108, 109, 111
Cuthbert Joseph Giles Martinez 87
Cynthia Lavinia Lynn Martinez 82, 93
Darina Martinez 16
Dativa Elizabeth Martinez nee Melendrez 81, 106
Delia Gloria Martinez 123
Dolores Martinez 92
Domingo Martinez 87
Elizabeth Martinez 81, 99, 106
Elliot Martinez 18, 22, 41, 58, 73, 92, 120
Elma Yvonne Arzu nee Martinez 8, 14, 27, 49, 50, 54, 94, 96, 105, 124, 127
Emily Ramirez nee Martinez 34, 49, 61, 67, 73, 74, 93, 108
Encarnacion Martinez 128
Epifania Martinez 3
Ernesto Martinez 25
Erwin Martinez 60
Estanislao Martinez 68
Eugene Pacelli Denny Martinez 54
Eugenia "Henny" Martinez 12, 23, 35, 73
Eulalia Martinez 20
Eustacia Martinez 92
Evangelista Martinez 127
Evilia "Ivy" Martinez nee Gonzalez 16, 36, 104, 112
Exzine Martinez 28
Facundo Martinez 49, 65, 127
Felix Martinez 23
Florentino Martinez 60, 76, 79, 84
Francis Benedict Martinez 8, 14, 27, 50, 53, 54, 70, 73, 83, 87, 88, 96, 108, 124, 125, 127
Francisco Martinez 3, 22, 50, 54, 65, 70, 84, 108, 125, 127
Francisco Xavier Martinez 118
Frederico Martinez 74

Fred Martinez 30
Genevieve Martinez 3, 4, 34, 114
George Martinez 56
Germaine Gloria Martinez 20, 22, 23, 34, 78, 80, 120, 122, 123
Geronima Martinez 20, 26, 52, 90, 101, 104, 105, 120, 127
Hazel Elinor Martinez nee Arzu 1, 8, 20, 41, 94, 95, 105, 114
Hipolito Martinez 18, 34, 41, 52, 58, 73, 81, 89, 93, 110, 118, 120
Hubert Aloyius Martinez 96
Inez Martinez 45
Ireneo Martinez 14, 42, 54, 74, 79, 106, 118
Isidora Martinez 40
Jacqueline Regina Martinez 66, 113
James Martinez 82, 107
James Wilfred Alexander Martinez 54
Jose Martinez 21
Joseph Martinez 33, 41, 70, 73, 121, 122
Juana Martinez 13
Julio Martinez 92
Justina Martinez 56
Keila Sharlene Martinez 30
Leona Martinez 42, 79
Liborio Martinez 3, 9, 16, 17, 40, 45, 46, 50, 83, 104, 112, 121, 122, 127
Llwelyn Martinez 50, 53, 73
Louis Franco Martinez 84
Louis Rosedo Martinez 27
Lucy Martinez 120
Luis Martinez 78
Lywelyn Martinez 17
Macario Martinez 12, 19, 20, 128
Macrina Martinez 3
Marcelina Augustina "Magiri" Garcia nee Martinez 4, 5, 7, 21, 24, 49, 53, 55, 58, 74, 83, 127
Marcos Oliver Martinez 121
Maria Tomasa Martinez 18, 46, 61, 62, 63, 116, 120, 128
Marlet Martinez 118
Martina Norma Arzu nee Martinez 91, 102, 105, 108, 110, 123
Martina "Obispa" Nunez nee Martinez 5, 16, 17, 28, 56, 57, 58, 78, 92, 105, 110
Martin Martinez 2, 5, 16, 58, 66, 81, 89, 100, 110, 111, 113, 118
Melvinia "Grandma Mi" Martinez 12, 16, 22, 24, 35, 50, 56, 64, 68, 72, 77, 85, 92, 93, 95, 100, 102, 105, 107, 110, 116, 120, 126
Michael Alejandro Martinez 1, 93, 105, 114
Michael A. Martinez, Jr. 114

Monica Martinez 43, 50
Myrna Martinez 30
Nadeth Michelle Martinez 7, 100, 105
Nicasia Martinez 47, 50, 78, 122
Nicolasa Nolberto nee Martinez 9, 16, 23, 30, 37, 42, 44, 45, 50, 57, 71, 73, 83, 118, 122, 128
Nolberto Martinez 12
Norma Estefania Martinez 87
Otilia Lucia Martinez 51, 122
Pasqual Martinez 50
Paula Martinez 68, 85, 100, 105
Pedro Martinez 16, 22, 56, 74, 107
Pedro Nicasio Martinez 12, 23, 50, 68, 72, 92, 107, 116
Prudencio "Brown" Martinez 3, 12, 21, 22, 23, 34, 35, 41, 52, 81, 92, 120, 124
Rafael Martinez 82
Raheem Martinez 5
Recillia Martinez 44, 78
Regina Martinez nee Lorenzo 118
Remigio Martinez 98
Rosalia "Baby Rose" Martinez 28, 92, 122
Samuel Hipolito Martinez 18
Santiago Martinez 60, 76, 79, 91, 109
Saturnino "Senerial" Martinez 17, 25, 26, 33, 34, 66, 70, 71, 74, 102, 122, 123
Secundino Joseph Martinez 17, 33, 70, 73, 102, 122
Serapia Martinez 111
Serveriano Martinez 23
Shane Martinez 115
Simon Martinez v, 20, 22, 23, 34, 39, 44, 63, 78, 80, 108, 111, 120, 125, 127
Stephen Martinez 87
Telesfora Martinez 3, 65
Teofila "Wana" Martinez 23, 108
Thomas Joseph Martinez 121
Tiana Ebony Martinez 44
Tomasa Martinez 18, 44, 46, 61, 62, 68, 96, 107, 116, 120, 128
Tomas Martinez 125
Tranquilino Martinez 71
Trinidad Martinez 60
Ursula Martinez 104
Victoria Martinez nee Barcelona 98, 105
Victoriana "Vicky" Nolberto nee Martinez 14, 17, 22, 23, 42, 43, 45, 48, 50, 52, 53, 54, 56, 57, 68, 74, 79, 90, 118, 128
Victoriano Martinez 32, 46, 73, 104, 108, 111, 127

Viola Martinez 3, 21, 23, 34, 41, 93, 120
Virgen M. Martinez 18, 25, 87
Virginia Patricia Martinez 8
Wilfred Martinez 94
Zacaria Rose Martinez 88
Zaira Mierelli Martinez 17, 22, 53, 70, 73
Salomie Maximo 91
Andaiye Colynn McAndrew 37
Neville McAndrew 37
Darlene McDonald 47
Parlet McFadzean 66, 100, 118
George McKensie 25, 38, 55
William D. McKensie 38
Olga McKoy 121
Antonio Medina 60
John Luis Medina 60
Abraham Bernard Mejia 3, 23, 32, 37, 50, 79, 85
Alexandra Mejia 46
Ambrosine Mejia 20, 22, 23, 39, 44, 63, 78, 80, 108, 111, 120
Apolinaria Mejia 24, 30, 37, 75, 111, 123
Cirilo Mejia 3, 32
Concepcion Mejia 90, 102, 115, 118
Eluteria Mejia 23, 30
Florencia Mejia 2
Gloria Mejia 1
Hilaria Palacio nee Mejia 7, 33, 40, 47, 53, 55, 8, 80, 81, 82, 88, 112
Ignacio Mejia 77
Isabela Mejia 5, 44, 85, 89, 118
Leon Mejia 23
Luciano Mejia 2
Marcelina Mejia 127
Nicolas Mejia 102
Pantaleona Mejia 2, 20, 41, 55, 70, 76, 77, 94, 105
Rachel Mejia 52
Santiaga Mejia 68, 118
Simeona Palacio nee Mejia 3, 8, 27, 29, 31, 34, 44, 52, 56, 76, 78, 79, 80, 83, 85, 88, 99, 123, 124, 125
Simon Mejia 5, 7, 17, 23, 27, 30, 44, 46, 55, 58, 63, 70, 75, 76, 77, 80, 82, 102, 108, 111
Sofia Mejia 98
Telesflora "Stella" Simeona Mejia 3, 29, 34, 56, 79, 85
Victoria Mejia 30
Zoila Mejia 7
Dativa Elizabeth Martinez nee Melendrez 17, 53, 73, 81, 106, 119
Evaristo Melendrez 73, 74, 81, 106, 119
Felix Melendrez 96

Gregoria Mena 39, 72, 128
Andrea Middleton 101
Denzel Miller 29, 47, 107, 122
Joycelyn Miller 8, 27, 29, 33, 107, 109, 115
Rosita Miller 29, 47, 122
Adranie Miranda 37
Emily Miranda 26
Liraine Miranda 79
Lorn Miranda 87
Miraine Miranda 79
Phyllis Miranda 23, 74, 81, 88, 96
Thomas Miranda 22, 26, 37, 79, 87
Ziolyne Miranda 22
Jose Maria Montero 63
Maria Los Angeles Montero (Juana Nunez) 63
Maria Nicolasa Moralez 13, 19, 36, 40, 71, 95, 103, 121
Erick Dionisio "Moon" Moreira 63, 64, 107
Marcelino Moreira 122
Myra Moreira 4, 72
Santos Moreira 4
Christina Moreria 50, 122
Rosita Moreria 122
Govel Morgan 8, 13, 14, 32, 108
Modesto Morgan 108
Paul Morgan 8
Henry Moriera 14
Sotera Moriera 14, 83, 111

N

Ignacio Nichoas 64
Adriano Nicholas 28, 71, 77
Alberta Nicholas 12, 35, 62, 78, 106
Alexandra Nicholas 50
Alice Casimiro nee Nicholas 6, 16, 45, 48, 63, 66, 77, 79, 87, 110, 111
Andrea Nicholas 7, 30, 46, 55, 58, 82, 102, 111
Andres Nicholas 70, 73, 95
Angelina "Angie" Nicholas nee Alvarez 2, 55, 64, 65, 76, 105, 125
Aniceto Nicholas 44
Arcilia Nicholas 81
Arnold Nicholas 46
Avelina Nicholas 7, 10
Balbina Nicholas 37
Benjamin Nicholas 44, 79
Casimira Nicholas 2, 4, 16, 22, 28, 42, 55, 56, 83, 92, 106, 108
Casimiro Nicholas 65, 74
Christine Nicholas 119
Cipriano Nicholas 70, 73, 95, 104
Cornelio Nicholas 90
Crescencio Nicholas 1
Cynthia Nicholas 78

Index

David William Nicholas 41, 46, 67, 119

Dorotea Nicholas 79

Egbert Nicholas 37

Erlinda "Delane" Ogaldez nee Nicholas 13, 23, 27, 34, 44, 49, 57, 74, 78, 85, 96, 110, 111, 127

Eugenia "Henny Girl" Nicholas 31

Eulogia Nicholas 30, 42, 79, 87, 114, 121

Fermina Nicholas 51, 100

Frederick Mervin Nicholas 114

Frederick Nicholas 9, 30, 34, 37, 46, 50, 51, 64, 74, 78, 79, 80, 81, 84, 88, 98, 110, 114

Gabriel Nicholas 33

Gilbert Nicholas 18

Ignacio Nicholas 21, 33, 41, 43, 67, 77, 79, 108, 110, 119, 125

Inocenta Nicholas 34, 49, 65, 67, 106, 127

John Nicholas 18, 62

Joseph Alexander Nicholas 2, 10, 28, 50, 60, 65, 66, 79, 111, 118, 119

Justin Nicholas 79

Justina Nicholas nee Ramirez 4, 53, 67, 83, 88

Leonarda Nicholas 112

Leoncio Nicholas 12, 33, 43, 44, 49, 51, 55, 60, 62, 77, 102, 111, 112, 118

Louis Nicholas 84

Lucius Nicholas 10

Martin Victor "Game and Gone" or "Tin-Tin" Nicholas 12, 18, 49, 62, 77, 79, 89, 95, 110, 125

Maximo "Maxie" Nicholas 41, 771

Merejildo Nicholas 43

Orson Lucious Nicholas 7, 115

Pablo Nicholas 1, 28, 45, 47, 51, 62, 77, 84, 85, 90, 100, 111

Paul Nicholas 47, 90, 99

Philip Nicholas 12, 13, 18, 30, 47, 49, 62, 89, 90, 95, 99, 109, 114

Prudencia Nicholas 47

Seferino Nicholas 85

Severiano Nicholas 109

Shirley Nicholas 21

Sonya Nicholas 36

Sotera Nicholas 46, 48, 60, 85, 88, 118

Sotero Nicholas 41, 43, 46, 49, 60, 65, 73, 80, 88, 95, 110, 111, 127

Stanley Nicholas 67

Teodora Nicholas 9, 30, 110, 127

Tiburcio Nicholas 37, 41, 64, 74, 79, 80, 98

Victor Joseph "Master Vic" Nicholas 2, 12, 44, 64, 68, 79, 118, 125

Victor Leonard Nicholas 12, 18, 30, 36, 77, 79, 89, 95, 110, 125

William "Country" Nicholas 104

Alberta Nolberto 33, 43, 51, 77, 118

Anacleta "Da" or "Da Cleta" Nolberto 11, 18, 28, 30, 16, 36, 46, 49, 73, 87, 105, 123

Bernadina Casimiro nee Nolberto 5, 18, 20, 43, 46, 49, 62, 67, 73, 85, 92, 98, 104, 108, 114, 115

Bruno Nolberto 99

Christina Nolberto 9, 12, 17, 18, 24, 43, 45, 76

Dionisio Nolberto 9, 16, 23, 30, 37, 42, 45, 51, 55, 57, 71, 73, 83, 122, 128

Elodia "Loya" Nolberto nee Palacio 64, 71

Fabiana Nolberto 9, 30

Felipa Nolberto 57

Francisco Nolberto 8, 12, 20, 22, 29, 36, 43, 46, 55, 56, 65, 68, 72, 76, 84, 92, 93, 104, 108, 116, 117, 119, 126

Gregoria Nolberto 2, 3, 33, 35, 37, 43, 56, 60, 66, 84, 92, 99, 100, 106, 117, 122, 127

Gregorio Nolberto 46

Hilario Nolberto 43, 45, 52, 57, 128

Hilma "Nana" Nolberto 45, 57

Inocenta Nolberto 126

Ireneo Nolberto 126

Isabel "Beans" Nolberto 56

Isabel Nolberto 71

Juana "Gubida" Nolberto 2, 12, 14, 16, 51, 53, 56, 71, 74, 78, 117, 120, 124, 128

Lorenzo "Thunder" Nolberto 4, 29, 65

Luciana Nolberto 4, 11, 22, 31, 47, 55, 101, 106, 109, 127

Macario Nolberto 4, 21, 29, 46, 65, 78, 99, 104, 126

Maria Nolberto 79, 87, 114

Nicolasa Nolberto nee Martinez 50

Paula Nolberto 2, 9, 21, 22, 23, 29, 44, 46, 50, 51, 56, 57, 65, 68, 71, 84, 100, 104, 106, 116, 119, 124, 127

Pio Nolberto 2, 4, 16, 20, 22, 28, 42, 55, 56, 65, 74, 83, 92, 106, 108

Roberta Nolberto 36

Romana Nolberto 65, 78

Valentino Santos Nolberto 21

Venancia Nolberto 12, 68, 105, 116, 119

Victoriana "Vicky" Nolberto nee Martinez 14, 17, 22, 23, 42, 43, 45, 48, 50, 52, 53, 54, 56, 57, 68, 74, 79, 90, 118, 128

Ambrosio Noralez 68, 121

Antonia Noralez 9, 52

Atanacio Noralez 49, 90

Bruno Noralez 114

Dionisio Noralez 16

Dominica Arzu nee Noralez 7, 32, 62, 76, 78

Emeteria Noralez 27

Eugenia "Jean" Zuniga nee Noralez 3, 9, 11, 27, 37, 41, 44, 45, 52, 60, 61, 68, 72, 75, 81, 87, 91, 108, 115, 121

Feliciano Noralez 62

Felix "Aska" Noralez 2, 8, 12, 14, 16, 53, 56, 57, 66, 74, 76, 78, 98, 117, 120, 124, 128

Florencio Noralez 39, 72, 127

Gregoria Noralez 57, 120, 128

John Noralez 2, 53

Leonarda "Leoni" Noralez 98, 117

Martina Noralez 14

Martin Benjamin Noralez 9, 11, 27, 39, 49, 70, 88, 90

Melvinia Noralez 47, 90

Paula Casimiro nee Noralez 1, 11, 13, 14, 18, 30, 32, 33, 35, 43, 44, 52, 56, 58, 60, 62, 63, 65, 73, 88, 96, 98, 100, 107, 108, 114, 115, 128

Sebastian Noralez 72

Secundino Noralez 70

Soledad Noralez 124

Teresa "Tandu" Noralez 2, 12, 14, 16, 41, 56, 57, 74, 78, 98, 117, 120, 124, 128

Timoteo Noralez 12

Tomasa Noralez 18, 62

Tomas Noralez 41, 74

Venancio "Ben" Noralez 27, 32, 39, 52, 62, 68, 70, 72, 76, 78, 121, 127

Alexine Nunez nee Loredo 51

Alfonso Nunez 16

Andrea Nunez 48

Augustina Nunez 12, 23, 50, 68, 72, 92, 107, 116, 120

Barbarin Nunez 55

Benita Ariola nee Nunez 1, 4, 9, 17, 20, 24, 29, 34, 52, 60, 85, 87, 101, 114, 115, 116, 117, 121

Bonifacio Nunez 83

Carmelo Nunez 3, 4, 34, 114

Casimiro Nunez 28

Catarina Nunez 64, 65, 95, 98

Clarence Nunez 33

Claudina Nunez 51

Claudio Nunez 51
Clemencia Nunez 55, 58, 101, 118
Cleofa Nunez 6
Clotilda Nunez 17, 51, 60, 88
Curt Nunez 33
Elorine Nunez 5, 14, 33, 47, 58, 105, 110, 127
Eretia Nunez 95
Evangelista Nunez 4, 12, 53, 83, 88, 103, 107
Evaristo "Bob Steele" Nunez 5, 14, 16, 28, 33, 47, 51, 56, 57, 58, 73, 105, 110, 127
Felicita Nunez 41, 74
Felix Nunez 16
Florencio Nunez 53
Francisca Nunez 12, 95, 101
Francisco Nunez 5, 16, 17, 28, 56, 57, 58, 78, 92, 105, 127
Francis "Chico" or "Cronic" Nunez 14
Gregoria "Gogo" Nunez nee Paulino 61
Ignacio Nunez 16
Irene Nunez 84
Isabel Nunez 6, 35, 97, 128
Isidora Nunez 11
Jameel Nunez 117
Jose Maria Nunez 3, 62
Juana Nunez 63
Judith Nunez 112
Juslin Nunez 109, 115
Karen Nunez 91
Leonarda Nunez 4, 45, 102, 109, 111, 117, 120, 122, 124, 126
Leonard Nunez 58, 73, 91, 98
Lucia Nunez 28
Luisa Nunez 22, 56
Luis Nunez 18, 62
Mackie Nunez 27, 33, 109, 115
Margarita Nunez 82
Martha Nunez 40
Martina "Obispa" Nunez nee Martinez 5, 16, 17, 28, 56, 57, 58, 78, 92, 105, 110
Martin Nunez 107
Narcisa Nunez 64
Neil Nunez 117
Nelson Leonard Nunez 98
"Nimla" Nunez 34
Paula Nunez 41, 43, 46, 49, 60, 65, 73, 80, 95, 110, 111, 127
Pedro Nunez 47
Presentacion Nunez 17, 51, 57, 86
Ron Nunez 27
Sebastian Nunez 17, 41, 95
Sharon Loredo nee Nunez 28, 43, 72, 73, 80, 92, 93, 114
Teresa Nunez 28

Thomas Nunez 28, 47, 60, 92, 109, 118
Tomas Nunez 47
Virginia Nunez 78, 92
Viviana Nunez 118

O
Agapito Ogaldez 66
Anthony Alexander "Tony" Ogaldez 34, 49, 66, 96, 112
Apolinaria Ogaldez 8, 66, 76, 128
Archangela Ogaldez 32
Arlene Ogaldez 96
Cyril Ogaldez 49
Erlinda "Delane" Ogaldez nee Nicholas 13, 23, 27, 34, 44, 49, 57, 74, 78, 85, 96, 110, 111, 127
John Ogaldez 66
Joseph Lucy Ogaldez 122
Secundino Ogaldez 44, 68, 76, 87, 122
Victoria Ogaldez 44, 53, 55, 58, 68, 83, 85, 87, 93, 94, 96, 98
Lucia Ordonez 4, 5, 18, 61, 63, 88, 104, 113, 122, 126
Francisca Sacasa (Ortiz) 17, 30, 37, 43, 46, 52, 65, 71, 95
Tomasa Ortiz 28, 47, 60, 118

P
Agapito Palacio 49
Agnes Felicita Palacio 6, 45, 87
Alejandro Palacio 20, 23, 42, 46, 103
Alexander Palacio 36
Allen Palacio 85, 87
Allison Steven Palacio 94
Aloysius Alan Palacio 88, 112
Anastacio "Baibai" Palacio 6, 10, 11, 16, 23, 31, 36, 39, 44, 49, 55, 58, 60, 61, 62, 63, 71, 74, 76, 79, 82, 94, 96, 99, 102, 108, 116, 117, 118, 120, 124
Andy Vivien Palacio 6, 10, 31, 32, 43, 50, 65, 70, 79, 95, 115, 117, 118, 125, 126
Angela Palacio 7, 55, 56, 60, 80, 92, 102, 103, 125
Aniceta Palacio 4
Aniki Patrick Palacio 25
Antonia Palacio 1, 2, 4, 5, 22, 39, 98
Antonio Palacio 17, 65, 95
Arcadio Palacio 6
Arreini Paula Palacio 19, 80
Augustine "Baba Titi" Palacio 8, 27, 29, 31, 44, 52, 76, 78, 79, 80, 83, 85, 88, 99, 123, 125
Augustus Palacio 88, 90, 121
Basilia Palacio 65
Basilio Palacio 68

Beatrice Palacio 19, 47, 71, 72, 77, 78, 120
Benito Palacio 84
Bernabe Apostol Palacio 30, 63
Candida Palacio 37, 41, 64, 74, 79, 80, 98
Carciana Palacio 40, 55, 68, 91, 100
Carlos Palacio 22, 93, 107
Catarino T. Palacio 17, 23, 29, 30, 31, 37, 42, 43, 46, 52, 65, 71, 95
Damasio Joseph Palacio 121
Demetrio Palacio 74, 124
Dionisio Palacio 64, 65, 95, 98
Elida Palacio 16, 42, 109
Elodia "Loya" Nolberto nee Palacio 64, 71
Emeri Palacio 6
Esteban Palacio 42, 57, 87
Eulogia "Nitu Mamie" Palacio 13, 30, 63
Eustaquia "Bilacu" Palacio 2, 15, 53, 64, 70, 83, 88, 107, 117, 121
Fabiana Palacio 18, 30, 47, 49, 62, 89, 90, 95, 99, 109, 114
Felicita Palacio nee Reyes 14, 72, 78, 120
Francisca Palacio 13, 33, 93
Francisco Palacio 13, 21, 31, 37, 39, 50, 53, 58, 61, 63, 65, 66, 68, 70, 75, 88, 90, 91, 95, 117, 124
Froylan Palacio 82, 99, 123
Gabian Sebastian Palacio 10
Georgiana Palacio 5, 39, 44, 60, 78, 88, 125
Gieri Palacio 90
Gladys Palacio 70, 94
Gregoria "Ponana" or "Go da Night" Palacio 2, 3, 10, 14, 25, 28, 41, 49, 58, 73, 78, 80, 89, 102, 103, 126
Gregorio Palacio 115
Gumercinda Palacio 6, 32, 60, 62, 76, 78, 128
Hilaria Palacio nee Mejia 7, 33, 40, 47, 53, 55, 8, 80, 81, 82, 88, 112
Hipolito "Puludu" Palacio 3, 6, 31, 40, 43, 50, 56, 71, 103, 115
Ignacia Palacio nee Arana 7, 13, 16, 18, 20, 30, 33, 40, 42, 46, 54, 55, 57, 58, 68, 80, 81, 85
Iris Palacio 27
Isabel Palacio 71
Jacinta Palacio 3, 4, 6, 17, 29, 39, 46, 55, 67, 70, 77, 88, 91, 94, 104, 118
Jacob Palacio 50, 65, 84, 95, 111, 126
Jermaine "Lily" Palacio 124, 125
Joan Palacio 22
John Baptist Palacio 82
John de Malha Palacio 7, 18

John Palacio 30, 43, 47
Joseph Orlando Palacio 19, 25, 53, 80, 88
Joseph Palacio 22, 64, 121
Joseph Pollard Palacio 7, 33, 40, 47, 53, 57, 58, 64, 80, 81, 82, 88, 107, 112
Juana "Jane" Palacio 24, 29, 31, 34, 39, 41, 60, 70, 73, 89, 91, 96, 106, 108, 114
Juana Palacio 16, 39, 76, 79, 101, 127,
Julia Palacio 19, 21
Kalin Palacio 77
Leon Palacio 121
Leroy Leo Palacio 34, 62
Liberato Palacio 6, 11, 18, 60, 74, 101, 124
Louis Palacio 44, 78, 80, 82, 83
Ludwig Palacio 27, 62, 65, 76, 80, 85, 88, 90, 121
Luis Palacio 49, 74, 82, 107
Magdalena Palacio 101
Margarita Palacio 70
Maria Ascencion Palacio 52
Martha Palacio 29, 31, 37, 65
Martina Cornelia "Mamita" Alvarez nee Palacio 2, 19, 27, 68, 80, 106, 115, 124
Martires Coronado Palacio 55, 118
Mercedes Paulino nee Palacio 23, 62, 91, 99, 100
Natividad Palacio 43, 113, 126
Nicanora Palacio nee Garcia 58
Nicodemus Palacio 49
Nicolasa Palacio 5, 31, 41, 44, 55, 63, 70, 76, 77
Nolberto Palacio 7, 13, 16, 18, 20, 30, 33, 40, 42, 46, 54, 55, 57, 58, 62, 64, 68, 75, 79, 80, 81, 85, 92, 100, 106, 115, 121
Olivia Prudencia "Aunti Olive" Avila nee Palacio 13, 30, 41, 47, 88, 93, 105, 107, 121, 127
Pamela Palacio 62
Patrocinia Palacio 3, 7, 19, 38, 54, 98, 99, 128
Paulina "Mayo" Palacio 51
Pauline Palacio 20, 27, 30, 127
Paul Palacio 2, 18, 27, 34, 40, 41, 55, 62, 68, 70, 75, 80, 115, 118, 121, 124
Pedro Palacio 103
Peter Palacio 11, 36, 39, 75
Petrona "Peti"Joseph nee Palacio 2, 8, 10, 34, 46, 52, 55, 85, 93, 99, 104, 126
Philip "Percy" Palacio 49
Phyllis Palacio 23, 65, 84, 90, 94, 109
Prajedes Palacio 75, 100, 106

Randal James Palacio 75
Rasheed Hassan Palacio 106
Robert Palacio 52
Ruben Palacio 1, 3, 6, 9, 22, 31, 40, 46, 50, 56, 71, 84, 87, 91, 95, 103, 111, 115, 118, 124
Runulfo "Roman" Nelson Palacio 42, 57, 87
Ruth Palacio 20
Sarah Palacio 46
Saturnina Palacio 65, 108, 124
Saturnino Palacio 14, 72, 78, 120
Sean Palacio 124
Simeona Palacio nee Mejia 3, 8, 27, 29, 31, 34, 44, 52, 56, 76, 78, 79, 80, 83, 85, 88, 99, 123, 124, 125
Stephen Palacio 35, 47
Susanne Palacio 56
Tecla Palacio 95
Telesforo Palacio 3
Teodoro "Joe Young" Palacio 17, 3, 27, 36, 40, 42, 46, 61, 62, 94, 124
Teofila Palacio 82, 107
Theodore Palacio 6, 21, 35, 40, 47, 53, 58, 60, 63, 68, 82, 85, 88, 112, 116, 124, 125
Timothy Palacio 6, 16, 77
Tolentina Palacio 28, 91
Valentina Palacio 20, 34
Vicenta Palacio 12, 41
Vicente Rebide Palacio 40
Virgen Palacio 103
Viviana Palacio 6, 21, 32, 39, 49, 52, 55, 56, 67, 76, 77, 78, 81, 88, 96, 100, 101, 114
Zena Palacio 47
Maria Luisa Palma 101
Benita Pascual 55
Ascenciona "Da Sola" Paulino 6, 10, 13, 32, 36, 51, 83, 90, 92, 106, 107, 111, 112, 114, 115
Augustin "Big Ease" Paulino 13, 14, 20, 26, 31, 33, 35, 37, 42, 43, 47, 51, 52, 56, 58, 59, 67, 70, 71, 75, 76, 81, 83, 85, 87, 94, 96, 105, 110, 112, 121, 122, 123, 124, 125
Basilia Paulino 112
Bonifacia Paulino 4
Braulio Paulino 35
Brigida Marin nee Paulino 13, 16, 46, 47, 53, 56, 57, 58, 70, 91, 93, 100, 103, 107, 117, 125
Catalina Paulino 48
Catarina Paulino 4, 8, 105, 112
Celestino Paulino 62, 91, 99, 100
Damiana Paulino 24
Delfina Paulino 125

Diego Paulino 10, 15, 19, 20, 37, 50, 51, 58, 61, 62, 67, 81, 85, 91, 94, 106, 125
Dolores Paulino 93
Elena Paulino 83
Elfreda Sideroff nee Paulino 79
Eugenio Paulino 10, 17, 18, 38, 48, 51, 57, 61, 86, 93, 112, 117
Eusebio "Macoshin" Paulino 12, 13, 19, 24, 27, 35, 52, 73, 79, 87, 114, 122
Eustaquio Paulino 94
Filomena Paulino 28, 44, 49, 94, 115
Francisca Paulino 52
Francisco Arsido Paulino 61
Francisco Sales Paulino 13
Genaro Paulino 117
Gregoria "Gogo" Nunez nee Paulino 17, 20, 51, 57, 61, 63, 86, 93, 107, 115, 125
Guadalupe Paulino 79, 121
John Paulino 14, 31, 76, 110
Josefa Paulino 25, 33, 34, 35, 66, 70, 71, 74, 76, 85, 97, 102, 123
Juana Paulino nee Luis 26
Julian Paulino 5, 31, 41, 44
Leandra Paulino 5, 31
Manuel Carmen Paulino 15
Marciana Paulino 27
Maria Magdalena Paulino 75
Matea Paulino 43, 96, 105, 121
Mercedes Paulino nee Palacio 23, 62, 91, 99, 100
Obispa Florentina Paulino 33, 56, 59, 67, 107, 124
Obispo Paulino 41
Octaviano Paulino 73
Pablo Paulino 13
Pascual Paulino 107
Pastora Paulino 38
Paula Paulino 6, 12, 24, 49, 50, 66, 92, 103, 112
Peter Canuto Paulino 10
Petrona Paulino 33, 56, 85, 91
Policarpio Paulino 10
Prudencia Paulino 47
Saturnino Paulino 19
Stephen Paulino 30, 42, 79, 87, 114, 121
Thomas Paulino 25
Victor Paulino 26, 30, 37, 42, 60, 87, 114, 122, 124
Viviano Paulino 117
Anastacia Petillo 53
Aniceta Petillo 124
Berta Petillo 42, 124
Bonifacio Petillo 1, 9, 21, 27, 32, 49, 65, 67, 73, 74, 84, 109, 112
Cornelia Petillo 87, 91, 93, 105

Cosme Petillo 61, 71, 93, 95, 109
Epifania Petillo 1
Faustino Petillo 21
Francisco Petillo 61
Gertrude Petillo 112
Joseph Margarito Petillo 67, 74
Juan Petillo 73, 95, 109
Julia Petillo 32, 49, 114
Leonard "Mr. Pete" Petillo 1, 21, 27, 46, 61, 63, 67, 73, 74, 84, 107, 108, 109
Macrina Petillo 65
Martin Petillo 63, 81, 107
O'Dillan Petillo 1, 84
Pedro Petillo 9
Shay Petillo 107
Sheridan Arzu nee Petillo 6, 9, 10, 20, 24, 25, 27, 37, 42, 46, 54, 65, 67, 80, 94, 108, 109, 127
Veronica Petillo 71
Guillemo Plummer 37
Apolonio Polonio 3, 5, 61, 86, 104, 119, 126
Bartolo Polonio 4, 10, 14, 18, 24, 32, 33, 61, 63, 72, 74, 84, 85, 88, 99, 104, 111, 113, 117, 122
Benedictina Polonio 33, 70, 91
Bobby Polonio 4
Cecilio "Dick" Polonio 10, 14, 18, 24, 32, 74, 84, 98, 113, 126
Epifania Polonio 3
Eusebio Polonio 4, 5, 18, 24, 61, 63, 88, 104, 113, 122, 126
John Polonio 63, 88
Justa Polonio 7, 23, 28, 29, 39, 47, 49, 55, 58, 76, 77, 84, 90, 112, 119
Justo Polonio 56, 119
Leonarda Polonio 10
Martin Polonio 14, 32
Pantaleon Odway Polonio 4, 33, 56, 85, 91, 111, 126
Ramona Polonio 86
Seferino Polonio 85
Timoteo Polonio 10
Tomasa Polonio 50, 65, 84, 95, 111, 126
Ursula Polonio 5, 6, 18, 32, 36, 49, 54, 58, 63, 78, 86, 98, 99, 104, 119, 121, 126
Ursulus Polonio 104

Q

Quiteria 124

R

Alejandro Ramirez 46
Anastacia Christina Castillo nee Ramirez 50, 113, 126
Anastacia Christina Ramirez 43, 53, 81, 105, 123

Angela Ramirez 27
Angel Ramirez 27
Bonifacia Ramirez 19, 29, 39, 55, 75, 84, 115
Bonifacio Ramirez 4, 12, 18, 53, 83, 84, 88, 103, 107
Carla Ramirez 99
Carlos Ramirez 2, 99
Carmen Ramirez 2, 13, 15, 53, 64, 70, 83, 88, 107, 117, 121, 123
Cecilia Ramirez 16
Cecilio "Nudi" Ramirez 43, 126
Cecilio Ramirez 24, 61, 88, 113
Celestino Ramirez 54
Christino Ramirez 113
Daniel Ramirez 2
Dorotea "Sista" Ramirez 13, 18, 22
Eduviges "Auntie Bia" Ramirez 2, 4, 12, 63, 84 103, 114, 121
Emily Ramirez nee Martinez 34, 49, 73, 74, 93, 108
Emily Williams Ramirez 67, 75
Eufemia "Tecki" Ramirez 88
Fulgencio Ramirez 117
Jesbert Ramirez 84
Joseph Ramirez 64, 121
Justina Nicholas nee Ramirez 4, 53, 67, 83, 88
Loreto Ramirez 4
Loriana Ramirez 9, 20, 70, 78, 122, 123
Luciano Ramirez 4
Marcos Ramirez 89
Martha Ramirez 12
Mauricio Linford "Linsy" Ramirez 24, 61, 67, 88, 113
Olga "Lettie" Ramirez 64, 111
Pasquala Ramirez 8, 12, 13, 19, 24, 51, 53, 64, 121, 123
Paula Ramirez 12
Pedro Ramirez 13, 16, 27
Peter Ramirez 24, 84, 113
Ricardo Ramirez 107
Sebastian Ramirez 4, 12, 46, 54, 63, 89
Valentino Ramirez 64
Victor Ramirez 111, 113
Amanda Ramos nee Zuniga 25, 33, 36, 96
Frances Ramos 81
Jarreen J. Ramos 62, 90, 109, 111
Leroy Ramos 44
"Pants" Ramos 33
Wasany Wellington Ramos 78, 95
Wellington Ramos 62, 78
Alfredo Rash 4, 32, 40, 98, 126
Emelda Rash 32
Francisco Rash 98
Juan Rash 126

Maria Rash nee Makin 4, 32, 40, 98
Ricardo Rash 40
Derona Requena 9, 11
Esme Requena 9
Anastacio Reyes 8, 43, 112
Aniceto Reyes 34
Estanislao Reyes 67, 102
Evangelisto "16" Reyes 34
Felicita Palacio nee Reyes 14, 72, 78, 120
Martin Reyes 2, 25, 36, 37, 38, 43, 55, 67, 72, 82, 99, 102, 112
Paulina Reyes 25, 38, 55, 58, 77, 111
Santita Reyes 2
Santos Reyes 36
Helen Reynolds 51, 110
Charlotte Rhaburn 117
Cecilia Rhys 12, 73, 124
Cayetana Rivas 128
Margarita Rivas 3, 32
Crescencio Roches 33, 56
Elijio Roches 67, 94
Luisa Roches 2, 25, 36, 37, 43, 67, 72, 102, 112
Maria Roches 92
Mauricio Roches 94
Pablo Roches 67
Yuancio Roches 37
Luisa Rochez 113
Benjamin Rodriguez 37, 111
Cardinal George Rodriguez 28, 61
Clinton Rodriguez 51, 53, 77, 115, 122
Dwayne Michael Rodriguez 51
Dwayne Rodriguez 122
Estanislada Rodriguez 37, 45, 85, 111
John Rodriguez 36
Loma Rodriguez nee Sanchez 33, 36
Lynette Valerie Rodriguez nee Valerio 31, 46, 51, 53, 77, 115, 122
Mariana Rodriguez 48, 77
Quinton Paul Rodriguez 115, 122
Leopoldo Rogers 77
Nicholas Rogers 64
Rosanna Martinez Rogers 35, 77
Roy Rogers 12, 64
Ermeterio Romero 19, 92
Rosa Angela 13, 111
Estela Rubio 42, 87

S

Hayworth Sabala 29
Francisca Sacasa (Ortiz) 17, 29, 37, 43, 46, 52, 65, 71, 95
Simeon Sampson 54
Sylvia Sampson 46, 54
Beatrice Cayetano nee Sanchez 36, 42, 58, 96, 113, 123
Bonlea Martina Sanchez 22. 94

Cecilia Sanchez 39, 51
Custodio Sanchez 98
Eluteria Sanchez 94
Francisco Xavier Sanchez 2, 119
Ishmael Sanchez 121
Jane "Kim" Sanchez 42
John Sanchez 39, 40, 77, 98
Leonides Sanchez 79
Loma Rodriguez nee Sanchez 33, 36
Roberto Sanchez 35
Sebastian Sanchez 2, 6, 17, 25, 35, 44, 119
Seferino Sanchez 40
Vicenta Luisa "Lulu" Sanchez 6, 20, 25, 28, 40, 42, 55, 59, 63, 75, 83, 91, 100, 101, 118, 121, 128
Amenigi Sandoval 117
Dercy Sandoval 9, 14, 28, 91, 101, 117, 120
Inebessi Sandoval 14
Xavier "Harvey" Sandoval 7, 39, 114
Anastacia Vicenta Santiago 17, 33, 70, 73, 102, 122
Andrea Avelina Santiago 9, 11
Raymond Santiago 73, 102
Agatha Santino 30
Augustin Santino 20, 27, 30, 51, 127
Bernardina Santino 13, 14, 17, 33, 42, 54, 56, 74, 79, 80, 90, 106, 118
Catalina Santino 20
Dionisia Marin nee Santino 20
Dionisia Santino 35, 47, 63, 70, 71, 76, 100, 112, 117, 120
Escolastica "Ka" Martinez nee Santino 111
Escolastica "Ka" Santino 128
Escolastica Santino 12, 19, 20
Eusebio Santino 4, 5, 20, 28, 30, 47, 70, 82, 100, 102, 111, 112, 122, 123
Francisca Santino 30
Frank G. Santino 78, 127
Henry Santino 78, 92
Jacinta Santino 82, 99, 123
Jacinta Trigueno nee Santino 4, 12, 19, 20, 28, 30, 35, 39, 50, 54, 69, 78, 82, 95, 99, 100, 102, 118, 120, 122, 123
Julius Santino 47
Lazaro Santino 122
Luisa Santino 20
Monico Santino 50, 122
Nicasio Santino 100
Petrona Santino 121
Philip "Kamuru Kamuru" Santino 5, 12, 19, 27, 28, 37, 39, 47, 50, 51, 54, 62, 74, 78, 80, 95, 111, 122
Polonia Santino 55, 98
Thomas Santino 62, 111

Tomas Santino 39
Victoriana Santino 3, 23, 32, 37, 50, 79, 85, 111
William Santino 47
Clemente Satuye 6, 17, 94, 116, 127
Estanislao Satuye 116
Eustaquia Satuye 1, 24, 27, 34, 37, 44, 54, 58, 65, 71, 76, 94, 108, 111, 122, 123, 127
Jacob Satuye 6
James Satuye 6
Harriet Scarborough nee Arzu 54
Andres Sebastian 11, 16, 18, 74
Secundino Maximo 45
Paula Serano 16, 103, 107
Francisca Serapia 8, 9, 12, 20, 22, 29, 36, 46, 55, 56, 65, 76, 108
Ambrosia Servio 128
Marcelina Pamfila Servio 73, 102
Petrona Severia 27, 76, 80
Elfreda Sideroff nee Paulino 79
Stephen Sideroff 79
Maria Juana Socorro 2
Suzette Staine 80, 102
Errol Suazo 36
Marsha Margaret Suazo 36, 93

T
Caroline Tasher 82
Casimiro Teo 3
Juan Bautista Teo 22, 23, 94
Lucas Teo 100
Simeona Teo 1, 2, 3, 4, 22, 23, 28, 88, 94, 100
Maria Teresa 41
Byron Leo Thomas 35
Damien Tingling 29
Edward Tingling 29, 47, 122
Fred Trigueno 82, 123
Isidro Trigueno 68, 85, 100, 105
Jacinta Trigueno nee Santino 4, 12, 19, 20, 28, 30, 35, 39, 50, 54, 69, 78, 82, 95, 99, 100, 102, 118, 120, 122
Marco Trigueno 105
Rosita Trigueno 85
Simeon Trigueno 100
Carla Tucker 67
Elroy Tucker 39
Carlson John Tuttle xi, 62, 68, 78
Farice Tuttle 68, 78
Valerie Delcy Tuttle nee Valencio 62, 68, 78 , 106

U
Charlotte Underwood 92
Godfrey Underwood 80
Kareem Davon Underwood 54, 80

V
Luis Valencia 25

Sebastiana Valencia 25
Britney Valencio 91
Daisy Mae Valencio 107
Egbert Anthony Valencio 8, 9, 11, 31, 32, 37, 55, 72, 91, 102, 106, 107, 114
Eufamio Valencio 19, 47, 71, 72, 77, 120
Felicita Valencio 28, 71, 77
Guillermo Valencio 19
Haneefa Kerian Valencio 82
Lauruni Lucille Valencio 9, 11
Leolin Elma Valencio 34, 37, 42, 56, 112
Liselle Celine Valencio 34
Lucille Luciana "Chilagu" Valencio nee Zuniga 4, 7, 8, 16, 18, 21, 22, 26, 28, 29, 31, 37, 42, 44, 55, 56, 62, 65, 68, 71, 72, 87, 92, 99, 106, 113, 115, 120, 126, 127
Lumar Valencio 4, 126
Marciana Valencio 83
Raymond Valencio 2, 8, 10, 14, 19, 25, 28, 36, 42, 43, 56, 62, 68, 71, 72, 77, 78, 106, 107, 112, 120, 123
Raynor Verne Valencio 112
Rudolph "Rudy" Valencio 68
Valerie Delcy Tuttle nee Valencio 62, 68, 78 , 106
Martin Valentine 73
Pantaleona Valentine 73, 108
Ainsworth Philip Valerio 100
Althea Marie Valerio 79
Ian Dane Valerio 3, 82
Lynette Valerie Rodriguez nee Valerio 31, 46, 51, 53, 77, 115, 122
Peter Philip Valerio Junior 101
Peter Valerio 3, 46, 77, 79, 82, 100, 101, 122
Santiago Valerio 46, 82
Nicasio Vargas 40, 60
Nicasio "Yao Daguwasi" Vargas 34
Victoriana Vargas 34
Domingo Velasquez 78
Elsie Velasquez 61
Elvira Cris Velasquez 8, 77, 79, 99
Faustino Velasquez 8, 23, 31
Gabriel Velasquez 23
Isaac Velasquez 79
Joseph Velasquez 8, 90, 122
Romana Velasquez 78, 127
Solomon Velasquez 31, 54, 63, 77, 79, 89, 102
Faustina Villafranco 44, 59
Gertrude Villafranco 28
Jane Victoriana Villafranco 12, 43, 58, 61, 72, 88, 89, 110, 120
Juan Villafranco 13
Luis Majin Villafranco 13, 37, 44, 58, 72, 89

Pastora Villafranco 37, 58, 119
Victoriana Villafranco 12, 47, 58, 61, 72, 88, 89, 110, 120

W

Andrew Williams 38, 40
Claudio Alonzo Williams 34, 50, 88
Dionisio Williams 12, 23, 73
Eleuterio "Linford" Williams 23
Jason Paul Williams 124
Kenisha "Kenny" Williams 73
Loretta Williams 7
Muriel Williams nee Casimiro 18, 62, 96, 114
Paul A.M. Williams 12, 73
Paul Williams 124
Santo Williams 43, 50
Sharron Gelobter nee Williams 29, 34, 43, 88
Walter Alfonso Williams 71
Acilla Withworth 38
Lisa Woodye 25, 62, 105
Marjorie Woodye 62

Y

Joy Young 5, 16

Z

Abeline Shashta Zelaya 55
Ernie Zelaya 55
Abraham Zuniga 9, 20, 70, 78, 122, 123
Alfonsa Zuniga 11, 55, 77, 109, 111
Alvin Zuniga 107, 113
Amanda Ramos nee Zuniga 25, 33, 36, 96
Antolino Zuniga 11
Antonette "Neti" Zuniga 22, 70, 112, 121
Antonia Zuniga 13, 37, 44, 58, 72, 89, 95
Ascencion Zuniga 9, 17, 25, 29, 85, 102
Balbino Zuniga 28
Bonifacio Zuniga 78
Canuto Zuniga 9, 20, 70, 78, 123
Carlos Zuniga 56
Carmen Zuniga 91, 98, 114
Catarino Claude Zuniga 2, 8, 103, 107, 114, 117, 121
Cesaria Zuniga 6, 24, 52, 56, 127
Christina Zuniga 40, 122
Claro Zuniga 4, 7, 18, 19, 21, 22, 29, 39, 65, 71, 74, 81, 92, 99, 101, 102, 105, 115, 127
Clotildo Zuniga 7, 9, 11, 12, 18, 21, 24, 25, 37, 38, 40, 43, 44, 45, 48, 61, 65, 70, 75, 81, 88, 92, 107, 112, 114, 118, 123, 126, 127

Crescencia Zuniga 5, 19, 22, 25, 27, 50, 68, 92
Delvarene Zuniga 34, 56, 85, 88
Derrick Zuniga 2, 14, 18, 83, 111
Eudora "Dora" Zuniga 37, 44, 60, 75, 81, 115, 127
Eugenia "Jean" Zuniga nee Noralez 3, 9, 11, 27, 37, 41, 44, 45, 52, 60, 61, 68, 72, 75, 81, 91, 108, 115, 121
Eulalia Zuniga 81
Faustina Zuniga 21
Faustino Zuniga 26, 39, 104
Felicita "Nitu" or "Cita" Zuniga 7, 14, 20, 21, 22, 29, 31, 32, 39, 54, 65, 80, 101, 115, 120
Felipa Zuniga 25
Felix Zuniga 4, 105, 112
Francesca Thomasina Zuniga 65
Francisco Zuniga 65
Francis Zuniga 65
Gabina Zuniga 3, 21, 22, 23, 34, 35, 41, 52, 81, 92, 120, 124
Henry Peter Zuniga 14, 83, 111
Inocente "Mafia" Zuniga 4, 11, 18, 22, 31, 47, 55, 100, 101, 105, 106, 112, 109, 127
Isaac Zuniga 44, 92
Isabela Zuniga 32, 73, 76, 104, 108, 111, 127
Eugenia "Jean" Zuniga nee Noralez 3, 9, 11, 27, 37, 41, 44, 45, 52, 60, 61, 68, 72, 75, 81, 87, 91, 108, 115, 121
John Jacob Zuniga 3, 9, 14, 20, 22, 25, 28, 29, 31, 32, 33, 34, 44, 56, 65, 79, 80, 85, 88, 101, 102, 118
Josefa Zuniga 3, 6, 31, 40, 50, 56, 71, 94, 103, 115
Katrina Maria Zuniga 2
Kevin Zuniga 13, 20, 21, 23, 25, 44, 45, 53, 61, 76, 87, 88, 92, 125, 127
Lamarta Zuniga 100
Lauriano Zuniga 70
Lazarus Zuniga 123
Leonarda Zuniga 76, 100
Lucille Luciana "Chilagu" Valencio nee Zuniga 4, 7, 8, 16, 18, 21, 22, 26, 28, 29, 31, 37, 42, 44, 55, 56, 62, 65, 68, 71, 72, 87, 92, 99, 106, 113, 115, 120, 126, 127
Luisa Zuniga 21, 96
Luis "Butter" Zuniga 112
Malik Zuniga 87
Marcelo Zuniga 4, 8, 105
Marcos Zuniga 7, 21, 24, 40, 45, 61
Marcus Garvey Zuniga 89
Mariano Zuniga 7, 39, 65, 71, 102
Marie Zuniga nee Casimiro 71

Martin Zuniga 95
Marti Zuniga 13
Matildo Zuniga 31
Modesto Edilberto Zuniga 25
Modesto Zuniga 9
Natividad Zuniga 9, 12, 17, 18, 24, 26, 39, 40, 43, 45, 65, 76, 102, 107
Nazaria Enriquez nee Zuniga 1, 19, 48, 64, 75, 77, 81, 103, 122
Nicholas Zuniga 48, 64, 77, 81
Nicolasa Zuniga 10, 17, 18, 38, 48, 51, 57, 61, 86, 93, 107, 112, 117
Nolasco Zuniga 98
Petrona Zuniga 48
Policarpio Zuniga 12
Polonia Zuniga 29
Rafael Zuniga 4, 8, 105, 112
Rodney Robert Zuniga 6, 59
Rodney Zuniga 121
Romalda Zuniga 11, 16, 18, 60, 74, 124
Rosa Zuniga 22
Rossele Ortilia Zuniga 101
Sebastiana Zuniga 26
Sharon Zuniga 81
Shermaine Amber Zuniga 18
Teresa Zuniga 98
Thomas Zuniga 56
Tiburcio Zuniga 43
Toribia Zuniga 44
Tranquilina Zuniga 11, 36, 39, 75
Valentin Zuniga 20
Vicente Zuniga 92
Victoria Zuniga 7, 49
Viviano Toribio Zuniga 28, 44, 49, 94, 115
Viviano Zuniga 28, 44, 49, 94, 115
Wilbert Zuniga 70

Back Cover: Ominique Castillo

Ominique Castillo was the youngest Baranguna when this book was being finalized in April, 2013. She is shown with her mother, grandmother, and great-grandmother. Here are some of her ancestors:

Parents
Rheena Castillo

Grandparents
Dercy Sandoval and Augusto Castillo

Great-grandparents
Felicita Zuniga and Matildo Sandoval; Elogio Castillo

Great-great-grandparents
John Jacob Zuniga and Tomasine Loredo; Cornelio Castillo and Melvinia Martinez

Great-great-great-grandparents
Ascencion Zuniga and Eleuteria Cayetano; Eulalio Loredo and Gregoria Palacio; Inez Castillo and Martha Fuentes; Pedro Nicacio Martinez and Augustina Nunez

Great-great-great-great-grandparents
Sebastian Sanchez and Vivciona Cayetano; Anastacio Palacio and Magdelana Cesario; Pedro Martinez and Regina Virgen Luis; Martin Nunez and Ascenciona Paulino

Great-great-great-great-great-grandparents
Vincente Sanchez; Julian Martinez; Pedro Luis and Marti Reyes; Diego Paulino and Dominga Cayetano

Great-great-great-great-great-great-grandparents
Juan Pedro Cayetano and Maria Nicolasa Moralez

www.ingramcontent.com/pod-product-compliance
Lightning Source LLC
Chambersburg PA
CBHW080646270326
41928CB00017B/3205